Mark Twain

AS A LITERARY ARTIST

Mark Twain

AS A LITERARY ARTIST

By Gladys Carmen Bellamy

NORMAN

UNIVERSITY OF OKLAHOMA PRESS

Acknowledgment is hereby made for permission most generously given by Harper and Brothers, publishers, and the Samuel Langhorne Clemens estate to quote from the following published works by Mark Twain:

The uniform edition of Mark Twain's works, which comprises twenty-five volumes (1899–1910) and includes the following: *Adventures of Huckleberry Finn; The Adventures of Tom Sawyer; The American Claimant and Other Stories; Christian Science; A Connecticut Yankee in King Arthur's Court; Following the Equator; The Gilded Age; The Innocents Abroad; Literary Essays; Life on the Mississippi; The Man That Corrupted Hadleyburg; Personal Recollections of Joan of Arc; The Prince and the Pauper; Pudd'nhead Wilson; Those Extraordinary Twins; Roughing It; Sketches New and Old; The $30,000 Bequest and Other Stories; Tom Sawyer Abroad; Tom Sawyer, Detective, and Other Stories; A Tramp Abroad.*

Also *Mark Twain's Autobiography*, 1924; *Mark Twain in Eruption*, 1940; *Mark Twain's Letters*, 1917; *Mark Twain's Notebook*, 1935; *Mark Twain's Speeches*, Stormfield edition, 1929; *The Mysterious Stranger and Other Stories*, 1922; *What Is Man? and Other Essays*, 1917. Also writings by Mark Twain included in Volume III of Albert Bigelow Paine's *Mark Twain: A Biography*, 1912, 3 vols.

Excerpts from *Mark Twain's Letters from the Sandwich Islands*, edited by G. Ezra Dane (copyright 1938 by the Board of Trustees of the Leland Stanford Junior University), are reprinted with the permission of the editor and Stanford University Press.

Excerpts from *My Mark Twain*, by William Dean Howells (copyright 1910 by Harper and Brothers; copyright 1938 by Mildred Howells and John Mead Howells), are reprinted by permission of the copyright owners.

Excerpts from *Mark Twain's Travels with Mr. Brown*, edited by Franklin Walker and G. Ezra Dane (copyright 1940 by Alfred A. Knopf, Inc.), are reprinted by permission of Alfred A. Knopf, Inc.

Excerpts from *San Francisco's Literary Frontier*, by Franklin Walker (copyright 1939 by Alfred A. Knopf, Inc.), are reprinted by permission of Alfred A. Knopf, Inc.

To the Memory of

THEODORE HAMPTON BREWER

PROFESSOR OF ENGLISH IN

THE UNIVERSITY OF OKLAHOMA

FROM 1908 TO 1940

Who first awakened my interest in Mark Twain

and then made it possible for me

to follow that interest

Foreword and Acknowledgments

THIS BOOK is an attempt to evaluate Mark Twain as professional author, as craftsman, indeed as literary artist. Its starting point was my conviction that Mark Twain was much more the conscious craftsman than is generally believed; but the phase of the subject which became most interesting to me was the way in which Mark Twain's work reflects his basic attitudes towards mankind, towards life itself; finally, the study led to the application of certain aesthetic principles to that work. At the risk of overemphasis, I have stressed a side of Mark Twain which has hitherto been largely overlooked. It is not that many things formerly said of him have not been true; it is only that these things, too, need to be said. In the light of much new material by Mark Twain, published since 1935, a revaluation is called for. The analysis I have made has required extensive quotation, since I believe that the reader should view the evidence which has led me to certain formulations about Mark Twain. In using this method, I echo F. O. Matthiessen in saying that "Only thus can the reader share in the process of testing the critic's judgments, and thereby reach his own."

Excellent studies of special phases of Mark Twain's life and work have been published, notably those of Ivan Benson, DeLancey Ferguson, and Effie Mona Mack. The Mark Twain specialists to whom I am most heavily indebted, however, are Bernard DeVoto, Walter Blair, Minnie M. Brashear, Van Wyck Brooks, and Edward Wagenknecht. In fact, I have read and re-read Mr. DeVoto, Mr. Blair, and Mr. Wagenknecht, and my debt to them is profound. Mr. Brooks, too, I have found stimulating, even when I have disagreed with him, just as I have occasionally disagreed with Mr. DeVoto and Mr. Wagenknecht. Other numerous indebtednesses I have tried to list in my text or notes. A flood of Mark Twain criticism has poured through the literary journals in recent years; I have read a good part of it, and I am deeply grateful to the various writers who have worked with perception in this field. The book lying outside my subject which has been of greatest benefit is F. O. Matthiessen's *American Renaissance;* its author's sensitive treatment and competent handling of his subject have demonstrated the rewards to be gained from studying a writer's view of the relation of the individual to society and of the nature of good and evil. I have attempted, so far as I was able, to study Mark Twain in these two connections.

For my own investigations, I owe particular thanks to the Rockefeller Foundation of New York for a grant made to me in the spring of 1948 to enable me to complete this study. Among my obligations nearer at hand, I am grateful to Professors Ernest C. Ross, Leonard B. Beach, Lawrence N. Morgan, and John P. Pritchard, all of the University of Oklahoma, for much helpful critical comment. Professors Joseph P. Blickensderfer, Charles C. Walcutt, and Robert W. Daniel, all formerly connected with the University of Oklahoma, gave critical guidance and suggestions in the early stages of the work. Professor Floyd Stovall, formerly of North Texas State Teachers College and now of the University of North Carolina, has permitted me to use some material which is specifically cited in the notes. Miss Elizabeth Halbert and Mrs. Wynona Smith of the University of Oklahoma Library have been generous of their time in looking up materials for me.

In addition, I owe thanks to a number of authors and publishers who kindly permitted me to quote at length from copyrighted works. In addition to permission to quote extensively from the works of Mark Twain published by them, Harper and Brothers have given me permission to quote from the following: *Mark Twain: A Biography*, by Albert Bigelow Paine; *My Father, Mark Twain*, by Clara Clemens; *Literary Criticism*, by Philo Buck; and the letters of William Dean Howells published in *Mark Twain's Letters*.

Besides Harper and Brothers, the following publishers and copyright owners have granted me permission to quote from the sources named: Atlantic Monthly Press for "Bret Harte and Mark Twain in the Seventies," by Mrs. James T. Field, *Atlantic Monthly*, Vol. CXXX. Bobbs-Merrill Company for *The Delight of Great Books*, by John Erskine; for *Mark Twain, Man and Legend*, by DeLancey Ferguson. Liveright Publishing Company for *The Curious Republic of Gondour and Other Whimsical Sketches*, by Samuel L. Clemens. Collier's Publishing Company for "Painting the Portrait of Mark Twain," by S. J. Woolf, *Collier's*, Vol. XLV; for "The Last Day at Stormfield," a poem by Bliss Carman, *Collier's*, Vol. XLV. Crown Publishing Company for *The Adventures of Thomas Jefferson Snodgrass*, edited by Charles Honce, published by P. Covici, Inc. Curtis Publishing Company for the lines from Mark Twain's letter to the little French girl in "Mark Twain's Private Girls' Club," *The Ladies' Home Journal*, Vol. XXIX. Bernard DeVoto for *Mark Twain's America*, published by Little, Brown and Company. Dodd, Mead and Company for *Humor: Its Theory and Technique*, by Stephen B. Leacock (copyright, 1935); for *Our American Humorists*, by Thomas L. Masson (copyright, 1913). Doubleday, Doran for *Midstream*, by Helen Keller; for *From Sea to Sea: Letters of Travel*, in The Writings in Prose and Verse of Rudyard Kipling; for *Many Celebrities and a Few Others*, by William H. Rideing. E. P. Dutton for *The Ordeal of Mark Twain*, by Van Wyck Brooks. George Fields, Publisher, for *The Washoe Giant in San Francisco*, edited by Franklin Walker. Harcourt, Brace for *A Lifetime with Mark Twain*, by Mary Lawton. Archibald Henderson for *Mark Twain*, published by Frederick A. Stokes. John Howell for *Sketches of the Sixties*, by Bret Harte and Mark Twain edited by John Howell. Mildred Howells for *My Mark Twain*, by William Dean Howells. Huntington Library for *The Letters of Mark Twain to Mrs. Fairbanks*, edited by Dixon Wecter. Alfred A. Knopf for *Mark Twain's Travels with Mr. Brown*, edited by Franklin Walker and G. Ezra Dane; for *San Francisco's Literary Frontier*, by Franklin Walker. The Macmillan Company for *American Fiction*, by Joseph Warren Beach; for *Humor of the Old Deep South*, by Arthur P. Hudson; for *The American Novel*, by Carl Van Doren. Modern Philology Press for "On the Structure of *Tom Sawyer*," by Walter Blair, *Modern Philology*, Vol. XXXVII. Charles Scribner's Sons for *Green Hills of Africa*, by Ernest Hemingway; for *The Saga of the Comstock Lode*, by George D. Lyman; for *Mark Twain in Nevada*, by Effie Mona Mack; for *Mark Twain, A Portrait*, by Edgar Lee Masters; for *The Sense of Beauty*, by George Santayana. Harvard University Press for *Mark Twain at Work*, by Bernard DeVoto. Oxford University Press for *The Problem of Style*, by J. Middleton Murry; for *American Renaissance*, by F. O. Matthiessen. Stanford University Press for *Mark Twain's Letters from the Sandwich Islands*, edited by G. Ezra Dane. The University of Texas and the author, Joseph Jones, for "Josh Billings: Some Yankee Notions on Humor," *Studies in English*. Edward Wagenknecht for *Mark Twain: The Man and His Work*, published by Yale University Press. Samuel C. Webster for *Mark Twain, Business Man*, published by Little, Brown and Company, as well as for the portrait of Olivia Clemens which he generously permitted me to use.

In closing, I must say a final word of appreciation to all who have aided me in countless important ways. Without their help, this book could not have been completed.

GLADYS CARMEN BELLAMY

Weatherford, Oklahoma

Contents

Foreword and Acknowledgments vii

   Book I : *The Mark Twain Problem*

1. The Man Mark Twain 3
2. The Critical Questions 25
3. The World Within 41
4. The Four "Bases" of Mark Twain's Mind 55

   Book II : *The Humorous Sketches*

5. A "Born Humorist" and a "Born Reformer" 67
6. The Humorist as Reformer 80
7. The Humorist as Moralist 105
8. The Humorist as Technician 119
9. The Humorist as Character Painter 141

   Book III : *The Travel Books*

10. The Moralist Abroad 159
11. The Traveling Determinist and Pessimist 182
12. Ugliness as Reality, Beauty as Dream 201
13. The Twofold Aspect of Life 223
14. Life as Broad Spectacle 238
15. Mark Twain's Style 249

   Book IV : *The Reminiscences*

16. Looking Backward 269

   Book V : *The Fiction*

17. Revolt from the Village 287
18. Moralism *versus* Determinism 305
19. Acceptance *versus* Rejection 326
20. The Microscope and the Dream 352

Bibliography 377
Index 383

Illustrations

Mark Twain as a young man   *facing page* 18
Mark Twain and "Colonel Sellers"   50
Virginia City in its heyday   82
Mark Twain and the Jumping Frog   114
Townsend, Twain, and Gray   146
Livy   178
Samuel Langhorne Clemens   210
Mark Twain and Lewis at Quarry Farm   242
A saddened humorist   274
Mark Twain and Dorothy Quick   306
Mark Twain in a familiar pose   338
Mark Twain and his daughter Clara   370

BOOK I

The Mark Twain Problem

CHAPTER I

The Man Mark Twain

Mark Twain remains to this day America's most picturesque literary figure. He still keeps his hold on the public mind, a hold so secure that few are the days when one does not somewhere see his name in print, or hear someone remark, "As Mark Twain said," even if it be but to repeat that apocryphal comment on the weather. Perhaps a part of his appeal to the mass-imagination lies in the fact that he himself was the embodiment of what many cherish as "the American dream": from commonplace beginnings he had struggled up to a towering, dazzling fame, to stand, as he himself once said of Daniel Webster, "for a single, splendid moment on the Alps of fame, outlined against the sun."

Although the splendid moment of his fame is still prolonged and extends immeasurably far into the future, that fame was only a small part of his power. There was something about him that moved people who knew nothing of his renown, who did not even know who he was. Mark Twain's personality was of a sort that compelled those about him so strongly that wherever he went, as his biographer Albert Bigelow Paine said, he seemed a being from another planet, a visitant from some remote star.

It was a matter of pride to him that he was born when Halley's comet hung in the night sky. He "came in with it," he said, and he confidently expected to "go out with it." And he did, although he did not know, as he lay on his deathbed, that it was again shining in the heavens. Life was always marking him out for unusual adventures which occurred at moments of dramatic effect. He was dynamic, irrepressible, unpredictable; and he was irrefutably a genius.

What manner of man was Mark Twain?

Born in Florida, Missouri, on November 30, 1835, "Little Sam" was "a wild-headed, impetuous child of sudden ecstasies," who was

3

constantly running away in the direction of the river and, as he later wrote, was "drowned nine times in Bear Creek and was suspected of being a cat in disguise"; a vividly imaginative child, who loved the companionship of the good-natured slaves and visited the Negro quarters beyond the orchard as a place of ineffable enchantment; a child whose sympathy included all inanimate things; a child who, Paine said, "pitied the dead leaf and the murmuring dried weed of November" because for them the summer was over forever; a child who, Van Wyck Brooks remarked, was "to retain through life that exquisite sensibility of which so many have spoken."

At the age of nine Sam Clemens "grew up" and became the leader of his boy companions, roving the hills and woods around Hannibal and yielding unreservedly to the fascinations of the Mississippi. He had a thatch of light, sandy hair, which he vainly tried to keep from curling, keen blue-gray eyes, a delicate complexion, and a winning smile. His slow, measured way of speaking—"Sammy's long talk," his mother called it—had an arresting quality even then; Paine tells us that, although Sam's mental attainments were not highly regarded and he did not talk much, "for some reason, whenever he did speak every playmate in hearing stopped and listened."

As a young man he was slender and loose-limbed, with a great tangle of hair which had deepened from sandy into the rich, mahogany tone called auburn. He could drum on piano or guitar, singing songs in a pleasant tenor voice; and his frank nature and the jokes he told in his slow, quaint fashion made him a general favorite. By the time he was twenty-one, some unusual quality of his mind or heart was making itself felt: when Horace Bixby took him on to "learn the river," the last thing Bixby wanted at that time was a "cub pilot." But he yielded to something in young Sam Clemens.

At twenty-three, a full-fledged pilot on the *City of Memphis*, "the largest boat in the trade," Sam dressed in dandified fashion in blue serge, white duck, fancy shirts, and patent leathers. He wrote to his brother Orion about feasting at a French restaurant in New Orleans, "dissipating on a ten-dollar dinner—breathe it not unto Ma!" He confessed to Orion that he derived "a *living* pleasure" and "a stern joy" from showing off a bit before the young pilots, then unemployed, who had once told him patronizingly that he could never "learn the river." But, employed and unemployed, the pilots of St. Louis and New Orleans regularly gathered around him when

4

he began spinning his yarns and telling the droll tales which convulsed his hearers while his own face remained perfectly sober.

Three years later he accompanied Orion Clemens west when Orion was appointed territorial secretary of Nevada. They arrived in Carson City in August, 1861, and Sam Clemens soon became a conspicuous figure on the Carson streets. No longer a dandy, he was then fashionable in the Western mode; clad in old slouch hat, flannel shirt, and rough trousers half in and half out of heavy cowhide boots, he had become, in Paine's phrase, a paragon of disarray. His bushy head of auburn hair, his piercing eyes, and his lounging gait drew the instant attention of strangers and made them turn for a second look, followed by quick inquiries about his identity. Carson City citizens who saw him leaning for hours at a time against a corner awning, smoking a clay pipe and watching the human motley of the Plaza, did not prophesy much for his future; but at night those same citizens clustered about the stove in Orion's office to hear him tell river yarns in his inimitable drawl.

When he had temporarily abandoned the study of human nature to succumb to the Western mining mania, he once sought diversion from the discomforts of a winter cabin and the disappointments of a miner's life by attending a dance in the mining camp of Aurora. His behavior there, recorded by an onlooker, shows his characteristic ability to lose himself in the present moment. "In changing partners, whenever he saw a hand raised he would grasp it with great pleasure and sail off into another set, oblivious to his surroundings. Sometimes he would act as though there was no use in trying to go right or to dance like other people, and with his eyes closed he would do a hoe-down or a double-shuffle all alone, talking to himself and saying that he never dreamed there was so much pleasure to be obtained at a ball. It was all as natural as a child's play. By the second set, all the ladies were falling over themselves to get him for a partner, and most of the crowd, too full of mirth to dance, were standing or sitting around, dying with laughter."[1] He was an innate actor, of course. Although his natural personality had a magnetic quality, he frequently reinforced nature with art, and by his manner and voice secured the effects he desired to make on others.

In August, 1862, the disgruntled seeker after gold abandoned

[1] Calvin H. Higbie, recorded by Albert Bigelow Paine in *Mark Twain: A Biography*, I, 195 (hereafter referred to as *Biography*).

mining to become a reporter and feature writer on the *Territorial Enterprise,* the leading newspaper of Virginia City, Nevada. Early in 1863 Joseph Goodman, editor of the *Enterprise,* sent Sam Clemens up to Carson City to report the doings of the territorial legislature. With this added dignity, he once more became a fashion plate, arraying himself in a long broadcloth coat, a starched shirt, and polished boots. His biographer described him during the period of his newspaper work on the Comstock as "high-strung and neurotic," with a highly organized nervous system that made him an easy prey to the tortures of noisemakers and practical jokers. Many were the jokes played on him in the Far West, mostly designed to draw forth an exhibition of his profanity; but, then and throughout his life, he was never able to appreciate fully a joke played on himself.

His performance in profanity seems to have been billed as a stellar attraction first in the West. When he was blowing off steam by swearing, it was his custom to begin a slow, circular walk, a habit earlier acquired within the confines of the pilothouse, and then his "rotary denunciations" were something both to hear and to see. An eyewitness, W. H. Rideing, described the spectacle thus: "When anger moved him, you could see his lean figure contract and his eyes ominously screw themselves into their sockets. Every fibre in him quivered, and for the moment his voice became acid and sibilant and out of tune—almost a whine. Then he would let himself out in a break like that of a dam unable to hold the flood, in language as candid and unshrinking as the vernacular of the Elizabethans." The change in voice became less noticeable with the years; finally he seems to have conducted these profane interludes in the same beautiful speaking voice that was his by nature. Upon his remarkable gift of phrase he had overlaid refinements gathered first from the printing office, later from the river, and finally from the mining camp. According to Paine, "To hear him denounce a thing was to experience the fierce, searching delight of galvanic waves. . . . And somehow his profanity was seldom an offense. His selection of epithet was always dignified and stately, from whatever source— and it might be from the Bible or the gutter. . . . Mark Twain's profanity . . . seemed, in fact, the safety-valve of his high-pressure intellectual engine. When he had blown off he was always calm, gentle, forgiving, and even tender." Katy Leary, a servant in his home for thirty years, insisted that his swearing "never seemed really bad" to

her: "It was . . . a part of him, somehow. Sort of amusing it was—
and gay—not like real swearing, 'cause he swore like an angel." And
Katy related that when Baby Jean, Mark Twain's youngest daughter, was shocked at hearing a man swear in the street and was reminded that she had often heard her father swear, she replied gravely: "Oh, no Katy! You're mistaken. That wasn't swearing. That
was only one of papa's *jokes!*" The deliberate quality of his profanity was accented by Miss Elizabeth Wallace, who had occasionally heard him holding forth in the privacy of the billiard room:
"Gently, slowly, with no profane inflexion of voice, but irresistibly
as though they had the head-waters of the Mississippi for their source,
came this stream of unholy adjectives and choice expletives."
Howells underscored the lofty effect of Mark Twain's swearing by
calling it his "pious profanity."

His eyes, his splendid head, his voice, his hands, and his walk
were the features that most impressed his acquaintances. Bret Harte
described him as he was upon their first meeting in San Francisco:
"His head was striking. He had . . . the aquiline nose, and even the
aquiline *eye*—an eye so eagle-like that a second lid would not have
surprised me—of an unusual and dominant nature."

Leaving Nevada and the *Enterprise* in May, 1864, Mark Twain
had gone to San Francisco to do newspaper work. From March to
July, 1866, he was in the Sandwich (Hawaiian) Islands, and upon
his return he launched himself in a new profession, one which displayed him in some of the most brilliant aspects of his career. In
October, 1866, he delivered in San Francisco his first public lecture,
"The Sandwich Islands," beginning a series in California and Nevada; and in May, 1867, he gave his first lecture in New York City.
He was chary of appearing before strangers, but he found that the
Eastern audience responded as eagerly to his odd, slow style as
had his old friends in the West. He loved to sway his hearers by his
oral art; and forty years later, recalling how that New York audience had laughed and shouted, he remembered, "For an hour and
fifteen minutes I was in paradise." His personal power he had carried
with him from the West to the East.

On June 8, 1867, he sailed on the *Quaker City* on the excursion
which resulted in *The Innocents Abroad*. On board, he was described by Mrs. A. W. Fairbanks, one of his first literary critics, who
wrote: " . . . all eyes are turned toward Mark Twain. . . . Sitting

7

lazily at the table, scarcely genteel in his appearance, there is something, I know not what, that interests and attracts." That this quality
was present in him even in those early days is attested more forcibly
still by a curious fact. When the *Quaker City* lay in the harbor of
Yalta, the Emperor of Russia decided to pay a visit to the American
ship. There was a perfect furor of preparation on board. A committee was appointed to draft an address of welcome to the Emperor;
and from the ministers, educators, and prominent people among the
passengers, Mark Twain was elected chairman and commissioned
to write the entire address. That the important task of welcoming
the Czar of all the Russias was entrusted to one recently known to
fame as "The Wild Humorist of the Pacific Slope" is significant.
Significant, too, is the fact that Mark Twain accepted the task without qualms and without apparent self-consciousness.

Among the *Quaker City* passengers was Dr. W. F. Church, an
orthodox deacon who thought Mark Twain irreverent, profane,
and therefore sinful. Years later, Church paradoxically summed up
his impressions, formed at this time: "He was the worst man I ever
knew. And the *best*." Mark Twain, it appears, attracted ministers
particularly. They seemed to love him, though they did not always
approve of him. He once wrote characteristically to his mother that
he was "as thick as thieves" with various ministers and added: "I am
running on preachers now altogether, and I find them gay." Henry
Ward Beecher sought his acquaintance, and the Reverend Joseph
Twichell of Hartford was his closest friend for forty years and
more.

When the travelers had returned from the Holy Land, Elisha
Bliss of the American Publishing Company wrote to Mark Twain
suggesting a book to be compiled from the *Quaker City* letters.
Mark Twain went to Hartford for an interview with the publisher.
Bliss, who had been eager to meet him, was disappointed in what
he saw. Mark Twain's traveling clothes, says Paine, were "neither
new nor neat, and he was smoking steadily a pipe of power." But
when this strange visitor began to talk, Bliss fell a victim to his charm,
invited him to stay at the Bliss home, and decided that personally
Mark Twain was even greater than the sought-after letters.

Certainly, when Mark Twain first settled in the East, he was
heretical towards most of the conventions of the polite society of
that day. This heresy was no more noticeable in his clothes than in

his speech, which was frequently brilliant and occasionally startling. The latter quality is illustrated by the remark he made in the sedate offices of the *Atlantic Monthly* at his first meeting with William Dean Howells. Howells had written a review praising *The Innocents Abroad*, and Mark Twain called and delivered his thanks in these words: "When I read that review of yours, I felt like the woman who was so glad that her baby had come white."

From that first meeting dated a friendship that lasted more than forty years. Howells was always his closest friend, next to the clergyman Joe Twichell. The Westernisms of the frontier still clung to him in those early years. When Thomas Bailey Aldrich took Mark Twain home with him one evening, Mrs. Aldrich did not invite the visitor to dinner because she thought him drunk; he "showed marked inability to stand perpendicular, . . . swayed from side to side, and had also difficulty with his speech; he did not stammer exactly, but after each word he placed a period." This was Mark Twain's natural manner, which he never lost; some of his rough edges, however, were polished away in a process of attrition against Eastern customs. In commenting on Mark Twain's "sealskin coat, with the fur out," worn then to gratify his love of strong effect, Howells said that in spite of Mark Twain's own warmth in it, it "sent the cold chills through me when I once accompanied it down Broadway, and shared the immense publicity it won him." His down-tilted hat and up-tilted cigar were a common sight on the streets, where, no doubt, he came and went on a wave of lifted eyebrows. But even in those days he was conventionally attired for his evening lectures and had already carried his art on the platform to the point where it was probably, as Paine called it, "the purest exemplification of the platform entertainer's art which this country has ever seen. It was the art that makes you forget the artisanship." In later years Howells declared, "He was the most consummate public performer I ever saw, and it was an incomparable pleasure to hear him lecture." When H. R. Haweis went to hear him, not knowing what to expect, he was rather disappointed; yet Haweis himself gave testimony to Mark Twain's spell by relating his surprise when his watch told him he had sat listening for an hour. It had seemed no more than ten minutes, at most.

In 1872, Mark Twain paid his first visit to England, and the intellectual aristocracy of that country took him to their hearts at once. He was "shy as a girl" at first, when he found the great of London ready to pay him homage. Van Wyck Brooks remarked that he was not gulled in England as Joaquin Miller had been, "because the beautiful force of his natural personality would have commanded attention anywhere." In England, said Howells, "rank, fashion, and culture rejoiced in him . . . and his bold genius captivated the favor of periodicals which spurned the rest of our nation." England could turn out cultured humorists aplenty, but not Mark Twains. He returned there in 1873 to lecture to the Londoners on "Our Fellow Savages of the Sandwich Islands" and was greeted with high enthusiasm.

After his emphatic success in England, the fastidious and "refined" of America were more ready to welcome him. Now his fame was so wide that when travelers first arrived in this country, they often expressed a desire to see two things: Niagara Falls and Mark Twain. By the time he was forty, his name was familiar everywhere, in every sort of environment. Countless Mark Twain anecdotes were being passed around the clubs, many of them illustrating his penchant for what Howells termed "the Southwestern, the Lincolnian, the Elizabethan breadth of parlance." In the luxurious home in Hartford where he lived with his wife and three daughters and elaborately entertained his guests, it was his custom to rise from the dinner table between courses and walk up and down the room, waving his napkin and talking the marvelous talk that for him was just a way of killing time. Sometimes he complained that his expenses in the Hartford house were "ghastly"; he spent money lavishly and then had thrifty intervals marked by small economies. In one of these seizures, after a long evening spent with pencil and paper, he announced that he could find but two items on which a saving was possible: the family must cancel its subscription to *Harper's Magazine* and buy a cheaper brand of toilet paper.

Mrs. J. T. Fields, wife of the editor of the *Atlantic Monthly*, described Mark Twain at forty years of age: "His eyes are grey and piercing, yet soft, and his whole face expresses great sensitiveness. He is exquisitely neat also, but careless, and his hands are small, not without delicacy. He is a small man, but his mass of hair seems the one rugged-looking thing about him." A decade later he was described by his thirteen-year-old daughter Susy as having "beautiful curly grey hair, . . . kind blue eyes, and . . . a wonderfully shaped head and profile. . . . He . . . has got a temper, but we all of us have in this family. He is the loveliest man I ever saw, or ever hope to see, and oh so absent-minded!" Mark Twain once essayed a description of himself: "Twenty-four years ago, I was strangely handsome . . . so handsome that . . . even inanimate things stopped to look—like locomotives, and district messenger boys. . . . In San Francisco, in the rainy season I was often mistaken for fair weather." Howells' carefully done portrait dates from the same period as Susy's: "Clemens was then hard upon fifty, and he had kept, as he did to the end, the slender figure of his youth, but the ashes of the burnt-out years were beginning to gray the fires of that splendid shock of red hair which he held to the height of a stature apparently greater than it was, and tilted from side to side in his undulating walk. He glimmered at you from the narrow slits of fine blue-greenish eyes, under branching brows which with age grew more and more like a sort of plumage, and he was apt to smile into your face with a subtle but amiable perception, and yet with a sort of remote absence; you were all there for him, but he was not all there for you." Hamlin Garland, too, found in Mark Twain a curious aloofness of glance, as though he spoke through a mask.

Kipling, who pictured himself "smoking reverently" through their meeting "as befits one in the presence of his superior," presented the Mark Twain of fifty-four as "a man with eyes, a mane of grizzled hair, a brown mustache . . . a strong, square hand shaking mine, and the slowest, calmest, levelest voice in all the world. . . . The thing that struck me first was that he was an elderly man; yet . . . in five minutes, the eyes looking at me, I saw that the gray hair was an accident of the most trivial. He was quite young."

Kipling, on a round-the-world tour, insisted that he had traveled fourteen thousand miles to meet Mark Twain. A few years earlier, however, a visiting Britisher had harbored no such eagerness. When Matthew Arnold came to Boston, he called upon Howells and was told that Howells was at Hartford, visiting Mark Twain. Surprised, he said, "Oh, but he doesn't like *that* sort of thing, does he?" Howells recorded what happened later at a reception in Hartford, where Arnold had gone to lecture: "While his hand laxly held mine in greeting I saw his eyes fixed intensely on the other side of the room. 'Who—who in the world is that?' I looked and said, 'Oh, that is Mark Twain.' I do not remember just how their instant encounter was contrived by Arnold's wish, but I have the impression that they were not parted for long during the evening, and the next night Arnold, as if still under the glamour of that potent presence, was at Clemens's house." On the night of Arnold's visit, Mark Twain was at his best and kept going a string of comment and anecdote of a kind which Joe Twichell declared the world had never seen before and Howells maintained it would never see again. "Arnold seemed dazed by it," wrote Paine. On his way home Arnold "repeated some of the things Mark Twain had said; thoughtfully, as if trying to analyze their magic."

In this way Mark Twain impressed, even dazzled, almost everyone who came into contact with him. Most of those Easterners who had first looked askance at him yielded in time, as Bernard DeVoto says, "to the personality that seems to have been the most glamorous of our literature." That his personality did not need to be strengthened by his reputation is shown in an incident related by George Bernard Shaw. When Mark Twain visited him at Adelphi Terrace, Shaw's parlor maid "did not know him from Adam, yet she admitted him without question and unannounced."[2]

People were most impressed, apparently, by his eyes and his voice. W. H. Rideing tried to describe the latter: "It was not a laughing voice, or a light-hearted voice, but deep and earnest like that of one of the graver musical instruments, rich and solemn, and in emotion vibrant and swelling with its own passionate feeling." Mark Twain told Rideing he had discovered that the Jumping Frog story was two thousand years old. "Two thousand years never seemed so long to me, nor could they have seemed longer to anybody than they did in his enunciation of them which seemed to make visible and tangible all the mystery, all the remoteness . . . of that chilling stretch of time. His way of uttering them and his application of them often gave the simplest words which he habitually used a pictorial vividness, a richness of suggestion, a fullness of meaning with which genius alone could endow them." He did not keep this art of his merely for parading in public. Talking at home, for instance, he once mentioned a word "that perfectly disgusts me"—the word was *optimist*—and as he spoke his voice and his features seemed to materialize the disgust he felt.

He still accompanied himself at the piano and sang occasionally.

[2] Edward Wagenknecht, *Mark Twain: The Man and His Work*, 143.

In the West his one song had been "I Had an Old Horse Whose Name Was Methusalem," but in the Hartford house in the evenings he would sit at the piano and sing the old Negro songs, spirituals and jubilees, that he had loved in his childhood. In memorable words his servant Katy Leary tells of a summer evening, a lovely night with a full moon, when the Warners had entertained friends at dinner. Afterwards the company assembled in the music room, with no lights inside the house, and sat looking out upon the moonlight. "And suddenly Mr. Clemens got right up without any warning and begun to sing one of them negro Spirituals . . . he just stood up with both his eyes shut and begun to sing kind of soft like—a faint sound, just as if there was wind in the trees . . . kind o' low and sweet, and it was beautiful and made your heart ache somehow. And he kept on singin' and singin' and became kind of lost in it, and . . . when he got through, he put his two hands up to his head, just as though all the sorrow of them negroes was upon him; and then he begun to sing, 'Nobody Knows the Trouble I Got, Nobody Knows but Jesus' . . . and when he come to the end, to the Glory Halleluiah, he gave a great shout—just like the negroes do. . . . They said it was wonderful and none of them would forget it as long as they lived."

Here he is portrayed in a mood of sadness, but his moods were myriad. He never got too old for clowning, and one of his letters tells how he "caught it" from Olivia Clemens, his wife, for impersonating a drunken colonel in the Howells home. He boyishly teased the exquisite Olivia as he had earlier teased his mother. Howells remembered seeing him "come into his drawing-room at Hartford in a pair of white cowskin slippers, with the hair out, and do a crippled colored uncle to the joy of all beholders." Say, rather, to the joy of most beholders; for Howells remembered, too, "the dismay of Mrs. Clemens, and her low, despairing cry of 'Oh, Youth!'" She called him "Youth" throughout their thirty-four years of married life, recognizing thus the youthful strain that was always in him, although he was ten years older than she; and he called her "Livy" as her family had done. She was physically frail, and Mark Twain followed her about with a chair. Their friends found his love for her one of his most moving qualities. As a father he was fun for his children, often playing with them as unrestrainedly as a frolicsome boy. In her biography of him, his little daughter Susy wrote, "The difference between papa and mama is, that mama loves morals and papa loves cats." Mark Twain belongs with Richelieu and Dr. Johnson, among the great cat-lovers of all time.

In 1877 his personal imp of the burlesque betrayed him into his greatest fiasco—the Whittier birthday-dinner speech in which he burlesqued Longfellow, Emerson, and Holmes with those gentlemen present, to the horror and consternation of all reverent Bostonians. Later, he sent humble apologies to the august trinity concerned and wrote in penitence to Howells: "My sense of disgrace does not abate. It grows." But he was freely forgiven by the authors themselves; and the resiliency of his spirit was such that, before many days passed, he wrote again to Howells: "I haven't done a stroke of work since the *Atlantic* dinner. But I'm going to try tomorrow. How could I ever— Ah, well, I am a great and sublime fool. But then I am God's fool, and all His works must be contemplated with respect."

Restless in temperament, he roamed about the world. He lived in Europe for one continuous period of nine years and for several shorter periods. He crossed the Atlantic fourteen times in three and one-half years and at various times resided in London, Vienna, Paris, Berlin, and Florence, with summers in Switzerland and Sweden. During these intervals he was sought after by the wealth, nobility, and even royalty of Europe. The family spent the winter of 1891–92 in Berlin, where Mark Twain was invited to dine with Emperor William II. Little Jean, awed by such royal favor, declared, "Why, papa, if it keeps on like this, pretty soon there won't be anybody left for you to get acquainted with but God"—a statement whose complimentary value her father questioned. When Mark Twain settled down in Vienna for the winter of 1897, Paine says, his apartments were "like a court, where with those of social rank assembled the foremost authors, journalists, diplomats, painters, philosophers, scientists, of Europe. . . . Mark Twain's daily movements were chronicled as if he had been some visiting potentate." During the second winter in Vienna, the Clemens drawing room became known as "the Second Embassy."

Mark Twain had no head for business. He lost the fortune which he had sunk in the Paige typesetting machine, that marvelous piece of machinery, that "cunning devil" of steel that could all but think; it proved impracticable because of its extreme delicacy and its high cost of manufacture. When his publishing company, managed by others, ran into difficulties during a business depression and declared bankruptcy, Mark Twain wrote: "The law recognizes no mortgage on a man's brain, and a merchant who has given up all he has may take advantage of the laws of insolvency and start free again for himself. But I am not a business man, and honor is a harder master than the law. It cannot compromise for less than 100 cents on the dollar, and its debts never outlaw." Resolving that his creditors should lose nothing, he determined to "go platforming around the world" to pay his debts, and he set off, accompanied by his wife and his daughter Clara. He was nearing sixty when he assumed this stupendous task, a task that would have tried the courage of a far younger man. While they were away, tragedy struck back home in the death of the eldest daughter, Susy, the one who seemed most of all to have inherited her father's genius. Mark Twain's daughter Clara tells how, with a father's natural feeling that if Susy's parents had only been there, her death might somehow have been averted, he walked the floor in grief and cried out in bitterness against the way God runs this world:

Do you remember, Livy, the hellish struggle it was to settle on making that lecture trip . . . ? To pay debts that were not even of my making . . . . But once the idea of that infernal trip struck us we couldn't shake it. Oh, no! for it was packed with sense of honor—honor—honor . . . plenty of honor, plenty of ethical glory. And as a reward for our self-castigation and faithfulness to ideals of nobility we were robbed of our greatest treasure, our lovely Susy.

Financially, however, the undertaking was a success, and by 1898, Mark Twain had completed the payment of his debts.

When he returned to America after following the equator around the world, the public hailed him with renewed affection. "He had behaved like Walter Scott," said Howells, "as millions rejoiced to know who had not known how Walter Scott behaved till they knew it was like Clemens." His opinion was sought on everything under the sun, and he was unfailing copy for reporters. But when a plan was under way for forming a Mark Twain Association and having a Mark Twain Day at the St. Louis World's Fair, he would have none of it, refusing on the ground that "such compliments are not proper for the living; they are proper and safe for the dead only." There was always the chance, he said, that "while I am still alive . . . I might . . . do something which would cause its members to regret having done me that honor. . . . I shall be a doubtful quantity, like the rest of our race."

Despite the honors heaped upon him, he always retained a certain modesty, a sort of humility even. At seventy he served as pall-bearer for his former coachman, taking his place along with his own gardener and some neighbor coachmen. A few days later, addressing a group of young men, he gave them the characteristics of the dead coachman, Patrick McAleer, as his idea of an ideal gentleman. "It was the sort of thing that no one but Mark Twain has quite been able to do," commented his biographer, "and it was the recognized quality behind it that had made crowds jam the street and stampede the entrance to be in his presence—to see him and to hear his voice."

In 1904 the death of his wife left him, as he said, "washing about on a forlorn sea of banquets," and there was a period when he felt little interest in what the world could offer. But when Oxford University requested the honor of conferring upon him the degree of Doctor of Literature, he eagerly accepted the proposal, saying, "Although I wouldn't cross an ocean again for the price of the ship that carried me, I am glad to do it for an Oxford degree." When his ship stopped at Tilbury, the stevedores stood on the dock and gave him a round of cheers, a welcome which he said "went to the marrow of me."

This was the beginning of an unprecedented demonstration on the part of the English people, an ovation which continued throughout the four weeks of his stay. His London hotel became not only a royal court but also, perforce, a post office; Paine said that two skilled men were required, working from sixteen to twenty hours a day, to receive callers and reduce the pile of correspondence. Acquiring Oxford degrees along with Mark Twain were Rudyard Kipling, Auguste Rodin, Saint-Saëns, Sidney Lee, and others; but, according to Sidney Lee, the crowd centered its attention chiefly on Mark Twain, and the Oxford pageant held on the following day was called "Mark Twain's Pageant" by the London papers.[3] Upon his leave-taking the London *Tribune* declared: "Mark Twain has triumphed, and in his all-too-brief stay of a month has done more for the cause of the world's peace than will be accomplished by the Hague Con-

[3] Paine, *Biography*, III, 1394-95.

ference." Perhaps it is true that, as Paine said, England had paid him "the greatest national tribute ever paid to a private citizen."

The rich scarlet of his Oxford gown did not lessen the value of the Oxford degree in his eyes. "I like the degree well enough," he said, "but I'm crazy about the clothes! ... Think of the gloomy garb I have to walk the streets in at home, when my whole soul cries out for gold braid, yellow and scarlet sashes, jewels and a turban!" He had once likened to a garden the rainbow colors of women's dresses in an opera audience, with the men "clothed in odious black, scattered here and there like so many charred stumps." About the time of his seventy-first birthday he put off his dark suits in favor of white clothes for both winter and summer wear. Though he pined for a costume of silks and velvets resplendent with stunning dyes, he compromised on the white, a striking complement to his white hair.

He loved a spectacle always, particularly if he formed a part of it. He was not above making an entrance with studied theatrical effect, and he preferred the "Peacock Alley" corridor leading into a Washington hotel dining room to the quiet entrance-way Paine had recommended. His height was only medium, says Paine, but "with his head thrown up, and like a lion's, rather large for his body," he gave the impression of being tall. Dressed in his snowy flannels, he made an impressive figure striding up and down the stage of the world. On Sundays, he loved to mingle in the streets with the crowds; when Paine suggested that by going home a roundabout way he could avoid the throng, he replied quietly, "I like the throng."

Mark Twain liked women who were comely and attractive in appearance. He was superstitious beyond all telling. He was a perfect fury of energy, generating power like a dynamo. Two years before he was sixty, he wrote to Livy of attending a New York ball and reported: "By half past four I had danced all those people down —and yet was not tired." That was 1893, the year he first became known as "The Belle of New York." Apparently, he could do on much less sleep than the average person needs. Billiards was the game he loved best, and his love for it amounted to a passion. In his old age, he himself asserted that he walked ten miles a day around the billiard table, with a cue in his hand. He could play at "the science of angles" all night without tiring, another sign of his appalling energy, and he always took great delight in his conquests. But sometimes when his shots were bad, the air turned blue, temporarily. After such outbursts he would try to make amends to his opponent. Once, playing with Paine, he angrily seized the cue and literally mowed the balls across the table. Immediately afterward "he was very gentle and sweet, like the sun on the meadow after the storm has passed by"— as meek as a little child in his remorse.

But when that violent temper flared, profanity was likely to be accompanied by action, in or out of the billiard room. One Sunday morning he hurled out of the window all his shirts that he found with buttons off; and Katy Leary declared that "if he found a shirt that didn't have the proper cuff buttons in, he'd tear it up." Little things rent him completely apart, though he could be calm and courageous in the face of great trouble. His love of color, already mentioned, was but one of his many artistic traits. He had an abnormal sensitiveness to sound: the ticking clock, the gnawing mouse, the rustling paper, the barking dog, the cackling guinea hen—these things tortured him and led to outbreaks of temper. Unpleasant human voices made him suffer, but the liquid beauty in certain rare voices was compensation.

The intensity of his moods was remarkable. His sudden savage impulses might bring hardship, sometimes even injustice, to others; if he discovered the wrong, he could not rest until he had atoned for it. But he held an indignation that amounted to malevolence towards those he believed his enemies and wore himself out in the vehemence of his resentments. Of Paige, the inventor whose typesetter cost him a fortune, of Paige, the smooth talker who "could persuade a fish to come out and take a walk with him," Mark Twain wrote in his memoranda: "Paige and I always meet on effusively affectionate terms, and yet he knows perfectly well that if I had him in a steel trap I would shut out all human succor and watch that trap until he died." Howells said that Mark Twain went beyond Heine, who forgave his enemies when they were dead: "Clemens did not forgive his dead enemies; their death seemed to deepen their crimes, like a base evasion, or a cowardly attempt to escape." But he was more relentless to himself than to anyone else; he pyramided his shortcomings into mountains of crime and kept his conscience perpetually clothed in a hair shirt as penance for his sins.

He could be unexpectedly patient with those whom he considered underprivileged. Howells told how Mark Twain once inadvertently sat down upon a notebook a brakeman had left on a

Mark Twain as a young man
From a photograph by Gurney

train seat; the brakeman was abusive to him and came back again and again to berate him. "The patience of Clemens . . . was so angelic that I saw fit to comment, 'I suppose you will report this fellow.' 'Yes,' he answered, slowly and sadly. 'That's what I should have done once. But now I remember that he gets twenty dollars a month.' " In philanthropy and charity he was extremely magnanimous. J. N. Larned of the Buffalo *Express* once characterized him with accuracy: "What one saw of him was always the actual Mark Twain, acting out of his own nature simply, frankly, without pretense, and almost without reserve. It was that simplicity and naturalness in the man which carried his greatest charm."[4]

Paine noted that "age and misfortune and illness had a tempering influence on Mark Twain's nature." Instead of becoming more harsh, more severe and bitter with the blows the passing years rained upon him, he grew "more gentle, more kindly." Nevertheless, he remained both trenchant and intrepid. He could still indulge, privately or semipublicly, his Southwestern or Elizabethan breadth of parlance. At seventy-two he attended a dinner given for Andrew Carnegie at the Engineer's Club and verbally cuffed Carnegie for his proposal to simplify spelling, protesting that "simplified spelling is all right enough, but, like chastity, you can carry it too far."

S. J. Woolf, the artist who painted him in 1906, described his appearance in his last years: "Instead of the weather-beaten face which I had expected, I saw one softer and calmer, but no less strong, while the delicacy and refinement of his features were most noticeable. His hair, too, which I had always thought wiry, was glossy and silken. Never have I seen a head where it seemed more an integral part—its ivory-like tones melting imperceptibly into the lighter hues of the skin so that the line of juncture was almost entirely lost. Even his hands betrayed a more actively nervous man than one would . . . imagine a former river-pilot could be."

His friends appreciated the innate fineness that was unknown to the world at large. Joseph Twichell, who accompanied him on the European tour which produced *A Tramp Abroad*, wrote in a letter home: "He has coarse spots in him. But I never knew a person so finely regardful of the feelings of others. . . . He hates to pass another person walking, and will practise some subterfuge to take off what he feels is the discourtesy of it." Twichell told how their guide

[4] *Ibid.*, I, 386.

had wished to pass ahead of them, yet hesitated to do so. "Mark paused, went aside and busied himself a minute picking a flower. In the halt the guide got by and . . . Mark threw the flower away, saying, 'I didn't want that. I only wanted to give the old man a chance to go on without seeming to pass us.' " And Twichell summed him up: "A strange Mark he is, full of contradictions."

Howells admired his delicate, shapely hands, and noted that he "had the fine instinct of never putting his hands on you . . . ; he did not paw you with them to show his affection." But perhaps the best record of his extreme sensitivity is preserved in the words of Helen Keller: "He knew with keen and sure intuition many things about me; how it felt to be blind and not to be able to keep up with the swift ones—things that others learned slowly or not at all. He never embarrassed me by saying how terrible it is not to see, or how dull life must be, lived always in the dark."

There was always, of course, another side to the picture. There were always those who did not like Mark Twain, who in fact disliked him intensely. Senator William H. Stewart of Nevada, whose Washington secretary Mark Twain had once been for a brief period distasteful to both men, described him as a disreputable looking person of sinister appearance, with an evil-smelling cigar butt protruding from the corner of his mouth. Robertson Nicoll was shocked at "his habitual, incessant, and disgusting profanity."[5] And Waldo Frank, who sat unresponsive through one of Mark Twain's humorous speeches at a benefit entertainment for the blind, objected to his humor and found his performance somehow shameful: "He stood there almost still . . . and dropped the ungainly humor from his mouth. And the audience before him snouted it, guzzled it, roared with delight." Mr. Frank is at some pains to make clear that he "hated this noble-looking fool."

Howells recognized that Mark Twain's effect on some persons was unpleasant: "His casual acquaintance might know him, perhaps, from his fierce intensity, his wild pleasure in shocking people with his ribaldries and profanities . . . as anything but exquisite, and yet that was what in the last analysis he was. They might come away loathing or hating him." Yet Howells maintained to the last that "Clemens's central and final personality was something exquisite."

[5] Wagenknecht, *Mark Twain: The Man and His Work*, 102.

Mark Twain liked to lie in his huge, carved bed in a room with deep red walls. He had acquired the habit of working in bed long before he grew old. He read there, he wrote there, and he frequently gave dictations to Paine from there; or sometimes he merely lay in his bed and talked what his friends considered the world's most remarkable entertainment. This talk of his was accompanied by incessant smoking, in bed or out. Missing him, Howells once wrote from England: "I would rather have you smoke in my face and talk for half a day than to go to the best house or club in London." A house where he had visited had to be aired from top to bottom, Howells said, for "he smoked all over it from breakfast to bedtime."

One spring morning when he was seventy, as he lay propped in bed, clad in his beautiful Persian silk dressing gown with his white hair spread against the pillows, a worshipful woman begged to be admitted to his presence for a moment. As she was leaving, she exclaimed reverently, "How God must love you!" Mark Twain answered softly, "I hope so"; but after she had gone he remarked in an odd, half-pathetic voice, "I guess she hasn't heard of our strained relations."

Sometimes in the dictations to Paine he went back to his earlier habit of walking up and down, resuming "the ceaseless slippered, shuffling walk" with its rocking, rolling movement. With that great mane of white hair, walking a regular measured beat in the habit acquired in the pilothouse, he must have resembled an aged lion, pacing up and down, just the length of his cage.

But he had, too, a lion's courage. In those last months, with all his immediate family dead except his daughter Clara, who had married the pianist Gabrilowitsch and gone abroad, Mark Twain was at best a somewhat pathetic figure. He retained to his last years, however, his faculty of living in the present. Howells recalled that on his last visit to Stormfield Mark Twain sang "Go Down, Daniel," in his quavering tenor and was up early in the mornings, swaying up and down the corridor in his long nightgown, "wagging his great white head like a boy that leaves his bed and comes out in the hope of frolic." Later, when the pain of the angina pectoris which killed him had kept him awake, he would remark, "Well, I had a picturesque night." But, nearing the end, he said once: "I am like a bird in a cage: always expecting to get out, and always beaten back by the wires." He got out on April 21, 1910, in his seventy-fifth year. His faithful servant Katy Leary insisted, "It was a terrible, cruel thing to have him die, really, because he was too young—that is, he *felt* young . . . and he could have said a good deal more." Attempting to explain why the world united in sorrow at his death, Paine suggested that it was "because he was so limitlessly human that every other human heart, in whatever sphere or circumstance, responded to his touch."

Howells, practiced writer though he was, admitted his failure at putting into words anything of the essence of Mark Twain: "It is in vain that I try to give a notion of the intensity with which he pierced to the heart of life." And Howells, who had known Emerson, Longfellow, Lowell, and Holmes—"I knew them all and all the rest of our sages, poets, seers, critics, humorists; they were like one another and like other literary men"—Howells pronounced Mark Twain's nature "rich and fertile beyond any I have known." In Howells' final judgment, "Clemens was sole, incomparable."

I have tried to set down here, in my turn, something of the man the world knew as Mark Twain, much that was good, some that was bad. I have emphasized his personality and the sway it held over others, using the testimony of those who knew him, those who heard him speak, and giving it mainly in their own words. But what of his writing, his literary work? His friends sometimes indicated that they felt it the lesser part of his career. John Macy wrote that it was "a pleasure to hear him in one of his coolly passionate tirades, speaking sentences amazingly finished and constructed, as if a prose style were as natural to him as breathing." Paine said that in the dictations Mark Twain delivered his sentences with a "measured accuracy" that seldom called for change; but in making his transcriptions, Paine found it hard to preserve "the bouquet, the subtleness of speech" of the original; "there is always lacking the wonder of his personality."

In fact, Paine went so far as to declare that he talked "in a strain and with a charm that he could never quite equal with his pen. It is the opinion of most people who knew Mark Twain personally that his impromptu utterances, delivered with that ineffable quality of speech, manifested the culmination of his genius." Sir Henry Irving told him that he would have made a greater actor than a writer. Apparently there was a tendency among his contemporaries to put the rare quality of the man himself above his literary work. Mr. Brooks, recalling that Howells had compared him with Cervantes and Swift and that Bernard Shaw had likened him to Voltaire, suggested that they gave the work more than its due because of the man: "Did they not, under the spell of that extraordinary personal presence of his, in the magnetism, the radiance of what might be called his temperamental will-to-satire mistake the wish for the deed?" A danger, it will be perceived, for those who were subjected to his charm. The danger has been recognized elsewhere. Edward Wagenknecht noted that "it was often his personality, rather than his art, by which his contemporaries were enthralled" and that he looms "more impressively in American literature as a personality than he does as a writer."

What great writer since his time has been able to capture the imagination of the public as he captured it and to hold it so long? Mr. Brooks prophesies that he will continue in the mass-mind for many generations as "a sort of arch type of the national character. . . . By whom, however, with the exception of two or three of his books, is he read?" But with each generation that unique figure is farther removed from us, growing more dim and shadowy with time. Anecdotes lose their force with the passing of eyewitnesses. His voice was recorded in his seventieth-birthday speech, but the records, made of wax and stored by his secretary in a warm attic, were unfortunately ruined. One record of his voice still exists but is inaccessible to many people.[6] What remains to us? His books.

By his books he must be known to us, as to those who come after us. Mark Twain the man has too long overshadowed Mark Twain the writer. And he would have wished it otherwise. A year before he died, glancing retrospectively over the long way he had come, he wrote: "To me, the most important feature of my life is its literary feature." Let us, then, put the emphasis where it really belongs—upon his books, for better or for worse.

Mark Twain, perhaps, is the only Southwesterner to command a world audience, to attain world significance in the field of literature. In view of his eminence it is surprising that so little attention has been paid to his actual writing itself, surprising that no study of the aesthetic and technical aspects of his work has ever been made. Yet, beginning with 1920 when Van Wyck Brooks opened a new

[6] Mort Weisinger, in "Listen! Mark Twain Speaking," *Saturday Evening Post*, Vol. 221, No. 1 (July 3, 1948), disclosed that the Voice Library at Yale University, collected by G. Robert Vincent, contains a record of Mark Twain's voice.

cycle of Mark Twain criticism, a new Mark Twain book has appeared every few years.

Mr. Brooks psychoanalyzed him and found that the humorist had frustrated the artist within him; Bernard DeVoto turned the spotlight on "Mark Twain's America," the sociological and economic background which produced him, studying his work in its broad effects, but not minutely; Edward Wagenknecht wrote on *Mark Twain: The Man and His Work*, but the emphasis throughout is on the man rather than the work; DeLancey Ferguson presented *Mark Twain: Man and Legend*, tracing the autobiographical material which appears in much of his work, but neither an autobiographical nor a documented biographical approach to that work can be fully adequate, for reasons which will later appear. An entire book has already been devoted to Mark Twain's views on religion, another to Mark Twain as a businessman. Surely, it is time to examine Mark Twain as an author, as a professional writer, even as a literary artist.

CHAPTER 2

The Critical Questions

IF it be true, as is often said, that controversy over an author is an indication of his genius, then surely Mark Twain can claim the divine spark, for he has occasioned much disagreement among the critics. The battle first raged about various endeavors to "place" him, to determine his status and rank as a writer. There were those who saw him only as a frontier humorist and therefore, with elevated noses, relegated him to a seat below the salt. But Mark Twain, one of the most complex of literary personalities, refused to stay there; and now that criticism has accorded him a place nearer the head of the board, the critical effort has sought to "explain" him, to account for his being what he was and writing the sort of works he produced.

Critics have found it difficult to explain why Mark Twain—a man of genius, fame, wealth, happy domestic relations, and pleasant social environment—should have become a pessimist. He did not, in fact, become a pessimist, for pessimism flares out occasionally even in his early work. Surely, from an external view, life had brought him all that he could have hoped for. He had proved that a man might go just as far in America as his own talent and energy would take him. But he recoiled from the spiritual ugliness that grew up in the country in the years following the Civil War. Some of it escaped him, but what he had the vision to see he excoriated with force and power. His indictment of civilization is both explicit and implicit in his work. He was one of the first writers to sense what lay ahead of the United States in the course on which she was set. And, because to him America had long embodied the hope of the world, his fear and despair were for all the world. America as a democracy amid certain social conditions, under certain dominant factors of economics, politics, and religion, and the life he lived in such a setting—these elements make up the background. The foreground must remain his works themselves.

Critics have generally viewed him as an "unconscious artist," if the term may be admitted, explaining his faults of structural disharmony on the ground that he was merely the improvisator, the careless writer, unconcerned and working by impulse. In her book *American Humour*, Constance Rourke stated unequivocally: "He was never the conscious artist, always the improviser." Edward Wagenknecht agrees emphatically with Miss Rourke. Van Wyck Brooks charges Twain with habitual "indifference" and even "insolence" towards his own work, insisting that in all the endless pages of his writing "there is scarcely a hint of any concern with the technique, or indeed with any other aspect, of what was nothing else, surely, than his art." Seeming to agree with Mr. Brooks's comment that Mark Twain's interest was confined to the "purely or mainly verbal aspects" of writing, Bernard DeVoto asserts in *Mark Twain's America* that "it is unlikely that he ever analyzed, beyond its mere grammar, an effect of his own or anyone's else."

My personal interest in Mark Twain was, at first, an attempt to determine whether he was a "conscious" or an "unconscious" literary artist. Although the latter term seems an obvious contradiction within itself, since the word *artist* implies a selection and control of material, criticism has on occasion applied it to Mark Twain. But the evidence shows that, although he was never conscious of his art in the sense in which such self-conscious artists as Henry James and Joseph Conrad wrote, he was much more the conscious craftsman than is generally believed. To read his works is to sense the genius of the man and also to realize that many of his works fail to do justice to that genius. Having had that experience, I grew interested in a more inclusive question: Why was it that the combination of a native endowment that was remarkable and a literary craftsmanship that was by no means slight, working together in Mark Twain, still produced a number of works of mediocre quality and a good many others which fall short of complete artistic success? The attempt to answer this question satisfactorily has proved a fascinating study.

Aside from the question of his working consciously, other questions interested me: Was Mark Twain's boyhood in a raw Missouri frontier town warped and stunted, as Mr. Brooks holds, or was his boyhood environment beneficial for his development, as Miss Minnie M. Brashear holds? Did the Far West further stultify and thwart his artistic growth, as Mr. Brooks maintains, or did the West develop him, as Mr. DeVoto maintains? Was he really "imprisoned" in his boyhood, as both Brooks and DeVoto hold? Is Brooks right in believing that Mark Twain impaired his artistic and satiric talents by becoming a humorist, or is DeVoto right in believing that he fulfilled himself through the writing of humor? Was his native endowment for becoming a great writer really as fine as Mr. Brooks believes? or was there something lacking, something at the very core of his being, that frequently held him back from achieving the highest peak of mastery in literary work?

In the arena devoted to contests over Mark Twain, the two chief antagonists have been Van Wyck Brooks and Bernard DeVoto. In *The Ordeal of Mark Twain*, Mr. Brooks pictured his subject as an "artist born" who betrayed the artist within him to become a humorist—not only because the West demanded humor as a psychical defense against the frustrations inherent in frontier life, but also because humor was popular enough to bring him money; as a satirist for whom satire became impossible because he must, perforce, be one of the crowd; as a writer stunted first by the narrowness of his Southwestern frontier village and later by the raw and violent crudeness of the Far West; as a case of arrested development who remained always a child and who could write well only when producing books for boys. Yet, says Mr. Brooks, this pitiful figure was potentially one of the greatest of men, and his gifts, his "unbounded energy, his prodigal fertility, his large utterance, . . . his powers of feeling, the unique magnetism of his personality were the signs of an endowment, as one cannot but think, more extraordinary than that of any other American writer." In brief, Mr. Brooks finds the secret of Mark Twain's pessimism in the fact that he had betrayed the artist within him by writing humor; he holds that Mark Twain regarded his humorous writing "as something external to himself, as something other than artistic self-expression; and it was in consequence of pursuing it . . . that he was arrested in his moral and aesthetic development."

In *Mark Twain's America*, Mr. DeVoto admits that Mark Twain was a humorist but finds no indication of artistic unfulfillment implicit in that fact. In his introduction to *Mark Twain in Eruption*, he says that Mark Twain "had a coherent development up to *A Connecticut Yankee*," but was later crushed under an avalanche of personal calamities which so impaired his writing talent that for a long time it seemed to have been destroyed; and, when it was integrated again, "there is . . . a new Mark Twain, the author of *What Is Man?* and *The Mysterious Stranger*." On this particular point Mr. Brooks had asserted, "Of the misfortunes of life he had neither more nor less than other men, and they affected him neither more nor less."

Mr. DeVoto insists that Mark Twain fulfilled himself abundantly as a writer, but grants that he had many faults as an artist—among them sporadic composition, painful disharmonies, failure to objectify his material enough to give it the discipline of form, negligence in revision, rambling improvisation, intrusion of burlesque into magnificent literary material, failure to subordinate impulse to plan, and, finally, lack of structure. And Mr. DeVoto finds the explanation of these weaknesses, as of many of Mark Twain's strengths, in the frontier that produced him.[1] In one passage DeVoto writes: "He left San Francisco at the end of 1866 and the frontier, having completed him, was done with him forever." That the frontier "completed" Mark Twain is a conception that cannot be granted.

Mr. Brooks sees Mark Twain's birth on the Southwestern frontier as the first step in life's betrayal of the artist he was destined to be. To Brooks, Hannibal was a desolate, barren place devoid of aesthetic possibilities, where the child Sam Clemens had only, on the one hand, the narrowness of his mother's iron-clad Presbyterianism and, on the other, the nerve-shattering voodoo tales of the Negro slaves. It is Miss Brashear who has done the most careful research for the purpose of bringing to life again Mark Twain's Missouri. She finds that Hannibal possessed "a more distinctly literary atmosphere than towns in Missouri have today." It had seven churches, an English and Classical School, a "female academy," five newspapers, three bookstores, and a public library which Sam Clemens's father had been instrumental in founding. At the time Sam left it at seventeen, it was the second city in the state in population. Miss Brashear maintains that the legend that Mark Twain sprang unaccountably from a western wilderness must be revised: "As a matter of fact, it is doubtful whether, anywhere in America, there could have been found in the forties and fifties a small section of country more favorable for his start in life than northeast Missouri."

[1] See, for example, Bernard DeVoto, *Mark Twain's America*, 154.

The critics who look on Mark Twain's early environment as antagonistic to his artistic development make the old error of assuming that the content of his imagination was a more or less literal copy of his actual surroundings. Never completely true of any mind, the assumption is much less true in cases involving the artistic temperament. And for that matter, much of his actual environment was of a kind potentially rich in imaginative quality. By his boyhood village there flowed the Mississippi, "the majestic, the magnificent Mississippi, rolling its mile-wide tide along, shining in the sun"; and his literary treatment of the river testifies to the power which its beauty and its grandeur exerted over his imagination. As for the fact that he grew up among Negroes, that fact, too, is important for the artist; for, as Mr. DeVoto has said, much that is fruitful in his art springs from the slaves—from "the melancholy, the music, the laughter, the terror, and the magic of the slaves." Mr. Wagenknecht stated the case admirably when he wrote that to hear the marvelous ghost tales of the Negroes and "to thrill to them afterward, was probably the intensest form of emotional stimulation that young Sam Clemens ever received." The influence of the Negro on Mark Twain was not only deep; it was sustained throughout his life.

At first glance it would seem that Mr. Brooks and Mr. DeVoto are in opposite corners of the ring, that they are diametrically opposed in their views concerning Mark Twain. There are a few points, however, on which they appear to have agreed from the first. Mr. Brooks's belief that Mark Twain's interest in writing was confined to its verbal aspects and Mr. DeVoto's doubt that he ever analyzed any effect beyond its mere grammar have already been mentioned. In the next place, Brooks complains that Mark Twain is "still obsessed with the morbid fears of that old Western village of his"; and DeVoto has emphasized, in all his writings on Mark Twain, "the dread that was Hannibal" as the obverse side of the idyllic charm of that village. Further, Brooks pictures the child Sam Clemens as a high-strung, neurotic child of exquisite sensibilities and then shows him "abandoned to the fervid influences of the negro slaves," crouching in their cabins drinking in "wild, weird tales of blood-curdling African witchcraft," with the suggestion that this early subjection to such a fearful stimulus was a bad thing for his normal development; and here again DeVoto follows Brooks in part. He writes that the boy Sam Clemens entered wholly into the slave's world, a world which contained "abysses of horror"; he then amplifies that horror through fourteen pages and concludes that "it is not granted here that the nervous instability of Mark Twain requires explanation. But if it does . . . a nervous organism that has been racked from its beginning by the Negro's midnight magic need not depend on American contempt of art for its discords." And the two have agreed from the first in holding the frontier responsible for some of Mark Twain's literary defects. Brooks charges that the raw environment of the frontier stunted his artistic growth; and DeVoto, while maintaining that the frontier developed him as a writer, nevertheless seems to feel that his faults of structure and technique were largely derived from the characteristic practice of the tall tale and the frontier anecdote.[2]

Recently, these critics appear to have drawn closer together than they were a decade ago; and, surprisingly enough, it is Mr. DeVoto who has moved towards his opponent. Although in 1933 Mr. Brooks revised *The Ordeal*, following the appearance of DeVoto's *Mark Twain's America* in 1932, his central position remained the same: Mark Twain, halted in his artistic development by the stultifying conditions of life on the frontier, had sold his artist's birthright for a mess of materialistic success, had wasted himself on his milieu, had descended to the writing of humor when he had been intended for a great satirist. "The making of the humorist," asserts Mr. Brooks, "was the undoing of the artist."

The first of these more recent agreements concerns the question of sex in Mark Twain's work. Mr. Brooks contends that the frontiersmen lived a life which blocked their instincts on every side: "There were so few women among them . . . that their sexual lives were either starved or debased"; and he concludes that Mark Twain's verbal obscenities were the expression of that "vital sap," which, because of taboos, had been driven inward and left there to ferment— "the waste of a priceless psychic material." In 1932, Mr. DeVoto insisted that the sex expression of the frontiersmen had been free and natural, that among them there was no suppression of emotion, fear of passion, repression of instincts, or abstinence from joy; and he concluded his remarks on the sex life of the frontier with a reference to the social activities of young Sam Clemens in Hannibal, with the clear implication that in such respects Sam was not inhibited. But in

---

[2] *Ibid.*, 92, 240; see also pp. 127, 154, 158, 243, 245, and 252.

his more recent book, *Mark Twain at Work*, he finds Twain "almost lustfully hypersensitive to sex in print," as a writer "rather more prudish than Howells," and guilty of timorous circumlocutions that are "astonishing." Quoting Mark Twain's statement that no girl in Hannibal was ever insulted or seduced, or even scandalously gossiped about, he observes finally: "Whatever the defect of experience or recognition that made him thus libel a full-blooded folk, that is how he remembered Eden." In hinting at some defect of experience or recognition, he implies that this "sexual queasiness" of Mark Twain's was somewhat abnormal; thus he approaches Mr. Brooks's diagnosis.

Whatever the source of the defect, most of Mark Twain's women characters float through his pages on pink-tinted clouds of sentimentality, with all the verve and zest and passion of bisque dolls. They are of charming purity, but they have no life. In the *Autobiography* he tells of meeting in Calcutta an acquaintance out of "the pathetic past, the beautiful past, the dear and lamented past," and his description of her is typical of his attitude toward Woman in general: "Mary Wilson . . . was dainty and sweet, peach-blooming and exquisite, gracious and lovely in character." He could draw with finality an old pioneer woman, or a middle-aged frontier woman, or a young slave woman; but in dealing with women who could be objects of desire, as Mr. DeVoto defines them, he could only sentimentalize the "virtuous" and ignore altogether their sisters of the opposite persuasion. In his young manhood he must have seen sex blatant and unveneered often enough. Tawdry queens of Natchez-under-the-Hill and broken-down beauties from the New Orleans dives undoubtedly traveled on the river boats, and the lights-o'-love of the western Gold Coast did not exactly hide their lights under bushels. Life must have shown him many a woman with a fascinating though irregular story, but one would never suspect it from reading his books; that is, with the single exception of *Pudd'nhead Wilson* and its courageous portrayal of Roxy, concubine and slave. The circumspect taste of his period cannot completely account for this tendency in Mark Twain, for his contemporary Henry James acknowledged in his novels the existence of sex and even his friend Howells, as Mr. DeVoto notes, was not so prudish in print as Mark Twain. It is both odd and significant that he practically excluded such material from his fiction, otherwise so amazingly full

31

of the life of his times. There was a psychological block, apparently, which held him from the use of this material for literature.

Mr. Brooks charges Mark Twain with spending his life on the leading-strings first of his mother and later of his wife, submitting himself to feminine dominance in any available guise. Brooks asserts that Twain was the Eternal Child, devoted to the mother complex, afraid to stand alone—forgetting that he left home and mother at seventeen, that he did not marry until he was almost thirty-five years old, and that in the intervening years, despite his brief show of deference to Mrs. A. W. Fairbanks as his literary mentor, no one woman looms large in his life. Add to this will-to-obey-Woman another ingredient Mr. Brooks has emphasized—namely the sex fear which he believes existed on the frontier—and we draw near the formula which Mr. DeVoto has suggested for solving "the dark, sensitive, and complex consciousness" which was Mark Twain's mind. In *Mark Twain at Work*, speaking of "the book that someone must eventually devote to the bases of Mark's mind," Mr. DeVoto prophesies that perhaps its central effort "will be to determine why death . . . colored his phantasy from childhood on," and that perhaps the answer, if it is found, "will show that the threat of death was twined in his phantasy . . . with the fear of woman's sex," Mr. Brooks earlier believed that Mark Twain lived in subjugation to woman's sex; now Mr. DeVoto approaches him in the surmise that the fear of woman's sex was embedded in Mark Twain's mind.

Another charge of Mr. Brooks's was that Mark Twain was a case of arrested development, able to write well only when producing books about boys and for boys. In *Mark Twain at Work*, Mr. DeVoto comments: "If ever a writer was imprisoned in his boyhood, clearly Mark Twain was." It is possible to offer artistic and aesthetic reasons for Mark Twain's literary emphasis on Hannibal and for his repeated use of his two boy characters. These reasons will appear later; the significant thing at this point is that in Mr. DeVoto's choice of the word imprisoned he approaches the idea advanced earlier by Mr. Brooks. The difference in context shades the meaning in each case: for Brooks, Mark Twain was "imprisoned" in frustration, while for DeVoto he was "imprisoned" in imaginative faculty. Nevertheless, despite the fact that Mr. DeVoto still views his own writing as "in part a refutation of Mr. Brooks's," it seems that he has made some admissions dangerous to his original position.

Mr. DeVoto appears pre-eminent as a source of Mark Twain criticism; but there remains—for me, at least—a residue of truth in the arguments of Mr. Brooks which his opponents have never quite been able to argue away. "One may agree with Mr. Brooks or one may disagree with him," says Edward Wagenknecht. "The only thing that one cannot do . . . is to ignore him. Nobody can write about Mrs. Clemens . . . as he might have written in 1919."[3] Although a good many years have gone by since *The Ordeal of Mark Twain* appeared in 1920, I would still agree with Mr. Wagenknecht that Mr. Brooks cannot be ignored; and I would add, "Nobody can write about *Mr.* Clemens as he might have written in 1919." Perhaps this is a good time to state my own position on two main points: I believe that Mr. Brooks was right in asserting that there was a strong internal conflict in Mark Twain; but I do not agree with him about the nature of that conflict. Again, I believe he was right in asserting that there was a certain amount of frustration in Mark Twain's literary work; but I do not agree with him about the nature of that frustration or the form it took. Mr. Brooks and Mr. DeVoto have each told part of the truth; each, however, has failed to consider certain evidence in Mark Twain's work.

As a reply to the joint charge of Messrs. Brooks and DeVoto that Mark Twain never analyzed any effect beyond its mere grammar, there exist his many letters to William Dean Howells, in which he discusses minute effects of dialect, characterization, and various other problems of writing technique. These references to technique are, I believe, valuable as an index to the conceptions he held concerning the nature and function of literature, since critics—from S. T. Coleridge to T. S. Eliot—have generally maintained that the writer's comment on the principles of his craft constitutes a fertile field for criticism.

In *Mark Twain at Work*, Mr. DeVoto describes certain un-

[3] Mr. Brooks speaks of Mark Twain as "a shorn Samson" led about by a "simple Delilah" who held complete sway over him and steadily weakened his literary strength. Both Livy and Howells toned him down somewhat, and their criticism was often sound; neither effected any real change in him. Early in their married life he gave up smoking to please Livy—"just as I would . . . quit wearing socks if she thought them immoral." The reform was short-lived, and he was soon back to chain-smoking. It should be noted that Livy, reared in strict orthodoxy, followed Mark Twain into religious unorthodoxy (Paine, *Biography*, II, 650–51). The turn of this vital issue I regard as conclusive evidence of which of the two wielded the stronger influence over the other.

published manuscripts; he has there himself offered the most conclusive refutation of his own earlier doubt that Mark Twain "ever analyzed, beyond its mere grammar," an effect of his own or anyone else's. He presents a series of efforts made by Mark Twain to portray certain ideas in fiction. The two themes which then obsessed Mark Twain—and had long obsessed him—were man's helplessness in the grip of inexorable circumstance (or of the passionless, indifferent forces of the universe) and man's own pervading pettiness and cruelty. He was struggling to find the correct form for the embodiment of these ideas, ideas which Mr. DeVoto says are "repeated over and over in the various manuscripts, modulated, changed, adapted, blended, and in the end, harmonized." These ideas will be treated fully in connection with Mark Twain's fiction. Here it is noted merely that his struggle was an artist's attempt to objectify as art the innermost materials of his mind and heart, and that all this striving represents, surely, an effort on a much higher level than a mere preoccupation with grammar. Yet, in this same book, Mr. DeVoto indicates that when the drive of Mark Twain's genius and his impulse to write were "in circuit with the deeper levels of his phantasy things went well, but when the circuit was broken he could only improvise." In other words, when he was "right," he was wonderful; but he exerted no conscious control over his writing.

Aware of the importance of form in writing, Mark Twain says in the *Eruption* volume that there are "some books that refuse to be written. . . . It isn't because the book is not there and worth being written—it is only because the right form for the story does not present itself. There is only one right form for a story." The passage does not exhibit a comprehensive grasp of writing discipline, but at least the concern with technique is there.

His light-handed attitude towards his own literary work, so much deplored by Mr. Brooks, must always be taken with a grain of salt, just as his disparagement of his own knowledge of books must be. Miss Brashear has made the pertinent comment that "it was a part of the legend he deliberately created about himself, either because it pleased his vanity to believe that what he had read had been of small value in his development, or because he knew that he was more interesting to his American public in the role of an original than as a man who had from boyhood extended his powers . . . by diligent reading. He was unacademic, but not unliterary." Speaking of his own assets as a novelist, he once wrote: "I surely have the equipment, a wide culture, and all of it real, none of it artificial, for I don't know anything about books." Again, he insisted that he did not know "enough to hurt" about books, "Only a few languages and a little history." Yet the compilations of his reading by Henry A. Pochmann, Miss Brashear, and Mr. Wagenknecht show that he had considerable familiarity with books. As Mrs. J. T. Fields recorded in her diary on April 6, 1876, after a visit from him, "he reads everything." Indeed, Miss Brashear goes so far as to declare that, leaving out of account all aspects of his training except the literary aspect, "Sam Clemens became a reader and critic of the best in literature by the time he was twenty-five years old."

Mr. Wagenknecht, whose book is devoted to the thesis that Mark Twain was not a conscious artist, states that "he did not take himself very seriously as a man of letters." Mr. Wagenknecht finds Mark Twain "abnormally sensitive, aesthetic, creative," although different from the general run of writing men. He follows Mr. De-Voto in his opinion of the frontier as the thing basically determinative in Mark Twain and perhaps goes beyond DeVoto when he declares: "To say that Mark Twain was an 'improvisator,' a *raconteur*, is . . . virtually equivalent to saying that he was a talker and not a writer."

This, it seems to me, is going a bit too far. Of the element of orality in Mark Twain's work there can be no question. He could copy to the life the anecdotal technique of the frontier raconteur, reproducing carefully the vocal emphasis, the speech rhythms, the authentic idioms. But there can be no question, either, of his knowledge of the distinctions between talking and writing. He made distinctions even between the methods of handling frontier anecdotes which he intended for use on the platform and for printing in his books, because he knew, as he said in the *Eruption* book, that "written things are not for speech; their form is literary; . . . they have to be limbered up, broken up, colloquialized, and turned into the common forms of unpremeditated talk." He used as illustration the anecdote he called "Grandfather's Old Ram," which he revised night after night upon the lecture platform until its final form for oral delivery was quite different from the original version which he had printed for reading purposes in *Roughing It*. He remarked that if the reader will compare the two, he will notice how different the spoken version is from the reading version. He confessed himself unable to explain "why the one can be effectively *recited* . . . and the other can't; there is a reason but it is too subtle for adequate conveyance. . . . I sense it but cannot express it; it is as elusive as an odor, pungent, pervasive, but defying analysis."

Conversely, he held that spoken things are not for print. His reluctance to give interviews stemmed from his belief that what would sound satisfactory to reporters would not read well in print. The novelist Elinor Glyn once interviewed him, but he refused to let her publish her script, writing bluntly to her: "It . . . is a poor literary job. . . . Approximations, synopsized speeches, translated poems, artificial flowers, and chromos all have a sort of value, but it is small." Edward W. Bok also interviewed him, but when Mark Twain read the result, his refusal to let it be published was adamant. His letter to Bok reads in part:

For several . . . reasons, an "interview" must, as a rule, be an absurdity. . . . It is an attempt to use a boat on land or a wagon on water. . . . Spoken speech is one thing, written speech is quite another. Print is the proper vehicle for the latter, but it isn't for the former. The moment "talk" is put into print, you recognize that it is not what it was when you heard it; . . . an immense something has disappeared from it. That is its soul. You have nothing but a dead carcass left on your hands . . . everything that gave that body warmth, grace, friendliness, and charm . . . is gone and nothing is left but a pallid, stiff, and repulsive cadaver. Such is "talk" almost invariably, as you see it lying in state in an "interview." The interviewer seldom tries to tell *how* a thing was said; he merely puts in the naked remark. . . . When one writes for print his methods are very different. He follows forms which have but little resemblance to conversation, but they make the reader understand what the writer is trying to convey. And when the writer is making a story and finds it necessary to report some of the talk of his characters, observe how cautiously . . . he goes at that risky and difficult thing. "If he had dared to say that thing in my presence," said Alfred, taking a mock heroic attitude and casting an arch glance upon the company, "blood would have flowed."

"If he had dared to say that thing in my presence," said Hawkwood, with that in his eye which caused more than one heart in that guilty assemblage to quake, "blood would have flowed."

"If he had dared to say that thing in my presence," said the paltry blusterer, with valor on his tongue and pallor on his lips, "blood would have flowed."

So painfully aware is the novelist that naked talk in print conveys no meaning that he loads, and often overloads, almost every utterance of his characters with explanations and interpretations. . . .

Now, in your interview, you have certainly . . . set down the sentences I uttered as I said them. But . . . what my manner was at certain points is not indicated. Therefore, no reader can possibly know where I was in earnest and where I was joking; or whether I was joking altogether or was in earnest altogether. Such a report . . . can convey many meanings to the reader, but never the right one. To add interpretations which would convey the right meaning is a something which would require—what? An art so high and fine and difficult that no possessor of it would ever be allowed to waste it on interviews.

Such delicate distinctions and fine-drawn shadings between spoken art and written art should help to refute the general impression of Mark Twain as the careless writer who simply wrote as he talked.

In 1908 he wrote to a friend, "There are times—thousands of times—when I can expose the half of my mind and conceal the other half," and such mental legerdemain increases the complexity of the Mark Twain problem. Mr. Wagenknecht takes account of this quality in him in words which recall Jane Clemens's early joke about striking his average and accepting what was left as perfect truth without a flaw. Mr. Wagenknecht warns that at the outset we must keep in mind that we are dealing with a humorist and that "the problem is to decide just what percentage to take. It is always extremely difficult to tell when Mark Twain is reporting and when he is elaborating, when he is actually conveying information to his auditor and when he is 'stringing him along.' " Yet Mr. Wagenknecht himself apparently gives serious consideration to Mark Twain's letter to a little girl, Elsie Leslie Lyde, in which he tells her that he began a slipper he has embroidered for her "with the first red bar . . . without ulterior design, or plan of any sort—just as I would begin a Prince and Pauper or any other tale"; he compares the making of a story and the putting together of the slipper, until finally "there's your book all finished up and never cost you an idea." Elsewhere Mr. Wagenknecht implies that to Mark Twain the business life was "worth two" of the literary life, since in business he could feel power in his hands: "When he finds in himself even a little aptitude along this

line, he swells up like a pouter pigeon; no purely literary achievement could for a moment be compared with it."

A good deal of the evidence tends to refute this statement. In
1909, in "The Turning Point of My Life," as he looked backward
over a long life spaced with various business ventures and acquisitions of wealth, he said, "To me, the most important feature of my
life is its literary feature." And in 1902 he wrote congratulating his
old friend Joe Goodman, who had devoted years to a study of the
Mayan civilization and inscriptions: "You think you get 'poor pay'
for your twenty years? No, oh no. You have lived in a paradise of
the intellect whose lightest joys were beyond the reach of the longest
purse in Christendom." That he himself had experienced those joys
he revealed to his daughter Clara. In *My Father, Mark Twain*, she
tells how he once complimented her for being so absorbed in her
musical studies that she cared for no other pleasures; then he continued: "It is as I used to be with the pen long ago, and it is life, *life*,
LIFE—there is no life comparable to it for a moment. Genius lives
in a world of its own. . . . Everybody lives, but only Genius lives
richly, sumptuously, imperially." He was speaking with the voice
of authority and experience. His own power of absorption in his
writing will be attested in the pages to follow.

But in praising Howells for the particular excellences in fiction
that he felt he himself lacked, he once declared, "I can't write a novel,
for I lack the faculty." Mr. Brooks considers this statement in connection with another of Mark Twain's: "I like history, biography,
travels, curious facts and strange happenings, and science. And I
detest novels, poetry, and theology." In spite of the declaration that
he couldn't write a novel, he repeatedly referred elsewhere to his
own books as novels. And the kind of novels he detested included
the namby-pamby products of sentimental "lady authoresses" and
books blighted by what he called "niggling analysis" and "jejune
romanticism." Mr. Brooks, however, was led to write: "Do we ask,
then, why Mark Twain 'detested' novels? It was because he had been
able to produce only one himself and that a failure."[4]

But it is time to turn from the critics to Mark Twain—this man
who "detested" novels, who was "indifferent" to literary effects and

[4] Quoted in Wagenknecht, *Mark Twain: The Man and His Work*, 48. In justice to Mr. Brooks, it should be noted that Mr. Wagenknecht used the 1920 edition
of *The Ordeal of Mark Twain*, not the revised edition of 1933.

"insolent" toward his own literary work. In 1894, in an essay called "What Paul Bourget Thinks of Us," he wrote a reasoned discussion on the importance of the novel which gives it an authority only recently yielded to it by men of our own time. He placed the novelist above the mere compiler of data (the statistician) or the "naturalist" with his collection of bugs which he studies and labels (the equivalent of our modern sociologist with his case studies):

The Observer of Peoples . . . , when he is at home, observing his own folks, . . . is often able to prove competency. But . . . when he is abroad observing unfamiliar peoples the chances are heavily against him. He is then a naturalist observing a bug. . . . He could explain . . . the bug to himself. But to explain the bug to the bug—that is quite a different matter.

A foreigner can photograph the exteriors of a nation, but . . . no foreigner can report its interior—its soul, its life, its speech, its thought. I think that a knowledge of these things is acquirable in only one way . . . *absorption;* years and years . . . of intercourse with the life concerned; of living it, indeed. . . . Observation? . . . One learns peoples through the heart, not the eyes or the intellect.

There is only one expert who is qualified to examine the souls and the life of a people and make a valuable report—the native novelist. . . . How much of his competency is derived from conscious "observation"? The amount is so slight that it counts for next to nothing. . . . Almost the whole capital of the novelist is the slow accumulation of *un*conscious observation—absorption. . . .

To return to novel-building. Does the native novelist try to generalize the nation? No, he lays plainly before you the ways and speech and life of a few people grouped in a certain place—his own place—and that is one book. In time he and his brethren will report to you the life and the people of the whole nation. . . . And when a thousand novels have been written, *there* you have the soul of the people, the life of the people, the speech of the people; and not anywhere else can these be had. And the shadings of character, manners, feelings, ambitions, will be infinite.

Mark Twain brought to the writing of such books as *Huckleberry Finn* and *Pudd'nhead Wilson* the sort of "unconscious observation —absorption" that he specifies here as the equipment of the novelist. But that he also gave a deal of time to thinking about the writing craft must begin to be evident.

Nevertheless, it must be freely admitted that much of his work

39

shows artistic weaknesses. In his first book about Mark Twain, Mr. DeVoto comments on his intrusion of burlesque into superb literary material and, more recently, on his "painful disharmonies." The most damaging charge made by Mr. Brooks is that the true satirist must substitute a new and personal ideal for the satirized "racial ideal" (as he terms it) and that Mark Twain has no ideal to set up as the measure of society; in other words, he lacks a "norm." Mr. Wagenknecht says that he lacked the ability to project himself very far and that there is an intermediate stage in the creative process that he seemed never quite able to master. His abundant creative energy was "never more than imperfectly under his own command. The natural result is that hardly any of his books achieve unity of tone or succeed in maintaining anything like a standard of uniform excellence." Painful disharmonies, lack of a norm, failure to achieve unity of tone—there is a basic similarity in these critical strictures against the work of Mark Twain. Granting that much of the time he worked consciously towards a foreseen and desired end—and this is what the evidence shows—how are we to explain such weaknesses in his work?

The shadowy outlines of the Mark Twain problem begin to appear. Obvious questions concern the effects of this disharmony, this lack of unity, upon the artistic quality of his literary work. But, beyond that, an analysis of what Mr. DeVoto calls "the bases of Mark Twain's mind" seems called for. And then, what conflict or conflicts existing at the "bases of his mind" made it impossible for him to achieve the norm demanded by Mr. Brooks, the harmony found lacking by Mr. DeVoto, or the unity of tone desired by Mr. Wagenknecht?

CHAPTER 3

The World Within

THE spectacular externals—particularly the effect of Mark Twain on other men—are significant and interesting; but it is necessary, too, to focus on the world within, in order to learn, so far as is possible, something of his aesthetic tastes, always important to the inner life of the artist. Mr. Brooks has charged that his spirit was closed to experience; however, in the field of aesthetic experience he had some curious adventures. There was a deep sensitiveness to beauty in him, but he would not always let his responses have full sway. Sometimes, in fact, he could not because of his prejudices.

In one field, however, his response to beauty was immediate and untrammeled—the beauty of nature, for which no special training is necessary for appreciation. In a letter to Elizabeth Wallace he describes the splendors of an autumn landscape as "heaven and hell and sunset and rainbows and the aurora all fused into one divine harmony," and his reaction is so intense that he cannot "look at it and keep the tears back." Again, in a letter to Clara Clemens, he is "drunk . . . with the autumn foliage"; and he says, "I have to shut my eyes to shave; this painted dream distracts my hand and threatens my throat. And I have to stop and write this postscript to quiet my mind and lower my temperature, so that I can go and stand between the windows again and without peril resume." Running water excited him, as it did Emerson; and to see rural England filled him with "rapture and ecstasy." Stormfield, his last home, was designed by John Mead Howells, the son of his old friend William Dean Howells, so that it fitted naturally into a beautiful setting of dark pines and cedars. There, he would allow no pictures on the walls. "Pictures in this house would be an impertinence," he said. "No artist has ever equaled that landscape." His childhood glimpses of the Mississippi under starlight or shining in the sun had given him a criterion for the beauties of nature. But in other provinces of beauty, particularly in the fine arts where some special technical training is needed for fullest enjoyment, he was not so fortunate. Indeed, he remarked in *The Innocents Abroad* in a discouraged mood that if it were not for his love of the beauties of the natural world, he would think all appreciation for beauty had been left out of his make-up. Nevertheless, his sincere efforts to acquire a conventional culture may be traced from the evenings which the seventeen-year-old boy spent in the printers' libraries of New York on through his visits as a pilot to the picture galleries of St. Louis down to his continued wanderings through the domains of European art. And always there is a development, an unfolding of his latent capacities for aesthetic enjoyment.

In music, there was again one type for which he did not have to cultivate an appreciation—the Negro spirituals. In 1897 he wrote to Joe Twichell from Lucerne, Switzerland, about a visiting "detachment" of jubilee singers:

Arduous and painstaking cultivation has not . . . artificialized their music, but . . . to my surprise—has mightily reinforced its eloquence and beauty. Away back in the beginning—to my mind—their music made all other vocal music cheap. . . . It is utterly beautiful, to me; and it moves me infinitely more than any other music can. I think that in the Jubilees and their songs America has produced the perfectest flower of the ages; and I wish it were a foreign product, so that she would worship it and lavish money on it and go properly crazy over it.

Despite his characteristic tendency to superlatives, this passage reflects the fine sensitiveness within him; and twentieth-century America begins to share his appreciation for the quality of this music.

His feeling towards "classical music," however, is another story. In his early attendance at Wagnerian opera, he complained that "the banging and slamming and booming and crashing were something beyond belief." But he came to consider *Tannhäuser* a thing "so divinely beautiful" that he felt it should be used "as a religious service." In both *The Innocents·Abroad* and *A Tramp Abroad* he is seen marveling at the enthusiasms of musical and artistic circles, astonished at the deep response elicited by works of art, and frankly envious of that enjoyment. On one occasion he wrote, "I have never heard enough classical music to be able to enjoy it, and the simple truth is I detest it"; but he wrote also, "I dislike the opera because I want to love it and can't," a confession notable for both its frankness and its humility. In time he grew to love Beethoven, Schubert, Chopin, and Brahms so much that the unwieldy Orchestrelle which played their compositions must be moved from the winter home to the summer home so that he would not be separated from his favorites.[1]

In the field of art criticism he reviled the "snuffling old masters" especially Raphael and Botticelli. But here again he admitted his own shortcomings: "As I have had no teaching in art . . . I am obliged to depend on my own crude standards." He refused, however, to imitate what others had said, or to claim dishonestly a pleasure he did not feel. In *The Innocents Abroad* he generally liked the copies better than the originals, their colors were "so bright and fresh." But when he revisited the galleries twelve years later in *A Tramp Abroad*, he found "a mellow richness, a subdued color" in the originals which the copies could not imitate.

In literature he learned early to use what books held in store for him, and he had a remarkably retentive memory. Mrs. J. T. Fields commented that in the early days he read "everything." By the time Paine knew him in 1906, he had restricted his reading largely to a group of old favorites which he read again and again, keeping them ever at hand. These included Suetonius, Saint-Simon, Pepys, Lecky, Malory, and Carlyle. Copies of Suetonius and Carlyle lay on his bed the day he died. Great favorites of a somewhat earlier period had been Cervantes, Plutarch, Casanova, Darwin, Macaulay, and Dickens's *Tale of Two Cities*. Goldsmith's *Citizen of the World* he heartily admired, but he detested *The Vicar of Wakefield* as heartily. He liked the work of H. G. Wells, George Bernard Shaw, Thomas Hardy, Olive Schreiner, Elizabeth Robins, John Hay, Willa Cather, Booth Tarkington, William Allen White, and James Branch Cabell. Hardy's *Jude the Obscure* was his last continuous reading, shortly before his death. Among literary allusions in his work, Pochmann counted many more from the Bible than from any other source, with Shakespeare next in order.[2] He particularly liked history and biography, astronomy and geology. Paine wrote: "I am constantly amazed at his knowledge of history—all history—religious, political,

[1] Wagenknecht, *Mark Twain: The Man and His Work*, 29.
[2] *Ibid.*, 43, 35.

military. He seems to have read everything in the world concerning Rome, France, and England."

Among novelists, he lauded his friend Howells, praising his skill in characterization: "The creatures of God do not act out their natures more unerringly than yours do." He admired Howells' ability to make emotions and motives clear "without analyzing the guts out of them, the way George Eliot does."

There were, of course, books he disliked, and his vigorous denunciations of them were so characteristically Twainian that they stick in the memory. He classed George Eliot and Hawthorne together because of their "niggling analysis": "I see what they are at a hundred years before they get to it, and they just tire me to death." He declared he had "rather be damned to John Bunyan's heaven" than to read Henry James's *The Bostonians*. He soberly charged James Fenimore Cooper with breaking eighteen out of nineteen rules of good writing. Godwin's theories annoyed him, and he remarked that from Godwin's point of view the last syllable of his name was superfluous. He held that the "mincing, smirking procession" of words in Dowden's *Life of Shelley* turned it into "a literary cakewalk." Howells, who remembered that Mark Twain was "always reading some vital book," remembered as well his distinct loathings in literature: "there were certain authors whose names he seemed not so much to pronounce as to spew out of his mouth." One of these, alas, was Howells' great favorite, Jane Austen. Perhaps because Howells praised her so constantly, Mark Twain went to the other extreme. He maintained stoutly, "A very good library may be started just by leaving Jane Austen out of it"; and he said, "When I take up one of Jane Austen's books, I feel like a barkeeper entering the kingdom of heaven." He confessed, "I often want to criticize Jane Austen, but her books madden me so that I can't conceal my frenzy from the reader; and therefore I have to stop every time I begin." He declared he could read Poe "on a salary," but not Jane Austen: "Jane is impossible. It seems a great pity that they allowed her to die a natural death."

Another pet abhorrence was Sir Walter Scott. In *Life on the Mississippi* he holds that the South derived her "jejune romanticism" and "medieval chivalry silliness" from Scott, and he ends by holding Scott responsible for the Civil War. Once during a long illness he tried to read Scott himself; after a few days he despairingly drew up a set of twelve questions on Scott and sent it to Brander Matthews with a plea for "help and elevation." Matthews, he pointed out, would not waste his time; he could make lectures out of the results to give to his students at Columbia University. The letter ends: "Brander, I lie here dying, slowly dying, under the blight of Sir Walter. I have read the first volume of *Rob Roy* . . . and I can no longer hold my head up or take my nourishment. Lord, it's all so juvenile! so artificial, so shoddy; and such wax figures and skeletons and specters. . . . but I will reflect, and not quit this great study rashly." Certainly, he was willing to receive instruction. But before Matthews could reply, Mark Twain wrote again: "I finished *Guy Mannering*—that curious, curious book, with its mob of squalid shadows gibbering around a single flesh-and-blood being—Dinmont; a book crazily put together out of the very refuse of the romance artist's stage properties—finished it and took up *Quentin Durward*. . . . It was like leaving the dead to mingle with the living; it was like withdrawing from the infant class in the College of Journalism to sit under the lectures in English literature in Columbia University. I wonder who wrote *Quentin Durward?*"

Born of Southern parents on the Southwestern frontier, Mark Twain was the direct inheritor of a group of Southern and Southwestern humorists that included Augustus Baldwin Longstreet, William Tappan Thompson, Johnson J. Hooper, Joseph G. Baldwin, George W. Harris, Thomas B. Thorpe, and others. These men wrote many sketches that were, as Franklin J. Meine has called them, the earliest literary realization of the frontier. Finding the incongruities of their daily lives to be sources of humor, they became skilled local-colorists who seized on the oddities in rustic or pioneer character in productions that went across the country in the columns of newspapers and were ready at hand for use as fillers in the newspaper exchanges. Sam Clemens knew this frontier humor well; he knew also the comic verbal devices of such literary comedians as George H. Derby, the California humorist better known as "John Phoenix."

He made free use of all this frontier humor in his own work. He believed himself to be highly original and once spoke of plagiarism as "a crime I never committed in my life." When he was holding any European work in his mind strongly enough for it to become an "influence," he himself was usually conscious of the fact and tried painstakingly to make acknowledgment. Apparently, he recognized a real debt to Cervantes; hence we have the acknowledgments to *Don Quixote* woven into *Huckleberry Finn*. In *A Connecticut Yankee*, Sandy relates a medieval fight in the style of Malory and Mark Twain footnoted his borrowing from *Morte d'Arthur*. The "Double-Barrelled Detective Story," which he traced to his reading of Conan Doyle, has in it a character named Sherlock Holmes. His use of the frontier humor, however, remained unacknowledged because he was not conscious of doing any borrowing. This humor invaded him completely, lived in his memory, and permeated his thought. He used the frontier humorists who preceded him freely and gladly, with no thought of plagiarism; and they play a larger part in his writings than do any other sources. But with Mark Twain the genre of the tall tale reached the level of genius.

In the appreciation of poetry, he progressed from a lowly stage in which the one poem he really cared for was C. F. Alexander's "The Burial of Moses" to an abiding love for the poet Browning. At his home in Hartford he held "Browning evenings" at intervals during 1886 and 1887. His hearers found his readings from Browning exquisite; it is doubtful, however, that they realized what those readings cost him in time and effort. Paine testified that his impromptu reading of some verses on Negro life could not have been improved upon: "We were held breathless by his dramatic fervor and power." But there was nothing impromptu in his approach to Browning. Robert Underwood Johnson wrote, "His voice was peculiarly musical and . . . his clear rendering of meanings in the most involved versification was sometimes like the opening of a closed door." Nevertheless, he had worked to pry open that door. During the Browning evenings he wrote to Mrs. A. W. Fairbanks: "It is very enjoyable work: only it takes three days to prepare an hour's reading. It takes me much longer to learn how to read a page of Browning than a page of Shakespeare. . . . The other day I took a glance at one of his mature pieces, to see how I am likely to fare when I get along over there. It was absolutely opaque!" Apparently, his ability to do something was measured by his desire to accomplish it. Before reading a Browning poem, according to Paine, "he studied it line by line, even word by word; dug out its last syllable of meaning . . . and indicated with pencil every shade of emphasis which would help to reveal the poet's purpose." The idea of a Mark Twain who willingly consigned himself to a task of such painstaking delicacy as his graduated underscorings and carefully scaled tonal values demanded is at variance with the popular idea of the negligent, the careless Mark Twain. Grace King wrote, "To him there were no obscure passages . . . no guesses at meaning. . . . He understood Browning as did no one else I ever knew."

His aesthetic experience no doubt still leaves much to be desired; but his attainment shows that he recognized his deficiencies, tried to keep an open mind, and attempted a sort of self-culture with a result that is in no wise contemptible.[3] In addition to his aesthetic conversions, the evidence presents a record of his intellectual progression on many subjects. Sometimes over a period of time he even reversed himself, as he did, for example, in his views on woman suffrage. His switch on the Spanish-American War was not long delayed. Despite his hatred for wars in general, he was at first favorably disposed to this one. From Vienna, he wrote to Joseph Twichell in June, 1898:

I have never enjoyed a war—even in written history—as I am enjoying this one. For this is the worthiest one that was ever fought, so far as my knowledge goes. It is a worthy thing to fight for one's freedom; it is another sight finer to fight for another man's. And I think this is the first time it has been done.

He desired to do homage to the soldiers and sailors who were enlisted for a "most righteous war," and he hoped that they might make "decisive work of it and leave Cuba free and fed when they face for home again." But when American designs for economic exploitation filtered to him across the sea, he wrote in January, 1900, again to Twichell: "Apparently we are not proposing to set the Filipinos free and give their islands to them. . . . If these things are so, the war out there has no interest for me." Later, when he found that the United States meant to annex the Philippines, he saw its imperialism for what it was; in that sorry realization, the disappointed idealist in him flamed: "When the United States sent word to Spain that the Cuban atrocities must end, she occupied the highest moral position ever taken by a nation. . . . But when she snatched the Philippines she stained the flag."

[3] *Ibid.*, 20–49, presents a chapter with the heading "The World Within" which traces Mark Twain's developing appreciation of the fine arts in more detailed fashion than the space available here allows.

He sometimes experienced reversals of opinion on certain books he read. He told Paine of reading *The Age of Reason* as a cub pilot "with fear and hesitation, but marveling at its fearlessness and wonderful power. I read it again a year or two ago . . . and was amazed to see how tame it had become." Another case in point appears in a letter to Howells in 1887. Because it reveals certain characteristic turns in the mind of Mark Twain, it is quoted here almost in full:

When I finished Carlyle's French Revolution in 1871, I was a Girondin; every time I have read it since, I have read it differently—being influenced and changed, little by little, by life and environment (and Taine and St. Simon): and now I lay the book down once more, and recognize that I am a Sansculotte!—And not a pale, characterless Sansculotte, but a Marat. Carlyle teaches no such gospel: so the change is in *me*—in my vision of the evidences.

People pretend that the Bible means the same to them at 50 that it did at all former milestones in their journey. I wonder how they can lie so. It comes of practice, no doubt. . . . *Nothing* remains the same. When a man goes back to look at the house of his childhood, it has always *shrunk;* there is no instance of such a house being as big as the picture in memory and imagination call[s] for. . . .

Well, that's loss. To have house and Bible shrink so, under the disillusioning corrected angle, is loss. . . . But there are compensations. You tilt the tube skyward and bring planets and comets and corona flames a hundred and fifty thousand miles high into the field. Which I see you have done, and found Tolstoi. I haven't got him in focus yet, but I've got Browning.

This letter presents several favorite themes of Mark Twain's: the Bible, the constellations, the influence of environment, and the idea of diminishing or magnifying something. All of these ideas appear as recurrent themes, some of them in his travel books, all of them in his fiction. At this point, the important thing is the letter's emphasis on his capacity for mental change and development.

If he could grow and learn and change and adapt himself in so many other fields, why could he not perfect his own craft—the craft of writing? He did, of course, show considerable progress in its techniques; as a writer he was always alert for any means of improvement. In 1887, after a complimentary notice published by Howells, Mark Twain wrote to him: "I haven't as good an opinion of my work as you hold of it, but I've always done what I could to secure and enlarge my opinion of it." To dismiss, as DeVoto does in *Mark Twain's America,* the whole list of his disharmonies, mixtures of genres, lack of unity, and various faults of technique with the implication that they all stem from the frontier practice of tale-telling is to deny Mark Twain any capacity for improvement in the craft he himself labeled "the most important feature of my life."

It is true that as a boy in the print shop in Hannibal he set type for fillers derived from the humorous sketches of backwoods life which were even then opening up new fields of realism; but the fillers were derived also from the classic wit of Dr. Johnson, the polished aphorisms of Pope, and the easy-flowing prose of Addison.[4] In other words, Mark Twain must have assimilated at an early age something of the rudiments of what is known as *form* in literature. In "The Turning-Point of My Life," he asserted: "One isn't a printer ten years without setting up acres of good and bad literature, and learning—unconsciously at first, consciously later—to discriminate between the two."

Howells was surely right when he wrote in 1872 of *Roughing It* that "the grotesque exaggeration and broad irony with which the life is described are conjecturably the truest colors that could have been used, for all existence there must have looked like an extravagant joke, the humor of which was only deepened by its netherside of tragedy." And much of Mark Twain's writing is imbued with the very spirit of the West—grotesque, violent, ironic. But as early as the summer of 1872 he could drop the Western manner completely to produce his little vignette, "A True Story," which signaled his first appearance in the pages of the *Atlantic Monthly.* Although it deals with material which could easily have become melodramatic —a slave auction in Richmond where a black mother's seven children are sold away from her, one by one—he manages to key the whole thing down to a point where it is not only tolerable, but even beautiful. He begins: "It was summer-time, and twilight," and, after describing his preliminary chaffing of old Aunt Rachel, he allows her to tell her story in her own words up to the point where, warming to her subject, she arose and "towered above us, black against the stars." Exhibiting a touch of artistic restraint, he closes the story with

[4] Minnie M. Brashear, *Mark Twain, Son of Missouri,* 203, 231 (hereafter referred to as *Son of Missouri*).

the black woman's words, without any additional comment: "Oh no, Misto C——, *I* hain't had no trouble. An' no *joy*."

And here a certain emphasis appears to be warranted: Let it be remembered that Mark Twain left frontier Hannibal at seventeen; that he went east, not west; that he spent some time in New York and Philadelphia and Cincinnati before he ever saw Carson and Virginia City and San Francisco; that he lived in the West for six years only and then left it never to return; that he passed the rest of his life either in eastern cities or in Europe. It should be emphasized also that there is no intention here to minimize the tremendous importance of the West and the Southwest in the literary development of Mark Twain. But there is something more than the episodic, unformed nature of the Western and Southwestern literature then current which must be brought forward in an effort to explain his deepest weaknesses as a writer. That so much of his work either slides off into artistic failure or just misses artistic success can be charged neither to frontier thought-patterns and tall-tale techniques nor to the fact that he wrote humor.

"The making of the humorist," reiterates Van Wyck Brooks, "was the undoing of the artist." Despite the fact that Mr. Brooks denounces the West as another link in the chain which fettered the artistic soul of Mark Twain and bound him to frustration, there can be little question that the West richly developed his gift of humor and led him to the methods of anecdotal narrative; more—and this point Mr. Brooks appears to have missed altogether—the West sharpened his natural satiric gift and set him to tracking down "the damned human race" as the quarry for his satire, a hunt in which he was to grow as keen as a bloodhound on the trail.

Humor, technicians say, has its foundation in contrasts; and Mark Twain's mind was a homeland for extremes. His favorite color was a warm brilliant red; his next favorite, a snowy white. White faces, however, wearied him; he preferred brown skins, even black, to the pale-faced Caucasians. He argued to his daughter Jean that "white was not a favorite complexion with God" since he made so many dark-skinned people, "two-thirds, you see, of the human race":

To my mind one color is just as respectable as another; there is nothing important, nothing essential, about a complexion. I mean, to *me*. But with the Deity it is different. He doesn't think much of white people, He

Mark Twain and "Colonel Sellers" (John T. Raymond)

prefers the colored. Andrea del Sarto's pink-and-lily Madonnas revolt Him. . . . That is, they *would*, but He never looks at them.[5]

Mr. Wagenknecht hails his quick response to strong contrasts as one marked characteristic of the artist's temperament. But in Mark Twain the elicited response sometimes differs from the expected one, and this fact signifies the natively humorous turn of mind. He writes in the *Autobiography*: "A thoroughly beautiful woman and a thoroughly homely woman are creations which I love to gaze upon, and which I cannot tire of gazing upon, for each is perfect in her own line, and it is *perfection*, I think . . . which is the quality that fascinates us." He found a thrilling perfection in "hogwash," his name for bad poetry. *The Sentimental Song Book*, masterwork of Mrs. Julia A. Moore, "the Sweet Singer of Michigan," he carried with him when he followed the equator, reveling in its inanities; he said, " . . . the one and unfailing great quality which distinguishes her poetry . . . and makes it precious to us is its stern and simple irrelevancy." He could find the peak of enjoyment in some things, not because they were good but because they were "tranquilly, serenely, symmetrically" bad. Mark Twain was a born humorist thus far: he was born with this whimsical type of mind.

So far, only the lighter aspects of his humor have been touched upon, but there is another side which must not be ignored. The innate complexity of humor, as Thomas L. Masson has pointed out, is not lessened by the fact that it often arises from grim beginnings; it may be so closely interwoven with pathos that the two elements appear to be inextricably mixed. Masson maintains that, instead of being spontaneous as is popularly supposed, "humor is either long premeditated, or . . . the result of a background of such solemnity and gloom that the flashes of humor that come out of it only seem to be spontaneous by contrast." The genuine humorist is an intense individualist who feels his own powers and yet "recognizes the utter hopelessness of circumventing Fate. This being so, he . . . resolves to laugh it off. It is the very depth of melancholy in the genuine humorist that compels him to take this course—otherwise he would go mad." Dickens was "sensitive almost beyond words," and his early life was spent in an atmosphere of such intense gloom that his very

[5] He reported his conversation with Jean in a letter to a French girl whom he addressed as "Dear France." See "Mark Twain's Private Girls' Club," *The Ladies' Home Journal*, Vol. XXIX (February, 1912), 54.

soul was seared with it; it was from the drab background of the misery of London that his humor came. Masson calls this the "law of humor" and applies it to Mark Twain, as well as to Dickens.

Under the operation of this law, Dickens's humor may be seen as an inevitable result for one possessing both a certain turn of mind and a certain background of experience. Mark Twain, too, had this turn of mind; like Dickens, he, too, was sensitive almost beyond words. But does he parallel Dickens by having a boyhood steeped in sadness, a background of such solemnity and gloom that it could generate apparently spontaneous flashes of humor? In most respects Sam Clemens appears to have had a delightful childhood. The family of John Clemens, though often in straitened circumstances, felt no actual want. Sam left school early and went to work in a print shop; but there was no workhouse in Hannibal. Yet anyone who knows Mark Twain's work recognizes in it much of the Dickensian brand of humor, the humor inextricably mixed with sadness. It is markedly different from his Western brand, the humor of exaggeration, anti-romanticism, and broad irony which was called out by the life of the Far West. Stephen Leacock, commenting on "the real marvel of Dickens's genius"—the art of blending humor and pathos—wrote: "Mark Twain reaches it in Huckleberry Finn and Nigger Jim. The soft haze in which it lies robs it of all anger. Huck Finn could have stepped across into the pages of Dickens." This aspect of Mark Twain's humor is integral in the nature of his art. What, then, is its source?

Howells, in a moment of clear-sightedness, half formulated a theory which may contain the answer to this question. In 1901, reviewing Mark Twain's literary work, Howells spoke of the "instinct of right and wrong which keeps him clear as to the conditions that formed him, and their injustice." What were the unjust conditions that formed Mark Twain? Howells suggested that it is conceivable that being always in the presence of the underdog, with a sort of clairvoyance he "came to feel for him as being under with him;" that it is supposable that the "ludicrous incongruity of a slave-holding democracy" quickened in him the sense of contrast which is the fountain of humor, and that if "the knowledge and vision of slavery did not tinge all life with potential tragedy, perhaps it was this which lighted in the future humorist the indignation at injustice which glows in his page."

In that childhood of Sam Clemens, mainly so delightful, there were moments which must have sunk deep into the mind of a sensitive child. He once saw a white man kill his slave with a lump of iron for some trifling offense. He vividly remembered seeing a dozen black men and women chained together, lying on the pavement, waiting shipment to a slave market: "They had the saddest faces I ever saw." That his vision of slavery was ever present in his submerged consciousness is illustrated by an incident which occurred in India, in 1896. He saw a burly hotel-owner strike a servant across the face; and instantly, back through threescore years, for just one moment, "All that goes to make the *me* in me was in a Missourian village, on the other side of the globe."

If Howells was right, it was the memories of slavery which life had hung up in the back of Mark Twain's mind that furnished the dull and somber curtain over which the flashes of his humor played. His vision of slavery had been for him what the London workhouse, the drab squalor, had been for Dickens. The flame of indignation at injustice which that vision had lighted in him burned to the last. In fact, as Brooks remarks, in his last years it was only the spectacle of the weak being oppressed by the strong which could move him to write.

On critical questions, we found Brooks asserting that Mark Twain was continually at war with his environment in the West, while DeVoto saw him as utterly at home in the Western surroundings that "completed" him. He generally appeared to be, externally at least, at ease in whatever surroundings he found himself. His uncouth appearance in his first contact with the East simply testified to his love of the irregular, the unexpected. The effect which he obviously had upon many Easterners amused him, perhaps. There is little evidence that he was ill at ease himself. From his pilot days on, he had been accustomed to the spotlight.

Still, there was much development to come. In *The Innocents Abroad* there is occasionally a trace of the brashness and uncertainty of what is known as the "typical American tourist." By the time of his residences abroad, however, this trace had vanished. He seems to have adapted himself to the life there with easy grace, always courteous and accepting homage without awkward protest, completely free from embarrassment.

This outward poise would seem to indicate a corresponding inward harmony and control. Unfortunately, the true condition of that inward life must have been far different. "Like Dickens, like Theodore Roosevelt," says Mr. Wagenknecht, "he lived in a storm. Not outwardly, exteriorly, as these men lived—he moved, he talked like a lord of the manor always—but inwardly." The bases of that inward storm, which Mr. Wagenknecht makes no attempt to define, are also, of course, the bases of whatever failings may be held against Mark Twain as a literary artist.

CHAPTER 4

The Four "Bases" of Mark Twain's Mind

THE effort to determine whether Mark Twain worked as a "conscious" and careful craftsman must be concerned with his intentions, with reading his purposes as they become legible; and even in the broader reaches of the subject, with reference to the mind of Mark Twain. For behind every literary work there is a conception in the mind of the writer, however vague; and the ultimate significance of the work depends upon the quality of this conception, just as the final form depends upon the writer's skill in translating the conception into words. Bliss Perry said in *A Study of Prose Fiction* that it is the province of criticism "to make clear, if possible, the relationship of the form or content of any work of fiction to the mind of the artist that produced it." It is a critical truism that content and form are intimately related to the artist's personality. And what is personality but the sum total of an individual's mental qualities and emotional tendencies? Nevertheless, the mind of an artist may be revealed through his work. It is the business of criticism to make him understood.

Mark Twain seethed with contradictions. A Puritan-Presbyterian by early training, he was temperamentally inclined to "free thinking." An inheritor of various Southern traditions as a scion of the Virginia Clemenses, he was more akin in spirit to the Western and Southwestern freedom from tradition, even hatred of it. His background and experience placed him squarely in the midst of the conflict between realism and romanticism which filled the later years of the nineteenth century: the adventures contingent upon settling the West invited a romantic coloring, but the vicissitudes of frontier life enforced a realistic point of view. Inasmuch as the realist's intent is to show man what he is, while the romanticist's is to show him what he should be, Mark Twain's work enrolled him among the realists; yet the romanticist in him sometimes fought the realist. But there was still another conflict even more influential, so far as his art was concerned, than any of these.

Paine was right when he said that Mark Twain's creed could be put into one word—humanity. From the early days in the West to the time when he last lays his pen aside, he is never long without some cause to champion, some wrong to right, some victim to defend. He is always fiercely stirred; he becomes a willing channel for what has been called the Anglo-Saxon corrective passion. Almost abnormally sensitive, he looks upon the woes of the world, and he suffers. He asks himself, Who has put these wrongs upon mankind? And he answers himself, Mankind. Very well, then; he will reform mankind.

Reasons advanced to explain this or that tendency in an author, to account for this or that quality in his work, must always remain speculative. But two tendencies in Mark Twain, each of which impaired his work from the artistic point of view, can be followed through his writings to the point where they come into violent conflict with each other. DeVoto, it will be recalled, has suggested the need for an analysis of what he calls "the bases of Mark Twain's mind." This analysis, which I have attempted, reveals a violent mental conflict, a logical dilemma, which forced much of his work into distorted patterns of both thought and structure, frequently making it impossible for him to achieve unity of any sort.

On the one hand, he was the rabid reformer, eager to uplift, instruct, and purify mankind. On the other, he was the dogmatic determinist, preaching as the text of his "Gospel" that the inborn disposition of mankind is "a thing which is as permanent as rock, and never undergoes any actual or genuine change between cradle and grave"—a doctrine which in effect renders useless all attempts to uplift, instruct, or purify mankind. The clash of ideas resulting from this logical dilemma was frequently great enough, the divergence in the two lines of thought was frequently wide enough, to furnish a plausible explanation for the structural defects, the lack of a norm, and the want of unity in tone which the critics have lamented as his chief failings as a literary artist.

As a reformer he has his own ways of administering reform: he will wrap it in a rollicking joke, sheathe it in bold burlesque, or clothe it in caustic satire. He knows that men will often accept in a jest what they will evade or ignore in a serious medium and that if the jest is repeated often enough they may even discover the truth at its core. DeVoto said truly that there were few elements of Mark Twain's age which he did not burlesque, satirize, or deride. From the first, he realized the humorist's opportunity as an instrument of social reform. It was the phase of his humorous work to which he most wholeheartedly dedicated himself and directed his efforts, sometimes successfully, sometimes less skilfully, sometimes bunglingly. Wagenknecht points out that Mark Twain was a born reformer. But he could not be satisfied in the role of the reformer-as-humanitarian. He must needs be also the reformer-as-moralist; for if the morals of mankind could but be reformed, all humanitarian reforms would become unnecessary. And the moralist in Mark Twain soon came to do violence to his literary art.

Much has been written of his rigid Calvinistic upbringing. In many ways, however, his was no rule-of-thumb morality. He maintained throughout his work a consistent praise of human nakedness. As Huck Finn put it, "Clothes is well enough in school and in towns, and at balls, too, but they ain't no sense in them where there ain't no civilization nor other kinds of bothers and fussiness around." Mark Twain retained these ideas. In an address near the end of his life he declared that "the finest clothing made is a person's own skin."

He encountered in Europe the practice of smoking by women and apparently did not disapprove. He himself smoked constantly. "Me, who never learned to smoke, but always smoked," he says; "me, who came into the world asking for a light"—and we are reminded of Rabelais' gigantic infant, Gargantua, who came into the world calling for a drink. As to drinking, Mark Twain seems to have indulged himself rather freely in his Western days. Later, a letter to Howells reports a Boston midnight dinner: "Osgood, full, Boyle O'Reilly, full, Fairchild responsively loaded, and Aldrich and myself possessing the floor and properly fortified. Cable . . . called it an orgy. And no doubt it was, viewed from his standpoint." Mark Twain used liquors as refreshment all his life.

He was not squeamish in giving his friendship. In the *Autobiography* he tells of Wales McCormick, a fellow apprentice, who "had no principles and was delightful company." On the *Quaker City* excursion he wrote to his mother of his roommate, Dan Slote, "I am fixed. I have got a splendid, immoral, tobacco-smoking, wine-drinking, godless roommate who is as good and true and right-minded a man as ever lived." Viewing these facts, it is the more surprising to find him reacting in the confirmed Victorian manner on the one particular subject—sex.

In his rambles in Europe he consistently confuses morals and art, as will be demonstrated more fully in the discussion of his travel books. He mentions Boccaccio's "improper tales" in the *Autobiography;* he speaks of "the loose but gifted Byron"; in *Life on the Mississippi,* when it becomes necessary for him to indicate sexual intercourse outside of marriage, he employs the stereotyped phrase, "they sinned." The crowning touch is the famous incident in which he abandoned his plans to aid Maxim Gorky in furthering the Russian revolution the instant he learned that Gorky's lady traveling companion was not his wife. He once admitted to having one racial prejudice, and one only—the French. He gave no reason for it; but the evidence indicates that it was founded on what he considered the sexual irregularities of the French people.

On the other side of the ledger appear "1601," a famous piece of pornography in American literature; the "Doleful Ballad of the Rejected Lover," which Mark Twain sang with Steve Gillis in the San Francisco streets at night; and the uncontestable Rabelaisianism of his conversation, occasional letters, and some speeches. He once complained, "Delicacy—a sad, sad false delicacy—robs literature of the best two things among its belongings. Family circle narrative and obscene stories."

Paradoxical Mark Twain! bewailing the loss to literature of "obscene stories," yet carefully, so carefully, detouring around an irregular bit of actual life with the pious pronouncement, "they sinned." But the sensitiveness to literary material, the perception of the artist, could still make him lament the "sad, sad false delicacy" of such circumlocutions. The perceptions of the artist, Wagenknecht remarks, by his very nature reach out "antennae-like, in all directions, and the first question he asks of a proffered stimulus is not whether it is 'good,' but whether it is 'strong.' " True enough, doubtless, as regards the artist. Suppose, though, that you have a moralist who asks of a proffered stimulus not whether it is "strong" but whether it is "good"? If your artist and your moralist live inside the same skin, there will be some curious results.

The genuine humorist is an intense individualist aware of his own powers. Sometimes he may try, as Mark Twain wrote to Andrew Lang, to uplift "the mighty mass of the uncultivated . . . that are best worth trying to uplift." He may be particularly impelled towards this task if he has shared with his fellows in a wide variety of experiences. During the period of westward expansion in the United States there grew up what Professor Lovejoy explains as romanticism's equivalent for universality: the insistence that "the great individual must possess a comprehensive knowledge of every activity of mankind and a sympathy to match his knowledge." Mr. Wagenknecht has noted that in equipping Mark Twain with his immensely varied range, life groomed him for the business of authorship as she has groomed few Americans. His rare repertory included the experiences of a boy growing up in a river village where he knew the slaves intimately; traveling "jour" printer who wandered from city to city; pilot on the Mississippi during the flush times; soldier for a few weeks in the Confederate Army, accompanied by "death-on-the-pale-horse-with-hell-following-after"; quartz-miller, pocket miner, prospector, silver miner; newspaper reporter for four years on city papers; reporter in a state legislature for two sessions and in the national Congress for one session; lecturer on the public platform; responder to toasts at banquets; inventor, publisher, businessman of the Gilded Age— And once, summing up all this, he characteristically added: "And I have been an author for twenty years and an ass for fifty-five." He knew his land and its idioms as few men have ever known it. He had lived in New York, Connecticut, Missouri, Iowa, Nevada, and California, thus actually living across its wide expanse. He had been an intimate part of three great phases of its folk experience—the Southwestern frontier, the steamboat era, and the rush to the Western mines. Clearly, his comprehensive knowledge of the activities of mankind leaves nothing to be desired.

And what of that other requisite for the great individual, the sympathy to match his knowledge? Mark Twain was ever one of the most humane, the most sympathetic of men. Howells relates meeting him when he had just been sickened at the sight of a blackbird brought down by a gunner; he described "the poor, stricken, glossy thing, how it lay throbbing its life out on the grass, with such pity as he might have given a wounded child." He suffered intensely at any injustice done to an animal or a Negro or any person low in the social scale. His hurt was often as deep as that of the injured one.

Writing in 1936, Walter Fuller Taylor found Mark Twain's "broad human sympathy" of a degree sufficient to rank him with Chaucer and Shakespeare as the three most "sympathetic" authors writing in the English language. A similar imaginative fellow-feeling with the lives of others is labeled by F. O. Matthiessen as "the greatest artistic asset" of Walt Whitman. And Mark Twain might have said with Whitman:

I am the man, I suffered, I was there.

It appears paradoxical, then, to say in the face of such evidence that it is in the requirement of sympathy that he is lacking; nevertheless, it must be said. His sympathy was deep and intense; but it was not broad enough to be all-inclusive, to embrace all mankind. Sensitive for humanity's sake and conscious of his own great potentialities, Mark Twain tries to uplift the "mighty mass" of mankind. But suppose mankind refuses to be uplifted? suppose human nature refuses to change? Then it will be remembered that mankind is, after all, only "the damned human race." Then the very Creator of such men will be called to account: "God had his opportunity. He could have made a reputation. But no, He must commit this grotesque folly."

There was constant war between his opinion of humanity in the abstract and his opinion of many individuals whom he knew and loved. It was the "damned human race"; yet it had produced Joe Twichell and Henry Rogers, Olivia Clemens and Joan of Arc, black Uncle Dan'l and Auntie Cord. He could pour a warm sympathy over erring individuals; but the volcanic lava of rage rose within him when he contemplated humanity-at-large. He was always pulled in two directions at once; and that pulling apart was detrimental to the artistic elements of his work.

His "damned human race" attitude begins quite early. One of his first letters from Carson City shows a touch of contempt for his ill-assorted new neighbors. As the years go by, he will lie awake nights, figuratively, to think up new adjectives with which to bedeck "God's most elegant invention"—a race not only "damned," but "mangy," too. In 1871 he described Niagara Falls and, conjointly, mankind. Niagara is that majestic presence which was monarch here "ages before this hackful of small reptiles was deemed temporarily necessary to fill a crack in the world's unnoted myriads," and will still be monarch here ages after they have joined "their blood-relations, the other worms, and been mingled with the unremembering dust."

"Small reptiles" and "worms," men were to him in 1871; in his later great purple passages of invective he could not reduce mankind to a status much lower than this. But he could try: "Man is a museum of diseases, a home of impurities," he wrote in 1898; "he begins as dirt and departs as stench." And in 1906: "But for the despised microbe and the persecuted bacillus, who needed a home and nourishment, he would not have been created. . . . let him do the service he was made for, and keep quiet." Sometimes he reveals a weary disillusionment, as in one of his maxims: "Man was made at the end of the week when God was tired." Such statements merely sear mankind with contempt; but others show the sting and bite and corrosive bitterness that express his pain at what he sees, as in this maxim of Pudd'nhead Wilson's:

If you pick up a starving dog and make him prosperous, he will not bite you. This is the principal difference between a dog and a man.

Other maxims exhibit a large portion of sorrow mixed with the bitterness:

All say, "How hard it is that we have to die"—a strange complaint to come from the mouths of people who have had to live.

Mark Twain's pessimism, like his attitude toward the "damned human race," appears early in his work. A letter to Mrs. A. W. Fairbanks on June 3, 1876, contains the gist of the most pessimistic outbursts he was ever to make. He comments, "What a curious thing life is," and goes on to speak of the misfortunes of a certain Mr. Benedict. He feels that Benedict's lot is "about the ordinary experience and must be fairly expected by everybody":

Grand result of a hard-fought, successful career and a blameless life: Piles of money, tottering age, and a broken heart. . . .

And yet there are people who would try to save a baby's life and plenty of people who cry when a baby dies. . . . all of us cry, but some are conscious of a deeper feeling of content. . . . *I* am, at any rate. . . . What a booming springtime of life it is for Charley [Fairbanks] . . . to all seeming. I rejoice in his gladness. . . . Never mind about that grisly future season when he shall have made a dazzling success and shall sit with folded hands in well-earned ease and look around upon his corpses and mine, and contemplate his daughters and mine in the madhouse, and his sons and mine gone to the devil. That is all away yonder—we will not bother about it now.

When one remembers that Langdon Clemens, his infant son—the only son he was ever to have—had already died when he wrote this letter, his comment on the death of a baby gains added significance. And his later pronouncements on the futility of life could hardly go much beyond this letter, despite the widespread opinion that his pessimism resulted largely from his personal tragedies in later life.

His determinism seems to have been a large factor in the growth of his pessimism, and there is evidence that the deterministic strain, too, had an early beginning. Miss Brashear believes that Sam Clemens's philosophy was forming itself while he was on the river. She refers to his cub-pilot reading of Tom Paine and of Voltaire's *Dialogues* and points out that his acquaintance with Paine and Lecky would have introduced him likewise to the doctrines of Newton, Hobbes, Locke, and Hume. To Newton, the perfect mechanism of the universe is the design of Providence; to Hume, any discernible pattern is only such a pattern as a kaleidoscope produces, with no intention back of it of good or evil; but to Mark Twain there is always direction back of the pattern and often it seems to him that of a malign power. In *Following the Equator* he describes "a ghastly curiosity"—a lignified caterpillar:

It happened . . . by design—Nature's design. This caterpillar was . . . loyally carrying out a law inflicted upon him by Nature—a law which was a trap; . . . he made the proper preparations for turning himself into a night-moth; . . . he dug a little trench . . . and then stretched himself out in it . . . then Nature was ready for him. She blew spores of a peculiar fungus through the air—with a purpose. Some of them fell . . . [on] the caterpillar's neck, and began to sprout and grow—for there was soil there —he had not washed his neck. The roots forced themselves down into the worm's person . . . ; the worm slowly died and turned to wood. . . .

Nature is always acting like that. Mrs. X. said . . . that the caterpillar was not conscious and didn't suffer. . . . No caterpillar can deceive Nature. If this one couldn't suffer, Nature would have . . . hunted up another caterpillar. Not that she would have let this one go. . . . No. She would have waited and let him turn into a night-moth; and then fried him in the candle.

Thus did Mark Twain peer into the frightful dark spaces of the universe.

Something of his determinism must have come from the Calvinistic background of his early years. His denial of free will, his feeling that life is controlled by an immovable power, may owe something to his mother's Calvinism; and his view of God (or Nature) as malign may show the effect on a sensitive nature of such Calvinistic beliefs as that which holds that God has selected a large part of the race to roast in eternal torment through no fault of their own. But whatever his initial impetus may have been, he evolved a determinism that explained, for him, a great deal about the "damned human race." He wrote it down in what he called his Gospel—that is, *What Is Man?*: "Whatsoever a man is, is due to his *make*, and to the *influences* brought to bear upon it by his heredities, his habitat, his associations. He is moved, directed, COMMANDED by *exterior* influences—*solely*. He originates nothing." And he carried the cause-and-effect chain to its last link in a conversation with Paine, remarking that "the first act of the first atom has led inevitably to the act of my standing here in my dressing gown at this instant talking to you." He told Kipling, ". . . neither religion, training, nor education avails anything against the force of circumstances that drive a man. Suppose we took the next four-and-twenty years of Tom Sawyer's life, and gave a little joggle to the circumstances that controlled him. He would, logically and according to the joggle, turn out a rip or an angel."

He wished to believe in the integrity of mankind; but the more he saw of mankind's shortcomings, the more his bitterness grew. He felt only pity for the caterpillar which loyally carried out "a law inflicted upon him by Nature"; yet when men acted in accordance with their petty natures, his pity was frequently tinctured with rage.

His extreme sympathy, the degree of which often approaches sentimentality, leads him into moralism: he will reform mankind so that such wrongs will not have to be suffered. Conversely, his "damned human race" attitude leads him into determinism: surely, man could not be so vile if he had a choice to make. And the threads of his moralism and his determinism entangle themselves in his pessimism: his own efforts to reform mankind have been futile, but mankind cannot help its worthlessness—it is simply unable to respond.

In such a philosophy there is no room for the motives and incentives that give meaning to life. There is no room for the great
law of adaptation which holds that man's duty is to live in harmony
with the universe. There is no room for the belief that man's capacity
is almost infinite, that pain itself is a necessary part of experience, that
out of the struggle between good and evil emerges man's moral
character. Mark Twain's determinism leads him only to a cynical
denial, an empty negation. Yet his cynicism was shaded with romance; his despair was tinged with yearning. He could never bring
himself to accept as final what his explorations seemed to uncover to
him as the essential nature of humankind.

The purpose here is not, however, to explain his determinism
but to show its effect on his literary work. The clash between the
moralist and the determinist, it seems to me, affected his art more
profoundly than any of his other conflicts. The realist-romanticist
conflict becomes superficial in comparison with it, as more concerned with literary manner and treatment; but the moralist-deter-
minist conflict goes deeper, determining not only literary content
but also his philosophy of life and even affecting the inner consistency of man and artist.

The primary "bases" of Mark Twain's mind, then—to employ
DeVoto's phrase once more—are four: moralism, determinism, pessimism, and patheticism.[1] These attitudes reflect thought-patterns
which dominate his mental processes, thought-patterns which assert
themselves again and again throughout his work. They are sometimes mutually influential, reinforcing each other—as do patheticism
and moralism, or determinism and pessimism. But when the contra-
dictory patterns of determinism and moralism are forced together,
the results are disastrous to his work. Four bases—the phrase suggests
a solid foundation, wholesome, four-square to the world. But its
wholesome sound is belied by its destructive effect on the artist.

---

[1] *Patheticism* is a coinage of my own which has seemed advisable and even
imperative, since the terms *sentimentalism* and *sentimentality* both have connota-
tions foreign to Mark Twain's attitude, which certainly does not subscribe to the
eighteenth-century doctrine that human nature is essentially good, or to the sentimental tendency to find enjoyment in "shedding a feeling tear." Although Mark
Twain sometimes wallows in patheticism, he appears to find no enjoyment, no release, in the process.

BOOK II

The Humorous Sketches

CHAPTER 5

A "Born Humorist" and a "Born Reformer"

THE complexity of Mark Twain has been commented on by all who have more than a casual acquaintance with his writings. His work does not lend itself readily to any sort of classification. It covers many levels and many degrees of significance, but most of it is pervaded by his humor, although that humor varies in its aims and importance. He was the possessor of a mind with a peculiar slant that would have been likely to make him a humorist, no matter what his surroundings. Wagenknecht noted that, despite Mark Twain's profound love for his wife, he could not avoid distressing her by playing the funny man in his family circle, in the absence of the gallery, simply because he could not avoid being himself.

The same natively humorous attitude was disclosed in his boyhood in Hannibal. His older brother Orion wrote that when their mother began a grave lecture directed at Sam, the boy would reply "with a witticism, or dry, unexpected humor, that would drive the lecture clean out of my mother's mind, and change it to a laugh."[1] During his early days in the West his letters show the spirit of humor alive and strong in him. Accompanied by John Kinney, he made an excursion to Lake Tahoe; his letter home tells of their adventures in getting lost and wandering for hours over dangerous rocks: "I couldn't keep from laughing at Kinney's distress, so I kept behind, so that he could not see me. . . . we would toil on in silence for a while. Finally I told him, 'Well, John, what if we don't find our way out of this today—we'll know all about the country when we *do* get out.' " Sam Clemens's bewilderment and physical discomfort must have been as great as those of his companion; but instead of "cursing the thieving country" as Kinney did, he saw the humor of their situa-

[1] Paine, *Biography*, III, Appendix A, 1592.

tion. Soon after, he wrote of getting lost again, this time with a man named Bunker. The same wild joy shows in his description of the "jolly time" his companion had trying to lead two horses through the sagebrush—"it does my *soul* good when I think of it." There is frequently a quaintness in his mode of expression. In 1872 he wrote to Howells from Munich, describing his arrival there with his tired family: " . . . then up at 6 in the morning and a noble view of snow-peaks glittering in the rich light of a full moon while the hotel-devils lazily deranged a breakfast for us in the dreary gloom of blinking candles." Save one striking word, almost any other writer might have written these lines; but the *deranging* of the breakfast is the typical Mark Twain touch that transforms the sentence.

Perhaps the strongest indication that he was a humorist by nature lies in the form of release his emotions followed in times of stress. Mrs. Clemens's father had died in August, 1870; soon after, spent with grief and sleeplessness, she had a premature confinement and was dangerously ill. Then a visiting friend fell ill and died in the house, leaving Olivia more worn than ever. Almost distracted with worry about his wife, Mark Twain experienced during this period sudden changes from deep melancholy to what he described in the *Eruption* volume as "tempests and cyclones of humor." In one of these "spasms of humorous possession" he sat down and wrote the burlesque sketch entitled "The Map of Paris." When fear and grief had keyed his feelings to the highest pitch, relief came in the form of a burst of wild humor that surged up from the depths of his despair.

His mother, perhaps, endowed him with the oblique glance, the quizzical slant through which he was always to view life; he copied, by his own testimony, her drawling manner of speech. Jane Lampton Clemens perhaps bequeathed him her own gaiety and charm, as well as the lively imagination and the consuming interest in people which formed so large a part of his stock in trade as a writer. But there was further endowment. Paine tells us, "Her sense of pity was abnormal. She refused to kill even flies, and punished the cat for catching mice." Mark Twain described her as the natural ally and friend of the friendless. Her abnormal pity and "gentle indignation" were to become in her son, perhaps, those elements of pity and rage which constantly wrestled for possession of his spirit. Among his vivid memories were some exhibitions of his mother's "soldierly qualities" when she rose to the defense of some helpless person or creature. He tells in the *Autobiography* how she went out into the streets of St. Louis and took the whip away from a cartman who was beating his horse; and how at home in Hannibal she defied, shamed, and wilted a burly Corsican who was about to whip his grown daughter with a rope. Jane Clemens obviously did not content herself with "shedding a feeling tear." Her spirit prompted her to militant action in an immediate attempt to end the suffering she saw about her. She was a reformer with humanitarian tendencies.

Very different from his dynamic wife was John Marshall Clemens. In *Following the Equator* Mark Twain described him as "a refined and kindly gentleman, very grave, rather austere, of rigid probity, a sternly just and upright man." As a lawyer, he was accustomed to feed his mind with books. He was appointed or elected judge, justice of the peace, county court clerk, and postmaster; he held other posts which testify to his intellectual activity and his public spirit. He was, for instance, the president of the Hannibal Library Institute and a trustee of the Florida Academy. His intellectual freedom is evidenced by the fact that in a community where "freethinking" was taboo and his own family circle Calvinistic, he remained a freethinker. Not much given to talking, he could always express himself well with a pen. He died at forty-nine, embittered by financial reverses. His obituary, reprinted by Miss Brashear, paid tribute to his "high sense of justice and moral rectitude," to the public spirit which he "exercised zealously . . . upon every proper occasion," and especially to his efforts for "the diffusion of learning."

There was a strain of melancholy in his make-up, but, in spite of it, John Clemens did not withdraw from the world. He felt his responsibility too keenly, apparently, to make a withdrawal possible. He engaged in no spectacular humanitarianism, however; he would take the long, slow way of educational improvement, striving to instill moral principles. Miss Brashear suggests that the paternal influence on Mark Twain's mind and temperament was more potent than he himself realized; he, however, recognized only his temperamental heritage from his mother.

The contrast between his parents is clear: Jane was coquettish, witty, a great talker, and interested in the little personal world around her; John was quiet, grave, austere, and interested in the world of books. Jane had a passionate hatred of cruelty; John, immersed in

principles, had a passion for avoiding hypocrisy. Jane was an orthodox Presbyterian, a rabid Calvinist even; John was a freethinker.
Jane had a piquant charm, John an immovable integrity. Their tem-
peraments, so mutually conflicting, were yet alike in one thing:
their activity in trying to make the world a better place. Jane's
sphere of influence was immediate and concrete; but John moved
by exercising his "public spirit" and by refusing to retreat from his
moral and intellectual standards. He appears to have been the same
sort of uncompromising idealist his son was to become. Mark Twain
writes amusingly in the *Autobiography* of his father's unsuccessful
attempts to reform the morals of Jimmy Finn, the town drunkard,
and of the degenerate Injun Joe.

Mark Twain, then, perhaps received from his mother an impetus toward patheticism and from his father an inclination toward
pessimism. But one thing is certain: in his early years he had always
before him the two living examples of his mother, the reformer-as-
humanitarian, and his father, the reformer-as-moralist. How could
he escape being what Wagenknecht has called him, a "born reformer"? The only question concerns the medium he will use; but if we
accept him as a "born humorist," too, that question is answered. He
will seek to reform his world through the medium of his humor. As
humorist and as reformer he will use both the public platform and
the printed page; but his first condemnation of the human race and
his first attempts at its conversion appear through the medium of
print.

He was early smeared with printer's ink. Apprenticed to the
trade at twelve, he worked on the Hannibal *Courier* under Joseph P.
Ament for two years and perhaps three, later working on his brother
Orion's paper, the Hannibal *Journal*. Along with his task of setting
up type, now and then in the *Journal* he set up efforts of his own. His
Hannibal work was chiefly comic, much of it being devoted to baiting rival editors in direct personal ridicule. During Orion's absence,
Sam, apparently in an effort to revive interest among subscribers,
staged a three-way readers' controversy involving a poem addressed
"To Miss Katie in H——l." All this was mere experimentation. But
it is surprising how early his satiric tendency, his desire to reform
mankind, and his moralizing strain all appear.

The *Journal* for September 16, 1852, carried his sketch, "Blabbing Government Secrets," signed "W. Epaminondas Adrastus

Blabb." It contains a Twainian hit at the state legislature. In the short-lived "Our Assistant's Column," he waxed mildly satiric about spiritualism and about the ambitions and amusements of women. In May, 1853, he excoriated a drunken brute in a way that drew reproof from a rival:

The Courier says we have been advocating mob law. Nonsense! A fellow who whips his wife is not a man, and therefore can be excused properly from a "ride on a rail," because "cruelty to animals" is objectionable, and not because it is "mob law."[2]

Thus, at seventeen, Sam weighed moral responsibility, suitable punishment, and applicable phraseology. The moralist appears in an item revealing both the fascination of the city and the revulsion felt for its wickedness: "From fifteen to twenty thousand persons are continually congregated around the new Crystal Palace in New York city, and drunkenness and debauching are carried on to their fullest extent."

The last "Our Assistant's Column" appeared May 26, 1853, and soon the young columnist left for St. Louis, secretly bent on getting a job to make money to take him on to New York. He wanted to see that Crystal Palace. By August, 1853, he was working in New York in the printing office of John A. Gray. His two New York letters of August, 1853, and his Philadelphia letter of October, 1853, all seem consciously designed with an eye to publication in the home-town papers. Full of sight-seeing and personal comment, they are really travel letters, containing in embryo the same elements that went into the *Quaker City* letters fifteen years later. His travels were broadening his horizons, mental and physical, and it is apparent that he felt an obligation both to entertain and to instruct his readers.

Somewhat later Orion Clemens opened a job-printing office in Keokuk, Iowa, employing Sam there as his assistant. By this time some of Sam's letters are consciously literary, notably one in 1855 to Annie Taylor, afterwards an English teacher in Lindenwood College, St. Charles, Missouri. Part of the letter is assuredly a carefully wrought essay, an account of a performance given by the bugs attracted by the flaring gas light above his head as he stood at the press for night work. The social satirist emerges here: the bugs are

[2] *Daily Journal*, May 26, 1853; reprinted in Brashear, *Son of Missouri*, 134.

likened to a group of human beings in religious assembly, and they are "showing off" in a way that forecasts the Sunday school scene in *Tom Sawyer*, a scene not to be written for almost twenty years:

> ... a religious meeting of several million was assembled on the board before me, presided over by a venerable beetle ... while innumerable lesser dignitaries ... were clustered around him, keeping order, and at the same time endeavoring to attract the attention of the vast assemblage to their own importance. ... good seats ... were in great demand; and ... small fortunes were made by certain delegates from Yankee land by disposing of comfortable places on my shoulders at round premiums.[3]

The big president beetle then gave the signal, and the congregation sang an anthem, with three dignified daddy longlegs beating time. A chorus, "Let Every Bug Rejoice and Sing," terminated the performance, while the congregation "split their throats from head to heels." In the fervent ecstasy of showing off, these devotees literally sang themselves to death, and he buried them "with musical honors in John's hat."

This letter appears to be Mark Twain's first extended burlesque of religious ceremonies. There is exaggeration in it, certainly; but it has little of the tall-tale quality of his later Western sketches involving animal grotesques made memorable by perversity or sheer "cussedness" or sometimes by mere size, as in *Life on the Mississippi* where he writes that two Arkansas mosquitoes could whip a dog and four could hold a man down. Here the effect of the whole is one of quiet humor and deep relish for the resemblances between the actions of these tiny creatures and those of humankind. The satiric tincture reveals a sharpening perception of the "damned human race," but there is a striking difference between the calm tone of these lines of 1855 and the strident note of flamboyant grotesquerie and shocking savagery which he was later to employ in the West. It is evident, however, that the twenty-year-old job printer exercised considerable care in reporting his bug meeting.

The Sam Clemens of 1855 was stigmatized by the Mark Twain of 1876 in a letter to Frank Burrough as "a callow fool, a self-sufficient ass ... imagining that he is re-modeling the world and is entirely capable of doing it right." Despite this ridicule of his youthful

---

[3] First published in the Kansas City *Star Magazine*, Sunday, March 21, 1926; reprinted in Brashear, *Son of Missouri*, 167–68.

zeal for reform, the writer of the letter was even then, in 1876, doing business at the same old stand, as will appear.

Sam Clemens's first definite expression of a literary ambition came in Keokuk—an ambition to write humor. When Ed Brownell once asked what he was reading, Sam replied: "Oh, nothing much—a so-called funny book—one of these days I'll write a funnier book than that, myself." Keokuk friends recalled often seeing him with a volume of Poe or Dickens under his arm; his mention of the so-called funny book seems to stamp it as probably by Dickens, a probability strengthened by the fact that his next appearance in print was through three letters published in the Keokuk *Post* and signed "Thomas Jefferson Snodgrass."

These early Snodgrass letters are marked by the sort of humor in vogue at the time, a humor based on misspelling, grammatical oddities, and crude attempts at reproducing the speech of the illiterate. The first letter, written from St. Louis, October 18, 1856, exhibits Sam Clemens's early interest in the backwoods character but has no bearing upon the reform motif important for this chapter. The second, sent from Cincinnati in November, 1856, contains an oblique reference to "a New Orleans 'lection riot"; but the third and last, dated from Cincinnati, March 14, 1857, is more fruitful for the present purpose. In it young Snodgrass satirizes the red tape and methodical delay by which public officials transact the public business. In idea it is remarkably similar to "The Facts in the Case of the Great Beef Contract," which Mark Twain was to write ten years later:

An indigent Irish woman—a widow with nineteen children and several at the breast, according to custom, went to the Mayor to get some of that public coal. The Mayor he gin her an order on the Marshall; the Marshall gin her an order on the Recorder; Recorder sent her to the Constable; Constable sent her to the Postmaster; Postmaster sent her to the County Clerk, and . . . she had sixteen places to go yet, afore she could git the coal . . . the unfortunit daughter of Eve. (I say "daughter of Eve" . . . as kinder figerative or poetastical like, for I forgit, now, whether the Irish come from our Eve, or not.)

This piece suffers from comparison with the bug assembly so carefully drawn for the young lady with literary tastes. Both are satiric in intent. But Sam Clemens knew the demands of the current newspaper humor. This was 1857, and in less than a year the Cleveland *Plain Dealer* would print the first letter from "Artemus Ward, the Genial Showman," with its eccentric spelling and grammar.

In April, 1857, when he was twenty-one years old, Sam Clemens became a cub pilot on the Mississippi. Van Wyck Brooks emphasizes the severe mental discipline required for learning the pilot's trade and memorizing twelve hundred miles of the Mississippi River, believing that by this means Sam Clemens first learned the joy that comes from perfecting oneself so far as possible in some undertaking —a "pure aesthetic feeling, produced by a supreme exercise of personal craftsmanship." Much earlier, however, Sam had set himself in the same fashion to excel in the craft of the printer. Writing from New York in 1853, he told his mother of the standards maintained in the printing office of John A. Gray, where he was employed:

They are very particular about spacing, justification, proofs, etc., and even if I do not make much money, I will learn a great deal. Why, you must put exactly the same space between every two words and *every line must be spaced alike*. They think it dreadful to space one line with three em spaces, and the next one with five ems. However, I expected this, and worked accordingly from the beginning; and out of all the proofs I saw . . . I can say mine was by far the cleanest. In St. Louis, Mr. Baird said my proofs were the cleanest that were ever set in his office. . . . I believe I *do* set a clean proof.[4]

Thus, long before the river epoch, he was experienced in the mastery of troublesome details. Note his willingness to subordinate the earning of a good salary to a chance for training and self-improvement; the passage disputes the view that he habitually subordinated such considerations to his inclination for making money.

According to Paine, Sam studied diligently during his river period, on the off-watch. At twenty-four he felt himself competent to disparage Tom Hood's humor: Hood's "wit (in his letters) has a savor of labor about it which is very disagreeable." He praised the humor of one of Orion's letters because its "quiet style resembled Goldsmith's 'Citizen of the World' and 'Don Quixote'—which are my *beau ideals* of fine writing." Earlier, perhaps in reply to a suggestion of Orion's, he had written, "I cannot correspond with a paper,

4 Hannibal *Journal*, September 8, 1853; reprinted in Brashear, *Son of Missouri*, 156.

because when one is learning the river, he is not allowed to do or think about anything else."

But Sam Clemens's pilot license was granted on April 9, 1859, and afterwards he would have more time for writing. Horace Bixby recalled that "Sam was always scribbling when not at the wheel," but how much he published is uncertain. The only piece which he later acknowledged was his Isaiah Sellers burlesque.

Before he left the river, there appeared in the New Orleans *Crescent*, between January 21 and March 30, 1861, a second Snodgrass series of ten letters, signed "Quintus Curtius Snodgrass." Mark Twain never acknowledged his authorship of them in later years, and they have not been authenticated as his work. Thomas Jefferson Snodgrass was a gawking up-country bumpkin, though slyly cynical; but Quintus Curtius Snodgrass is a city man, consciously literary, a satirist, even an elegant stylist. In keeping with his classical name, he adorns his lines with Latin, French, and German phrases and with allusions to Dickens, Cervantes, Tom Paine, Shakespeare, and the Bible. Miss Brashear suggests that Sam was making use of the knowledge lately acquired from his reading and his visits to the cultural centers of St. Louis and New Orleans.

A pronounced advancement in satiric quality is exhibited by Quintus Curtius Snodgrass: instead of the crudely personal ridicule of Hannibal days or the local-office hits of Thomas Jefferson Snodgrass, the satire here has a broader scope. It is directed at the love of martial glory which enhances the pomp and pride of war; the mechanical-doll effect of military life, which finally makes automatons out of men; and the ironic regard for a slain man's clothes and military supplies rather than for his life. Snodgrass recommends that men in action adopt fatigue dress, for it is a shame "to have bullets put through broadcloth and gold lace, when flannel answers all the purpose." After covering himself "with glory and a blue uniform" by joining the Louisiana Guard, Q. C. Snodgrass quickly acquires himself that "disregard of human life which particularly characterizes military men." Certainly, these views coincide with those held by Mark Twain at any period of his life.

He had already grown skeptical when he wrote to Orion in 1860: "What a man wants with religion in these breadless times passes my comprehension." In June, 1858, he had experienced his first great personal tragedy in the death of his younger brother

Henry under circumstances for which he blamed himself. He then prayed many an orthodox prayer to God to strike *him* down, but "have mercy on that unoffending boy." Henry's death set him to uttering his lifelong question: Why?

Alone in his pilothouse at night, he meditated on "life, death, the reason of existence, of creation, the ways of Providence and Destiny." Guarding freight left on the levees at night in New Orleans, he mulled the same questions over and over. Later he said of this period: "I used to have inspirations as I sat there alone those nights. . . . Those things got into my books by and by and furnished me with many a chapter. I can trace the effect of those nights through most of my books." In his notebook of the pilot days there long remained a well-worn clipping, preserved as a sort of creed, headed "How to Take Life": "Take it just as though it was—as it is—an earnest, vital, and important affair. Take it as though . . . the world had waited for your coming. Take it as though it was a grand opportunity to do and achieve . . . ; to help and cheer a suffering, weary . . . brother." Clearly, at this time Sam Clemens was sensing his own powers. The impulse towards life beat strong within him; life was "vital," "important," and he rose to the task of performing a part in it. He could still feel the poetry in the air he breathed. The nap was not yet worn off the world. But then came the Civil War.

In April, 1861, Fort Sumter was fired upon, and Sam Clemens left his pilot's post forever. His brief span of soldier life has been too often dismissed as a negligible factor in his development. He was a resident of a border state. By tradition and environment he belonged with the Confederacy; but, if his consistent condemnation of slavery means anything, his sympathies were partially with the Union. Various sketches and letters show what his sentiments about war must have been, on either side. The killing would have revolted him. Thus life provided him with a conflict which he would shortly resolve in the only way then open to him—an escape from an intolerable situation.

In "The Private History of a Campaign That Failed," he later told in facetious fashion the story of his brief, inglorious career as a Confederate soldier. One sober incident there, labeled by Paine as wholly fictitious, was introduced only to present the horror of war. It is no matter that it is untrue to the facts of his military service; it is infinitely true to his spirit. He represented himself as firing on a stranger in a panic-stricken moment, believing the man to be "the enemy." Watching the stranger die, the untried soldier realized that he had just killed a man who had never done him any harm:

... and I would have given anything then—my own life freely—to make him again what he had been five minutes before. . . . the taking of that unoffending life seemed such a wanton thing. And it seemed an epitome of war; that all war must be just that—the killing of strangers against whom you feel no personal animosity. . . . My campaign was spoiled. It seemed to me that I was not rightly equipped for this awful business.

The brevity of his contact with the Civil War takes no account of its possible effects on his imaginative, sensitive nature.

At this point, then, he had beheld the human race engaged in two of its unloveliest activities, the crime of slavery and the crime of war. Soon he was on his way to the West with Orion Clemens. His mental discipline in learning to be a pilot had sharpened his powers of perception; his river nights of meditation had deepened his capacities for thought. And whether or not the spectacle of fratricide he had just witnessed in the Civil War gave rise to new feelings of contempt for the human race at large, subsequently his letters and writings reveal a greater measure of that contempt.

One of his earliest letters from Carson City describes the country as "fabulously rich . . . in thieves, murderers, desperadoes, ladies, children, lawyers, Christians, Indians, Chinamen, Spaniards, gamblers, sharpers, coyotes, . . . poets, preachers, and jackass rabbits." Although his trips up and down the Mississippi must have brought him in touch with thieves, murderers, desperadoes, gamblers, and sharpers as bad as these, no mention of them appears in his river letters. The trace of bitterness here hints that some illusion concerning humanity has been destroyed. He had been in the West a month, hardly long enough for the impact of the frontier to have effected much change in his thought; he had not yet embarked on the mining attempts which brought him such disillusionment; and the only other event ascertainable from the records between this letter and those written on the river was his brief contact with the Civil War.

Later, his letters in his mining days alternate between hope and despair, mingled with brief accounts of shootings and murders, and objections to "the d——d laws of this forever d——d country." Plainly, his perception of human failings was growing keener. In speaking of himself, he remarked that "poor frail human nature is a sort of crazy institution anyhow." In July, 1862, the disheartened miner wrote grimly to Orion: ". . . if I can't move the bowels of those hills this fall, I will come up and clerk for you."

But the turn of events soon made such a clerkship unnecessary. From the mining camps of Esmeralda, he had sent to the Virginia City *Territorial Enterprise* several burlesque letters signed "Josh." One was a take-off on an egotistical lecturer designated as "Professor Personal Pronoun," whose lecture could not be reported in full because the type case did not hold enough upper-case *I*'s. Another began "I was sired by the great American eagle and foaled by a Continental Dam!" and Sam Clemens strewed through it the patriotic clichés of Territorial Judge George Turner, in his best flag-waving style.[5] Thus "Josh" caught the fancy of Joseph Goodman, editor of the *Enterprise*. Soon after, a letter dated August 7, 1862, informed Orion that Sam had been offered a place on the *Enterprise* and he "guessed he would take it." Near the end of August he arrived at the *Enterprise* office travel-stained and lame, announcing as he dropped into a chair: "My starboard leg seems to be unshipped. I'd like about one hundred yards of line . . . I'm falling to pieces. . . . My name is Clemens and I've come to write for the paper."

Critics point out that up to this time Sam Clemens had already served three "abortive apprenticeships"—as printer, pilot, and miner—and that his life work was still undetermined.[6] His biographer stated of an even later period, that of 1863, that "thus far" there was no evidence that he had "any literary ambitions." Although Sam Clemens's literary work up to this point leaves much to be desired, as regards ambition Paine's statement does not seem to be borne out by the evidence. For throughout the course of the three apprenticeships mentioned, the thread of a fourth turns up persistently; it is the only interest that survived in him through the years, through his other occupations—his interest in the writing craft.

It is clear that his early writings, however crude and unformed they may be, point toward the trend his later work will take. A glance over them will show that the apprentice writer already employed a variety of styles as well as a considerable range in subject

[5] Effie M. Mack, *Mark Twain in Nevada*, 172, makes the statement that the caricatured speaker was Judge George Turner, chief justice of the Territory.
[6] See, for example, Ivan Benson, *Mark Twain's Western Years*, 1, 113.

matter. Crude character portrayal; rival-editor baiting; satiric hits at government, at military life, at war itself, and at religious assemblies; descriptive "travel letters" with an instructive tone; a few literary essays; rough attempts at reproducing the dialect of the illiterate man; and burlesque sketches bearing the marks of the frontier humor—these are Sam Clemens's productions in his first decade of writing, from 1852 to 1862. His five and one-half years in the Far West were to deepen and intensify the serious purposes which had always lain beneath his humor.

CHAPTER 6

The Humorist as Reformer

IN August, 1862, when Sam Clemens began his connection with
the *Territorial Enterprise*, he was employed as a local reporter and
feature writer to substitute for William Wright, whose pseudonym was Dan de Quille. De Quille, given a leave in "the States," was
already famous locally for his "quaints." Following De Quille, Sam
Clemens would naturally feel it appropriate to furnish an occasional
hoax; but, beyond that, the extravagance and fantasy of the Western
humor undoubtedly struck a responsive chord in his own nature.
He seems to have forgotten his early praise of the quiet style in
humor; his own humor was anything but quiet. He indulged in
paper warfare, burlesques, and hoaxes of various kinds. The miners
were delighted; and, when Dan de Quille returned to his post, Joe
Goodman kept both of his humorous writers.

Mark Twain's Western period was of great importance to his
literary development. In 1910 he wrote of it: "In Nevada, circumstance furnished me the silver fever and I went into the mines to
make a fortune as I supposed; but that was not the idea. The idea was
to advance me another step toward literature." During the gold rush
a complete society came into being practically overnight on the
western frontier of the United States. Socially, the frontier was an
artificially democratized society, in part primitive, in part degenerated from much higher levels. As the economist Loria has expressed
it, "colonial settlement is for economic science what the mountain
is for geology, bringing to light primitive stratifications"; and the
colonial experiment in the Far West provided what Franklin Walker has called "the most concentrated cross-section to be found in history." Such surroundings would have been highly suggestive to any
intelligent observer. On the creative mind, the most sensitive mind,
the impact of this human and economic jumble must have been ter-

rific. Contrasts were heightened on the frontier; incongruous juxta-
positions were everywhere. Impinged upon by contrast and incongruity, the raw materials of humor, and impelled by the necessity of
the frontiersmen which made humor requisite for existence, numerous frontier humorists plied their trade. Mark Twain was among
them and of them; but his sketches frequently contained something
beyond humor.

He was able, certainly, to supply humor at a time when the
Westerners demanded it. Living in intimate contact with them as he
did, he must have realized their need for what he had to give; furthermore, the inclinations of his own temperament coincided with the
conditions of time and place. And not only did his impulse toward
humor reinforce the demand about him; his impulse towards reform
also sought an outlet by making his humor hide many a lesson at its
core.

Even among his earliest Western articles there are sketches in
which he satirized the general follies of mankind or derided what he
considered particular public wrongs. In fact, he consciously designed many of his humorous sketches as vehicles for what he termed
"preaching." But the early blend of humor and moralism failed to
provide the embryo artist with a form through which his genius
could find its fullest expression. Only by accident, as it were, did he
first fall into patterns of writing directed by his aesthetic impulses
and their needs rather than by the ulterior motive of reform. This
development will appear in a later chapter; at this point the emphasis
belongs on the strongly satiric turn Mark Twain's writing took in
the West.

The caliber of his associates on the *Enterprise* added incentive
to his satiric turn of mind. Joe Goodman, editor in chief, conducted
his paper courageously and honestly; it was rugged and fearless,
picturesque and individual. At the beginning of Sam Clemens's employment, Goodman advised him: "Never say we learn so and so,
or it is rumored, or we understand so and so; but go to headquarters
and get the absolute facts; then speak out and say it *is* so and so. In
the one case you are likely to be shot, and in the other you are pretty
sure to be; but you will preserve the public confidence."[1] The *Enterprise* became "the nerve center of Washoe, the brainiest sheet on the
Coast.... It was the mouth-piece of Sun Mountain—her final tribu-

[1] Paine, *Biography*, I, 206.

nal. . . . It could be loved; it could be feared like the plague. When it got angry, it had claws like those of a mountain cat. It was Comstock to the core."[2] Possessing enormous prestige, the *Enterprise* was the most powerful paper in the West, not excepting the San Francisco papers. Besides Goodman and De Quille, staff members included Rollin M. Daggett, previously a co-founder of the *Golden Era*, and little Steve Gillis, the fighting bantam cock. In this circle of high courage, Sam Clemens had his first opportunity to give full rein to his hatred of hypocrisy and sham. The loud guffaws his humor sent ringing round the mountain should not draw attention from this other side of his work in the West.

Murder and other crimes of violence occurred daily on the Comstock Lode; suicide, prompted by the shattering of some miner's dream of gold, was not infrequent. Here, perhaps, was sharpened the social consciousness which would one day create *Huckleberry Finn* and *Pudd'nhead Wilson*. Here, perhaps, was awakened the recognition of economic forces which, augmented by bitter personal experience of mining and by growing manifestations of greed everywhere, would one day produce *The Gilded Age* and, eventually, *The Man That Corrupted Hadleyburg*. Sam Clemens's Western sketches are but crude pencilings when compared with these later books; but his work is alive from the first with social, political, and ethical implications. The fact that much of this work fails artistically arises partly from the strength of his will-to-reform, joined with his perpetual impatience toward mankind. Nevertheless, the work fulfilled his intentions, it appears, at the time of writing.

He had been on the *Enterprise* but a few weeks when he wrote his "Petrified Man" hoax; and even this rollicking burlesque had a purpose behind it—a desire to punish the stupidity of a Humboldt coroner. Generally, however, the human weaknesses which drew his fire were of a graver nature than the pompousness of a Coroner Sewall.

One of his earliest sketches, the "Blabb" piece in Hannibal, had included a thrust at a state legislature. The doings of governmental assemblies—democracy in action—always interested him. That he was not content with writing humor alone is shown by his suggestion to Joe Goodman that he be sent up to Carson City to report the proceedings of the territorial legislature. Early in 1863, he became a

[2] George D. Lyman, *The Saga of the Comstock Lode*, 205.

Virginia City, Nevada, in its heyday

marked figure in the sessions there. The letters which he sent back to the *Enterprise* were widely copied in other papers. To the dispatch which appeared in the *Enterprise* of February 2, 1863, he signed for the first time the pseudonym "Mark Twain," which, with its dynamic force and its fitness to the writer and his work, soon displaced even among his personal friends the name he was born to.[3]

Upon examination, it will be found that most of his Western writings, no matter how sheathed in buffoonery and burlesque, contain satirical elements which can be grouped under the headings of social, political, and moral satire. Some perception of the weaknesses of what he was later to christen "the Gilded Age" is apparent quite early in his Western product.

In 1863 he spent a summer vacation at the fashionable Lick House in San Francisco, where he wrote "Those Blasted Children." Deciding the sketch was a "pearl which ought for the eternal welfare of my race to have a more extensive circulation than is offered by a local daily paper," he sent it east to the New York *Sunday Mercury*. Except for the juvenile "Dandy Frightening the Squatter," printed in Boston in 1852, the "Blasted Children" sketch was his first work to appear in an Eastern publication. Reprinted in the *Golden Era* for March 27, 1864, it brought much merriment to Western readers with its deadly remedies prescribed for ailing tots.

But the sketch is not all fun. It satirically discloses the ideals prevalent among the younger generation, ideals which bear close resemblance to those of their elders. Flora Low, daughter of the governor of California, and Florence Hillyer, child of one of the Western mine kings, wage a pitched battle about whose father has more money. Little Miss Low insists that she can have a thousand dolls if she wants them, " 'n gold ones, too, or silver, or anything," a claim which spurs Miss Hillyer to declare that her pa "could fill this house full of silver, clear up to that chandelier." Not wanting to be entirely overlooked, Susy Badger says that her Aunt Mary owns "horses 'n things—O, ever so many!—millions of 'em." The playful turn of the boys takes another direction and mirrors the resentment towards the Chinese which Mark Twain had noted in the grown-up world. This

[3] The name is a phrase from the leadsman's call as he measures the depth of the river: "Mark three! Quarter-less-three! Half twain! Quarter twain! M-a-r-k twain!" (See *Life on the Mississippi*.) The phrase means, literally, two fathoms or twelve feet of water. Mark Twain always felt that it was a "comforting sound" to hear on a dark night, for it meant "safe water" for any boat on the river.

seems to be his first recorded protest of the treatment accorded the Chinese of San Francisco, a subject which was to engage him for years:

Hi, boys! here comes a Chinaman. (God pity any Chinaman who chances to come in the way of the boys hereabouts, for the eye of the law regardeth him not, and the youth of California in their generation are down upon him.) Now, boys! grab his clothes basket—take him by the tail! (There they go, now, like a pack of young demons; they have confiscated the basket, and the dismayed Chinaman is towing half the tribe down the hall by his cue. Rejoice, O my soul, for behold, all things are lovely. . . .)

Aside from the thought of this passage, its style reveals Mark Twain's habit of dropping into Biblical language and Biblical rhythms, a device he would use until the end of his days.

In "The Lick House Ball," dated September 27, 1863, he slyly hit off the pretensions of the newly rich nabobs of the West in his reference to the "nobility" as represented by "his Grace the Duke of Benicia, the Countess of San Jose, Lord Blessyou, Lord Geeminy, and many others. . . . Owing to the press of imperial business, the Emperor Norton was unable to come." The last was an actual person, a one-time financier gone mad, who currently imagined himself the emperor of the United States. The mythical "Duke of Benicia" is Mark Twain's embodiment of a real-estate fiasco promoted in the so-called "city" of Benicia. His satiric glance at the Gilded Age then revolving about him is revealed in a conversation with the Duke on the number of diamonds displayed. His Grace says the ball reminds him of an occasion on which he visited all the jewelry shops for the purpose of renting diamonds for his wife to wear, but only one jeweler had diamonds; "he only had a quart left, and they had already been engaged by the Duchess of Goat Island." The Duke is, perhaps, a potential Colonel Sellers; but, in the immediacy of his satiric purpose, Mark Twain disdained any attempt to make a true character of Benicia. He is instead a mere name, a shadowy figure—hardly even a caricature—by the use of which Mark Twain laughed at that turbulent golden world, its shams and affectations, while its inhabitants joined in the laughter that mocked them. In reporting the ball he remarked: "Over in Washoe I generally say what I please about . . . everybody, because my fellow citizens have learned to put up with it."

The burlesque satire of the early Mark Twain touched not only the fashions, the manners, and the ideals of the Western Gilded Age, but its ethics as well. On October 28, 1863, he printed in the *Enterprise* the hoax known variously as the "Empire City Massacre" and the "Dutch Nick Massacre." Of all his *Enterprise* writings, this piece attracted most attention on the Comstock. It gives an account of one Philip Hopkins, who went berserk and, with an axe, a knife, and a "blunt instrument," killed his wife and seven of his nine children. He then cut his own throat from ear to ear, and "bearing in his hand a reeking scalp (his wife's) from which the warm, smoking blood was still dripping," rode wildly into Carson City to fall dead in front of the Magnolia Saloon. Despite the gory details, the factual style of this account makes it read like a piece of straight reporting.

The closing paragraph explains the reason for the rash act. Hopkins had formerly owned stock in the mines of Virginia City and Gold Hill; but, alarmed when the San Francisco *Bulletin* exposed the Washoe practice of "cooking dividends," he had sold out and bought up large stocks in the Spring Valley Water Company of San Francisco. That company soon cooked up a fancy dividend of its own, and Spring Valley stock went to nothing:

It is presumed that this misfortune drove him mad and resulted in his killing himself and . . . his family. The newspapers of San Francisco permitted this water company to go on borrowing money and cooking dividends, under cover of which cunning financiers crept out of the tottering concern, leaving the crash to come upon poor and unsuspecting stockholders, without offering to expose the villainy at work. We hope the fearful massacre detailed above may prove the saddest result of their silence.[4]

By saying that the newspapers "permitted" this thing to occur, Mark Twain registered his view of the public press as an institution responsible in matters of ethics—in this case, responsible for the warning and protection of the "unsuspecting stockholders." Bernard DeVoto remarks, "Social satire thus makes its appearance at the Enterprise office, completely embedded in the native joke." But even for a Western joke the piece contains an unusual amount of bloody violence. Mark Twain, unconcerned at this point with aesthetic effect, couched his satire in terms calculated to shock his readers into

[4] Paine, *Biography*, III, Appendix C, 1599.

an awareness of a situation he deplored: the laxness of the newspapers had left such occurrences entirely unnoticed; consequently, he designed a piece so horrific that it could not be overlooked and, once read, could not be forgotten.

He meant, however, to treat his readers with good faith. This is proved by the notice he printed the following day:

I take it all back. * * * * * Mark Twain.

He had posted signboards along the way to warn readers that they were being hoaxed. He did not intend his sketch to be believed, but he did intend it to have a moral effect. In *Sketches New and Old,* writing on "My Bloody Massacre," he himself afterwards underscored his satiric intent in this piece. He labeled it "my fine satire upon . . . 'cooking dividends,' a thing . . . frequent on the Pacific Coast":

Once more . . . I felt that the time had arrived for me to rise up and be a reformer. . . . And so, under the insidious mask of an invented "bloody massacre," I stole upon the public unawares with my scathing satire. . . .

Ah, it was a deep, deep satire, and most ingeniously contrived. But I made the horrible details so . . . interesting that the public devoured *them* greedily . . . missing the guide-boards I had set up to warn . . . that the whole thing was a fraud.

To drop in with a poor little moral at the fag-end of such a gorgeous massacre was like following the expiring sun with a candle.

He then learned that it is human nature to skip the dull explanations and "to revel in the blood-curdling particulars and be happy." His readers had swallowed the bait he had provided for them but had ignored the hook, the moral attached at the end. The sectional bias of the piece—San Francisco guilt *versus* Washoe guilt—loses significance in the face of his frequent accusations of Washoe imperfections.

The Western political scene furnished him a frequent source for satiric copy. His account of "The Great Prize Fight," published October 11, 1863, had a twofold purpose: in it he effectively burlesqued the pugilistic jargon of the day and also paid his oblique respects to certain political practices. He represented Leland Stanford, the governor of California, and F. F. Low, the governor-elect, as competing in the prize ring "for a purse of a hundred thousand dollars," ably seconded by an associate justice of the Supreme Court, Justice Stephen F. Field, and the Honorable William M. Stewart of Nevada. Stewart and Field had had their men in training for six weeks preceding the contest; and, when first one and then the other made bids for public favor, the changes in public opinion kept the citizens' minds in "such a state of continual vibration that I fear . . . they will never more cease to oscillate." Such is the characteristic mental state of many voters in what Mark Twain later called "this great big ignorant nation." Here, he wrote that the two champions both wore "the Union colors"—that is, both were Republicans. After engaging in "some beautiful sparring," they went down and "took a drink." But from the fifth round on, all rules were disregarded and the two politicians slugged it out in true prize-fight fashion. Mark Twain introduced many bloody details of the battle in the zestful Western manner, rising to new heights of ferocity: "so dyed were the combatants in their own gore," and they had "minced each other into such insignificant odds and ends that neither was able to distinguish his own remains from those of his antagonist." Such sanguinary debris becomes the aftermath of many a political campaign where personalities obscure issues; and Mark Twain exhibited once more his technique of getting public attention by the use of shock and of "blood-curdling particulars."

Back in Washoe, the territorial judges, headed by Judge George Turner, were notoriously corrupt, and few Washoe gunmen had reason to fear the law.[5] Objecting to the lax treatment of law violators, Mark Twain published a squib "On Murders":

We average about four murders in the first degree a month, in Virginia, but we never convict anybody. The murder of Abel, by his brother Cain, would rank as an eminently justifiable homicide up there in Storey county. When a man merely attempts to kill another there, and fails, . . . our Police Judge handles him with pitiless severity. He has him instantly arrested, gives him some good advice, and requests him to leave the country. This has . . . a very salutary effect. The criminal goes home and thinks the matter over . . . and concludes to stay with us. But he feels badly—he feels very badly.

He continued to ridicule the public officials through the public press.

[5] Franklin Walker, ed., *The Washoe Giant in San Francisco*, 54.

Shortly after his skit "On Murders" appeared, he wrote: "A teamster was murdered and robbed on the public highway, between Carson and Virginia, today. Our sprightly and efficient officers are on the alert. They calculate to inquire into this thing next week."[6] This heavy irony was long his favorite weapon in the cause of reform.

His satire touched not only dwellers in the world of officialdom but also those besotted souls who clamor at its gates for admittance. In "Concerning Notaries," he employed a variety of humorous devices to deride the zeal of the numerous applicants besieging Governor Nye of Nevada for commissions as notaries public, then most lucrative appointments. He described the voluminous "little petition" with which each applicant had provided himself: one looked like "a bale of dry goods"; another was so extensive that the county surveyor was "chaining it off." Placards advertised coaches leaving every fifteen minutes for the Governor's Mansion "for the accommodation of Notarial aspirants." The climax came when Mark Twain himself was seized with the "fatal distemper"—a longing for a notaryship: "I wrote a petition with frantic haste, appended a copy of the Directory of Nevada Territory to it, and . . . fled down the deserted streets to the Governor's office."

Lest it appear that an intention toward satire is here read into such burlesques rather than injected into them by Mark Twain, here is his own explanation of his theory and practice. It appears in his sketch, "A Couple of Sad Experiences," published in the *Galaxy* in 1870:

One can deliver a satire with telling force through the insidious medium of a travesty, if he is careful not to overwhelm the satire with the extraneous interest of the travesty, and so bury it from the reader's sight and leave him a joked and defrauded victim, when the honest intent was to add to either his knowledge or his wisdom. I have had a deal of experience in burlesques.

The thread of reform runs consistently through the early writings. Even so farcical a sketch as "How to Cure a Cold" begins significantly, "It is a good thing, perhaps, to write for the amusement of the public, but it is a far higher and nobler thing to write for their instruction, their . . . benefit." Couched in his humorous strain, these lines express the opinion he stated soberly elsewhere.

[6] Benson, *Mark Twain's Western Years*, 178.

Shortly after the Nevada Constitutional Convention adjourned on December 13, 1863, a night meeting was held to organize the "Third House," and Mark Twain was elected "Governor of the Third House." The opening of his inaugural address to this burlesque assembly suggests a kinship to Artemus Ward, who, in the phrase of Max Eastman, loved nonsense with a manly and mature love. Governor Twain began: "Gentlemen: This is the proudest moment of my life. I shall always think so. I think so still." But how far he was from sharing Artemus Ward's tendency towards Max Eastman's "pure humor"—the love of absurdity for its own sake—may be seen in the way he adjourned the Third House after an evening spent in riotous ridicule of the First House:

Gentlemen: Your proceedings have been exactly similar to those of the Convention which preceded you. You have considered a subject which you knew nothing about; spoken on every subject but the one before the House, and voted, without knowing what you were voting for, or having any idea what would be the general result of your action.[7]

As Governor Mark Twain, he added new plaudits to his growing reputation. In January, 1864, he went up to Carson City to report the territorial legislature for the second time. He watched the proceedings closely and wrote according to the merits of each law passed. Years later, he spoke in the *Autobiography* of the power his position then gave him: "I was there every day . . . to distribute compliments and censure with evenly balanced justice . . . over half a page of the Enterprise every morning; consequently I was an influence." Members of the legislature feared the ridicule at which he was becoming adept. He could now handle social satire effectively on the journalistic level, and his barbed editorials made him, according to a Nevada historian, Effie Mack, "the most feared political writer in the Territory."

In his product of these days, however, he concerned himself little with possible artistic effects. He could make his prose express his thoughts clearly and forcefully; more, he could make it sting and cut deep enough to linger in the reader's memory. He was nominally a newspaper reporter, and he combined his nominal business with his real business of writing humor and dispensing reform through that humor. But the biting satire in some of these Western pieces

[7] Mack, *Mark Twain in Nevada*, 276; see also p. 273.

completely submerges any truly humorous effect. C. C. Goodwin, a writer of the Comstock, suggested that Dan de Quille was more popular locally than Mark Twain because De Quille's humor lacked the cutting quality that edged Mark Twain's: "Dan had a softer way." Miss Mack reprints a squib from the rival *Evening Bulletin* of April 2, 1863, which denounces Mark Twain for his "merciless" humor and denies him the possession of wit on the ground that "when acrimony and bitterness is exhibited, wit is no more genuine than a bar of gilded brass is gold."

In the preceding paragraph I have spoken of Mark Twain as "nominally" a newspaper reporter. There are readers who view him as essentially a journalist—a good reporter, a superlative reporter even, but in the last analysis only a reporter. They maintain that his shortcomings are those of the journalistic writer and that critics need seek no high-flown explanation for his literary failures. Certainly, his journalism was invaluable to him in one way: it furnished him a ready outlet and kept him writing during his formative years. But the record shows that he intensely hated newspaper work; that by temperament and inclination he was badly fitted for it; that in such newspaper posts as he held, he managed to slant his work away from routine items toward either reformative or imaginative material; and that when he found himself unable to do so, he was ready to quit his job.

On the *Enterprise* he disliked writing reports which demanded exact facts and figures; he hated "solid facts." He liked to do human-interest stories or denunciatory articles. Consequently an agreement was made under which the feature material was handled by Mark Twain, the straight news by Dan de Quille. In his first reports of the Nevada legislative proceedings, he made some curious blunders, as technical matters were of minor concern to him. What he liked was to capture the flash and sparkle of the sessions, to picture the clash of personalities, and above all to consider the ethics and the justice of new laws, distributing "compliments and censure" accordingly. After writing scathing editorials about James L. Laird, editor of the Virginia City *Daily Union*, he found it best to migrate to San Francisco. Arriving there in May, 1864, he went to work for the *Morning Call* as a staff reporter. But he was dissatisfied with his position from the first. He missed the freedom he had enjoyed on the *Enterprise;* on the *Call* he was expected to handle definite assignments, to keep more or less regular hours—in short, to work as a newspaperman. All of this bored him immensely. Remembering it in later years, he wrote: "It was fearful drudgery, soulless drudgery, and almost destitute of interest." After four months of it, he rebelled. At his own suggestion, the *Call* publishers cut his salary and dispensed with his night work.

But it was not merely the irksome routine of a news machine that made him dislike his post on the *Call;* he himself makes that point clear. On arrival he had found San Francisco "weltering in corruption." He lost no time in putting his reforming pen to work. According to Paine, he wrote several severe articles, criticizing officials and institutions, but only one of them ever saw print in the *Call*. This was the true discord in his new connection: the silencing of his pen as an instrument of social reproof. Commenting in *Mark Twain in Eruption* on an article he wrote at this time, an article concerned with the stoning of a Chinese by "some hoodlums" while a policeman stood watching "with an amused interest," he said:

Usually I didn't want to read in the morning what I had written the night before; it had come from a torpid heart. But this item had come from a live one . . . and so I sought for it in the paper next morning with eagerness. It wasn't there; it wasn't there the next morning, nor the next. I . . . found it tucked away among condemned matter on the standing galley.

Then Mark Twain grew indifferent and lazy. George Barnes, publisher of the *Call*, sought to improve the situation by hiring a news gatherer, one Smiggy McGlooral, to act as assistant for Mark Twain; but this arrangement was of short duration. Even the great San Francisco earthquake of that day failed to awaken in him any enthusiasm for reporting for the *Call*. He had lost interest, and, by mutual agreement, his connection with the paper was terminated. He continued to write articles for the *Golden Era* and the *Californian* and through them to spread abroad his reforming ideas by way of burlesque. And he soon regained a former outlet by sending "philippics" back to the *Enterprise*.

A few years later, in 1870, while editor and part owner of the Buffalo *Express*, he conducted a department for the *Galaxy*, an ambitious New York magazine. Paine asserted that the *Galaxy* was really a fine magazine, with the best contributors obtainable, and that Mark Twain was soon "writing most of his sketches for it . . . better literature, as a rule, than those published in his own paper." This illustrates his preference for some other medium than newspaper work when both were open to him. But when writing a book, *Roughing It*, filled his days, he withdrew from both the *Galaxy* and the *Express*, selling his interest in the newspaper in April, 1871, for ten thousand dollars less than the purchase price. This incident marked his "farewell to journalism."[8]

Although the *Morning Call* did not see eye to eye with its reporter in his urge to reform the world, it did publish one of his civic criticisms on September 6, 1864, an item denouncing the coroner's office for refusing information to local reporters. Writing to his mother, he boasted that thereafter the reporters got any information they wanted. His success in this affair and his obvious influence during the legislative sessions at Carson City undoubtedly strengthened his belief in the power of the press. He viewed the newspaper as a powerful channel for moral reform; that office held its chief interest for him. His strongest expression of his conviction appears in his article, "The Indignity Put upon the Remains of George Holland by the Rev. Mr. Sabine," published in the *Galaxy* for February, 1871. Sabine had declined to hold Holland's burial service in his church because Holland had been an actor. Mark Twain vigorously upheld the theater, the press, and the novel as moral teachers of men:

Am I saying that the pulpit does not do its share toward disseminating the . . . gospel of Christ? . . . No. . . . The pulpit teaches assemblages of people twice a week—nearly two hours altogether—and does what it can in that time. The theater teaches large audiences seven times a week—28 or 30 hours altogether—and the novels and newspapers plead, and argue, and supplicate at the feet of millions and millions of people every single day, and all day long and far into the night; and so these vast agencies till nine-tenths of the vineyard, and the pulpit tills the other tenth.[9]

Another clear-cut expression of his belief in the power of the press appears in the burlesque sketch "Journalism in Tennessee," written in 1871. The editor of the *Morning Glory and Johnson County War-Whoop* stops his writing of an article on "The Encouraging Progress of Moral and Intellectual Development in Amer-

8 Paine, *Biography*, II, 434, 431.
9 *Ibid.*, III, Appendix J, 1626.

ica" to engage in a gun fight with a rival editor. The hot-headed duels of honor and the exaggerated courtesies of the Old South are lampooned: the editors, both wounded, politely discuss elections and crops as they reload. Foreshadowing certain passages in *Life on the Mississippi*, the sketch is important, too, for its statement of what Mark Twain believed a newspaper should be:

The heaven-born mission of journalism is to disseminate truth; to eradicate error; to educate, refine, and elevate the tone of public morals and manners, and make all men more gentle, more virtuous, more charitable, and in all ways better, and holier, and happier.

In spite of its farcical context, the opinion voiced here is the same as that soberly written at the time of the death of his actor friend, George Holland.

But this is anticipating, somewhat. It is necessary to go back seven years to San Francisco, where Mark Twain's first extended treatment of the American court system appeared in the *Golden Era* for June 26, 1864, in "The Evidence in the Case of Smith vs. Jones." There he commented ironically on "that nice sense of justice . . . among the masses," which he was confident would enable them to determine the guilty party merely by reading his transcription of the testimony. First, Smith and Jones were called. Each gave his account of the fight they had just had, accounts that half persuaded Mark Twain they "were talking about two separate and distinct affairs altogether." Variations appeared in all testimony given: One witness swore that the fight took place in the saloon, another that it was in the street. Some said the combatants fought with their fists, others said with knives, others revolvers, others clubs, others beer mugs, and others swore there had been no fight at all. His Honor, observing that this evidence resembled that brought before him in thirty-five cases every day, continued the case "to afford the parties an opportunity of procuring more testimony." Mark Twain affirmed his complete confidence "in the instinctive candor and fair dealing of my race," declaring his willingness to leave the case of Smith *versus* Jones to "the People," satisfied that their judgment would be righteous and impartial and their decision "holy and just": "I leave the accused and the accuser before the bar of the world." His ironic praise of "the masses" and of "my race" accents the scornful contempt with which he views these gabbling, lying people, blinded by ignorance, confused by self-interest, and impelled by sheer perversity. Let there be no mistake: it is the "damned human race" which Mark Twain leaves before the bar of the world in June of 1864.

In December of that year, embroiled anew in a row with the San Francisco police, he took advantage of an invitation from Steve Gillis's brother Jim and went up into the Tuolumne hills to stay until things cooled down. The visit with Jim Gillis lasted for three months and was to have great significance for his development as a writer. When he returned to San Francisco, there was a new note in his writing—a development to be discussed later. Meanwhile, he continued to write as well the same sort of humor as before, mainly sketches hiding his moral lessons deep in travesty and burlesque.

His first sketch after his sojourn in the Tuolumne hills, "An Unbiased Criticism," appeared March 18, 1865. In it he proposed to discuss the California Art Union and "its moral effects upon the youth of both sexes." Most of the sketch, however, relates events of his stay in the Big Tree region, digressing into his favorite device of the burlesque-bearing-a-moral. Because of the scarcity of reading matter at Angel's Camp, he said, the inhabitants had fallen to studying the advertising columns of newspapers. Reading of merits displayed by rival sewing-machine companies, they took sides so fervently that the issues involved settled all county elections along the same party lines. As to sewing machines, he represented himself as "a bitter Florence man" as opposed to the "unprincipled Grover & Baker cabal." He exhorted the men of Calaveras, all "enlightened Calaverasses," to join him in thwarting the "hellish designs upon the liberties of our beloved country" entertained by the members of the Grover & Baker Loop-Stitch Sewing Machine Party. The sketch becomes a satire against the customs prevailing at election time: "at the last moment fraudulent hand-bills were suddenly scattered abroad containing sworn affidavits" detrimental to his party's cause. But the Florence-machine men rallied and "deposited their votes like men for freedom of speech, freedom of the press, and freedom of conscience in the matter of sewing machines, provided they are Florences." Thus he satirizes "machine politics"—that brand in which votes are cast on prearranged lines having nothing to do with issues at stake—and ethical questions creep into his wildest burlesques.

I have already mentioned his assertion that one "can deliver a satire with telling force through the insidious medium of a travesty, if he is careful not to overwhelm the satire with the extraneous interest of the travesty." His article relates the difficulties which he himself has encountered in following this method. He laments that sometimes

... the "nub" or moral of the burlesque ... escapes notice in the superior glare of something in the body of the burlesque itself. And very often this "moral" is tagged on at the bottom, and the reader, not knowing that it is the key of the whole thing and the only important paragraph in the article, tranquilly turns up his nose and leaves it unread.

These lines were written a scant five years after his machine-election extravaganza. His flat statement that the tagged-on moral is often "the key of the whole thing and the only important paragraph" stamps the moral aim as a leading motive for his writing. He consciously designed his work as an instrument of reform, but because he was also potentially an artist he saw that his preaching should not be too obvious. Therefore he concealed his lessons in humor, flattering himself that his "ingenious satires" were very subtly contrived.

It will be recalled that he had earlier had trouble with reader reaction to his "Bloody Massacre" sketch. Since he so clearly recognized the accompanying difficulties, why did he pursue the attempt to deliver his moral teachings through the medium of humor? To this question, there are several possible answers: He had always had a predilection for humor; driven by the compulsion of the moralist, he wanted to reform his fellow man; and he honestly believed that humor offered the best means of carrying that reform to a wide and needy audience. Humor was best, too, for quick results. He never deviated from this early idea, as is shown by words he put into the mouth of the Mysterious Stranger, around 1899:

... your race, in its poverty, has unquestionably one really effective weapon—laughter. Power, money, persuasion, supplication—these can lift at a colossal humbug—push it a little—weaken it a little, century by century; but only laughter can blow it to rags and atoms at a blast.

Mark Twain's strong impatience—with mankind, with the existing plan of things, with almost everything—was one factor which determined his use of burlesque as a vehicle of reform. In the early years he relied on driving his moral lessons home with the bludgeon blows of grotesque humor, shocking "bloody" satires, and exaggerations tall enough to attract the public eye. All of this was at the expense of the potential artist within him, forced to yield to the get-results-quick schemes of the humorist-reformer. In time he would move slowly towards a more thoughtful type of work. In time he would try to embody his ethical teachings in characters carefully drawn. These characters and their backgrounds would be permeated with the humor of Mark Twain; it would become a quieter humor, an organic humor growing out of the character and the background. But that time was not yet.

In the early sketches he sometimes made a quick satiric sally out of his humorous manner with a plunge back into farcical humor again, but sometimes his reform was couched in articles more sustained, more direct. Occasionally the directness amounts to invective. In the fall of 1865 he sent a series of letters from San Francisco to the Virginia City *Enterprise*, letters assailing the civic corruption of San Francisco, calling specific names. Finally Martin G. Burke, the chief of police, filed a libel suit against the *Enterprise*. Mark Twain's answer was a vitriolic letter denouncing the police for openly permitting lechery. Beginning "The air is full of lechery," it continued in a strain, according to Paine, "which made even the *Enterprise* printers aghast." But Joe Goodman, unintimidated, published it in full.

One of these *Enterprise* articles bore the title "What Have the Police Been Doing?" Now available to readers in *The Washoe Giant*, it illustrates what the old-timers of San Francisco meant when they told Paine that the letters constituted a "series of daily philippics." Mark Twain's extravagant irony pretends to defend the city police, who are always "easy and comfortable . . . always leaning up against a lamp-post in the sun," or parading up and down with frightful velocity at the rate of a block an hour. He records the case of a poor wretch who had had his skull bashed in "for stealing six bits' worth of flour sacks" and had been jammed into a jail cell "in the most humorous way." As the ironic defense continues, all semblance of humor disappears:

And why shouldn't they shove that half-senseless wounded man into a cell without getting a doctor to ... see how badly he was hurt ... ? And why shouldn't the jailor let him alone when he found him in a dead stupor two hours after, ... sleeping ... with that calm serenity which is peculiar to men whose heads have been caved in with a club. ... Why shouldn't the jailor do so? ... the man was an infernal stranger. He had no vote. ... Ah, and if he stole flour sacks, did he not deliberately put himself outside of the pale of humanity and Christian sympathy by that hellish act? I think so. The Department think so. Therefore, when the stranger died at 7 this morning, after four hours of refreshing slumber in that cell, with his skull actually split ... from front to rear, like an apple ... what the very devil do you want to go and find fault with the prison officers for? ... Can't you find somebody to pick on besides the police? It takes all my time to defend them from people's attacks.

Mark Twain's rage is strongly evident in this sketch. The irony with which he builds the stranger's "hellish act" of stealing flour sacks into a crime that puts him outside the pale of human sympathy equals some of his invective of later years.

Other sketches which he then directed against civic laxness were "The Black Hole of San Francisco," "How They Take It," and "Not a Suicide." We have already noted his disappointment at not seeing in print his article describing the stoning of a Chinese under the idly amused gaze of a policeman. In *Sketches New and Old* the sketch entitled "The Disgraceful Persecution of a Boy" has a footnote which details similar circumstances. He probably kept his rejected article and later incorporated part of it in "The Disgraceful Persecution."

This sketch opens with the announcement that in San Francisco a boy on his way to Sunday school has been arrested and locked up for stoning a Chinese:

What a commentary is this upon human justice! What sad prominence it gives to our human disposition to tyrannize over the weak! ... How should he suppose it was wrong to stone a Chinaman? ... He was a "well-dressed" boy and a Sunday-school scholar, and therefore ... his parents were intelligent ... people, with just enough natural villainy in their composition to make them yearn after the daily papers ... and so this boy had opportunities to learn all ... week how to do right, as well as on Sunday.

Mark Twain then explains the sort of thing the boy has learned from the daily papers with a summary of the hard lot of the Chinese in California and a reminder that the Constitution specifies America as an asylum for all oppressed peoples. The newspapers get their share of his satiric attention: half of each day's local items would indicate that the police were either asleep or dead, and the other half that the reporters "were gone mad with admiration" of the effectiveness of that very police, especially when some wretched knave of a Chinaman was brought "gloriously" to prison and his misdemeanor was magnified "to keep the public from noticing how many really important rascals went uncaptured in the meantime." Reading the papers has been invaluable to this boy:

It was in this way that the boy found out that a Chinaman had no rights that any man was bound to respect; that he had no sorrows that any man was bound to pity; that neither his life nor his liberty was worth . . . a penny when a white man needed a scapegoat; that nobody loved Chinamen, nobody befriended them, nobody spared them suffering when it was convenient to inflict it. . . . And, therefore, what *could* have been more natural than for this sunny-hearted boy, tripping along to Sunday-school . . . to say to himself:

"Ah, there goes a Chinaman! God will not love me if I do not stone him."

This is not exactly buoyant mirth. Mark Twain must have suffered in the writing of it, as he was to suffer in later years when he longed for "a pen warmed up in hell" with which to paint the damnable meannesses of the human race. He was torn between pity for the Chinese and rage at his tormentors. But he abandoned the grim denunciation to slide back into the lighter mood in a final fling:

Keeping in mind the tuition in the humanities which the entire "Pacific coast" gives its youth, there is . . . a sublimity of incongruity in the virtuous flourish with which the good city fathers proclaim . . . that "The police are positively ordered to arrest all boys . . . who engage in assaulting Chinamen". . . . The new form for local items in San Francisco will now be:

"The ever vigilant and efficient officer So-and-so succeeded, yesterday afternoon, in arresting Master Tommy Jones, after a determined resistance."

His belief in the power of the press as an instrument for public good made him ever alert to its possibilities and correspondingly caustic when he felt his colleagues were neglecting their opportunities. In this single sketch he ridicules the newspapers, the police, the tradesmen, the legislature, and the city ordinances. Is this an example of his "noisy pride" in America the critics talk of?

His defense of the Chinese grew into larger proportions. By 1870–71 he was running a series of "Chinese Letters" in the *Galaxy* under the heading "Goldsmith's Friend Abroad Again," describing how Chinese arriving in America are fleeced of their small funds, have vicious dogs set on them by rowdies, and are thrown into prison on the slightest pretext. Thus he early showed his awareness of the structure of violence in our society and of the crumbling masonry of our human relationships erected on foundations of greed and racial prejudice. And his continued criticism of the treatment accorded by "civilized" society to the oppressed races—Negroes, Filipinos, Kanakas, and Maoris, as well as Chinese and Jews—finally comprises one of the largest connected bodies in his work. Such aspects of his literary beginnings are significant because they are related to subjects and ideas emphasized in his later work. The degree to which his early writing anticipates his later social and political commentary—in *Huckleberry Finn*, for instance—has not been adequately recognized by Mark Twain scholarship.

In the autumn of 1864 he temporarily ceased contributing to the *Golden Era* on the ground that it "wasn't high-toned enough," and began to write for the *Californian*, a literary magazine which had first appeared May 28, 1864. Founded by a couple of Easterners —C. H. Webb as editor and Bret Harte as chief contributor—the *Californian* was the outlet for a writing group that gave San Francisco its literary distinction. Besides Bret Harte and Webb, Paine names among the coterie of Mark Twain's writing acquaintances in San Francisco such men as Joaquin Miller, Prentice Mulford, Charles Warren Stoddard, Fitzhugh Ludlow, and Orpheus C. Kerr; elsewhere Mark Twain himself names Ralph Keeler, Henry George, and Ambrose Bierce.

The growing critical spirit of West Coast writers in this period belies the view of Van Wyck Brooks that the West was united in a conspiracy to hold all pioneer traditions sacrosanct, in order to inveigle settlers with "utterly mendacious pictures of their future." However that may be, Editor Webb followed heretical paths. As

Franklin Walker has noted, Webb made unkind remarks about forty-niners, patriotism, and literacy; he openly attacked the cult of "the honest miner," questioning "whether the individual who contributed a fund of impious slang to the national vocabulary was peculiarly estimable as a moral teacher." In the *Californian* he regularly showed little respect "for such sacred Western institutions as the climate, the hospitality, and the pioneer vigor." Not content with this, says Mr. Walker, Webb and his associates went deeper still; "they implicitly hinted that hard work did not always bring success and that virtuous living did not always bring a reward." Mark Twain followed his editor in impugning California's climate. In his humorous "Earthquake Almanac" he impishly caricatured the Californian tendency to extol all native features: residents are advised to expect "mild, balmy earthquakes" and "spasmodic but exhilarating earthquakes."

By the mid-sixties, Mr. Walker believes, San Francisco wore a critical attitude as part of its sophistication. Webb was influential in directing the city's literary impulses into the vein of satire. Mild-mannered journalists, not at all satiric by nature, tried painfully to adapt their writings to the satirical tone of established papers. It was here that Ambrose Bierce, "Bitter Bierce," was launched in December, 1868, as the new "Town Crier" for the San Francisco *News Letter*. Previously, his writings had not been markedly satiric; but he made his "Town Crier" column conspicuous by his penchant for the macabre, his special combination of irony and horror.

Western writing in general, so Mr. Walker maintains, passed through three stages: from naïveté to satire, and from satire to romantic nostalgia. The naïve period is illustrated by the *Golden Era* and the satiric period by the early *Californian*, while the tinge of romantic nostalgia colored the *Overland Monthly*. Mark Twain has in *Roughing It* some passages touched by nostalgia for the vanishing West, just as in *Life on the Mississippi* he caught the sunset glory of the steamboat era; but when the two men were in the West, it was Bret Harte who mined deepest in the nostalgic vein. In his Western days the bold, satiric note was always Mark Twain's strongest bent. Even his "naïve" period is marked by characteristics of the middle or satiric era: his gory sketches, such as the "Massacre" with its ghastly verisimilitude placidly recounted and "The Great Prize Fight" with its anatomical debris zestfully catalogued, anticipate the devices which Bierce later used so very effectively for causing shock to his readers.

Returning from his *Quaker City* excursion in November, 1867, Mark Twain stayed in Washington for a time as secretary to Senator William M. Stewart of Nevada. His heretical attitude toward Washington is demonstrated in numerous sketches satirizing various aspects of the United States government. "The Great Beef Contract" hits at red tape and official delay; "The Case of George Fisher" attacks the profiteer; "Facts Concerning the Recent Resignation" relates his thankless attempts to reform departments that were obviously wasting time and money. He tendered his resignation when asked to copy a report; this was too much: "Sir, do you suppose that I am going to *work* for six dollars a day?" Upon resigning, he filed a claim for consultation fees for advice given to department heads, and also for his mileage—mileage figured by way of the Holy Land. "Territorial delegates charge mileage both ways, although they never go back when they get here once. Why my mileage is denied me is more than I can understand," he confided plaintively.

Meanwhile, he was writing to Orion Clemens from Washington: "There are more pitiful intellects in this Congress! . . . I am most infernally tired of Wash." Orion wanted a job in Washington, and Mark Twain had earlier planned to help him get one. But, there on the sacred ground itself, he spoke out against such employment in words that might have been written by Thoreau: "I hope you will set type till you complete that invention, for surely government pap must be nauseating food for a *man*—a man whom God has enabled to saw wood and be independent."

In his skit about the "Judge's Spirited Woman," he surveyed satirically the judicial and jury system in the West:

. . . there warn't any interest in a murder trial . . . because the fellow was always brought in "not guilty," the jury expecting him to do as much for them some time; and, although the evidence was . . . square against this Spaniard, we knew we could not convict him without seeming to be . . . sort of reflecting on every gentleman in the community.

In "A Mysterious Visit" he twitted the perversity that prompts a man to boast of his property at the time of tax assessment and then perjure himself to avoid paying taxes on what he has acknowledged. This piece also ridicules the art of "deftly manipulating the bill of

deductions" until the exemption covers the tax. He had been in-
structed in this art by a gentleman

. . . of moral weight, of commercial integrity, of unimpeachable social
spotlessness—and so I bowed to his example. I went down to the revenue
office and . . . I stood up and swore to lie after lie, fraud after fraud,
villainy after villainy, till my soul was coated inches . . . thick with
perjury, and my self respect was gone forever.
 . . . It is nothing more than thousands of the richest and proudest
and most respected, honored, and courted men in America do every year.

  Sometimes the innate perversity he found in human nature was
of a deeper dye. Of such a tint is the trait exposed in "Lionizing
Murders," which begins with a ludicrous account of his visit to a
fortuneteller and ends in an excoriation of "the sentimental custom
of visiting, petting, glorifying, and snuffling over murderers." Mark
Twain could not stomach this nauseating practice. In "A New
Crime: Legislation Needed," he holds that the insanity plea has
swallowed up all chance of convicting a murderer who has "friends
and money": "Really, what we want now is not laws against crime,
but a law against insanity." This recalls his original dedication for
Roughing It, made "To the Late Cain," because it was his misfortune to live in an age "that knew not the beneficent Insanity Plea."
When he deals with the minor frailties of human nature as in "The
Late Benjamin Franklin" or "The Tone-Imparting Committee,"
his humor is delightful; but when he strikes at its darker vices, the
edge of his bitter satire cuts at the reader's nerves.
  Mr. Brooks, condemning Mark Twain for failing to recognize
that literature may be made "a great impersonal social instrument,"
writes of his days in the West: "whether in Nevada or California,
he was prohibited, on pain of social extinction, from expressing himself directly regarding the life about him." But, viewing his early
writings of both Nevada and California, it is difficult to see how anyone could have expressed himself more directly regarding the life
about him. Nor is there any evidence of his holding back on fear of
social extinction. The memorable picture which Bret Harte gave
of the early Mark Twain described his eye as that of a dominant
nature and his general manner as "one of supreme indifference to
surroundings and circumstances." This, surely, does not picture one
humbling himself in fear of not being accepted as one of the crowd.

The implication made by Mr. Brooks—that Mark Twain surrendered his integrity to the frontier, that he was swallowed up by his environment, unable to stand as an individual against it—is not borne out by the evidence. That he did not surrender himself to his milieu is proved, as the German critic Friedrich Schönemann points out, by the unusual books in which this very milieu is appreciatively but still critically reflected.

Calling the roll on Rabelais, Cervantes, Molière, Voltaire, and Swift, Mr. Brooks declares: "Satire is a criticism of the spirit of one's age, and of the facts in so far as the spirit is embodied in them. . . . Mark Twain satirizes the facts. . . . But when it comes to the spirit . . . that is quite another matter." There is some justice in this criticism; but the kind of world Mark Twain worked in must be considered. In the Far West, where he first wielded his pen with real satiric aim, nothing was stable. Everything was constantly changing. Everything existed on the superficial level merely.

Carl Van Doren remarks, apropos of Henry James, that certain American writers long felt "that the present at any given moment has lacked the stability . . . which alone might afford the novelist a firm texture of reality." In some degree, this applies also to the satirist. In his Preface to *The Marble Faun*, Hawthorne spoke of the difficulty of writing about America, "a country where there is no shadow, . . . no picturesque and gloomy wrong." Mark Twain never felt this lack; for him, slavery furnished the requisite picturesque and gloomy wrong. His thorough grasp of slavery as an institution enabled him to attack not only the mere facts of slavery itself, but also the spirit, the thing in human nature which makes slavery possible. That vision is constant in his work. But slavery was basic in Hannibal, as nothing was basic in Washoe. He should not be blamed too much for failing to ground his Western criticism on fundamental problems; in Washoe, it was the all-important surfaces that determined survival. Perhaps the fact that he spent formative years amid such kaleidoscopic scenes as the West offered was detrimental to his development as a writer. Those Western years doubtless made it easy for him in future to seek out and satirize the surfaces rather than the fundamentals. On that ground, it seems apparent that the West did not really mature him and "complete" him as DeVoto believes.

The West did, however, clarify both his intention and his

technique. His burlesque-bearing-a-moral could hardly have been improved, so far as it realized what he intended it to do. And Mark Twain, who was first called "the Washoe Giant" because he arrived in San Francisco when the town was talking prize fight, would before his departure be hailed as "the Moral Phenomenon."

CHAPTER 7

The Humorist as Moralist

A large body of Mark Twain's Western satire is distinguished by
its moralistic vein. From natural bent, perhaps because of
the questions posed in his mind by his own orthodox Presbyterian–freethinker parentage, he was always interested in theology
and the philosophy of religion, as well as in the problem of morals.

The *Californian* for May 6, 1865, carried his "Important Correspondence," purporting to be "Between Mr. Mark Twain of San
Francisco and Rev. Bishop Hawks, D.D., of New York, Rev. Phillips Brooks of Philadelphia, and Rev. Dr. Cummings of Chicago,
concerning the Occupancy of Grace Cathedral." He exhorted
Bishop Hawks to come west because San Francisco offered "such a
magnificent field . . . sinners are so thick." He ridiculed clergymen
who refused to fill empty pulpits in the West because of large-scale
speculations carried on in the East: Bishop Hawks is allegedly "in
cotton to some extent" and is already wedded to the splendors of
"St.-George-the-Martyr-Up-Town"; Doctor Cummings is "specu-
lating a little in grain"; and Phillips Brooks is "in petroleum." By
contrast, hordes of small-town ministers are eager to come out and
"fight the good fight" for larger salaries. Thus he probed the clergy
for hypocrisy and selfish love of money.

Woven into his Grace Cathedral correspondence is a picture of
his own demeanor in church as an average "sinner at large." He
stood there listening as the minister's long prayer wandered on and
on. He grew absent-minded and fell to conjecturing "whether the
buzzing fly that keeps stumbling up the window-pane and sliding
down backward again will ever accomplish his object to his satisfaction"—a passage which resembles lines from Tom Sawyer's day
in church, a day still far in the future. But finally the minister reached
Mark Twain's department, with a kind word for the poor "sinners

at large." Concerning prayers in church, Mark Twain advised ministers to adopt "the simplicity and the beauty and the brevity and the comprehensiveness of the Lord's Prayer as a model." This suggestion contains a stylistic mannerism which would grow on him with the years: the habit of linking nouns or adjectives into a chain, with the conjunction never omitted, thus producing long rhythms. Frequently, as here, the resultant rhythm is markedly Biblical.

During the furor of spiritualism which swept San Francisco in 1865–66, he devoted several articles to this "wildcat religion," contrasting the public attitude towards it with that manifested towards established religions. Methodist camp meetings and Campbellite revivals had earlier stocked the asylums with lunatics, and nobody said a word; but the public was ultra-critical over madness occasioned by "fighting the tiger of spiritualism." Although he did not really "own in the old regular stock," his strong leaning towards it made him feel somewhat prejudiced against all wildcat religions. Nevertheless, he recognized the unfairness of such an attitude: "I do not love the wildcat, but . . . I do not like to see the wildcat imposed on merely because it is friendless." He paid his compliments to orthodox Presbyterianism by using himself, the "brevet-Presbyterian," as an example. He could claim no credit for not going crazy over Presbyterianism, since all Presbyterians "go too slow" for that; and he satirized the lack of spiritual fervor, the sterile ritual of the complacent Calvinism of his boyhood surroundings:

Notice us, and you will see how we do. We get up of a Sunday morning, and put on the best harness we have got and trip cheerfully down town; we subside into solemnity and enter the church; . . . we sit silent and grave while the minister is preaching, and count the . . . bonnets furtively, and catch flies; we grab our hats and bonnets when the benediction is begun; when it is finished, we shove. . . . No frenzy—no fanaticism . . . ; everything perfectly serene. You never see any of us Presbyterians getting in a sweat about religion. . . . Let us all be content with the . . . safe old regular religions, and take no chances on the wildcat.

Ironically, he held up the placid indifference of the Presbyterian service as a model for the "wildcats"; such a course would have prevented all cases of fanatic insanity among them. Thus he began the cultivation of a literary field which would occupy him until his death, the ridicule of what he considered narrow and bigoted religions.

In "Reflections on the Sabbath," he skeptically explored the theological aspects of orthodox Presbyterianism. This sketch is apparently his first recorded objection to the ways of the Almighty. He often thought regretfully that the omnipotent Creator could have made the world in three days as easily as in six, and then we could have had more Sundays. If Providence "grew weary after six days' labor, such worms as we are might reasonably expect to break down in three." And he felt "a depraved inclination to question the judgment of Providence in stacking up double eagles in the coffers of Michael Reese and leaving better men to dig for a livelihood." Still, no man should meddle with Providence: "Let us take things as we find them—though I . . . confess it goes against the grain . . . sometimes." Mark Twain's later work continued to find fault with the ordering of man's universe until finally he arrived at his conception of a dark, hidden, deep-lying corruption in Nature. In the sixties his mind was already mulling over the problem of good and evil which he could never resolve.

As he was a "brevet-Presbyterian," having been sprinkled in infancy, he claimed that this circumstance gave him the right "to be punished as a Presbyterian hereafter." He emphatically preferred the substantial Presbyterian punishment of fire and brimstone to "this heterodox hell of remorse of conscience" of the wildcat adherents. Calling themselves "Friends of Progress," they expected to go on progressing and progressing in their Heaven; therefore he was confident it would be more hellish than hell. This perverse view appears in his later writings where hell is made to seem more attractive than certain aspects of Heaven.[1] "Heaven for climate, hell for society," he once remarked. His announced preference of the orthodox hell instead of the wildcat hell of remorse of conscience is likewise significant for his later work; an example is "The Recent Carnival of Crime in Connecticut," which pictures his struggles in the hell furnished by his taunting, tormenting conscience. The foreshadowing in these years of so many of his later preoccupations indicates the part the West played in developing his latent capacities.

In San Francisco, he did some direct moralizing. When he first met Adah Isaacs Menken in Virginia City, he complimented her as

[1] See, for example, *Mark Twain's Notebook*, 168.

a "fellow literary cuss" and attended her strip-tease performance in *Mazeppa;* but later, when he was presumably writing the unsigned dramatic reviews for the San Francisco *Call,* a review condemns *Mazeppa* on moral grounds: "Let a pure youth witness Mazeppa once, and he is pure no longer. . . . Strip the play of the obscene and as a theatrical display it is worse than a Chinese tragedy, wooden shoes, gongs, and all the rest."[2] Personally, he had enjoyed *Mazeppa,* as he had apparently enjoyed his acquaintance with Adah Menken. But he was coming to view himself, in his role of newspaperman, as holding the public morals in trust. He casts a second stone at Menken in his "Extraordinary Meteoric Shower," speaking of a certain constellation as "the Great Menken" because he considers the phrase "a more modest expression than the Great Bear," with the implication that the terms are synonymous. He attends seances and reports that the only departed spirits willing to commune with him are all named Smith. He finds there are "dead loads" of Smiths living in hell, which they call "the Smithsonian Institute."

"William" of Missouri requests information about Washoe, and Mark Twain gives him a serious warning to beware of mining stocks which he knows nothing about. The moralist probably dictated the warning answer to William's inquiry about what diseases people die of in Nevada: "they used to die of conical balls and cold steel," but recent statistics show the power of "erysipelas and the intoxicating bowl." The realistic picture of Nevada exhibits Mark Twain's desire to debunk the legends spreading eastward about the glories of the West:

Nevada . . . is a barren waste of sand, embellished with melancholy sagebrush and fenced in with snow-clad mountains. But these ghastly features were the salvation of the land, William, for no rightly constituted American would have ever come here if the place had been easy of access, and none of our pioneers would have staid here after they got here if they had not felt satisfied that they could not find a smaller chance for making a living anywhere else. Such is man, William, as he crops out in America.

The perversity of man, a subject which engrossed him much in his old age, here engages his attention; and the antiromantic colors in

2 Franklin Walker, *San Francisco's Literary Frontier,* 169.

which he paints the Nevada scene foreshadow the technique of
Innocents Abroad.

In a visit to the Cliff House the moralist again strikes a note:
instead of the superb view of ocean and sky which he had expected,
"There was nothing in sight but . . . a long row of bottles with Old
Bourbon, and Old Rye, and Old Tom, and the old, old story of man's
falter and woman's fall in them." Thus the moralizing strain appears
in a chance touch. He ponders momentarily on "the great law of
compensation. . . . Behold, the same gust of wind that blows a lady's
dress aside and exposes her ankle, fills your eyes so full of sand that
you can't see it."

"Daniel in the Lion's Den—and Out Again All Right," one of
the satiric-moralistic sketches of this period, recounts his adventures among the brokers of San Francisco. For several days he had
associated with brokers as freely as he would with the most respectable people in the world, in the hall known to disinterested persons
as "the Den of Thieves." Here there is a hint of the determinism
which becomes such a large factor in later work: he considers that
"a broker goes according to the instincts that are in him"; therefore
he has a right to live, "just the same as a better man"; and, since
brokers do "come into the world with souls," he has a right to repent
at the eleventh hour to save his soul, as others do:

I am of the opinion that a broker can be saved. . . . Lazarus was raised
from the dead, the five thousand were fed with twelve loaves of bread,
the water was turned into wine, the Israelites crossed the Red Sea dry-
shod, and a broker *can* be saved. True, the angel that accomplishes the
task may require all eternity to rest himself in.

Only by employing the language of Biblical miracle can Mark
Twain convey the idea of the rarity of a broker's chance at salvation. A delinquent on the board of brokers loses caste, "and that
touches his fine moral sensibilities"; he may even be expelled if his
delinquency "savors of blundering and ungraceful rascality . . . and
this inflicts exquisite pain upon the delicate nerves and tissues of his
pocket."

This sketch ends with an imaginative picture of the arrival of
"that band of Bulls and Bears into Paradise," showing the restrained
welcome accorded them by skeptical old St. Peter, who stands "with
his ponderous key pressed thoughtfully against his nose, and his head

canted critically to one side, as he looks after them tramping down the gold-paved avenue." Certain imaginative details have been blended with the satiric-moral aim of this picture. But Mark Twain was not yet able to view the world as spectacle, recording it objectively and without concern for wringing a moral lesson from what he saw. At this point the urgency of the reform drive within him, coupled with his impatience toward mankind, caused him to strike through the short circuit of rampant humor, eliminating the aesthetic distance necessary for artistic effect.

The moralizing strain creeps into his writings in unexpected places. One of the routine "Interior Notes" on the mines, written for the San Francisco *Bulletin*, breaks off to denounce practical jokes on the ground that they are "lies": "any idiot can tell a lie, and no practical joke is anything more than a spoken or acted deception."[3] But his moralism was certainly not that of the conventional moralist, as he made clear in a blast aimed at the "Moral Statistician":

I don't want any of your statistics; I took your whole batch and lit my pipe with it. I hate your kind of people. You are always ciphering out how much a man's health is injured . . . and how many pitiful dollars he wastes in the course of ninety-two years' indulgence in the fatal practice of smoking; and in the equally fatal practice of drinking coffee; and in playing billiards occasionally; and in taking a glass of wine at dinner. . . . Of course you can save money by denying yourself all those little vicious enjoyments . . . but then what can you do with it? What use can you put it to? Money can't save your infinitesimal soul. All the use that money can be put to is to purchase comfort and enjoyment in this life; therefore . . . what is the use of accumulating cash? . . . you people who have no petty vices are never known to give away a cent. . . . Very well, then, what is the use of your stringing out your miserable lives to a lean and withered old age? What is the use of your saving money that is so utterly worthless to you? In a word, why don't you go off somewhere and die . . . ? Now, I don't approve of dissipation . . . but I haven't a particle of confidence in a man who has no redeeming petty vices, and so I don't want to hear from you any more.

He turned aside from the physical ills of childhood, prescribed for in "Those Blasted Children," to its moral and spiritual necessities, writing sketches designed to give "profit to the rising generation," among them a most unconventional approach to the character of

3 Benson, *Mark Twain's Western Years*, 240.

"young George W." and an article questioning the validity of Ben Franklin's "attractive little poem on early rising." Thus he early began to impugn the tenets of conventional propriety.

He had read the moralizing Sunday school tales in his childhood and had found them dreary books: ". . . there was not a bad boy in the entire bookcase. They were all good boys and good girls and drearily uninteresting." He burlesqued the sentimentalized tales in his "Stories for Good Little Boys and Girls" by piling up examples of the success-at-any-price formula. In the *Californian* for December 23, 1865, he offered "The Christmas Fireside . . . by Grandfather Twain," which now appears in *Sketches New and Old* as "The Story of the Bad Little Boy." This piece contrasts the career of small "sinful Jim" with the lives of all the bad little Jameses in the Sunday school books, where bad boys "invariably get drowned" or are "infallibly struck by lightning." But this boy stole, lied, rose by cheating and rascality, and yet prospered to the point where, being "the infernalest wickedest scoundrel in his native village," he is also "universally respected and belongs to the legislature." It is the perversity of the human race, of course, which makes material success, however acquired, a sufficient endowment for universal respect and a seat in the legislature. In this same sketch Mark Twain glanced at George Wilson, the good little boy who learned, alas, that virtue is not its own reward. This paragon was wrongfully accused of theft; and, although innocent, he was punished and disgraced.

A companion piece, "The Story of the Good Little Boy," exhibits Jacob Blivens, an unnatural creature who was "so honest he was simply ridiculous," took no interest in any kind of rational amusement, and was looked on by the other boys as "afflicted." Jacob found his greatest delight in the Sunday school tales, and his ambition was to land in a Sunday school book himself; he consciously set about living a life that would put him there. But "somehow nothing ever went right with this good little boy." He tried to aid a blind man and got whacked with a stick; he fed a lame dog and was bitten for his pains; finally he admonished some bad boys who were tying cans of nitroglycerine to dogs' tails, and as a result he got "apportioned around among four townships."

These inverted fables of Mark Twain's contain a reversal of the creed which teaches that good must follow good deeds and evil follow evil. Further, they slyly question the spiritual quality of an age in which the recipe for success produces a scoundrel. Some years later he followed the success pattern step by step and depicted, in *The Gilded Age,* a full-blown rascal with a seat in the national Congress. The relations between Mark Twain's Western work and his later writings are remarkably sustained.

Franklin Walker observes that Mark Twain's frontier audience was surprised to find that beneath his burlesques of the Sunday school stories there "lurked a defense of natural morality as opposed to conventional propriety." But whatever may be said of the tardy awakening of his frontier readers, his fellow journalists early discovered the satirist and moralist hidden beneath his clown's motley. Bret Harte saw him in 1866 as "something of a satirist," and C. H. Webb, hailing him as The Wild Humorist of the Pacific Slope, still predicted he would go down to posterity as The Moralist of the Main. In fact, Webb told readers in his preface to *The Jumping Frog* that he was presenting its author in his secondary character of humorist, rather than in his "primal one of moralist."[4] In 1866 the *Californian* ran some fake applications for the editorship; the letter purporting to be Mark Twain's spoke of his "missionary labors" and emphasized his moral turn:

What you want is a good Moral tone to the paper. If I have got a strong suit, that is it. If I am a wild enthusiast on any subject, that is the one. . . .
. . . What the people are suffering for is Morality. Turn them over to me. . . . when I play my hand in the high moral line, I take a trick every time.

Yours,
"Mark Twain."
Surnamed The Moral Phenomenon.

John Howell attributes this letter to Mark Twain himself, though Franklin Walker believes it is bogus; but whether written by Twain or merely in imitation of him, it sounds a note with which he was by this time evidently associated.

Although his Western colleagues thus recognized from the beginning the complex nature of his work, most Eastern readers viewed him solely as a humorist for years to come. In 1901, upon his return after a sojourn in Europe, an editorial in the Louisville *Courier-*

---

[4] Paine, *Biography*, III, Appendix E, 1605. Webb added that in preparing the book for publication it had been necessary to detach "threads of humor . . . from serious articles and moral essays with which they were woven and entangled."

Journal commented upon the "remarkable transformation, or rather development" that had taken place in Mark Twain, changing the "genial humorist" into "a reformer of the vigorous kind, a sort of knight errant who does not hesitate to break a lance."[5] Actually, as a reformer Mark Twain had then been engaged in vigorously breaking lances for thirty-eight years.

In passages quoted in Chapter 6, he himself explained his practice of hiding his moral truths in burlesque. But when the pose suited him, he would disclaim any intention of giving either reform or instruction to his readers. His article "About Play Acting" contains one of his characteristic disclaimers: "Do I seem to be preaching? It is out of my line: I only do it because the rest of the clergy seem to be on vacation." In his long letter to Andrew Lang, making a plea for a system of aesthetics for the middle classes, he said: "I have seldom . . . tried to instruct them, but have done my best to entertain them"; but in the next breath he revealed the motive of that entertainment: "I had two chances to help to the teacher's one."

The weight of the evidence is heavy on one side. In the *Eruption* book, in which he spoke "from the grave" and thus, as he said, had no reason for pretense or evasion, he underscored once more his custom of "preaching" through humor. Speaking of an anthology which contained his own work and that of seventy-eight other American humorists, then forgotten, he analyzed their failure:

Why have they perished? Because they were merely humorists. Humorists of the "mere" sort cannot survive. Humor is only a fragrance, a decoration. Often it is merely an odd trick of speech . . . and presently the fashion passes and the fame along with it. There are those who say a novel should be a work of art solely, and you must not preach in it, you must not teach in it. That may be true as regards novels, but it is not true as regards humor. Humor must not professedly teach, and it must not professedly preach, but it must do both if it would live forever. By forever, I mean thirty years. . . .

I have always preached. That is the reason that I have lasted thirty years. If the humor came of its own accord and uninvited, I have allowed it a place in my sermon, but I was not writing the sermon for the sake of the humor. I should have written the sermon whether any humor applied for admission or not. I am saying these vain things in this frank way because I am a dead person, speaking from the grave.

[5] *Mark Twain's Letters*, II, 703.

That he had a clear and undeluded perception of this aspect of his work, that he consciously chose the humorous methods by which he put it into effect, can scarcely be doubted. He once jokingly referred to himself as a "Professor of Moral Culture and the Dogmatic Humanities"; but elsewhere he spoke of himself quite seriously as a moralist and a reformer. In reply to a letter from a French girl, he wrote: "Yes, you are right—I am a moralist in disguise; it gets me into heaps of trouble when I go thrashing around in political questions." In 1905 he wrote to his publisher, F. A. Duneka, that he was living in an artists' and writers' colony in the New Hampshire hills and was enjoying it: "any place that is good for an artist in paint is good for an artist in morals and ink." The following year, he and Helen Keller exchanged letters about a project to aid the blind, and he quoted a statement of hers:

You say, "As a reformer, you know that ideas must be driven home again and again."
  Yes, I know it; and by old experience I know that speeches and documents and public meetings are a . . . lame way of accomplishing it. Last year I proposed a sane way—one which I had practiced with success for a quarter of a century—but . . . the good old way will be stuck to. . . . Its function is to breed hostility to good causes.

In his own view, his way of administering reform was not only more subtle, but also much more effective. It did not impel the reader to an automatic resistance, as the more obvious way was likely to do.

In his later years he went so far as to announce himself from the public platform as "a chartered, professional moralist"; and his conception of himself in the role of reformer was so strong that even in the early years he was not content to be viewed as a mere humorist. When in 1870 the publishers of the *Galaxy* specifically asked him to conduct a humorous department, he as specifically refused to do so. After facetiously announcing his new department, he added seriously:

These MEMORANDA are not a "humorous" department. I would not conduct an exclusively and professedly humorous department for any one. I would always prefer . . . the privilege of printing a serious and sensible remark, in case one occurred to me, without the reader's feeling obliged to consider himself outraged.[6]

  [6] *The Curious Republic of Gondour and Other Whimsical Sketches*, 23.

Mark Twain and the Jumping Frog
Poster for a Brooklyn lecture, February 7, 1869

Evidences of his dissatisfaction at being known only as a humorist appear throughout his work.[7]

Commenting on the ephemeral quality of humorists who have no ideal higher than "that of merely being funny," he once remarked to Archibald Henderson:

The first great lesson of my life was the discovery that I had to live down my past. When I first began to lecture, and in my earlier writings, my sole idea was to make comic capital out of everything. . . . I treated my readers as unfairly as I treated everybody else—eager to betray them at the end with some monstrous absurdity or some extravagant anticlimax.

This was his keen conscience accusing him falsely. He was, as usual, too hard on himself when he said that in early years his sole idea had been to make comic capital out of everything. How far this was from the truth has been demonstrated here. Almost from the beginning, his leading idea seems to have been to turn every available joke to the profit of mankind.

His first really valuable lesson, he said, was the instruction given him by a Nevada orator, Tom Fitch: Never nullify an eloquent, moving description by following it with an atrocious anticlimax.[8] He had received, then, early and forceful warnings against this fault, which the critics object to in his writings. But the force of the natural humor within him and the reforming urge which motivated his work combined to make him vulnerable. He had explicitly marked out the lower middle classes for his converts. In 1889 he complained to Andrew Lang:

If a critic should start a religion it would not have any object but to convert angels; and they wouldn't need it. . . . It is not that little minority who are already saved that are best worth trying to uplift . . . but the

---

[7] Bernard DeVoto (*Mark Twain's America*, 99) makes this odd observation: "It is not only that Mark Twain never became anything but a humorist, realist, and satirist of the frontier; he never desired to be anything else." After a public lecture that was apparently highly successful, Mark Twain burst out to George W. Cable, "Oh, Cable . . . I am allowing myself to be a mere buffoon. It's ghastly. I can't endure it any longer" (Paine, *Biography*, II, 768; see also *Letters*, I, 264, 261, 236–37, 284).

[8] Archibald Henderson, *Mark Twain*, 99.

mighty mass of the uncultivated who are underneath. . . . And I . . . always hunted for bigger game—the masses.

His ludicrous humor was the lure, the bait, which he set to snare them.

But, from the beginning, the power and vigor of the reforming motif in Mark Twain are countered by his view of the general worthlessness of mankind and the essential futility of life. Much of his iconoclastic, destructive humor—and this element is particularly strong in his Western product—sets itself to tear the mask from the face of life, to show up the "mangy human race." The sorry picture of mankind presented in "The Case of Smith vs. Jones," the ugly passages which make use of offensive smells and vomiting, of eternal violence and omnipresent death—all show an awareness of the drab background before which he paraded his fury of reform.

In his review of *Roughing It,* Howells said that an honest man could treat the frontier conditions only with exaggerated humor or with bitter despair. Mark Twain's formula uses both: his Western humor compounds a skyscraper exaggeration with a singular ferocity which is assuredly a by-product of despair. A writer of Bret Harte's caliber could cast a haze of theatricality, like a veil of gauze, over the frontier life, softening it into the unreality of a stage set; but for Mark Twain in the West reality was the thing, although it might be painful to behold—reality intensified, heightened, piled up until it towered into grotesquerie. In 1868 he wrote to Mrs. A. W. Fairbanks, who had complimented him:

There is nothing that makes me prouder than to be regarded . . . as "authentic." . . . *I* don't care anything about being humorous, or poetical, or eloquent, or anything of that kind—the end & aim of my ambition is to be authentic—to be considered authentic.

In honesty, he pictured the world as he saw it; and often he saw it ugly.

Gradually the reform motive effected changes in his subject matter. In the early days he derived much humor from the topic of drunkenness. He enumerated as "natural features" of Calaveras the Big Trees, the Morgan gold mine, and a certain straight whiskey whose potency he celebrated. He used "washes" of Veuve Clicquot for his telescope, as an aid to astronomical observations. He introduced Jim Blaine, "tranquilly, serenely, symmetrically drunk," to tell the story of his grandfather's old ram. In later years, however, he generally excluded the subject from his pages; H. W. Fisher quotes him as saying, "I love a drink, but I never encourage drunkenness by harping on its alleged funny side." Thus a fertile subject is forbidden to the artist by the moralist; for Jim Blaine is a work of art, proving how fascinating, at least in literature, an expertly exhibited drunk can be.

In their turn, his reforming tendencies were constantly opposed by the beliefs set forth in other writings which voice his deterministic view that "neither religion, training, nor education avails anything against the force of circumstances that drive a man." And circumstances, he asserted, lie entirely beyond man's control. What, then, was the benefit to be derived from the mass of writings penned by Mark Twain the Moralist, the Reformer? If mankind is incapable of changing through training or education, then man is an impossible subject for reform. And Mark Twain's dilemma remains unsolved.

But Mark Twain the Moralist is not only set at cross purposes against Mark Twain the Determinist; frequently, the Moralist is also set at cross purposes against the Artist. Moral values embody the writer's perception of evil and his desire to escape it. He is prompted to shun certain ills to which humanity is subject, and he seeks to warn his fellows, that they also may escape the same dread ills—death, hunger, disease, loneliness, crime. In his essay on "The Nature of Beauty," Santayana shows the shadow forms of these specters standing behind every moral injunction. To the moralist their voices merge with the voice of conscience within him, urging him on to save his fellows; he cries out to mankind, "Do not!" So far as Mark Twain's work utters the warning, "Do not!" he becomes a naysayer to life.

To the ethicist the practice of ethics may become a satisfying end in itself, but in the realm of practical morality, morals serve mainly to confine human conduct within the narrow limits of security. But, if we could conceive of a life so ideal that practical morality is no longer necessary to give security, art in some form would still be needed to fill the leisure of that ideal existence as an element of our happiness—what Santayana calls "the clear profit of living."

There are two kinds of truth—practical truth and imaginative truth; and they confer two separate benefits. Moral values, based on a consciousness of benefits in some way involved, may be remote from the present moment; but the value of art is that it gives a sense of the immediate presence of something good, a good satisfying to some fundamental capacity of our minds. And art, in both its production and its appreciation, belongs to those free moments when, in Santayana's phrase, we are "redeemed from the shadow of evil and the slavery to fear, and are following the bent of our nature where it chooses to lead us." When the imagination of the artist is released and free, true creative art may be the result; the artisan, on the other hand, of necessity wrenches his ideas to fit his utilitarian pattern.

Moral values, then, embody the instinct for self-preservation; aesthetic values embody the impulse for self-realization. So far as self-preservation is concerned, spontaneous and delightful activity may be useless; but what is the advantage of self-preservation without self-realization? In other words, life cannot be prized unless its content is valuable. And here the moralist in Mark Twain suffers a defeat: he tries to save mankind to a life which he often paints as despicable and futile.

Aesthetic activity is its own justification, its own reward. But if through it art can be produced which embodies a deep knowledge of humanity, because it reveals both a self-knowledge and a self-respect, then art becomes a blending of the ethical and the imaginative. Straight utilitarianism is a deadly anti-aesthetic formula; but, although art does not aim essentially at moral edification, we are the better for that aesthetic exercise in which we learn about the world of man's spirit. From Mark Twain's work the reader gets a vast amount of self-knowledge, particularly that touching the darker side of human nature. But from much of that work he gets very little that increases his self-respect.

CHAPTER 8

The Humorist as Technician

MARK TWAIN'S mastery of the tricks of the professional
humorist is unquestionable. Through the patterns and
techniques of the world's humor he wandered at will,
adapting to his purpose now one device, now another. In the technique of humorous invective he was particularly proficient; his
specialty was exaggerated description, adorned with arresting epithets drawn from the Bible or the gutter. But in the field of invective and epithet he practiced long and polished carefully before he
began to turn out his distinctive product.

As late as 1901 he used a succession of adjectives to describe a
woman as "only an innocent, well-meaning, driveling vacancy."
Usually, however, he was selective, coupling a single powerful adjective with a comprehensive noun, sometimes linking them for
alliteration, as in "stupefying simplicity," "craven carcass," "disastrous donkey"; or for repetition of sound, as in "frozen effrontery."
He anticipated Hollywood in his early fondness for *stupendous*
and *colossal;* but he used these words mainly in derogation—"stupendous lies" and "colossal ignorance." Sometimes the adjective
gives the reader a slight sense of shock because of its unexpected connection with the accompanying noun; the same is true of adverbs,
as when he remarked that something was "intolerably interesting"
or that one need not expect to become, because of early rising, "in-
sufferably healthier and wealthier and wiser."

Humor rests on a reversal of things from the ordained condition, on startling juxtaposition and on bizarre incongruities. Mark
Twain linked adjective and noun in the incongruity which is basic
in humor in such combinations as "majestic ignorance," "charming
absurdity," "stately blunder," and "imposing insanity." By tying a
flattering adjective to an uncomplimentary noun he achieved such

119

striking epithets as "illustrious guttersnipe," "animated outrage," "immortal jackass," and "gentle idiot." The technique of thus bringing together two paradoxical elements in a sudden stroke is an old one, but a special pungency is added when such incongruities become terms of address. Exasperated with the incompetency he encountered in Washington, Mark Twain addressed one dignified official as "illustrious Vagrant" and another as "renowned and honored Imbecile." He employed the same device in such Indian names as "Beneficent Polecat." And the effect he achieved by calling someone a "festive ass" is more strongly humorous for its basic incongruity than the more ordinary term, "driveling ass." Based on this technique of incongruous elements, a form of *non sequitur* was one of his favorite devices. An example is his offhand mention of a man who "had a wart on his nose and died in the hope of a glorious resurrection." He practiced digression in his first three appearances in the *Californian*: "A Notable Conundrum," "Concerning the Answer to That Conundrum," and "Still Further Concerning That Conundrum." Like Artemus Ward's famous "Babes in the Wood," completely ignored in the lecture advertised under their name, that conundrum was slighted throughout the sketches while Mark Twain ranged far and wide.

The device of incredible exaggeration he used as early as 1856 in the first Snodgrass letters, which disclose a humor marked by a primitive imaginative power. Thomas Jefferson Snodgrass describes a race between "an old fellar with a carpet bag" and a steamboat that walked. Stuck on a sand bar, the steamboat finally got clear

... and away she went walkin down the river on four inches of water, and jumpin over three acre patches of dry land, just as though she had legs. The old man and her had a mighty tight race of it, and she only saved herself by takin a nigh cut across the bottom, comin in fifteen minutes ahead.

Here the image of the walking steamboat produces in the mind's eye a mythical creature resembling a great dragon or crocodile. This humor of the grotesque, a special form of the humor of incongruity, may present a thing out of its natural habitat—like Rabelais' drought-stricken fishes that wandered over the earth, "crying horribly." A steamboat that walks suggests a Caliban-like lumbering gait, and the imagination is instantly busy with the suggestion. This is part of the strength of humor, as of lyric poetry: its power of suggesting more than it says. Not, necessarily, that the early Mark Twain received ideas from Rabelais; yet, from his very beginnings as a writer he employed a grotesque fantasy depending on a subtle disharmony foreign to the crude directness of slapstick farce. In his "Fables for Good Old Boys and Girls," he conveys a sense of the speed of a train as it appeared to the simple creatures of the forest; a demoniacal shriek was heard, then a rumbling noise, and "a vast terrific eye shot by, with a long tail attached, and disappeared into the gloom, still uttering triumphant shrieks." Here the image suggests another creature of myth, a Cyclopean serpent or dragon.

Especially grotesque is the animalesque humor in which animals or reptiles are brought into unusual comparisons. In "Washoe, Information Wanted," he gave a vivid impression of the barren Nevada landscape, studded with sagebrush, by saying "the country looks something like a singed cat." He frequently derived humor from the ass, which, being a hybrid, is a bit of natural grotesquerie in the animal kingdom. One of Pudd'nhead Wilson's maxims is based on this excellent creature:

Observe the ass. . . . his character is about perfect, he is the choicest spirit among all the humbler animals, yet see what ridicule has brought him to. Instead of feeling complimented when we are called an ass, we are left in doubt.

This maxim introduces the technical device called litotes, meiosis, or understatement. Euphemism, too, was one of Mark Twain's most characteristic humorous devices. His "Burlesque Biography" is one long illustration of the device, as well as a triumphant glorification of rascality, a humorous technique at least as old as Reynard.

Comic hyperbole is the direct opposite to the dry humor of understatement, and Mark Twain's exaggerated similes and extravagant metaphors are among his distinctive features. His early Western sketches begin his long-continued drawings of perverse and decrepit horses. A horse proudly presented to him as a "Morgan" he saw as "a solemn, short-bodied, long-legged animal—a sort of animated counting-house stool." He encountered another horse "whose ridgy backbone stood out . . . like the croppings of a quartz ledge"; while his team-mates galloped, trotted, and paced, this horse walked

"with a martial stride that defied all imitation except with stilts."
Here the grotesque element appears in the picture the imagination
presents of that stiltlike walk in contrast with the other gaits.

Although exaggeration marked the first Snodgrass letters, it
was in the climactic life of the Far West that Mark Twain's exaggeration took on colossal proportions. There his sky-breaking humor
was a product of calculated detail and conscious elaboration. That
it was also consciously designed as a vehicle of reform—a point
demonstrated in preceding chapters—proves it the opposite of spontaneous and unpremeditated. In the West he shunned cacography,
for John Phoenix had taught the Western writers that humor need
not be illiterate. But amid that ferocious movement and swift color,
chaotic confusion became a salient quality of his writing. As a comic
artist, he cultivated disorder, making formlessness and comic verbosity his goals. As a burlesque technician, he piled up grotesque details
in patterns of absurd association. In *Roughing It* he tells of a dissolute
stranger who invaded Virginia City and worked briefly on Tom
Fitch's abortive novel; and his description of the stranger's writing
as "symmetrically crazy" and "artistically absurd" fits perfectly
many of his own sketches. Examples of his climactic accumulation
of detail are to be seen in "Those Blasted Children," in "Aurelia's
Unfortunate Young Man," and—perhaps best of all—in the "Extraordinary Meteoric Shower." Explosive stories such as "How I Edited
an Agricultural Paper" and "The Great Beef Contract" possess, as
G. K. Chesterton pointed out, one absolute essential for art: the
excitement in them mounts up and up; they grow more and more
comic, as a tragedy should grow more and more tragic. Mark Twain
employs both the surprise ending and the progressive form in which
the ending is foreseen. Some of his humorous conceits, doubling and
turning upon themselves, are as involved in nature as the conceits
of the Elizabethan poets. The reader's sense of humor is excited almost as much by the anticipation as by the final arrival of the climax.

A time-honored division of humorous technique is that which
deals with the humor of cruelty. Stephen Leacock suggests that
laughter originated as a sort of physical expression of triumph, and
that the savage "who cracked his enemy over the head and shouted
'Ha! ha!' as a release of pent-up emotion was our first humorist."
The primitive humor of cruelty in Mark Twain appears in such
savage bits as "The Great Prize Fight," already noted as a satire on

politics, where mutual attentions between Governor Low and Leland Stanford strew the battleground with odds and ends of human anatomy. There is also in his work a repulsive humor, exemplified in "Cannibalism in the Cars" and still more in "The Invalid's Story"—that adventure of the limburger cheese and the guns which Howells felt as grisly humor might "challenge all literature for its like." By emphasizing the stench of corpses, Mark Twain seems also to emphasize the indignity of human life, an attitude which he ultimately crystallized into the words, "Man comes into the world as dirt and goes out of it as stench." He exhibited a different facet of his death-humor when he viewed death in a pleasurable, almost playful mood in "The Undertaker's Chat," where the undertaker dwells on the merits of a certain corpse.

But there are quieter forms of humor at his command. Some passages have the flavor of that odd, gentle resignation to disappointment which Howells considered one of Mark Twain's finest touches. "Early Rising as Regards Excursions to the Cliff House" follows this pattern and deserves analysis as one of the earliest expressions of his realistic observation. The early-morning trip had been romanticized by summer tourists until Mark Twain felt that a visit to the Cliff House at a more comfortable hour was out of the question. Rising at four o'clock in the morning, he set forth with a companion, determined to delight in the popular features of a bracing atmosphere perfumed by flowers, a road free of carriages, and a drive on the beach while its smoothness was yet unmarred by wheels. But the atmosphere was freezing rather than bracing, and he soon added a horse blanket to his overcoats. Thereafter the fresh perfume of flowers in suburban gardens was mingled with the odor of horse blanket. True, the road contained no other travelers; this one feature was as advertised, but he was not content. He wanted it understood that when next he took an early voyage, the rest of the people should "be made to stand their share of the desperate lonesomeness of the thing." Through the fog the excursionists could see only the ears of their horse sticking up out of a white mist; if Mark Twain were forced to take another "ride in the clouds," he would go in a balloon:

I shall prefer to go in the afternoon, also, when it is warm, so that I may gape, and yawn, and stretch . . . without disarranging my horse-blanket and letting in a blast of cold wind.

Humor is almost indefinable, and its effects have a certain complexity; it broadens into a general notion of "disharmony between a thing and its setting, between its present and its usual accompaniment."[1] That is why we laugh at a naked savage in a silk hat. And the humor here rests on Mark Twain's obvious acceptance of a future in which he will be perpetually accompanied by his horse blanket. This sketch is one of his early Western pieces; and the contrast between its plaintive resignation and the bludgeoning blood-humor of his "scathing satires," as he called them, reveals the breadth of his range in humorous styles and techniques.

He often held himself up to laughter, either in self-vaunting or in self-depreciation. He was sometimes the debonair egotist, filled with a sublime conceit; one sketch reveals that he considered himself eminently well fitted to be king of Spain. But the humor of reversed egotism, the humiliation of self, he employed more frequently. Physical discomfiture, a fruitful source of humor from the days of Tyll Eulenspiegel to those of Sut Lovingood, forms the base for such sketches as Mark Twain's recital of his countless sprawls on the "granite-bound inhospitable shore" of the curb while "Taming the Bicycle."

But mental discomfiture, incomparably more complex than physical, proved a more engaging theme for him. In this field he was the forerunner of such American humorists as Robert Benchley, James Thurber, and S. J. Perelman. The favorite character of these devotees of the cult of lunacy, a character usually identified in their writings with the humorist himself, is the shy, bewildered, mentally ill-at-ease little fellow who is beset on every hand by the myriad complexities of modern life. Recall, for instance, Thurber's struggles with his recalcitrant overcoat. The technique in which Mark Twain is nearest to these moderns, these deadly enemies of common sense, is in the humor of a mild insanity, a mellow idiocy. In "Playing Courier" he revealed the gentle madness which had seized him when he attempted to act as courier for a party of seven from Aix-les-Bains to Bayreuth. His absent-mindedness got him into trouble with ticket agents, cabmen, hotel keepers, and telegraphers; he lost his head completely. Finally, he had to return to his waiting party and face them, having failed in everything entrusted to his care. Anticipating Benchley's technique, he tried to make light of his failure; he

[1] Stephen B. Leacock, *Humor: Its Theory and Technique*, 11.

shied his hat into the arena outlined by their stiff, forbidding figures, and shouted blithely,

"Ha, ha, here we all are, Mr. Merryman!"

Nothing could be deeper or stiller than the absence of applause which followed. But I kept on; there seemed no other way. . . . I tried to . . . soften the bitter resentment in those faces by throwing off bright and airy fun . . . but I . . . thawed nothing of the winter that looked out of those frosty eyes.

He united the themes of physical discomfiture and mental uneasiness in his sketch "About Barbers," which describes his agonies as he waits on the bench, fearful that his turn will bring him to the ministrations of a barber whom he dislikes and is afraid of, but lacking the courage simply to say he will wait for the next chair. His state of mind is recounted with all the minuteness of Robert Benchley's little piece detailing how Benchley was intimidated by some arrogant pigeons.

The timid creature depicted in such sketches embodies a satire on the failure of man to adjust himself to his environment or to mold it, to adapt it to his own ends; as such, he is one of the most significant products of modern imagination. The keynote of pieces centered in him is always the fear of the unfit; instead of primitive scenes in which man cowers before the fury of nature, red in tooth and claw, we are shown this ill-adjusted one shivering before a background of shrieking motorcars, grinding wheels, and barbers armed with sinister razors. In the technique of reverse egotism the humorist holds nothing back from his audience; he does not try to present himself in a favorable light or in palliating circumstances. Instead, his cringing, timorous little soul is laid bare in all its frail weaknesses, all its ill-defined fears. He falls back aghast from the multifold dangers of modern living. Mark Twain commented on this technique in his anonymous review of his own *Innocents Abroad*. He presented, not the fears, but the futility of the "fool" character;[2] either fear or futility will render him useless to society.

Our author makes a long, fatiguing journey to the Grotto del Cane . . . to test its poisoning powers on a dog—got elaborately ready for the ex-

[2] Walter Blair, *Horse Sense in American Humor*, 283 ff. Mr. Blair discusses the "fool character" and analyzes the moderns.

periment, and then discovered that he had no dog. A wise person would have kept such a thing discreetly to himself, but with this harmless creature everything comes out.

He often achieved verbal humor by an odd turn of phrase, a novel word application. An example is the opening sentence of his early "Biographical Sketch of George Washington": "This day, many years ago precisely, George Washington was born." He claimed to know all about the newspaper business, as he had "been through it from Alpha to Omaha." He reasoned judiciously about the powers of a dead whale on the beach at San Francisco; the whale was only thirty-five feet long, but "he smelt as much as a mile and a half longer, I should say." These lines were written in 1864; in 1897 he was still capable of the same whimsical conjecture. Someone had sent him a trick photograph showing Mark Twain seated in a dilapidated cart with two Negroes, and he returned grateful acknowledgment: "The picture has reached me, and has moved me deeply. . . . I consider that this picture is much more than a work of art. How much more, one cannot say with exactness, but I should think two-thirds more." The "William" who wrote for information about Washoe inquired if he thought it "advisable for a man who can make a living in Missouri to emigrate to that part of the country," and Mark Twain replied: "If you are not content in your present condition, it naturally follows that you would be entirely satisfied if you could make either more or less than a living. You would exult in the cheerful exhilaration always produced by a change." This reasoning has the same mad, yet unassailable, logic of Benchley's economic reports.

Much of the delightful craziness of Mark Twain's essay on "How to Make History Dates Stick" is akin to the nonsense humor, in spite of his sober purpose in writing it. His whimsical absurdity flavors such passages as that dealing with the "jamboree," his fanciful inspiration for representing King John. His drawing resembles a jackass more than anything else, but the creature's body is curiously twisted; it seems to be sitting down and galloping at the same time. Mark Twain explained:

Physically it has no representative now, but its mind has been transmitted. First I drew it sitting down, but have turned it the other way now because I think it looks more attractive and spirited when one end of it is galloping. I love to think that in this attitude it gives us a pleasant idea of John coming all in a happy excitement to see what the barons have been arranging for him at Runnymede, while the other one gives us an idea of him sitting down to wring his hands and grieve over it.

He closed the sketch by recommending that varicolored bits of paper be pinned on the parlor walls to represent the reigns of different kings: "This will make the walls interesting and . . . really worth something instead of being just flat things to hold the house together."

He used a satiric humor that laughs at men for being so ridiculously what they are; an ironic humor that laughs at them for not being what they should be; a grisly humor that derides the dignity of life; a macabre humor that mocks at the seriousness of death; a fantastic humor, seemingly too light in touch to be sinister, which yet degrades the lofty or raises the low to unmerited pretensions. As a master of every device of the professional humorist, he employed homespun aphorisms, anticlimax, comic implication, irreverence, solemn protestations of truthfulness, and, very rarely, cacography.[3]

There is occasional coarseness in his humor, the earlier sketches exhibiting much more of this element. In his "Kearney Street Ghost Story" a ghost came in the night to a servant girl's bedside, groaned, and "bet kittens" until it had "stacked up a whole litter of nine little bloody kittens" on the pillow. "What would you think of a ghost that came to your bedside in the dead of night and had kittens?" Akin to his "Bloody Massacre" in purpose, his ghost story was aimed at the credulity of West Coast followers of spiritualism and was designed to draw public ridicule to a current story of a servant visited at night by a "spirit." Critics say that grossness in literature "may be due either to the rollicking spirit of a gross age, or it may be due to an effort to satirize vice."[4] The first reason has too often been given to explain Mark Twain's coarseness, without enough attention to the second.

But his coarseness may have even more complexity than is lent to it by its nether side of satire. It is odd that so much of his humor

[3] In a review of Walter Blair's *Native American Humor*, DeLancey Ferguson holds that Mark Twain "was not a folk humorist but a highly skilled man of letters adapting the materials of popular humor to literary art" (*American Literature*, Vol. IX, No. 4 [January, 1938], 483).

[4] Philo Buck, *Literary Criticism*, 301 n.

should be concerned with nausea, vomiting, offensive smells, and ugly violence, when those who knew him best testified, as did his friend the Reverend Joseph Twichell, to his "exquisite refinement of taste and sentiment." But he was so sensitive that he suffered because of his sensibility. And by dragging out into the open what we normally wish to forget, he perhaps found a certain relief. In his coarse sketches, apart from their shock value for his reforming motives, he may have intellectualized painful things by introducing them into his humor. Thus he tried to free himself from them, and the attempt is an indication that he was temperamentally an artist, essentially concerned with the things which made him suffer.

In 1864, when he met Bret Harte, he found in Harte the most experienced literary craftsman he had yet known. Harte's finical care for details was proverbial: he was said to have filled a waste-basket in his efforts to concoct the "right" reply to an invitation.[5] Mark Twain solicited Harte for advice in the revision of his articles, and thus doubtless learned something of the value of form. Franklin Walker suggests that he may in turn have imparted some of his vitality to Harte. At any rate, in 1871 Mark Twain made his own obligation a matter of record:

. . . Bret Harte . . . trimmed and trained and schooled me patiently until he changed me from an awkward utterer of coarse grotesquenesses to a writer of paragraphs and chapters that have found a certain favor in the eyes of even some of the decentest people in the land.

Despite this testimony, it is difficult to find traces of great indebtedness. Harte's influence seems to have been an influence of manner rather than of spirit, of mere coaching rather than of literary inspiration. In California, it is true, the rampant vigor of the frontier in Mark Twain's sketches was somewhat toned down.

In the West his style soon attained an easy-flowing rhythm, marked now and then by a striking image or an arresting simile. He described the view of the ocean he had expected to see from the Cliff House, with "piles of picturesque rocks . . . garrisoned by drunken, sprawling sea-lions and elegant long-legged pelicans." The mincing, dignified gait suggested by "elegant" pelicans offers a striking contrast to the lumbering, reeling movements of the drunk-

5 Walker, *San Francisco's Literary Frontier*, 130.

en, sprawling sea lions. In his burlesque "Account of the Extraordinary Meteoric Shower" he washed his glass frequently with Veuve Clicquot and recorded what he saw after each "wash":

I applied the sixth wash. A sprinkle of sparkling fragments ensued— fragments of some beautiful world that had been broken up and cast out of the blue firmament—and then a radiance of noon-day flared out of the zenith and Mercury . . . came sweeping down like a banished sun. . . . you couldn't see the other side of the street for the hurtling tempest of stars.

In such passages, although the means so lavishly expended are far beyond the worth of the end obtained, there is indication of careful attention to word selection and sentence structure, with a strong underlying sense of prose rhythm.

His resources of vocabulary show up well in early sketches where he needed a contrast in style or language to embody contrasting ideas. As one phase of the humor of incongruity, he made use of an incongruous mixture of styles. A passage will begin in high-flown, poetic, or even Biblical language and then suddenly descend into colloquial phraseology that brings the reader up short with a surprising bump. Writing on the almost fatal effects of early rising, Mark Twain declared that after seeing the sun rise four times a week in Virginia City, he was so changed that his relatives became alarmed and grieved for him

. . . as one whose days were numbered—whose fate was sealed—who was soon to pass away from them forever, and from the glad sunshine . . . and go down into the dark and silent tomb—and they went forth sorrowing, and jumped a lot in the graveyard, and made up their minds to grin and bear it.

A similar technique appears in passages containing a sudden descent to an idea of lower level than that which has gone before, instead of a lowering of the writing style:

Ah me! Summer girls and summer dresses and summer scenes at the "Willows," Seal Rock Point, and the grim sea-lions wallowing in the angry surf; glimpses through the haze of stately ships far away at sea, a dash along the smooth beach, and the exhilaration of watching the white waves come surging ashore and break into seething foam about the startled horse's feet; reveries beside the old wreck, half buried in the sand, and compassion for the good ship's fate; home again in a soft twilight, oppressed with the odor of flowers—home again to San Francisco, drunk, perhaps, but not disorderly. Dinner at six, with ladies and gentlemen dressed with faultless taste and elegance, and all drunk, apparently, but very quiet and well-bred—unaccountably so, under the circumstances, it seemed to my cloudy brain.

Both passages, the first illustrating the mixture of high and low styles and the second the abrupt descent in ideas, were written in 1863 or 1864. Already Mark Twain appears, despite the utter disproportion of means to ends, a writer in fair command of his material, possessing an adequate vocabulary and a feeling for prose rhythm.

One of the chief excellences of his later style was his ability to express abstract ideas in concrete terms. His tendency to think in images began early. In his Western days, as later, his favorite figures were drawn from elemental sources, chiefly from fire and light and from the world's waters—seas, rivers, oceans, and the boats and ships that ride upon them, the latter class probably deriving from his steam-boating days. In the Jumping Frog story the "little small bull-pup" seemed of no account at first glance: "But as soon as money was up on him he was a different dog; his under jaw'd begin to stick out like the fo'castle of a steamboat, and his teeth would uncover and shine like the furnaces." And at the crucial moment, the shot-filled frog "couldn't no more stir than if he was anchored out." His figurative use of seasons and storms, moonlight and sea, cloud and wind, lava and ice, water and fire, is in keeping with the primitive quality of his imagination.

Another element of his early style is his use of Biblical language and cadence. He drops into it with an ease which seems to take the reader's knowledge of the Bible absolutely for granted. In "The Great Beef Contract" a searching clerk finally found the long-lost record—"the rock upon which so many of my ancestors had split." Sometimes there is merely a faint Biblical flavor, a reminiscence, as when the irreverent Tumble Bug "was driven away with stripes" by the other inmates of the forest. An early example of his concrete expression of an abstract idea occurs in "Daniel in the Lion's Den," in which he commends the eleventh-hour sagacity of Barabbas in "selling out of a worked-out mine of iniquity and investing in righteousness." In the matter of word choice, the early Mark Twain was partial to *unoffending, vast,* and *prodigious;* and the same words appear frequently in his later writings. But another early favorite, *slathered,* he soon abandoned; he had used it, apparently, for its humorous effect in sound, as in his "Earthquake Almanac," where he wrote of "worlds slathered around carelessly."

His early and continued interest in the writer's craft is shown by the number of sketches in which he burlesqued forms or styles of writing. Parody reproduces a particular piece, while burlesque reproduces a class, revealing the sickly sentiment or bombast of the literary works themselves; but a higher range is reached when burlesque is used to satirize not merely the books of a period "but the life and manners of the period itself."[6] It is but natural, then, that Mark Twain's talent did not run to parody so much as to burlesque.

His criticism of writing that affected him disagreeably appears first in sketches burlesquing various forms of journalism. In a lampoon of the ridiculous fashion reviews then current, Mark Twain the Moralist makes a reference to the women of the demimonde in the remark that the "circus-tent" hoops which render such a charming effect when one stands on the corner of Montgomery and looks up "any steep street" are worn by some who are not "virtuous ladies." He invented "correspondents" to enable him to deride their writing styles and ideas. Even his early "Petrified Man" sketch, besides settling a score with an egotistic coronor, had as its purpose the ridicule of a literary fad, as he explained in the *Galaxy* for June, 1870: "In . . . 1862 in Nevada and California the people got to running wild about . . . natural marvels. . . . I chose to kill the petrifaction mania with a delicate, a very delicate, satire."

His account of the "Distressing Accident" related to him by Johnny Skae gave him an opportunity to lampoon the ordinary run of "local items." He charged the *Californian* with being entirely too fastidious in its objections to Skae's item. In the light of what he later wrote about how Bret Harte had "trimmed and trained and schooled" him during this period, it is possible that in the guise of burlesque he was actually revealing his own current attitude, a somewhat resentful one, toward that critical training, especially in the lines concerning humor:

But it is just the Californian's style to be so disgustingly particular and

6 Leacock, *Humor: Its Theory and Technique,* 68.

so distressingly hypercritical. . . . They don't appear to know how to discriminate. They don't appear to understand that there are different kinds of jokes. . . . No; they give a man no credit for originality—for striking out into new paths and opening up new domains of humor.

Whether or not this passage is the aftermath of some difference of opinion between Bret Harte and Mark Twain, it is included in the article on Johnny Skae which Mr. DeVoto views as combining extended digression and *non sequitur* to produce a high point in a technique not found earlier than Mark Twain in American humor. Skae's "item" follows chains of association apparently quite mad; in his defense of it, Twain points out characteristic weaknesses of certain journals with a side commentary on their readers: "It is after the same style . . . as the articles published every day in the city papers. It has got all the virtues that distinguish those articles and render them so acceptable to the public."

In a "novelette" called "Uncle Lige," Mark Twain caricatured those affecting incidents (later called sob stories) which staff writers descend to when there is a shortage of news. Aimed at tear-jerkers which sentimentalize maudlin old drunkards, the article gives the drunken speeches of "poor blind-drunk Uncle Lige," accompanied by an obbligato of hiccoughs which shows an early attempt of Mark Twain to render speech realistically. The moralist is evident in "The Wild Man Interviewed," which pillories newspaper sensationalism in a most sensational style. The wild man has been forced to do an atrocious murder and to perpetrate various humbugs, from writing the Junius letters to playing sea serpent, all to create news for "quill-driving scum." He is now on his way to dig up the Byron family.[7]

Mark Twain's use of burlesque as literary criticism by no means confines itself to journalism. He burlesqued travel folders, learned articles, astronomical reports, and scientific jargon in general. In "My Late Senatorial Secretaryship" he caricatured the noncommit-

[7] Reference to an intent "to dig up the Byron family" is as close as Mark Twain could come to the subject of incest. In an early essay he speaks of the Byron scandal as not susceptible of burlesque "because the central feature of it, incest, was a 'situation' so tremendous and so imposing that the happiest available resources of burlesque seemed tame and cheap in its presence. Burlesque could invent nothing to transcend incest, except by enlisting two crimes, neither of which is ever mentioned among women and children, and one of which is only mentioned in rare books of the law, and there as 'the crime without a name'—a term with a shudder in it." Quoted in Wagenknecht, *Mark Twain: The Man and His Work*, 121.

tal epistles with which congressmen are wont to pacify the demands of their constituents back home. In a remarkably deft missive he answered a letter demanding that a certain post route be changed, by seeming to promise everything while actually promising nothing. His reply, sheer nonsense couched in official-sounding phrases, winds on and on about the Mormon trail that "leaves Mosby's at three in the morning," and concludes:

... thus making the route cheaper, easier of access to all who can get at it, and compassing all the desirable objects so considered by others, and, therefore, conferring the most good upon the greatest number, and, consequently, I am encouraged to hope we shall.

The allusion to the great tenet of democracy—the greatest good to the greatest number—is jargon thrown in to still the petitioners.

His review of *Ingomar, the Barbarian*, entitled "Ingomar Over the Mountains," is amusing in its mingling of Greek characters and local Indians, but it is also literary analysis; for, as DeLancy Ferguson observes, Mark Twain had realized that in spite of Greek costumes and inflated speeches, the play "was no different from Beadle's dime novels, and his parody underscored the resemblances." On October 15, 1864, he reviewed the opera *The Crown Diamonds*. He points out that current reviewers make no difference between gifted and mediocre performers, allowing the true artist to "sink from sight ... in the general slough of slimy praise" in which they cause all performers to "wallow once a week." For his part, he praises the talented work of Signor Bellindo Cellini, "the accomplished basso-relievo furniture-scout and sofa-shifter." But his burlesque is also a vehicle for his condemnation of newspaper critics who evade their responsibilities. In his critique he declares:

I feel the importance of carefully-digested newspaper criticism in matters of this kind—for I am aware that by it the dramatic and musical tastes of a community are moulded, cultivated, and irrevocably fixed—that by it these tastes are vitiated and debased, or elevated and ennobled, according to the refinement or vulgarity and the competency or incompetency of the writers to whom this department of the public training is entrusted.

"The Story of the Good Little Boy" represents the effect of

reading a certain kind of romantic literature—the Sunday school books—as definitely as *Madam Bovary* and *Don Quixote* display the effects of other romantic stories. Its companion piece, "The Story of the Bad Little Boy," anticipates in caricature the Horatio Alger series destined to ennoble boy readers for years to come. A memorable passage follows sinful Jim's action in stealing the teacher's penknife and hiding it in the cap of George Wilson, most moral boy of the village. When the knife has been discovered there and the teacher is just ready to bring down the switch upon the shoulders of poor innocent George,

. . . a white haired, improbable justice of the peace did not suddenly appear in their midst, and strike an attitude and say, "Spare this noble boy —there stands the cowering culprit! I was passing the school door at recess, and, unseen myself, I saw the theft committed!" And then Jim didn't get whaled, and the venerable justice didn't read the tearful school a homily, and take George by the hand and say such a boy deserved to be exalted, and then tell him to come and make his home with him, and sweep out the office, and make fires, and run errands, and chop wood, and study law, and help his wife do household labors, and have all the balance of the time to play, and get forty cents a month, and be happy.

Mark Twain thus, albeit in burlesque of a sentimental literature he loathed, pointed to the irrationality of human existence in which mere force of circumstance, instead of moral law, determines man's fate.

Expressing a kindred philosophy of life is his article on "Magnanimous-Incident Literature." He had often wondered what happened to the benefactors and beneficiaries after the happy climaxes ended their stories; he had sought out the sequels with "great labor and tedious research" and now laid the results before his readers. The sequels end with such warnings as "Whom God sees fit to starve, let not man presumptuously rescue to his own undoing." The piece candidly expresses an underlying philosophy which gives the lie to the maxim "A good deed cannot fail to benefit the doer." The moralist is once more probing his problem.

An emphasis is necessary at this point. Whether Mark Twain burlesques fashion reviews or inane question-and-answer departments or maudlin sob stories or sensational journalism, one thing is clear: it is the fatuity of the human mind that he parodies. He insists that the very faults of "Johnny Skae's Item" should most endear it to the public. In these literary caricatures the human intellect is held up to scorn in a scathing derision that applies to both writers and readers. He exhibits in his calculated burlesques that profound stupidity or laziness of men which leads them to accept such imperfect modes.

"The Recent Carnival of Crime in Connecticut" he labeled as "an exasperating metaphysical question . . . in the disguise of a literary extravagazna." This short study of the human conscience he had written in two days; but, as he wrote to Howells, he later spent three more days "trimming, altering, and working at it. I shall put in one more day's polishing on it." This is contrary to the accepted belief that he was either careless in revision or shunned it altogether. Howells felt that Hawthorne or Bunyan "might have been proud to imagine that powerful allegory, which had a grotesque force beyond either of them." Yet the sketch shows little variance in humorous technique from many other Mark Twain sketches. All the trimming, altering, and polishing were doubtless designed, as usual, to deliver a moral lesson "with telling force through the insidious medium of a travesty," to quote once more his own words explaining his practice in writing humor.

His extravaganza called "The Canvasser's Tale" satirizes the "exquisite enjoyment" of the confirmed collector, here a collector of echoes. Mark Twain, in planning it, weighed the relative values of absurdities. He wrote to Howells:

Yes, the collection of caves was the origin of it. I changed it to echoes because these, being invisible and intangible, constituted a still more absurd species of property, and yet a man could really own an echo, and sell it, too, for a high figure—such an echo as that at the Villa Siminetti, two miles from Milan, for instance. My first purpose was to have the man make a collection of caves and afterwards of echoes, but perceived that the element of absurdity . . . was so nearly identical as to amount to a repetition of an idea.

Although the final form of the sketch is completely wild and absurd, this letter is evidence that its author carefully worked toward that end. If the burlesque in it towers into the sky, it is because Mark Twain consciously blueprinted it as a humorous skyscraper dedicated to one more gigantic folly of mankind.

A recent study of Josh Billings refers to him as "a rather severely self-disciplined artist, just as every superior humorist is disciplined by the exacting regulations of the craft." Its author, Joseph Jones, insists that humor, which seems so effortless when done well, is "really very arduous, and the mortality rate among humorists is unusually high." In fact, a literature boasting a single great humorist is lucky; many nations are denied even one. Mr. Jones feels that this fact is explained by the inherent difficulty of the art. The widespread opinion that Mark Twain was a funnyman who merely wrote down whatever happened to come into his head needs revision. Carl Van Doren, in closing his chapter on Mark Twain in *The American Novel*, sums him up as "a natural force which . . . moved through the world laughing, an American Adam with the eye of innocence giving new names to what he saw." Such a view of Mark Twain, it seems to me, is untenable.

As a literary form, burlesque itself is neither easy nor simple. It entails a double vision: the thing itself is seen and judged; then a new version is viewed at a different angle, so that it is thrown out of perspective, with a caricature as the result. Mark Twain was an artist in burlesque.

He was a humorist by virtue of his quizzical slant on life. But the easy facility in seizing on disharmonies, the quick perception of the fundamental incongruities in human existence which he cultivated as part of his humorist's technique, may have contributed to his failure to achieve harmony and unity in some of his more serious writings. Perhaps this facility and this perception made it difficult for him to effect the reconciliation necessary for a complete view and a true perspective of life itself—life with its innate dignities, its myriad possibilities so sadly jumbled with obvious stupidities and injustices. The nature of humor itself, however, does not involve such a failure. The assertion of Mr. Brooks that "the making of the humorist was the undoing of the artist" cannot be granted. Humor may make for a balance in art which has its analogue in life; it may, in one blinding flash, slice through differences and conflicts to the basic common denominator on which all things rest. Mark Twain recognized the value of humor as the great reconciler, the great catalyst, as he makes clear in his article on Paul Bourget: "Well, humor is the great thing, the saving thing. . . . The minute it crops up, all our hardnesses yield, all our irritations and resentments flit away, and a sunny spirit takes their place." Nevertheless, it was just this use of humor of which Mark Twain seemed frequently unable to avail himself.

He was wit as well as humorist; and it was as a wit, particularly, that he was the careful craftsman. His Western writings show an outpouring of words, a reveling in sheer verbosity. He probably regretted his Western practice by 1876, when he wrote to Howells: ". . . how often I do use three words where one would answer—a thing I am always trying to guard against." Working towards a concise mode of expression, he formulated, as Pudd'nhead Wilson, pungent maxims which are the essence of Mark Twain—worded in his droll phraseology, permeated with his bleak cynicism. His conscious practice in pruning and condensing resulted in epigrams which have become stock phrases in American conversation. In the group below appear some of his finest crystallizations:

Be virtuous, and you will be eccentric.
Truth is our most valuable possession. Let us economize it.
Gratitude and treachery are merely the two extremities of the same procession.
Truth is more of a stranger than fiction.

Other maxims, couched in unpretentious phrasing and not so polished in form, reveal his deep knowledge of human nature:

Few things are harder to put up with than the annoyance of a good example.
There isn't a Parallel of Latitude but thinks it would have been the Equator if it had had its rights.
There are several good protections against temptation, but the surest is cowardice.
You can't depend on your judgment when your imagination is out of focus.
Everyone is a moon and has a dark side which he never shows to anybody.

The following homely injunctions have the quaint cast of thought which marks the "cracker-box philosopher":

It is better to be a young June-bug than an old bird of paradise.
It is difference of opinion that makes horse races.

There are maxims which testify to his passionate belief in the efficacy of reform, the power of training to remold men:

Training is everything. The peach was once a bitter almond; cauliflower is nothing but cabbage with a college education.

And there are others which reflect his bitter belief in the natural depravity of man and the futility of training to change natural disposition:

If the desire to kill and the opportunity to kill came always together, who would escape hanging?

The care which he expended on his maxims is graphically shown by a facsimile page from his notebook, included in *Following the Equator*. As the cuckoo clock is a noisy clock, it had often incurred his displeasure. The facsimile shows five different versions of a maxim celebrating the death of the clock's inventor. The first draft follows: "The man that invented the cuckoo clock is dead. It is old news, but good." He tried four more versions, besides making various deletions and substitutions. Finally he surrendered, writing across the notes: "Give it up. Am sorry he died." These difficulties, however, inspired a new maxim, duly added to Puddn'head Wilson's Calendar. Its first form stood, "It is more difficult to construct a maxim than it is to do right"; but the final form reads, "It is more trouble to make a maxim than it is to do right." The revision is here, as it is so often, toward the colloquial level, substituting *trouble* for *difficult* and *make* for *construct*.[8] Brander Matthews gave early warning that Mark Twain's deliberate colloquial ease should not hide from us his mastery of all the devices of rhetoric.

Speaking "from the grave" in a passage quoted in Chapter 8, Mark Twain attributed his longevity as a humorist to the fact that he had "always preached." In a conversation with Archibald Henderson in 1907, he laid his success to his efforts to be not an American humorist so much as a "human humorist":

8 The care with which these colloquialisms are substituted for more formal usage recalls Mark Twain's advice to Howells, who was about to set out on a reading tour. In effect, this advice was "thoroughly memorize the things you want to say and then deliver them as if they were mere improvisations" (*Letters*, II, 684). The record steadily discloses that Mark Twain's apparently artless product was actually studied in detail.

"Many so-called American humorists . . . have been betrayed by their preoccupation with the local. Their work never crossed frontiers because they failed to impart to their humour that universal element which appeals to all races of men. . . . My secret—if there is any secret—is to create humour independent of local conditions. In studying humanity as exhibited in the people and localities I best knew and understood, I have sought to winnow out the encumbrance of the local." And he significantly added—musingly—"*Humour, like morality, has its eternal verities.*"

Thus it becomes a matter of record that humor and morality remained entwined in Mark Twain's thoughts in his last years, just as they had been in the gorgeous and robust burlesques of his early days in Washoe.

Nevertheless, as I have already said, most of his early writings are not true humor but satire—satire with a contemptuous laughter too bitter, a bright blade too nakedly exposed, to allow the work the universality of pleasure that marks real humor. Aristotle defined the laughable as any mistake or deformity not productive of pain; the comic mask that excited laughter was something ugly and distorted without causing pain. "When sympathy with the ludicrous or grotesque object is felt, the tone of the laughter changes and we have what we call humor"; in this humorous laughter, "the incongruous is softened, and the grotesque becomes an object even of affection."[9] This true humor of the humorous character Mark Twain afterwards produced abundantly, but it is not much in evidence in the early sketches. His "scathing satires," having as their hidden purpose reproof and castigation, were designed to give pain. But, moved by subconscious aesthetic impulses, perhaps, Mark Twain the Technician manipulated the devices at his command to sugarcoat his pill, to dress his satire in a fantastic clownish garb that would assure it a welcome from the unwary reader.

Some other early sketches, not so bitter, I have classed as moralistic rather than satiric: their object is not to give pain, but to prevent it. But neither in the cutting satires nor in the moralizing sketches was Mark Twain able to realize his fullest artistic possibilities. His work was set too much at cross-purposes: As a moralist he tries to save mankind for a life which he often shows as not worth the living; as a satirist he expends his scorn on men whom he makes too con-

[9] Buck, *Literary Criticism*, 293.

temptible to be worth the trouble. The cat-o'-nine-tails castigates by a blow, and the prison punishes by loss of freedom; but derisive laughter castigates by its implication "that the victim is worth neither a blow nor the trouble of confining."[10]

In the Tuolumne hills Mark Twain was to rediscover a familiar mode of expression which held neither the scorn of the satirist nor the escapism of the moralist.[11]

[10] *Ibid.*, 317.
[11] For my discussion of moralism as one form of escape, see p. 156.

CHAPTER 9

The Humorist as Character Painter

MARK TWAIN appears to have been drawn into the field in which he was most the artist—the genre of native portraiture—by a combination of native gifts, background, and experience. He possessed an ear sensitively tuned to the rhythms and idioms of speech, an alert eye, and a consuming interest in people. In his maturity his highest reaches were to come in character portrayal. Hence it is fitting that his first writing extant, "The Dandy Frightening the Squatter," should be an attempt at character drawing. True, it is a fumbling attempt. Sam Clemens was sixteen years old when "The Dandy" appeared in the May 1, 1852, issue of *The Carpet-Bag*, a humorous weekly published in Boston.[1] The scene of the sketch is Hannibal; a steamboat stops there and "a spruce young dandy, with a killing moustache" sees a tall, brawny woodsman leaning against a tree. Showing off before the steamboat passengers, the dandy takes a bowie knife and two horse pistols and swaggers ashore to intimidate the squatter. He blusters and threatens until the unmoved squatter knocks him into the river, commandeering his knife and pistols. Typical of the humor of the Southwest, the sketch is the sort of thing Sam Clemens saw frequently in the exchanges.

This first effort is a crude attempt not only at character drawing, but at character contrast—the city slicker worsted by the hardy rustic. "Blabb," his next character, is an egotistic monologist who expresses some opinions characteristic of his creator. As early as the first Snodgrass letters, Sam Clemens gave flash portraits of some of his characters; in the second letter of 1856, for instance, there is an "old fellar with a carpet bag, who calculated it was good exercise to

---

[1] "The Dandy Frightening the Squatter" is reprinted by Franklin J. Meine, ed., *Tall Tales of the Southwest*, 447–48. Meine discovered this sketch, which is four months earlier than the earliest items extant in the Hannibal papers.

walk to Quincy." The line shows a knowledge of the habits of thrifty old age.

The one piece written during Sam Clemens's river days which Mark Twain later acknowledged was a burlesque on Isaiah Sellers, an old pilot whose custom was to publish paragraphs of river information beginning, "My opinion for the benefit of the citizens of New Orleans."[2] The burlesque exhibits "Sergeant Fathom," who has been on the river longer "than any other 'cub' extant," setting forth his experiences of 1763. In this sketch, published in the New Orleans *True Delta* in May, 1859, Sam Clemens catches the plodding, methodical workings of the old man's mind, its quaintly oracular note, its naïve conviction that all men are eagerly awaiting its pronouncements—catches all this in a way which forecasts Mark Twain's later skill in exploring the minds of his characters.

His descriptive gift enabled him to compress a good deal about his characters, their appearance and traits, into the compass of a line or two. Writing in the West on February 28, 1864, he introduced "a pompous little man with a crooked-handled cane and sorrel moustache" who spoke effusively: "How do you do, Mr. Twain—how do you do, sir? I am happy to see you, sir—very happy indeed, sir." His ability to draw a pen picture on a larger scale comes out in "Daniel in the Lion's Den," in his graphic description of the scene in the brokers' hall in San Francisco. It has a Dickensian flavor. The brokers are ready for business,

. . . some with a leg thrown negligently over the arms of their chairs, some tilted back comfortably with their knees against their desks, some sitting half upright and glaring at the President, hungry for the contention to begin. . . .

. . . And while the storm of ejaculations hurtled about their heads, these brokers sat calmly . . . but when a sale was made . . . down came legs from the arms of chairs, down came knees propped against desks, forward shot the heads of the whole tribe with one accord, and away went the long ranks of pencils dancing over the paper! the sale duly recorded by all, the heads, the legs, and the knees came up again, and the negligent attitudes were resumed once more.

This same sketch, published in 1864, shows Mark Twain's delight in transferring to paper a dialect, a vernacular, or any oddity of

[2] Paine, *Biography*, III, Appendix B, 1593–96.

speech. Here the speech of the president of the brokers is presented to show the rapidity of his enunciation. Mark Twain attempted to write down just what he heard: "Fift'naitassfrwahn fift'nseftfive bifferwahn fift'naitfive botherty!" which an obliging member translated as meaning: "Fifteen-eighty (fifteen hundred and eighty dollars) asked for one (one foot), fifteen-seventy-five bid for one, fifteen-eighty-five buyer thirty (thirty days' time on the payment)."

Speech and the manner of speaking became increasingly important to him because he found it possible to tell a great deal about his characters by carefully recording what they said and how they said it. One of the earliest group drawings in which he used differentiated speech as a means of characterization is his "Case of Smith vs. Jones" (1864). The first encounter between witness and officials forecasts the "Buck Fanshaw's Funeral" episode in *Roughing It*, where Scotty Briggs and the parson talk at cross-purposes, since neither understands the other. In the Smith-Jones case the first witness, Alfred Sowerby, is a rough-and-ready saloon loafer who employs robust metaphor and strongly prefers it to the stilted legal vocabulary thrust at him by lawyer and judge:

Witness: "I was in the saloon at the time, your honor, and I see this man Smith come up all of a sudden to Jones, and split him in the snoot—"
Lawyer: "Did what, sir?"
Witness: "Busted him in the snoot."
Lawyer: "What do you mean . . . ? When you say that the plaintiff suddenly approached the defendant . . . and 'busted him in the snoot,' do you mean that the plaintiff *struck* the defendant?"
Witness: "That's me—I'm swearing to that very circumstance. . . . Well, Smith comes up to Jones all of a sudden and mashed him in the bugle—"
Lawyer: "Stop! Witness, this kind of language will not do. I will ask you a plain question, and I require you to answer it simply, yes or no. Did—the—plaintiff—*strike*—the defendant? Did he *strike* him?"
Witness: "You bet your sweet life he did. Gad! he gave him a paster in the trumpet—"
Lawyer: "Take the witness! take the witness!"

Mr. McWilliamson, next witness, is an emotional man whose fervid imagination prompts some sensational testimony; the third witness is Washington Billings, the most illiterate of the lot; the fourth, Jeremiah Driscoll, is the most polished in speech and manner, but his testimony is no more accurate than that of his predecessors. Mark

Twain's observation of mankind enabled him to exhibit these specimens of "the damned human race"; but they appear secondary to his prime purpose of presenting a lesson for social improvement. They are not lovingly drawn for their own sakes, as some later creations were to be.

The frontier society in the Far West, as described earlier, was in part primitive, in part degenerated from higher levels. Bret Harte found literary material in men of culture and education who had fallen on evil days, black-sheep scions of old families who had drifted westward to become cardsharps and drunkards. Mark Twain, however, characteristically sought not the degenerate but the primitive. His immediate resources were his quick eye, his sensitive ear, and his keen insight into human nature; but to turn them to their full use he must first be confronted with fundamental human patterns.

On December 4, 1864, he arrived at Jim Gillis's cabin on Jackass Hill in the Tuolumne region. The three months' stay which he divided between Jackass Hill and Angel's Camp was to have a marked effect on his development as a writer. The southern mines were no longer in their flush times. The tide of activity had swept onward, leaving behind it scattered handfuls of old-timers whose dreams had not yet died. From force of habit, they kept on panning for gold and lingered on in the mines because they were happy there.

Emerson observed that the function of the artist in society is to seek the elemental and to renew the primitive in racial experience. Some such opportunity was now manifested to Mark Twain. In the Tuolumne hills he was able to get away from the tawdry tinsel and glitter of Gold Hill and Nob Hill; and there he found "natural" men, men untouched by artificialities. The simple lives they led seemed far removed from the pressures of the environment he had left with its political corruption, racial strife, and social tension. He felt no urge to moralize among them. They had no need of his "preaching." It was Mark Twain the satirist, the social critic, who had fled from San Francisco; but on Jackass Hill he was in a relaxed mood, able to take comfort in these mining men because he felt no responsibility for them. For the moment he was free to follow his own inclinations. He ferreted among the indigenous materials, the primitive folk scorned by such writing men as C. H. Webb, to uncover forgotten sources important for his own art.[3] He had been familiar all his life

[3] Walker, *San Francisco's Literary Frontier*, 181–82.

with the anecdotal technique of the frontier raconteur; now he seemed to realize at last its literary possibilities.

At Angel's Camp he scribbled the first of his notebook entries which became the bases for later stories, items dealing with incidents and people: one about a squatter whose house slid downhill, loosened from its foundation by rooting hogs; another about a crazed man who asked for his wife, long dead (this memorandum years later became "The Californian's Tale"); and a third brief jotting about a frog, filled with shot to prevent its winning a jumping contest. This entry commemorated one of the unimpassioned monologues which Ben Coon, former river pilot, delivered before the fire in the hotel barroom. Jim Gillis, Mark Twain's host, was a master yarn spinner in his own right. Gillis told the story of the bluejay and the acorns; another concerning the intellectual prowess of Dick Stoker's cat, Tom Quartz; and a third, "The Burning Shame," which Walter Blair believes was related to a folk yarn of the old Southwest, based on the fabulous gyascutus, seemingly a very phallic beast. Meanwhile, Stoker and Mark Twain sat and listened. This entertainment, too, would prove valuable to Mark Twain in years to come; but the note on the jumping frog was the mother lode of his literary strikes.

On February 25, 1865, he returned to San Francisco and resumed the writing of burlesques and extravaganzas for the *Californian*, most of them the moral-bearing kind. His first sketch published after his fateful interlude in the Big Tree region appeared on March 18, 1865, under the title "An Unbiased Criticism." It contains his initial anecdote in the frontier vernacular, accompanied by a thumbnail sketch of the narrator. The skit begins with promise of a criticism upon a current art exhibit; then it digresses to Mark Twain's recent Tuolumne visit and the scarcity of reading material at Angel's Camp. In desperation one day he had tried to borrow a book from Ben Coon, "a nice bald-headed man." Coon was silent a moment and then launched into the traveling adventures of his one book—"a mighty responsible old Webster-Unabridged," which had gone "sloshing around" the camp at Angel's. The demand for reading matter was so great that the men "kept her sashaying around from shanty to shanty and from camp to camp," but nobody ever spoke a good word for her. Coon recalls bleakly the faultfinding of her finicky readers:

Now Coddington had her a week, and she was too much for *him*—he couldn't spell the words; he tackled some of them regular busters . . . and they throwed him; next, Dyer, he tried her a jolt, but he couldn't *pronounce* 'em—Dyer can hunt quail or play seven-up as well as any man, understand me, but he can't *pronounce* worth a d——n; he used to worry along . . . till he'd flush one of them rattlers, with a clatter of syllables as long as a string of sluice-boxes, and then he'd lose his grip and throw up his hand; and so, finally Dick Stoker harnessed her, up there at his cabin, and sweated over her, and cussed over her, and rastled with her as much as three weeks, night and day, till he got as far as R, and then passed her over to 'Lige Pickerell, and said she was the all-firedest dryest reading that ever *he* struck; well, well, if she's come back from San Andreas, you can get her and prospect her, but I don't reckon there's a good deal left of her by this time; though time was when she was as likely a book as any in the State, and as hefty.

And then former corporal Coon "proceeded cheerlessly to scout with his brush after the straggling hairs on the rear of his head and drum them to the front for inspection and roll-call." In this early sketch appear the distinctive features of many others to follow: the carefully copied vocal emphasis, preserving the rhythm of speech; the authenticity of the idiom, drawn from the mine and the card table; the indication that to the raconteur himself there is no humor in the tale he tells. The yarn of the "old Webster-Unabridged" is a rehearsal for the Jumping Frog, for Jim Baker's Blue-jay yarn, for the story of Grandfather's Old Ram. In this part of the sketch Mark Twain has found the center of his interest in character. Above all else, he is absorbed with the individual Ben Coon, and with Coon's intricate conditioning by environment and experience. There is no moralizing here; in its place is the serene and steady enjoyment of the writer—the almost-artist—working with malleable material. In the remainder of the sketch, however, he slides back into his earlier manner of the burlesque-bearing-a-moral: he uses the scarcity of reading matter at Angel's Camp as an approach to his sewing-machine election, a burlesque overlying a social criticism directed at "machine politics."

In Mark Twain's frontier yarns there is no taint of the self-consciousness, the patronizing tone, which blemishes the native portraiture of Bret Harte. Instead, Mark Twain's work is distinguished by its complete naturalness, a quality belonging to the art which

George Alfred Townsend, Mark Twain, and David Gray

seems no art; but art of that sort is rarely attained except by pains-taking care. Among these native materials, he appears to have worked with utter freedom. Harte, Easterner as he was, seems to have been gripped by the theatrical aspects of the California scene. Mark Twain, too, appreciated the drama of that life, but he did not seek for scenes heightened in dramatic intensity. He realized that, strange and odd as some of these creatures might appear before the painted backdrop of mountain and sea, down underneath they were actually people. The same sort of naturalness covers his oddest characters.

His early frontier figures are presented with a primitive spontaneity. He makes no effort at the realization of an extended character, as yet. Still, in his early isolated portraits he exhibits a serenity that offers a striking contrast to the impatience with mankind that pricks him on in his satiric or moralistic sketches. We find here no cynical sport arrayed in the verbal pyrotechnics of the humorist virtuoso. "The struggle has ended, the pain has died away,"[4] and the writer dominates and controls his material to the point where serenity at last becomes possible. He neither admires nor abhors the creatures of these frontier sketches; he simply understands them. And his complete understanding of their behavior and thought gives him an enjoyment reflected in his work—leads him finally into the true aesthetic attitude, which challenges the writer to present his material artistically, taking his joy in the authenticity of his product without concern for the didactic element. With his facility in copying speech rhythms, vocal intonations, native idioms and mannerisms, he was rapidly approaching artistic performance in native portraiture. It was in this field that he would become an artist.

Almost from the first he touched up his frontier portraits with an imaginative brush. Ben Coon appears in his own person to tell the story of his dictionary; but by the time of "The Jumping Frog" he has become, for literary purposes, "good-natured, garrulous old Simon Wheeler." In the earlier sketch Mark Twain gave but a passing glance to the "shade of melancholy" which flitted across Coon's face before he began his recital; but in the Frog, one of the most effective bits is the powerful spotlight which is turned on the narrator and his method:

He never smiled, he never frowned, he never changed his voice from the

4 The phrase is Santayana's, in "The Nature of Beauty."

gentle-flowing key to which he tuned his initial sentence, he never be-trayed the slightest suspicion of enthusiasm; but all through the inter-minable narrative there ran a vein of impressive earnestness and sincerity, which showed me plainly that, so far from his imagining that there was anything ridiculous or funny about his story, he regarded it as a really important matter, and admired its two heroes as men of transcendent genius in *finesse*. I let him go on in his own way and never interrupted him once.

As Walter Blair has observed, a part of the excellence of "The Jump-ing Frog" arises from Mark Twain's skillful management of the narrative framework. This frame holds three successive personali-ties: first there is Mark Twain, writing in his own person to Artemus Ward; Mark Twain then presents Simon Wheeler; Wheeler, in his turn, presents Jim Smiley and the stranger. And, as Miss Brashear points out, the tale gets its peculiar quality from being the report of one oddity by another; for Jim Smiley is as intensely interesting to Simon Wheeler as Wheeler himself is interesting to Mark Twain. Within the Wheeler yarn, there is a careful climactic arrangement: first we have that talented mare, the "fifteen-minute nag"; then the "little small bull-pup" that would have "made a name for hisself if he'd lived, for the stuff was in him, and he had genius"; and finally the educated frog, Dan'l Webster: "You never see a frog so modest and straight-for'ard as he was, for all he was so gifted." Yet these distinct personalities fade into the background when the clash be-gins between the two men, with its surprising climax. No moral is pointed, no lesson taught. What followed is literary history. Arriv-ing in New York too late for inclusion in Artemus Ward's new book, the sketch was printed instead in the last issue of the expiring *Satur-day Press*, November 18, 1865. From the *Press* it was speedily copied in papers all over the country.

By the time Mark Twain wrote the Ben Coon and Simon Wheeler anecdotes in 1865, he had arrived at most of the knowledge which he incorporated in 1894 into "How to Tell a Story." There he says that the humorous story—the most difficult kind—is Ameri-can, the comic story is English, and the witty story is French:

The humorous story depends for its effect upon the *manner* of the tell-ing; the comic story and the witty story upon the *matter*.... The humor-ous story bubbles gently along, the others burst.

The humorous story is strictly a work of art—high and delicate art —and only an artist can tell it; but no art is necessary in telling the comic and witty story; anybody can do it. The art of telling a humorous story . . . was created in America, and has remained at home.

The humorous story is told gravely; the teller . . . conceal[s] the fact that he even dimly suspects that there is anything funny about it; but the teller of the comic story . . . is the first person to laugh when he gets through. . . . To string incongruities and absurdities together in a wandering and sometimes purposeless way, and seem innocently unaware that they are absurdities is the basis of the American art.

Mark Twain then comments on the skill with which James Whitcomb Riley told a story in the guise of a dull-witted old farmer whose rambling technique followed the humorous method. He adds: "This is art—and fine and beautiful, and only a master can compass it; but a machine could tell the other story."

His belief that the narrative pattern, the frame which encloses a humorous story, is the important thing rather than the story itself, appears in his 1881 correspondence with Joel Chandler Harris. Mark Twain frequently read the "Uncle Remus" tales from the platform, having heard many of them from the Negro companions of his childhood. He appreciated Harris's manner of presenting them and wrote a letter expressing his admiration. In reply Harris disclaimed any originality for the stories, maintaining that his "relations toward Uncle Remus are similar to those that exist between an almanac maker and the calendar." Mark Twain sought to convince Harris that the art that had gone into his creation of the old Negro as narrator and the child as audience constituted him more than an almanac maker:

You . . . argue *yourself* into the delusion that the principle of life is in the stories themselves and not in their setting. . . . In reality the stories are only alligator pears—one merely eats them for the sake of the salad-dressing. Uncle Remus is most deftly drawn, and is a lovable and delightful creation; he and the little boy, and their relations with each other, are high and fine literature and worthy to live for their own sakes; and certainly the stories are not to be credited with *them*.

The realism of Harris's framework contrasts with the fantasy of the enclosed tales in the same way in which Mark Twain's anecdotes— such as Jim Baker's Blue-jay yarn—display a blend of realism and fantasy. By 1881 he could argue thus that Harris's characters were worthy to live for their own sakes, but this perception had come to him only gradually. Before his stay with Jim Gillis, such characters as he introduced had been only necessary adjuncts to his purposes of burlesque and reform—grotesques such as "his Grace the Duke of Benicia," a satiric incarnation of the ideals of the gold-mad Western world; or fantastic figures like those of Governor Low and Leland Stanford, slugging each other in the blood-spattered ring of current politics. These caricatures have no life as persons in his pages.

After his return from Jackass Hill and Angel's Camp, however, his growing interest in characterization flashes through his reforming burlesques, albeit briefly. Huckleberry Finn exists in rough outline in a sketch of January 21, 1866, "Fitz Smythe's Horse," written to ridicule Evans, an *Alta* reporter whom Mark Twain lampooned for sententious overwriting. Fitz Smythe feeds his horse on nothing but old copies of the *Alta* and the *Bulletin*, and this dry-as-dust fare is starving the animal. As Mark Twain stands pitying it, an unnamed boy appears and gives him its history in a vernacular which crudely forecasts Huck Finn's. The sketch contains Mark Twain's early efforts to convey into print the tonal inflections of the narrator: the hoss will eat "a-n-y-thing he can shet his mouth on," and "*he* don't care a dam." If he should be turned loose, "he'd eat up m-o-r-e goods-boxes," also animals, including cats. The boy shows something of Huck's pictorial art in his description of Fitz Smythe, riding his ravenous animal:

. . . you ought to see him with his soldier coat on, and his mustashers sticking out strong like a cat-fish's horns, and them long legs of his'n standing out so, like them two prongs they prop up a step-ladder with, and a jolting down street at four mile a week—oh, what a guy!—sets up stiff like a close pin, you know, and thinks he looks like old General Macdowl.

But the entertaining boy, to Mark Twain's regret, is called to duty by the stern voice of his "old man."

A week later Mark Twain had a letter from old Mrs. Chapman, one-time actress on a broadhorn theater. The memory of that Mississippi showboat led him back into the past to Captain Ed Montgomery and his kindness to Mrs. Utterback, owner of a riverside wood lot. The Captain often went ashore to talk with her, Mark Twain remembered, and sometimes took his lady passengers along to enjoy her startling conversation. Mark Twain recorded one such visit, "as it may let in the light of instruction to some darkened mind." Captain Montgomery had brought some "fine ladies" with him, and the old woman was transported with delight:

"Good morning, Captain Montgomery!" said she with many a bustling bow and flourish. "Good morning, Captain Montgomery; good morning, ladies all; how de do, Captain Montgomery—how de do—how de do? . . . Fly around, gals, fly around! You Bets, you slut, highst yoself off'n that candle-box and give it to the lady. How *have* you ben, Captain Montgomery?—make yoself at home, ladies all—you 'Liza Jane, stan' out of the way—move yoself! Thar's the jug, help yoself, Captain Montgomery; take that cob out and make yoself free, Captain Montgomery—and ladies all. You Sal, you hussy, git up f'm thar this minit, and take some exercise! for the land's sake, ain't you got no sense at all?—settin' thar on that cold rock and you jes' ben married last night, and your pores all open!"

Mother Utterback, who had lived "in the bend below Grand Gulf, Mississippi," lives briefly in the *Golden Era* for January 28, 1866; but she is the ancestress of Mark Twain's more fully detailed frontier women—warm-hearted, talkative, overflowing with a rough hospitality. At this early date he was able to embody in her the two characteristics requisite for true humorous characters: she is completely unconscious of her own failings, and she inspires a sort of affection rather than contempt. The gusto with which he put her on paper is apparent in the result he achieved. But his hesitancy in using her as literary material is also evident from his apologetic introduction: "I do not know that this incident is worth recording." And his reluctance may be attributed to the fact that he can think of no way to link her up with a moral. He succumbs to her fascinations, nevertheless; and his interest in the frontier vernacular is obviously growing.

His snapshot impressions of people run through the humorous sketches from 1865 on. With devastating contempt, he described "The Office Bore," sunk in "a tranquil, mangy animal contentment," infesting the metropolitan areas; but he admired the "spirited woman" who lightens his page in a burlesque inveighing against the Western court system. She was bright and pretty, but she was also a

... nervous, uneasy devil of a Mexican woman—because you know how they love and how they hate, and this one had loved her husband with all her might, and now she had boiled it all down into hate, and stood here spitting it at that Spaniard with her eyes; and I tell you she would stir *me* up, too, with a little of her summer lightning occasionally.

And Mark Twain selected from the natural world the figure of summer lightning to express the flashing, intermittent danger of this woman's glance.

It was neither to urban figures nor to foreigners, however, that he gave his best efforts in character creation. It was to the stolid, steadfast creatures of the frontier. Southwestern frontier "originals" must have engaged his attention often in his Missouri boyhood days. During his years on the river this bedrock of observation was over-laid with a stratum of knowledge concerning the hodgepodge of human drift that came floating down; over this, in turn, was laid a layer of familiarity with human variants met in the Far West. From this material he learned to quarry figures containing what he called "the principle of life."

In the beginning he drew directly from life, concentrating on minute characteristics of appearance, behavior, and, finally, thought. Something in the primitive quality of the frontier people appealed to the vitality of his imagination. In his Western milieu, as I have said, he did not picture the prostitutes, the gamblers, the "delirium tremens specimens" which Walt Whitman objected to in Bret Harte; neither did he select the "heroic personalities" which Whitman had demanded as most illustrative of "this great outgrowth of Western character." Instead, he concerned himself with individuals drawn from the great common mass. In his day, perhaps, time had not yet given the perspective necessary for setting up a heroic tradition; but it is likely that his chosen material would have been the same in any event. He addressed his literature of reform to the common man rather than to what he called "the thin top crust of humanity"; he considered "the mighty mass of the uncultivated . . . best worth trying to uplift." And in the same way, in creative moods, he apparently felt that it was the mighty mass that he must paint with all the art that he could release for such a purpose.

His reaction against the early celebrity of "The Jumping Frog" throws an interesting light on his main objectives during this period. It appears in a letter to his mother, dated January 20, 1866:

To think that, after writing many an article a man might be excused for thinking tolerably good, those New York people should single out a villainous backwoods sketch to compliment me on!—"Jim Smiley and His Jumping Frog"—a squib which would never have been written but to please Artemus Ward, and then it reached New York too late to appear in his book. But no matter. His book was a wretchedly poor one, generally speaking, and it could be no credit to either of us to appear between its covers.

This letter has been much discussed by critics who seek to account for Mark Twain. Paine wrote that Twain was disappointed because he felt the Frog's Eastern success meant "failure for his more highly regarded work." Mr. Brooks interprets the disappointment as arising from the fact that the Frog was a humorous story and that Mark Twain instinctively felt himself above the writing of humor. Still, Mark Twain had only recorded his chagrin that the East had praised a backwoods sketch instead of "many an article a man might be excused for thinking good," and, as Mr. DeVoto points out, "nothing he had written before . . . was anything but the humor that offends Mr. Brooks." DeVoto himself says only that Mark Twain's letter attests the inaccuracy of his self-criticism. Ivan Benson believes that Mark Twain was disappointed at not having achieved book publication. Yet Twain specifically stated his opinion of Ward's book as such a poor one that it could be no credit to appear in it. What, then, is the best explanation for Mark Twain's letter?

Mr. DeVoto is unquestionably right in holding that Mark Twain's previous articles had been humorous ones, almost without exception. But upon examination, most of these articles, ridiculous burlesques and riotous extravaganzas as they are, will be found to contain social reform or moral lessons. "Those Blasted Children," which Mark Twain had pronounced "a pearl" and sent east to the *Sunday Mercury*, satirized the Western money-madness and the unjust treatment of the Chinese. Even the original appearance of Ben Coon is embodied in a sketch which derides the practices of machine politics. Up to this point "The Jumping Frog" stands almost alone as character drawing, pure and simple, with its native portraiture unalloyed by the tincture of social reproof. In this respect the Frog's only companion had been Mrs. Utterback, for whose existence in his pages Mark Twain had apologized. In writing the Frog, he had forgotten his reform purpose, momentarily, in a new enjoy-

ment; but he was bewildered and somewhat disgruntled when his
"ingenious satires" were overlooked in favor of a backwoods sketch
lacking the moral element. That he should at this stage prefer preaching to painting is understandable when one remembers the sort of
work demanded by the publications for which he was writing. C.
H. Webb, editor of the *Californian*, scorned indigenous materials
in favor of satire. But, working on the Frog, Mark Twain for once
relaxed his will-to-reform in the unhampered, unhurried outpouring of a wealth of long-accumulated observation. It may be said of
him, as F. O. Matthiessen has said of Whitman, that his ripest creations did not spring from the desire to reform society but from "the
discovery of the previously unexpressed abundance of ordinary
American life." When he heard Ben Coon yarning solemnly before
the fire at Angel's Camp, he was moved to a realization of literary
values hitherto ignored; but only with time and use would he grow
to prefer them to his customary materials.

Although his final achievement in the art of characterization is
remarkable, his interest was never so much in individual men as in
man in general, in the possibilities and limitations of the human race.
It was unfortunate for Mark Twain as an artist that his attention was
centered on the limitations of mankind rather than on the possibilities. His characters, being composite pictures, are broad types of
humanity; but as each type is presented, it is portrayed with minute
consistency. His thumbnail sketches of Ben Coon, Simon Wheeler,
and Mother Utterback were his first creative writing. In such isolated
portraits his sensitive treatment of common life was first manifested,
the beginnings of the memorable tale he had to tell of primitive men
and women, unmellowed, unrefined. As time went on, he passed
beyond these isolated literary snapshots to a study of such figures
against the background appropriate to their concerns. Man in his
village then became the center of interest for Mark Twain—man as
a member of society, yes, but chiefly as a member of village society.
Ethical activity had motivated his work almost from the beginning;
but when he stumbled on Ben Coon during the rainy season in the
Tuolumne hills, he was moved—almost against his ethical will—to
reproduce Coon with pen and ink. He then assuredly experienced
something of the joy of artistic creation, although that first creation
was but a spontaneous exercise of his gift for physical imitation.

But there were frequent conflicts of standards which resulted in damage to his art. His ethical standard was set by his keen conscience, reinforced by his will, that burning will to reform mankind; and his artistic standard, inevitably affected, was controlled much more by ethical ends than by aesthetic imagination. Some strong instances of this effect have already been noted: his expressed reluctance to encourage drinking "by harping on its alleged funny side" in print; his apologetic attitude in setting down old Mrs. Utterback; his assertion that if a pure boy is allowed to see *Mazeppa*, he is pure no longer; his customary exclusion of sexual material from his fiction—all these are straws in the wind.

"The Dandy Frightening the Squatter" and "The Jumping Frog" both carry the theme of the tables turned, but thirteen years elapsed between them. In between came the slightly satirical Hannibal column, the cynical Snodgrass letters, the gaudy Washoe reform burlesques, the stinging San Francisco philippics. For years he had witnessed the spectacle of life before he began to record that spectacle as an aesthetic activity. Although his moral preoccupation was as steady as that of Hawthorne, he lacked what Matthiessen calls the "enchanted wholeness" which Hawthorne's mind possessed; therefore he had difficulty in fusing the artistic and the ethical aspects of his work. His first creative work consisted of character studies drawn from the surface only, as a sort of playful holiday exercise. But as he advanced into a preoccupation with man in his village, his artistic interest in character and his ethical interest in reform were gradually to become blended in studies that are by no means simple. As will appear later in the discussion of his fiction, he is finally able to combine the aesthetic inclination which leads him to create and the ethical inclination which leads him to teach—or, as he put it, to "preach." It is only when the two are fused that his imagination can work with the freedom necessary to the artist.

Van Wyck Brooks explains Mark Twain's determinism as an avenue of escape from the self-condemnation contingent upon the betrayal of his artistic ideals. Mr. Wagenknecht feels that a man of Mark Twain's temperament would derive comfort "from throwing his responsibilities back in the face of the universe." And Bernard DeVoto sees Twain's determinism as a means by which he sought to exonerate himself from blame for the catastrophes that engulfed him in the late nineties. Various critics are agreed, then, that determinism was for him a form of escape.

His moralism, it seems to me, was also a sort of literary escape, in the sense that it offered the easier of two possible roads he might have traveled. With the oversimplification of the moralist, viewing everything in terms of black or white, he possessed a mind that rebelled at the twofold nature of life with its grayed intermingling of good and evil, its inevitable mixture of beauty and ugliness. It was easier to praise some individuals and condemn humanity in bulk than to attempt the synthesis necessary for recognizing and bringing together both good and evil in fictional characters as life brings them together in the same persons. Although he sometimes shirked this task, in his greatest books he did attempt the difficult synthesis and carry it through with marked success.

With the mass of common men Mark Twain elected to cast his literary lot. They finally became for him the center of interest in his artistic consciousness, as they had long been in his ethical consciousness. And when his interest in humanity leads him to explore man in his village and to record what he finds there, the character painter becomes the novelist.

BOOK III

The Travel Books

CHAPTER 10

The Moralist Abroad

BEFORE he was eighteen years old, Sam Clemens was investigating the ways of New York City and Philadelphia with his type stick in his hand as his ticket of admission. He was devoting his evenings, however, to reading in city libraries and to composing letters to send back home, some of them plainly written with an eye to publication in the home-town papers. In these letters the youthful writer exhibits a sense of responsibility for furnishing both entertainment and instruction to those who have not had his opportunities for travel.

Even his early "Thomas Jefferson Snodgrass" letters are travel letters, anticipating his later travel books, and he apparently planned to develop them into a book. The second letter, dated from Cincinnati, November 14, 1856, explains that the writer "took a notion to go a travelin, so as to see the world, and then write a book about it—a kind o' daily journal like—and have . . . on the back of it 'Snodgrass' Dierrea' . . . like other authors that visits forren parts." He was to get five dollars a letter from the Keokuk *Post* and was excited at the prospect of receiving, for the first time, money for his writing. Paine suggested that the fact that there are only three of the letters indicates the young humorist found them hard work; perhaps their labored misspelled humor palled on him.

From the Far West, Sam Clemens's first letters home are undisguised travel letters, studded with pictorial bits and items of general information. Often they exhibit a satiric note, as does his earliest Carson City letter, written in September or October of 1861:

It never rains here, and the dew never falls. No flowers grow here, and no green thing gladdens the eye. The birds that fly over the land carry their provisions with them. Only the crow and the raven tarry with us.

Our city lies in the midst of a desert of the purest—most unadulterated and uncompromising *sand*—in which infernal soil nothing but that fag-end of vegetable creation, "sage-brush," ventures to grow.

Mark Twain sailed from San Francisco for Hawaii on the *Ajax*, March 7, 1866. The letters recording that journey, by their publication in the Sacramento *Union*, won him his first praise from the polite world for his ability as a writer of descriptive prose. At the beginning of the voyage he appears to have been in a rare holiday mood: "It was a pleasant, breezy afternoon, and the strange new sense of entire and perfect emancipation from labor and responsibility coming strong upon me, I went up on the hurricane deck so that I could have room to enjoy it." On the steamer he began gathering information about the islands, and his *Notebook* entries show that upon arrival he suffered no disappointment. A journal note reads:

No careworn or eager, anxious faces in the land of happy contentment— God, what a contrast with California and Washoe. . . .
"O, islands there are on the face of the deep,
Where the leaves never fade and the skies never weep."

In Honolulu he stood for the first time in a foreign land with an assignment, as newspaper correspondent, to record his impressions of its manners and customs. The bias in favor of his own country which criticism is accustomed to find in him in such a situation is not much in evidence here. Instead of the mud-colored, brownstone fronts of San Francisco, he saw neat white cottages with green shutters; instead of "the customary infernal geranium languishing in dust and general debility on tin-roofed rear additions," he saw banks of fresh flowers; instead of roughs and rowdies staring and blackguarding on the corners, he saw long-haired native maidens sitting in the shade; instead of crowded streetcars, he saw fleet horses sweeping by, with dusky, brightly clad women astride them; instead of the stenches of Chinatown and the Brannan Street slaughterhouses, he breathed the fragrance of jessamine and oleander; instead of the noisy confusion of San Francisco, he "moved in the midst of a Summer calm as tranquil as dawn in the Garden of Eden." When he rode across the bridge and down the gleaming, white-coral turnpike, he saw a massive building, the government prison. In appearance, it might have been the king's palace, so neat and clean it was; and as for the prison yard, "that sad inclosure which, in the prisons of my native America, is a cheerless barren and yieldeth no vegetation save the gallows-tree, with its sorrowful fruit," it was a very garden.

Since he felt a certain responsibility for the American tourists, he early began to pick flaws in their conduct. When admitted to watch the funeral ceremonies for a Hawaiian princess, they had acted shamefully; in their eager collecting of bones from a native battlefield, they had shown no respect for the dead; and he questioned whether they gained anything from gazing, in unreflective mood, at spots of historic interest. In contrast with selfish, curiosity-seeking Americans, he found the simple-hearted natives especially charming.

And the beauty of the natural surroundings remained a constant delight to him. As a change from the sand hills skirting San Francisco Bay, he admired the view of mountains and valleys and the sweep of the ocean:

a brilliant, transparent green near the shore . . . further out, the dead, blue water of the deep sea . . . and in the far horizon, a single, lonely sail—

At this moment . . . Brown, who has no better manners than to read over one's shoulder, observes:

"Yes, and hot. Oh, I reckon not (only 82 in the shade)! Go on, now, and put it all down. . . . just say, 'And more "santipedes," and cockroaches, and fleas, and lizards, and red ants, and scorpions, and spiders, and mosquitoes and missionaries—' Oh, blame my cats if I'd live here two months."

Mr. Brown, that "bitter enemy to sentiment" who is Mark Twain's constant companion in the islands, thus frequently calls him back to reality from his flights of fancy. Brown becomes an alter ego for Twain, as well as an incarnation of antiromanticism. A typical passage is that in which Brown tries to squelch Mark Twain's enthusiasm for a majestic palm tree silhouetted against a smooth gray sky: " 'A beautiful, beautiful tree is the cocoa-palm!' I said fervently. 'I don't see it,' said Brown resentfully. 'I don't see what there is about it that's handsome; it looks like a feather-duster struck by lightning.' " Brown was created whole cloth, it appears, out of Mark Twain's imagination. Perhaps it was the expression of his own antiromantic moods through Brown; or perhaps it was simply the reformer awakening to the shortcomings of the natives upon closer acquaintance with them; but at any rate he soon realized that they were not so lovely as he had at first believed. Even the rainbow-clad girls he found, at close quarters, to "smell like thunder with their villainous cocoa-nut oil."

He soon came to suspect them of failings worse than addiction to coconut oil. A *Notebook* entry reads: "Kanakas will have horses and saddles and the women will fornicate—two strong characteristics of this people." One of his letters describes the hula-hula, a dance performed as part of the "funeral orgies" honoring the dead Princess Victoria. Mark Twain and some other Americans watched

... the lascivious dance that was wont to set the passions of the men ablaze in the old heathen days. . . . About thirty buxom young Kanaka women . . . shook the reefs out of their skirts, tightened their girdles, and began the most unearthly caterwauling . . . the noise had a marked and regular time . . . and they kept strict time to it with writhing bodies; with heads and hands . . . then . . . quicker time, faster and more violently excited motions . . . (the words of their fierce chant meantime treating in broadest terms, and in detail, of things which may be vaguely hinted at in a respectable newspaper but not distinctly mentioned)—then a convulsive writhing of the person, continued for a few moments and ending in a sudden stop. . . .

. . . I could not disguise from myself that . . . the heathen orgies resurrected by the Lord Bishop of Honolulu were not warranted by the teachings of the Master whom he professes to serve.

The last lines refer to Bishop Staley's re-establishment of certain native customs, the hula-hula among them.

Mark Twain's moralism, once aroused and brought into action, soon became a prominent feature of the Sandwich Islands letters, especially in criticism of sexual laxness. Commenting on the fact that in the islands the female line takes precedence of the male in tracing lineage, he wrote: "Their reason for this is exceedingly sensible, and I recommend it to the aristocracy of Europe: They say it is easy to know who a man's mother was, but, etc." The civil courts imposed fines for adultery—thirty dollars for each offense—and Mark Twain "would remark, in passing, that if the crime were invariably detected and the fines collected, the revenues of the Hawaiian Government would probably exceed those of the United States." The surface humor of such passages is obvious; yet the humorous veneer is actually very thin. Although his criticism of sexual excesses predominates, he presents the natives as cruel to their horses, dishonest in trades, and innate liars:

They still believe in . . . the Great God Shark, and pray each other to death. When sworn by the Great God Shark, they are afraid to speak anything but the truth; but when sworn on the Bible . . . they proceed to soar into flights of fancy lying that make the inventions of Munchausen seem . . . trifling by comparison.

His treatment of the missionaries shows a divided opinion. He wrote in his *Notebook* that the first white landed on the islands was a "curse" to the natives, and his early letters berate the missionaries for tampering with their lives; but the better he knew native ways, the more sympathy he felt for the labors of the missionaries. The reformer-as-moralist approved the efforts of the American missionaries to modify the lascivious habits of the natives; and the reformer-as-humanitarian endorsed the movement by which the missionaries had emancipated the common people from oppression by the hereditary hierarchy of the islands.

His moral theories gained a new application when he saw the father of the current king. He contrasted the present condition of this old man, the president of the Hawaiian legislature, with his past, thinking to himself:

This man, naked as the day he was born . . . war-club and spear in hand, has charged at the head of a horde of savages against other . . . savages . . . has worshiped wooden images on his bended knees; has seen hundreds of his race offered up . . . as sacrifices to hideous idols . . . and now look at him: an educated Christian . . . handsomely dressed; a high-minded, elegant gentleman. . . . Look at him, sitting there presiding over . . . a legislative body . . . a grave, dignified, statesmanlike personage. . . . Lord! how the experiences of this old man's strange . . . life must shame the cheap inventions of romance!

Thus the moralist implicitly emphasized the power of moral training and education to change a man from earlier habits of life.

Mark Twain's Hawaiian correspondence, his first sustained writing, shows a clear development in three ways: his humor rises from the low level of jokes on seasickness to the level of his dialogues with Mr. Brown, which contrast the romantic and the realistic points of view and thus foreshadow the later debates of Tom and Huck; his modeled descriptive prose becomes more effective; and his satire grows keener in attacks on the missionaries, the legislature, the established church, monarchies, politicians, and the exploitation of the natives by the whites.[1] In the Sandwich Islands by 1866, he had arrived at the formula with which he would measure civilization for the rest of his life, his standard being the "economic and moral state of the masses."

Between his return from the Sandwich Islands and his departure on the *Quaker City* voyage in June, 1867, he wrote a series of letters for the *Alta California*. Since his ramblings were still shared by his fictitious and irreverent fellow traveler, the title chosen for these letters upon their recent publication in book form was *Mark Twain's Travels with Mr. Brown*. This series forms a link between the *Letters from the Sandwich Islands* and *The Innocents Abroad*.

He visited both Nicaragua and Panama on his way to New York. The steamer *America* was barely out at sea when a "luscious sensation" was discovered on board: "it was whispered about that our young couple who passed . . . as 'Mr.—— and wife' and occupied a stateroom together were really not married!" Scandalized, Captain Ned Wakeman straightway hauled them up and married them himself, before witnesses. The passengers bickered over the captain's action, some viewing it as sheer meddling. Mark Twain's shocked but humorous comment was: "God help me! I am an orphan and many . . . a league at sea—with such a crowd as this!"

He noted that the Nicaraguan girls were always dressed in a single flowing gown, gathered across the breast—"they are singularly full in the breast, the young ones"—and that they had winning faces:

They are virtuous according to their lights, but I guess their lights are a little dim. Two . . . were exceedingly beautiful—such liquid, languishing eyes! such pouting lips! such glossy, luxuriant hair! such ravishing, incendiary expression! such . . . voluptuous forms, and such precious little drapery about them! such—

"But you just prospect one of them heifers with a fine-tooth—"

This interruption is, of course, from that confirmed antiromanticist,

---

[1] Walker, *San Francisco's Literary Frontier*, 243–44.

Brown, who, Franklin Walker observes, could always be relied on to make the crude remarks which passed through the mind of his creator.

During Mark Twain's stay in New York in 1867, the country's first great girl show was holding the male population entranced, while Uncle Tom drew only "critical, self-possessed groups of negroes and children at Barnum's museum":

> I fear me I shall have to start a missionary society here. . . . In '53 they called that horrid, immoral show . . . the "Model Artists" . . . but now they call that sort of thing a "Grand Spectacular Drama." . . . It is the wickedest show you can think of. . . . I warn you that when they put beautiful clipper-built girls on the stage . . . with only just barely clothes enough on to be tantalizing, it is a shrewd invention of the devil. It lays a . . . siege to public morals.
>
> The name of this new exhibition . . . is the "Black Crook." . . . seventy beauties arrayed in dazzling half-costumes and displaying all possible compromises between nakedness and decency, capture the men and boys. . . . The scenery and the legs are everything. . . . Those girls dance in ballet, dressed with a meagerness that would make a parasol blush. And they prance around and expose themselves in a way that is scandalous to me.

Sally Hinckley, late of San Francisco, was then playing in New York in "a nude fairy piece," in the last act of which she made a statue of herself and stood aloft, practically naked. Mark Twain was keenly concerned about the moral results of such shows. Almost a year later, on March 3, 1868, he reported in a news letter the shocking effects of the *White Fawn*: "The best thing New York can do now, and the other . . . towns of America as well, will be to build . . . houses of ill-fame—let them build thousands and tens of thousands of them, and the Black Crook, the White Fawn, and the infernal literature they have bred will stock them all."[2]

He related his adventures at Harry Hill's Club House, where there were music, dancing, and drinking. Signs on the walls forbade the use of obscene language and profanity and announced that "lovers" were not allowed. Mark Twain considered how irregular these people must be in their habits, to make such ordinances necessary. Finally, a young man in a Highland costume came out on a

[2] Walter Blair, "Mark Twain, New York Correspondent," *American Literature*, Vol. XI, No. 3 (November, 1939), 257.

stage and danced, "and he ought to have danced moderately, because he had nothing in the wide world on but a short coat and short stockings. This was apparent every time he whirled around." The visitor later found that he had been in "one of the worst dens in all New York," where the men were a hard lot and the girls were "streetwalkers and the most abandoned in the city." Speaking of "the prostitutes that infest the alleys," Mark Twain confessed: "I had rather face the guns of Fortress Monroe than brave the tongues of those foul-mouthed she dragons." Another passage ridicules the "woodenheaded louts . . . who fall in love with every old strumpet who smiles a flabby smile at them in a street car." The preoccupation of the moralist with sexual matters in these travel letters makes all the more striking the almost complete exclusion of sex as a subject for his fiction.

In *Travels with Mr. Brown*, one little sermon studies the moral effects in Hoboken of the New York excise law forbidding the sale of liquor on Sunday:

It is a great thing for the morals of New York, but it . . . inflicts twenty thousand beer-swillers upon Hoboken every Sabbath. You remember the pious girl who said, "I found that my ribbons and gew-gaws were dragging me down to hell, and so I took them off and gave them to my sister." . . . We found that beer drinkers were debauching our morals, and so we concluded to turn them over to our neighbors.

In Biblical phraseology, one passage blends the motives of the reformer-as-moralist with those of the reformer-as-humanitarian. Denouncing the indifference of the rich for the "criminally, sinfully, wickedly poor," Mark Twain warned that the slums were a breeding ground for the cholera: "it will sweep those sinks of corruption like a conflagration. . . . its lodgings are set apart and made ready for it—and in the fullness of time it will enter in."

He analyzed the materialism of the postwar era, pointing out that five thousand men had been made wealthy, while for a "good round million citizens" it now took "the closest kind of scratching" for them to get along in their accustomed style:

The brown-stone fronter and the rag-picker of the Five Points have about an even thing of it. . . . both struggle desperately to hold their places, and both grumble and grieve to much the same tune. . . .

The old genuine . . . pedigreed aristocracy of New York stand stunned and helpless under the new order of things. They find themselves supplanted by upstart Princes of Shoddy, vulgar and with unknown grandfathers. The incomes which were something for the common herd to gape at . . . once, are mere livelihoods now—would not pay Shoddy's house rent. They move into remote new streets up town, and talk feelingly of the crash which is to come.

A satiric flavor permeates many passages. At the Travelers' Club cosmopolitans gathered to lend an air to the "worshipful five-story brownstone front on ineffable Fifth Avenue, far up town in the midst of the odor of sanctity that prevails in that thoroughfare . . . so peculiarly sacred to greenbacks and fashion." Sometimes, as in the Western sketches, the *Mr. Brown* letters grow coarse in an attempt, it appears, to shock the public into a realization of the need for certain reforms. The stench of corpses is apparently used for its shock value in a plea for better sanitary regulations in St. Louis.

The last letter in the *Travels with Mr. Brown* series was soon followed by the first in the *Quaker City* series, which later became the basis for *The Innocents Abroad*. Most of these letters, too, were written for the *Alta California*, although the book includes letters sent to the New York *Tribune* and the *Herald*.

Much has been written about *The Innocents Abroad*, but two important points concerning it have not been given sufficient attention. One of these is the degree to which Mark Twain injected criticism of American ways and American civilization into his running commentary on the foreign scene. The book has been called the American literary declaration of independence from subservience to Europe's superiority. In part, this is true; but Mark Twain, feeling himself more responsible for Americans than for Europeans, directed his camouflaged "preaching" wherever he felt there was need for it.

One point at which he found Europe infinitely superior to America was the leisure for living which Europeans allowed themselves. In Milan he strolled about, "enjoying other people's comfort and wishing we could export some of it to our restless, driving, vitality-consuming marts at home." In America we hurry constantly; we worry nightly over business cares until we "either die early or drop into a lean and mean old age." And Mark Twain continues in words that might have been written by Thoreau: "What a robust people, what a nation of thinkers we might be, if we would only lay ourselves on the shelf occasionally and renew our edges!" In this atmosphere a change is already creeping over the American tourists: "Day by day we lose some of our restlessness and absorb some of the spirit of quietude and ease that is in the tranquil atmosphere about us. . . . We grow wise apace. We begin to comprehend what life is for."

He derided the aura of self-importance that hangs about the American tourist:

None of us had ever been anywhere before; . . . travel was a wild novelty to us, and we conducted ourselves in accordance with the natural instincts that were in us. . . . We always took care to make it understood that we were Americans—Americans! When we found that a good many foreigners had hardly ever heard of America, and . . . knew it only as a barbarous province away off somewhere . . . we pitied the ignorance of the Old World, but abated no jot of our importance.

The people of those foreign countries were very, very ignorant. Why, in Paris those idiots could not understand their own language —that is, the *Quaker City* version of it. "The people stared at us everywhere, and we stared at them. We generally made them feel rather small, too, . . . because we bore down on them with America's greatness until we crushed them." It would seem that the ironic flavor of such passages is too strong to be mistaken; yet that feat has been accomplished.

At Marseilles a certain American talked very loudly at dinner, laughing boisterously while all others were well behaved. He ordered wine "with a royal flourish" and said, "I never dine without wine, sir," looking about for admiration:

All these airs in a land . . . where wine is nearly as common among all ranks as water! This fellow said: "I am a free-born sovereign, sir, an American, sir, and I want everybody to know it!" He did not mention that he was a lineal descendant of Balaam's ass; but everybody knew that.

At Nain in the Holy Land, the American "pilgrims" must break souvenir specimens from the walls of an Arabian mosque, even though they had to step upon the sacred prayer rugs with booted feet to do it:

It was almost the same as breaking pieces from the hearts of those old Arabs. . . . Suppose a party of armed foreigners were to enter a village church in America and break ornaments from the altar railings for curiosities, and climb up and walk upon the Bible and the pulpit cushions? However, the cases are different. One is the profanation of a temple of our faith—the other only the profanation of a pagan one.

In the heavy irony of the last lines, he reverts to his Western technique.

There are some things which, for the credit of America, should be left unsaid; but these are the very things which, for the benefit of Americans, should be said. In Egypt, in the solemn presence of the Sphinx, "We heard the familiar chink of a hammer. . . . One of our well-meaning reptiles . . . was trying to break a 'specimen' from the face of . . . the great image [which] contemplated the dead ages as calmly as ever, unconscious of the small insect . . . fretting at its jaw." Mark Twain ridiculed foreignized Americans through his comments on an "enterprising idiot" named Gordon who spent eight weeks in Paris, returned home, and allowed himself to be hailed three times in the street before he begged pardon and said that he had grown so accustomed to hearing himself addressed as "M'sieu Gor-r-*dong,* with a roll to the *r,*" that he had forgotten the native sound of his own name.

It is not pleasant to see an American thrust his nationality forward *obtrusively* in a foreign land, but oh, it is pitiable to see him making of himself a thing that is neither male nor female, neither fish nor fowl—a poor, miserable, hermaphrodite Frenchman!

Mark Twain was reminded of his homeland during a visit to Tangier: "We visited the jail and found Moorish prisoners making mats and baskets. This thing of utilizing crime savors of civilization." He saw as one of the most pitiable things about Americans the pride they take in their slight speaking acquaintance with the world of art. Europe is full of "old connoisseurs from the wilds of New Jersey who . . . feel privileged to void their critical bathos" on all the fine arts.

The question of the arts brings us to the second point concerning *The Innocents Abroad* which has not received sufficient consideration: the degree to which Mark Twain's critical strictures on art were influenced by his conviction that the economic and moral state of the masses must serve always as the measure for any civilization. In the preceding generation the American sculptor Horatio Greenough had anticipated Mark Twain by demanding social and economic equality as the only right foundation for art. Greenough believed that in a healthy society "everything is generative, everything is connected," and that some abnormal development had always followed the theory that "out of a prostrate humanity, as out of a bank and magazine," a nation could draw the materials for culture to a class. He insisted that this theory was "a lie, and had the effect of a lie," and that the artist must find his impulse in the community, must consign the seed of his talent "to the earth which we all despise so truly—the hearts and heads of common men." Greenough felt that there was the ground where the artist's talent must "find the soil and the moisture, blood and tears, which burst its rind" and finally permit it to flower. In the architecture of Egypt and the Middle Ages he saw only "cost to the constituency," the soul-searing toil of oppressed peoples.[3]

I do not know that Mark Twain ever read this theory of Greenough's; but the similarity of his ideas to this doctrine will be evident to anyone who has read thus far. He, too, had consigned the seed of his talent to the hearts and heads of common men, that earth which he felt the literary critics so unwisely despised. Criticism usually charges his lack of appreciation for the masterpieces of European art to mere Western philistinism, to want of aesthetic judgment, to insensitivity to beauty, to an untrained eye and an untrained spirit. He himself wondered at his inability to enjoy Europe's artistic treasures. Lack of training doubtless played its part; but his denunciations of art and architecture were entangled with both his humanitarian impulses and his moralistic leanings. His responses to the art of Europe were not mere surface responses governed by the eye and the ear; they arose from the deepest substratum of his mind and were too complex and too deeply significant to be now lightly dismissed.

His reiterated conviction was that there is only one thing that can "make or save countries or . . . build them to greatness—it is clean men, clean ordinary citizens, rank and file, the masses." He was

3 Passages quoted from Horatio Greenough's essays are taken from F. O. Matthiessen, *American Renaissance*, 147–52.

engaged with the masses to such a degree that he could not approve of an art that achieved its beauty in the midst of their want. Turning away from the Louvre and "The Last Supper," he was disturbed by the poverty of street beggars, the low wages of European workmen, and the hovels crowding to the very feet of the great cathedrals. He viewed Italy, the home of the world's greatest artistic treasures, as "a land which has groped in the midnight of priestly superstition for sixteen hundred years." His condemnation of the established church as an oppressor of individual liberty has weight here, of course; but the reformer-as-humanitarian enters in such passages as that relating his visit to a great Jesuit church. All about the door wretchedness was clustered; a dozen hands were extended, appealing for pennies, an appeal aided by "sad eyes, and sunken cheeks, and ragged raiment, that no words were needed to translate. Then we passed within the great doors, and it seemed that the riches of the world were before us." Decorations of agate and jasper and lapis lazuli were lavished everywhere; the furniture of the altar was solid gold and silver; yet half of that community did not know how they could keep body and soul together. All the churches of an American city could not buy the "jewelled frippery" of one great Italian cathedral; and for every beggar in America, Italy could "show a hundred—and rags and vermin to match." Thus Mark Twain, the humanitarian democrat, found Italy "one vast museum of magnificence and misery." At sight of the splendid Duomo, he "fell down and worshiped it," like all other men; but when the filthy beggars swarmed around him, the contrast was too suggestive, and he said, "Oh, sons of classic Italy ... why don't you rob your church?"

Only the year before, the Italian Parliament had, in fact, taken over the property belonging to certain churches, and Mark Twain rejoiced at the results of this good deed: good turnpikes, comfortable railroad stations, and excellent railways for part of Italy. "These things win me more than Italy's hundred galleries of priceless art treasures"; for, generally speaking, he felt that there was in Italy "no real foundation for these great works" of art. How could there be, when Mark Twain's yardstick of civilization, the condition of the masses, showed such a low level? He could not approve a society that followed the will-o'-the-wisp of art while its people had neither bread nor clothes.

The points at which his conceptions of art coincide with the theories of Horatio Greenough serve to throw new light on the fact that his aesthetic sense was frequently subordinated to his humanitarian and ethical conscience. In the national cemetery of France were buried men and women who had been born to no title but had achieved fame through their own energy and genius. He was glad that both the "man who originated public gas-lighting, and that other benefactor who introduced the potato and thus blessed millions of his starving countrymen" could lie there amid "the royalty of heart and brain." This was the spirit which prompted him, on the occasion of Walt Whitman's seventieth birthday, to congratulate the poet for having lived in an age that had produced many benefactions to make life easier for all people; he listed among them the amazing products of coal tar, but neglected, as Mr. Brooks observes, to congratulate the age for having produced Walt Whitman. In this same spirit he contrasted, in the *The Innocents Abroad*, the aesthetic treasury of Europe with the utilitarian treasury of the United States. Time would show him the folly of the early idea that the progress of machinery may be identified with the progress of humanity. His friend the clergyman Joseph Twichell once insisted on the "steady progress from age to age of the coming of the kingdom of God and righteousness"; at that time Mark Twain wrote in reply:

"From age to age"—yes, it describes that giddy gait. . . .
     . . . the 19th century made progress . . . colossal progress. In what?
Materialities. Prodigious acquisitions . . . which add to the comfort of many and make life harder for as many more. But the addition to righteousness? Is that discoverable? I think not. The materialities were not invented in the interest of righteousness. . . . In Europe and America there is a vast change (due to them) in ideals—do you admire it?

But that was in 1905. In 1867 the young Mark Twain simply believed that for a civilization to make any real progress, the masses would have to be uplifted, too—and not only "uplifted," but fed and clothed as well.

Van Wyck Brooks denies that Mark Twain was a true satirist because, he says, Mark Twain had no ideal to set up as the measure of society, no new and personal ideal to substitute for the satirized "racial ideal," as he terms it. But it is clear that Mark Twain's measure of society was always the condition of the common people to whom he had dedicated his life and his art. By this personal standard he measured everything that came into his ken, at home or abroad.

His standard encompassed not only the economic status of the masses, but their moral status as well. With the sufferings of the common people under his eye, his reaction to Europe's art was dictated by the reformer-as-humanitarian; in other passages, however, the reformer-as-moralist was in command. In *The Innocents Abroad*, Raphael is denounced because he pictured "such infernal villains" as Catherine and Marie de Medici seated in Heaven and conversing familiarly with the Virgin Mary; "and yet my friends abuse me because I am a little prejudiced against the old masters—because I fail sometimes to see the beauty in their productions." He tried to be honest about his position:

I cannot help but see [the beauty] now and then, but I keep on protesting against the groveling spirit that could persuade those masters to prostitute their noble talents to the adulation of such monsters as the French, Venetian, and Florentine princes. . . . I am told that the old masters had to do these shameful things for bread. . . . If a grandly gifted man may drag his pride and his manhood in the dirt for bread rather than starve with the nobility that is in him untainted, the excuse is a valid one. It would excuse theft in Washingtons and Wellingtons, and unchastity in women as well.

He declared that some of the Louvre paintings, admittedly beautiful, carried "such evidences about them of the cringing spirit . . . that we found small pleasure in examining them." In such passages the moralism masks the intransigent view of the absolutist, demanding perfection. The narrow view, emphasizing ethical import, makes aesthetic enjoyment impossible to him. It is the old story of the moralist who sees everything as black or white.

This confusion of art and morals continues. The moralist's limited outlook on life helps to explain Mark Twain's commentary on literature, as found in *The Innocents Abroad*. A lively horror was aroused within him by Lamartine's "nauseous sentimentality" in treating the legend of that "dastardly seducer" and "abandoned villain," Abélard. As retold by Mark Twain, the story of Abélard and Héloise reverts to the technique of his Western sketches. It carries a heavy burlesque aimed directly at the masses, a burlesque arising from the fact that Fulbert, the uncle of Héloise, was a canon of the

Cathedral of Paris. Fulbert is called a mountain howitzer, an old gun "or son of a gun, as the case may be," and a good old swivel. This poor canon was "spiked" by the treachery of Abélard; but Mark Twain, at least, would "always respect the memory . . . of the old smooth bore." Mark Twain's power as a writer of prose during this period may be gauged by referring to his descriptive passages. It had been some years since Tom Fitch of Nevada had warned him against nullifying a piece of eloquent writing by an "atrocious anti-climax." Moreover, *The Innocents Abroad* was the first book edited for him by Olivia Langdon, who read the manuscript with him. Speaking to Archibald Henderson of her long service as his editor, he once commented upon her critical method:

After I had written some side-splitting story, something beginning seriously and ending in preposterous anti-climax, she would say to me: "You have a true lesson, a serious meaning to impart here. Don't give way to your invincible temptation to destroy the good effect . . . by some extravagantly comic absurdity. . . . Speak out your real thoughts as humorously as you please, but—without farcical commentary."

So much for his lessoning, in early years and later. The story considered here is certainly marred by its farcical accompaniment. The aesthetic flaw of injecting into the moving story of love and pain and death woven about Abélard and Héloise such a crude burlesque could hardly have escaped the critical notice of Olivia. Nevertheless, the burlesque survived. In fact, it was particularly in pieces where he had "a true lesson" to impart that he was most likely to hide his sermon in comic absurdity. He was ever stalking the "big game" he hunted, the "mighty mass of the uncultivated" who seemed to him best worth trying to uplift. Once more his moral had been delivered, as he doubtless considered, "with telling force through the insidious medium of a travesty." And in the story of Abélard and Héloise it may well be that his artistic conscience was sacrificed to his ethical conscience.

Approaching the burlesque technique and undoubtedly designed with a moralizing purpose is his reference to Petrarch and Laura. As he looks upon the handwriting of "the gentleman who loved another man's Laura," his thoughts stray from the deified lovers to the probable mental state of "poor Mr. Laura": "How do you suppose *he* liked . . . having another man following his wife everywhere and making her name a familiar word in every garlic-exterminating mouth in Italy with his sonnets to her pre-empted eyebrows? . . . it does not chime with my notions of right." This is buffoonery, of course; but, like the Western sketches, it is more than mere buffoonery.

The moralistic observation moves on, much of it dealing with sex. In ruined Pompeii he found the Pompeiian version of a bawdy-house and saw on its walls pictures "which looked almost as fresh as if they were painted yesterday, but which no pen could have the hardihood to describe"; here and there he saw Latin inscriptions, "obscene scintillations of wit, scratched by hands that possibly were uplifted to Heaven for succor in . . . a driving storm of fire before the night was done." In Versailles he saw the room where Louis XIV and his mistress Madame Maintenon, and after them Louis XV and Pompadour, had sat at meals "naked and unattended—for the table stood upon a trap-door, which descended—when it was necessary to replenish its dishes." He commented on the Mohammedan system of concubinage, observing that among the Turks "morals and whis-key are scarce": "The Koran does not permit them to drink. Their natural instincts do not permit them to be moral." The word *moral* frequently has for Mark Twain, as here, a sexual connotation only. A description of the Constantinople slave mart in which young girls were bought and sold has its accompanying burlesque: an American newspaper "Slave-Girl Market Report" lists a promising crop of Circassians, "prime to good"; several Georgians, fancy brands; and "one forty-niner—damaged—at £23, seller ten, no deposit."

In his horrified reaction to the Parisian cancan, he placed his hands before his face "for very shame." But the artist, living in hiding somewhere beneath the attitudes of the moralist, took an aesthetic delight in the spectacle afforded by that disgraceful dance at the same time that the moralist condemned it:

I moved aside and took a general view of the Cancan. Shouts, laughter, furious music, a bewildering chaos of daring and intermingling forms, stormy jerking and snatching of gay dresses, bobbing heads, flying arms, lightning flashes of white-stockinged calves and dainty slippers in the air, and then a grand final rush, riot, a terrific hubbub, and a wild stam-pede! Heavens! Nothing like it has ever been seen . . . since trembling Tam O'Shanter saw the devil and the witches at their orgies that stormy night in "Alloway's auld haunted kirk."

This description is more than a mere picture. It is a moving picture, with sound effects. But the aesthetic sensibility revealed in it cannot be realized in a great part of Mark Twain's work because of the restraining limits of the moralist's view of life. Too often his artistic standards are controlled by ethical ends.

Mr. Brooks charged him with lack of aesthetic discrimination in slighting Paris and Rome while he pictured Jerusalem as "full of poetry, sublimity, and . . . dignity." Mr. Brooks explained this rudimentary taste by saying that in Mark Twain's childhood his attention had been fixed upon Biblical lands, "and that is why they seemed to him so full of poetry and dignity," while his early attention had never been drawn to Europe, "and that is why it seemed to him so empty and absurd." But the reason for the preponderance given to the Holy Land in *The Innocents Abroad* is to be sought rather in Mark Twain's motivation. He designed the book to appeal to the common people, addressing to them whatever lessons it might contain; and he knew where their interests and preoccupations lay. Certainly, it was Europe in which he himself chose to reside; and his own private opinions of the Holy Land are revealed abundantly in the *Notebook* which he kept on the excursion:

Sept. 19 . . . Crossed a . . . plain . . . to Magdala, the birthplace of Mary Magdalene—the rattiest, rustiest, dirtiest little collection of mud hovels, tattooed women and sore-eyed children. . . .

Thence along the edge of a mountain, to Tiberius, another nasty mud-hovel village. . . .

Sept. 21 . . . On the hill where Ahab, King of Judah, lived in splendor with his awful heifer, Jezebel. . . .

Sept. 22 . . . Climbed a hill to visit the ruin of the city where the woman of Samaria conversed with Christ and gave him to drink. . . . It is rough stone, mud hovels, and camel dung as usual.

Sept. 24 . . . Village of Bethany. It is fearfully ratty. . . . No Second Advent—Christ been here once, will never come again.

Sept. 26 . . . The ravens could hardly make their own living [here], let alone board Elijah.

In *The Innocents Abroad* itself, his mood is almost as clearly indicated. There he spoke of "the God-forsaken barrenness . . . of Syria," saw the solitude of Gennesaret as repellent, found the "Madonna-like beauty" of the Nazarene girls actually a sad homeliness, and labeled Jerusalem as "mournful, and dreary, and lifeless." The very piece which Mr. Brooks points out as containing Mark Twain's confession of his preference for the Holy Land is so ironic that it is difficult to understand how its tone could be mistaken. This "Newspaper Valedictory," closing the book, derides the self-righteous ways of the "pilgrims," those zealots who broke into ecstasies over any place mentioned in the Bible (even, as Mark Twain declares elsewhere, over a spot "sacred to Balaam's ass")—and in this ironic vein continues:

... the Holy Land brought out all our enthusiasm. We fell into raptures by the barren shores of Galilee; ... we exploded into poetry over the questionable loveliness of Esdraelon; ... we rioted—fairly rioted—among the holy places of Jerusalem. ... After dismal, smileless Palestine, beautiful Egypt had few charms for us. We merely glanced at it and were ready for home.

In *A Tramp Abroad*, begun in 1878, with its pronounced intermingling of morals and art, Mark Twain rises to new heights of denunciation after his call in Florence at the world's "most visited little gallery," the Tribune. He fumes against "Titian's beast," the Venus, lying "there against the wall, without obstructing rag or leaf ... the foulest, the vilest, the obscenest picture the world possesses. ... there the Venus lies, for anybody to gloat over that wants to—and there she has a right to lie, for she is a work of art." He insists that this picture was unquestionably "painted for a *bagnio* and it was probably refused because it was ... too strong." He objects, not to the fact that she is naked and stretched out on a bed, but to the suggestive attitude of one of her arms and her hand. Young girls steal furtive glances at her; young men gaze long upon her; aged men "hang upon her charms." All this is bound to have a demoralizing effect upon patrons of the gallery. In the impossibilities of its iron cables floating on water, Turner's "Slave Ship" is a manifest lie, "and only rigid cultivation can enable man to find truth in a lie." This confusion of morals and art persisted as late as 1899, when he wrote to Howells from Vienna: "The office of art seems to be to grovel in the dirt before Emperors and this and that and the other damned breed of priests."

Following the Equator, his last sustained travel writing, was begun in 1896. By the time of this book, he was able to handle without his customary railing or restraint at least one subject involving the question of sex—the priapus worship connected with the Hindu religion. Shiva's symbol, the lingam with which Vishnu began the Creation, was worshiped in the form of an upright stone shaped "like an elongated thimble." In Benares it was on view everywhere, garlanded with flowers. If Vishnu had foreseen what his town was going to be, he would have called it "Lingamburg." In a Benares temple Mark Twain saw a devotee working for salvation in a curious way: "He had a huge wad of clay . . . and was making it up into little wee gods no bigger than carpet-tacks. He stuck a grain of rice into each —to represent the lingam, I think."

As for statesmanship involving land grabbing, he felt that the point there is to "get your formalities right—never mind about the moralities!" He commented ironically on "the quaint product called French civilization" in connection with the "snatching" of Madagascar. The European nations have been "raiding each other's territorial clothes-line for ages"; and when Russia "found a quarter of the world hanging out to dry on a hundred parallels of latitude . . . she scooped in the whole wash. She keeps a sharp eye on a multitude of little lines . . . and every now and then she snatches a hip-rag or a pair of pajamas." But usage, as Mark Twain pointed out, can accustom the human race to anything:

A crime persevered in a thousand centuries ceases to be a crime, and becomes a virtue. This is the law of custom, and custom supersedes all other forms of law. Christian governments are as frank today, as open and above-board, in discussing projects for raiding each other's clothes-line as ever they were before the Golden Rule came smiling into this inhospitable world and couldn't get a night's lodging anywhere.

During the Boer War he naturally sympathized with the underdogs; as he expressed it, "My head is with the Briton, but my heart and such rags of morals as I have are with the Boer." Still, his head was with the Briton; for, as he wrote to Howells in 1900 in words which seem to indicate that he foresaw the two world wars and the issues for which they were fought:

. . . England must not fall; it would mean an inundation of Russian and German political degradations which would envelop the globe and steep it in a sort of Middle-Age night and slavery which would last till Christ comes again.

LIVY

when she had been Mrs. Samuel Clemens for three years

He compared England's imperialism with that which America was exhibiting in the Philippines, and when young Winston Churchill visited the United States in 1900, Mark Twain introduced him at a dinner, remarking that their two countries were "kin in sin." The human race was displaying its usual depravity during these years: not only were the Boers and the Filipinos being oppressed; indemnities were being extorted from China following the Boxer Rebellion, and King Leopold was massacring the blacks in the Belgian Congo. Mark Twain's cup of bitterness ran over; and on New Year's Eve, 1900, he penned "A Greeting from the Nineteenth to the Twentieth Century":

I bring you the stately nation named Christendom, returning bedraggled, besmirched, and dishonored from pirate raids in Kiao-Chou, Manchuria, South Africa, and the Philippines, with her soul full of meanness, her pocket full of boodle, and her mouth full of pious hypocrisies. Give her soap and towel, but hide the looking-glass.[4]

A year later, in 1901, he prepared his Pageant of Progress, in which a "Stupendous International Procession" moves across the world led by The Twentieth Century, "a fair young creature, drunk and disorderly, borne in the arms of Satan," her banner bearing the motto: "Get What You Can, Keep What You Get." Her guard of honor includes Monarchs, Presidents, Tammany Bosses, and Land Thieves. She is followed by Christendom, "a majestic matron in flowing robes drenched with blood," who wears a crown of thorns; impaled on its spines are the bleeding heads of Boers, Boxers, and Filipinos; in one hand she carries a " slung-shot," in the other a Bible, open at the Golden Rule; protruding from her pocket is a bottle, labeled "We bring you the blessings of civilization"; she has two attendants, Slaughter and Hypocrisy; her ensign is the Black Flag, and her guard of honor is made up of missionaries and "soldiers laden with loot." The American flag appears, "furled and draped in black"; and finally Mark Twain moves the shade of Lincoln across the stage of the world, Lincoln, "towering vast and dim toward the sky, brooding with sorrowful aspect" over this Pageant of Progress.[5] Lincoln had signed an Emancipation Proclamation in 1863; but in 1901 Mark Twain realized that the world was still trying to exist half slave and

[4] Paine, *Biography*, III, 1127.
[5] *Ibid.*, 1149–50.

half free—that the world conflict between liberty and despotism was still being fought, the victory still unwon.

Nowhere does the essential conflict in his thought show more clearly than in his attitude toward the subjection of native races. From the Sandwich Islands letters on, he inveighed against the exploitation of the Fijis, the Kanakas, the Maoris, the black aborigines of Australia. In *Following the Equator* he held that the results of white-imposed reforms upon the native races have always been disastrous: the natives were unaccustomed to "clothes and houses and church and school and Sunday school and work and other misplaced persecutions of civilization." The Tasmanians and Maoris, transplanted to strange shores, pined for their lost homes and their wild free life; too late "they repented that they had traded that heaven for this hell." They sat homesick on their alien crags and gazed in the direction of their lost paradise until, one by one, they died of grief.

The Whites always mean well when they take human fish out of the ocean and try to make them dry and warm and happy and comfortable in a chicken-coop; but the . . . white man . . . if he had any wisdom . . . would know that his own civilization is a hell to the savage—but he hasn't any . . . ; and for lack of it he shut up those poor natives in the unimaginable perdition of his civilization, committing his crime with the very best intentions, and saw those poor creatures waste away under his tortures; and gazed at it, vaguely troubled and sorrowful, and wondered what could be the matter with them.

That is Mark Twain the Humanitarian, speaking out of his sympathy with the heartbreak of the natives. But soon we find in this same book, *Following the Equator*, a passage of the opposite tenor:

The signs of the times show plainly enough what is going to happen. All the savage lands in the world are going to be brought under subjection to the Christian governments of Europe. I am not sorry, but glad. . . . The sooner the seizure is consummated, the better for the savages. The dreary and dragging ages of bloodshed and disorder and oppression will give place to peace and order and the reign of law.

This is Mark Twain the Moralist, praising Christian law and order. Is it better, then, for the savages to be shut up in that "unimaginable perdition of civilization," if at such a price a systematized order can but be purchased? Is it better to have them waste away under its tortures if such a result can but insure "the reign of law"? The moralist seems to think so. In these conflicting passages, strangely enough, it is the moralist and the humanitarian that are pitted against each other; but the chief conflict in Mark Twain is reserved for the moralist and the determinist. For the moralist's reasoning rests on the assumption that the natives will respond to teaching—in other words, on the assumption that they are proper subjects for reform. And Mark Twain the Determinist denies the efficacy of all reform.

CHAPTER II

The Traveling Determinist and Pessimist

MANY passages in the travel books nullify all of Mark Twain's moralistic endeavors by the recurrent text of his "Gospel," either expressed or implied—his belief that the inborn disposition of mankind is "a thing as permanent as rock, and never undergoes any actual or genuine change between cradle and grave." This definition of man's nature was written in his later years; but in the Sandwich Islands in 1866 he advanced the same theory. Commenting on the "amazingly unselfish and hospitable" nature of the natives, he mentioned the hearty good will with which they "offer their houses, food, beds, and often wives and daughters" to the visiting stranger:

They are a strange race, anyhow, these natives. . . . The example of white selfishness does not affect their native unselfishness any more than the example of white virtue does their native licentiousness. Both are in their blood and bones, and cannot be educated out.

His Gospel itself is not more explicit. It should be noted that his granting of "virtue" to the whites, despite their selfishness and other failings, rests solely upon their greater sexual restraint.

To witness the rites held for the dead Hawaiian princess, Victoria, was to comprehend what a thin veneer of civilization lay over the savagery of these people. Outside, in the palace yard, "natives howl and wail, and weep and chant for the dead. . . . I hear them at it yet, poor, simple, loving, faithful Christian savages."

In the *Travels with Mr. Brown*, human nature is closely studied. On the train on a particularly chilly night, Mark Twain observed that "the usual mean man was aboard, who kept his window a little open to distress his fellows." Everywhere on the streets of New

York people were squandering time in the "miraculous triviality" of a new toy, merely a rubber ball attached to an elastic cord; yet everybody "neglected graver pursuits and revelled in the fierce intoxication of this amusement." Humanity-at-large gets some attention: "Verily, some things are stranger than others, and man is but grass, and a very poor article of grass at that." An exceptionally poor variety was the "sanctimonious old iceberg that looked like he was waiting for a vacancy in the Trinity," who took passage on the *Quaker City* and inquired whether the excursion would come to a halt on Sundays. A woman who believed herself to be watching a burning ship was disappointed when an officer, sent on a rescue mission, returned with a supply of sea food and the news that the ship was not afire after all. She exploded: "I've sot here and sot here . . . cal'latin' you'd fetch a boatload of sorrowful roasted corpses, and now it ain't nothing but a lot of nasty cussed mud-turkles—it's a dern thieving shame." Here Mark Twain isolates and records a repellent human trait: human nature's resentment at being cheated of a horrific sensation.

During his 1867 stay in New York he tried to separate a couple of fighting men, strangers to him, and as a result he spent the night with them in the station house. The company there consisted of "dilapidated old hags and . . . ragged bummers." There was one bloated old hag "with a wholesome black eye, a drunken leer . . . and nothing in the world on but a dingy calico dress." She had had a husband, she said, but he drifted off somewhere, and so she took up with another man. She had had a child, too, a little boy:

. . . but it took all her time to get drunk, and keep drunk, and so he starved . . . or froze, she didn't know which—both, maybe, because it snowed in "horrible" through the roof, and he hadn't any bedclothes but a window shutter. "But it was a d——d good thing for him, anyway," said she, "because he'd have had a miserable rough time of it if he'd a lived."

On the contemporary movement for "compulsory temperance," Mark Twain's conclusion was that "prohibition only drives drunkenness behind doors and into dark places, and does not cure it or even diminish it." The implication is that man is thus-and-so by nature and apparently unchangeable. Human depravity fascinated him.

He held both creating forces and environing circumstances accountable for fashioning the sorry creature the human animal is. The determinism of environment is particularly noticeable in *The Innocents Abroad*. The reader must be warned, however, that Mark Twain was never a determinist in the scientific sense of the term. The rage which filled him as the "mangy human race" passed in review before him usually prevented him from attaining the point of view of the true determinist, objective, calm, and detached. In the crooked little streets of the Faubourg St. Antoine, "they will murder a man for seven dollars and dump his body in the Seine. . . . they take . . . genuine pleasure . . . in cutting a throat or shoving a friend into the Seine." Such passages, predicting human behavior in terms of environment, emerge from that side of Mark Twain's mind which was tinged with the deterministic outlook. It was in the sordid side of existence that he was best able to display the operation of external forces upon mankind. Determinism of this sort is implicit in many passages of *The Innocents Abroad*. In Constantinople a father will recommend his son to a prospective employer as a deft cheater and a gifted liar; at Tangier the swarthy Riffs from the mountains are all "born cutthroats." Greeks, Turks, and Armenians are drawn toward lying and cheating by nature, "and then they go on and improve on nature until they arrive at perfection." At Magdala the entire population are abject beggars "by nature, instinct, and education." And the nomadic instinct, born with Adam, has proved so strong within the human race that "after thirty centuries of steady effort, civilization has not educated it . . . out of us yet."

Mark Twain's contention in *What Is Man?* that the human race is "moved, directed, COMMANDED, by exterior influences solely" is illustrated as early as 1877 by his words concerning a remarkable boy he met on his "Idle Excursion" to Bermuda. He said of the little white waiter at the hotel: "there is the making of a mighty man or a mighty rascal in this boy—according to circumstances." If his surroundings are conducive to virtue, a man will behave himself; change his surroundings, and his behavior will alter. All of this Mark Twain summed up neatly in the aphorism, "Prosperity is the best protector of principle."

But other passages, such as his statement that "the average human being is a perverse creature," reveal his belief in the innate perversity of the human race, beyond the mere force of circumstance.

This innate perversity sometimes manifests itself in curious religious forms. It furnished the groundwork for the Trappist Order to build upon in the large monastery near Durban, discussed in *Following the Equator*. The life there was a revelation of what mankind can endure: the rough work, the impossible hours, the scant food, the hard beds, the taboos of speech and relaxation and the presence of women. It was incredible, this suppression of human instincts, this extinction of the man as individual:

La Trappe must have known . . . the human race better than it knew itself. He set his foot upon every desire that a man has—yet he floated his project. . . . But La Trappe knew the race. He knew the powerful attraction of unattractiveness. . . .

Mark Twain himself had often felt the fascination of the unattractive, as will appear later.

Brown-skinned races, too, he believed, have their innate perversities. As a cloud of Indian crows will peck a sick vulture to death, so the natives of India will attack a fallen man. All the sycophants who have offered to lie for him, even kill for him, will turn against him the moment he loses his power, in "niceties of so subtle and delicate a sort that they lift . . . rascality to a place among the fine arts." He found India a strange and sinister land. There he heard of the killing of a young girl by a young man, aided by an old woman and two other men, for the sake of her worthless ornaments. The thing could have been done elsewhere, but not with "the cold business-like depravity, absence of fear, absence of caution, destitution of the sense of horror, repentance, remorse," that stamped it in India. This murder made the institution of Thuggee at last believable. Mark Twain treated Thuggee at length—Thuggee, that sect sworn to waylay and murder travelers "for the glory and contentment of the goddess Bhowanee." He based his discussion of Thuggee on the desire to kill, as a fundamental element of human nature. Sportsmen pit their skill against that of a tiger, or a poor trembling rabbit. How much higher game is the Thug's; he pits his skill against that of creatures of his own kind:

The joy of killing! the joy of seeing killing done—these are traits of the human race at large. We White people are merely modified Thugs;

Thugs fretting under the restraint of a not very thick skin of civilization.

By showing the depth at which such characteristics are embedded in human nature, Mark Twain sought to prove his theory that the innate depravity of the human race cannot be refined away. Human nature he viewed as largely of one pattern. Some of the English convicts sent to settle Tasmania had been "very bad people, even for that day"; still most of them were probably "not noticeably worse than the average of the people they left ... at home." And he molded into an aphorism his belief that every man recognizes within himself this innate depravity: "When people do not respect us we are sharply offended; yet deep down in his private heart, no man much respects himself."

This same aphorism, however, records simultaneously the power of the interior voice, the judge within man holding him to a strict accounting, never letting him off, a judge unaffected by the force of external circumstances. The power of that internal judge is reflected also in the statement that "we can secure other people's approval, if we do right and try hard; but our own is worth a hundred of it, and no way has been found out of securing that." Such lines express the basic conflict in Mark Twain which underlies so much of his fiction —a conflict between his deterministic contention that man is moved by exterior influences only and his moralistic belief in the power of the inward voice of conscience.

On the side of the latter belief belongs another passage from *Following the Equator* in which he recognized an innate self-respect, in contrast to the sense of innate depravity which he generally emphasized. This passage mentions a certain "holy feeling" inside a man, which may be equated with religion and yet is not the same as religion. For practical uses, this feeling may be called "modesty":

Without doubt modesty is nothing less than a holy feeling; and without doubt the person whose rule of modesty has been transgressed feels the same sort of wound that he would feel if something made holy to him by his religion had suffered a desecration.

But it is the depravity, the perversity, the pettiness, the cruelty of mankind that Mark Twain emphasizes most.

He often saw Nature as aligned against man in an interminable struggle, signs of which are found everywhere. Nature has awarded man no lavish generosities: "she has cut him off with the mere odds and ends of creation." Only one-fifth of the world's area is suited to his enterprises; yet man, in his characteristic simplicity and complacency, thinks Nature regards him as the favorite member of her family. "Surely, it must ocur to even his dull head, sometimes, that she has a curious way of showing it." But it would be difficult to show just which branch of Nature's family is her "favorite"; for, according to Mark Twain, the dark malignancy of Nature extends also to the helpless animals and insects:

Nature cakes a fish's eyes over with parasites, so that it shan't be able to avoid its enemies or find its food. She sends parasites into a starfish's system, which clog up its prongs and swell them and make them . . . uncomfortable.

I have mentioned his example of the lignified caterpillar and the malign intent of Nature toward the caterpillar when she set a death-trap for him while he was carrying out the laws inflicted upon him by Nature herself. Thus malevolence hides at Nature's dark heart.

Mark Twain's determinism acted as a strong reinforcement for his pessimism. The sensitivity of his nature also acted on his pessimism, precipitating intense reactions to what went on around him. Especially receptive to the beauties of nature, he fell an immediate victim to the charm of the natural setting in the Sandwich Islands. One island letter, written from a veranda shaded by great dark trees, records a mood: "If I were not so fond of looking into the rich masses of green leaves that swathe the stately tamarind right before my door, I would idle less and write more, I think." He described the blossoms of the ohia tree as having a color "so vivid as to be almost painful to the eye." But, for all his responsiveness to the beauty open to the eye, the ear was his most receptive organ. His sense of sound was as delicately attuned, perhaps, as that of Poe, although he never made Poe's claim to the ability to "hear" colors. His sensitive ear was a most valuable asset, but he paid a price for his gift by suffering frequently because of it. One Sandwich Islands letter breaks off suddenly: "I shall have to stop at this point and finish . . . tomorrow." For some "villain over the way" was playing "Get Out of the Wilderness" on a flute and skipping "the first note in the second bar

—skipping it so uniformly that I have got to waiting and painfully looking out for it. . . . Human nature cannot stand this sort of torture." Mark Twain's nature could not, at any rate.

The coarsenesses which obtruded themselves into his consciousness in the islands were revolting in contrast to his idyllic surroundings. In proportion to the degree of his revulsion is his emphasis: he dragged out into the open, as I have said before, the things he apparently found most revolting. His general earthiness, his delight in ribaldry, and his resentment against excessive gentility—these things add to the effectiveness of his writing. But many of his coarse passages are weak art because their effects may be equated with those of his moralizing strain: both reflect the extremes that held him back from achieving a perspective. His obsession with the object prevented him from placing it successfully in its literary framework. This is true of the passages concerned with the native fashion of eating poi from the communal bowl, the delicate subject of vomiting, and the humor of offensive smells.

Impatience and rage, as well as coarseness, deface many lines in the travel books. The violence of his reaction is frequently out of all proportion to the impetus involved. In one Sandwich Islands passage he fervently curses the saddle—"one might as well sit in a shovel"; the stirrups are only ornamental nuisances which fill him with nervous dread that they may slip: "But the subject is too exasperating to write about." In *Travels with Mr. Brown*, he tells of being annoyed in New York by an "irruption of blind people" that infested the streets for three days:

Blind people led by a friend; blind people led by dogs; blind people who felt their way with a stick; blind people who sat on doorsteps with horrid poetry labelled on their hats and a tin cup alongside with a penny nest-egg in it; blind men who tortured charity from foot passengers by grinding dismal music out of a thing like a mud turtle. . . . Everybody who had a blind friend borrowed him and trotted him out. It was a short-lived excitement, but it was fine while it lasted.

Here Mark Twain's shrinking from the horror of blindness brought a repulsion for these people, a repulsion that held in abeyance his usual sympathy for human suffering. The lines are marked far more by rage against these blind ones than by pity for or sympathy with their misfortunes.

In a chilly railway coach on a cold night, the train moved slowly:

... every time we stopped I cursed the railroad and that afforded me some little satisfaction. . . . I wished the Company would burst up so completely that there wouldn't be money enough left to give the Directors Christian burial, but I hoped they might need it shortly.

He grew tired of the same old question each time he visited a city: "How do you like San Francisco?—How do you like New York?" A man who has lived a long life and has been around a good deal, he reasoned, will probably meet twenty or thirty thousand acquaintances in the hereafter and will be bored "with that same wretched old question of 'how you like it.' . . . The subject distresses me beyond measure. . . . However, when one is tired hating anything he can always go to bed. I will." And there is no dependence to be put in waiters, or in the New York weather: "These things aggravate me beyond measure, sometimes." Cars and carriages always come along and get in the way just as one wants to cross a New York street; and that is the thing that "makes a man soar into flights of sublimity in . . . profanity. . . . There is one thing very sure—I can't keep my temper in New York." But the most annoying thing of all is to try to find a house number; the numbers do not follow any regular order, and always comes "that unaccountable jump": "You do not swear any more, now . . . because you can't find any words. . . . You feel degraded and ignominious and subjugated. . . . Then you wish you had never been born, to . . . suffer in this way."

Thus rage, impatience with mankind, and a spleen out of all proportion to the issue involved are regular features of the travel books. Although such passages are certainly exaggerated for humorous effect, there are far too many of them in Mark Twain's work to make them justifiable as mere humor. Their great number forbids explaining them by merely referring them to the technique of the humorist; they do, however, have a relationship to aesthetic principles. There is a raw and throbbing pain running through them which belies their apparent triviality and ties them up with the deeper levels of the writer's essential attitude towards life. In fact, their continued appearance indicates his failure to win to that partial victory over life, or at least temporary truce with it, which is the final effect of great humor. As we read such passages, we are reminded that the artist must possess the maximum of sensibility and feeling—and this Mark Twain unquestionably has; but the true artist must possess also the maximum of what we commonly think of as serenity, and here Mark Twain is woefully lacking.

This conception of the balance between sensibility and serenity has been subscribed to by various critics and authors, from William Wordsworth to Benedetto Croce. The sensibility relates to the rich material which the artist absorbs into his being; the serenity, to the form with which he subdues and dominates the tumult of the sensations and emotions. Because of his failure to achieve a detachment from the pettinesses with which life afflicts all men, Mark Twain was frequently unable to carry through the process of selection, simplification, and abstraction from the raw material of life—a process somehow required for the production of art. This, it seems to me, is a truer explanation of his failure to achieve adequate form than is his early addiction to the modes of the frontier anecdote.

The Innocents Abroad exhibits the same impatience which had earlier flared in the Sandwich Islands letters and in *Travels with Mr. Brown*. At Constantinople the boating "is calculated to drive an impatient man mad in a week. The boatmen are the awkwardest, the stupidest, and the most unscientific on earth, without question." At Jerusalem, Mark Twain visited the Fountain of the Virgin: "But the water was not good, and there was no comfort or peace anywhere, on account of the regiment of . . . beggars that persecuted us all the time for bucksheesh." The guide suggested that the Americans should give the beggars some money as alms, and they complied:

. . . but when he went on to say that they were starving to death, we could not but feel that we had done a great sin in throwing obstacles in the way of such a desirable consummation.

Doubtless the guide spoke truly of these people; but Mark Twain's irritation at their clamor for "bucksheesh" drove out of him all his humanitarian feeling, all his pity for their distress. At Annunciation, too, the people came crowding around and charged two cents for everything—opening a carriage door, bowing "with a lickspittle smirk," informing the tourists that it was a warm day: "They crowd you—infest you—swarm about you, and sweat and smell offensively, and look sneaking and mean and obsequious."

The pain that human beings inflict on each other was always sure to evoke from him a mixture of rage and pity. He found that the Moors have a "persuasive punishment" for a cattle thief; they cut off his right hand and his left leg. "Their surgery is not artistic. They slice around the bone a little; then break off the limb." But the cruelest pain of all, Mark Twain considered, is the needless pain we see around us every day, cruelest because there is no reason for it. An example of this sort was the pain inflicted in the theater of San Carlo upon an old woman who had once been a great actress and singer. A large crowd enthusiastically encored the old singer at the close of each song and then received her with hisses when she reappeared. "It was the cruelest exhibition—the most wanton. . . . What traits of character must a man have to enable him to help three thousand miscreants to hiss, and jeer, and laugh at one friendless old woman. . . . ? He must have *all* the vile, mean traits there are." Here Mark Twain obviously felt both pity and rage—pity for the old singer and rage at her tormentors.

In some curious passages, however, pity and rage are manifested simultaneously towards the same persons. At what he called the "Balaam's Ass Fountain" of Figia, there was enacted a scene recorded in his *Notebook*:

Wretched nest of human vermin about the fountain—rags, dirt, sunken cheeks . . . sores, projecting bones, dull, aching misery in their eyes and ravenous hunger speaking from every eloquent fiber and muscle from head to foot. How they sprang upon a bone, how they crunched the bread we gave them! Such as these to swarm about one and watch every bite he takes . . . and swallow unconsciously every time he swallows . . . hurry up the caravan!—I shall never enjoy a meal in this distressful country . . . it is worse punishment than riding all day in the sun.

A sense of guilt seems to invade the emotion of pity in such passages as this; guilt, perhaps, that one is part of a world in which such things are permitted. Modern psychiatrists may be right in holding that there is a tinge of guilt on every emotion of pity. Specifically, Mark Twain perhaps felt guilt that he was able to eat at all under such circumstances, and the guilt in him gave rise to the emotion of rage. His rage colored his view of these people until he described them in terms befitting animals: "How they sprang upon a bone, how they crunched the bread!" In the "execrable village" of Banias, a similar group of squalid humanity gathered about at the breakfast hour and "waited for such crumbs as pity might bestow" upon them:

They had but little clothing, but . . . any little absurd gewgaw or gim-crack they had they disposed in such a way as to make it attract attention. . . . They sat in silence, and with tireless patience watched our every motion with that vile, uncomplaining impoliteness . . . which makes a white man so nervous and uncomfortable and savage that he wants to exterminate the whole tribe.

Here, the very fact that the wretched natives are patient and uncomplaining adds to their "vileness." Mark Twain's comment on the way they had arranged their absurd little ornaments shows that their childlike simplicity had gone to his heart. But the demands they made upon his pity aroused his resentment as well, because of his suffering, because his response to them was so much in extremes. As a result, he sat there and grew so "savage" that he longed to exterminate them. But there seemed nothing to be done about their condition, and the emotion which they had aroused he spewed out in futile rage. His sense of being responsible in some way for all his fellow beings lies at the bottom of such passages as these, just as it lies at the bottom of his reforming and moralizing passages. It is his knowledge that there is little to be done for the world's unfortunates that gives to the thought of Mark Twain the final tinge of pessimism and at the same time prevents his attainment of the serenity and detachment necessary for the best literary handling of such material.

As early as 1866 in his New York letters, a mood of restlessness is sometimes exhibited which differs in tone from his customary impatience and rage. It is more philosophic in its efforts to analyze causes, but it arrives at no satisfactory conclusion:

There is something about this ceaseless buzz, and hurry, and bustle that keeps a stranger in a state of unwholesome excitement all the time, and makes him restless and uneasy, and saps from him all capacity to enjoy anything . . . a something which impels him to try to do everything, and yet permits him to do nothing.

There are so many attractions offered that the New York visitor is like a boy in a candy shop: he "starts to a library; changes and moves towards a theater; changes again and thinks he will visit a friend;

goes within a biscuit-toss of a picture-gallery . . . and finally drifts home without having really done anything or gone anywhere. . . . This fidgety, feverish restlessness will drive a man crazy, after a while, or kill him. . . . I have got to get out of it."

He takes note of the "serene indifference" of the average New Yorker to everything outside the pale of his private circle, concluding that New York is "a splendid desert—a domed and steepled solitude, where the stranger is lonely in the midst of a million of his race." But at any rate, he has "done" the city: he has attended horse races, billiard tournaments, and Sunday schools; he has visited the "dens of poverty, crime, and degradation that hide . . . in the Five Points and infinitely worse localities," but he blushingly declines to describe them. He has gone the rounds of newspaper offices and theaters; he has seen Brooklyn and the ferryboats and Staten Island and the bootblacks:

. . . I have been in the Bible House, and also in the Station House—pleasant experiences of a day, but nothing worth for a second visit; . . . I have . . . contrasted the feverish turmoil of Broadway with the still repose of Greenwood Cemetery; . . . and behold I . . . did contract to go up in a balloon, but the balloon didn't go. I have seen all there was to see—even the "Black Crook"—and yet, I say it . . . all is vanity! There has been a sense of something lacking, something wanting, every time—and I guess that something was the provincial quietness I am used to.

But the solution was not quite so simple. For wherever Mark Twain went about the world, there was always that sense of "something lacking," a quest for something that he never quite attained. Such passages show that in 1866 in the *Travels with Mr. Brown* he was already traveling the road of disillusionment that was to lead to what we now think of as "the modern temper"—the probing of the individual's ethical place in the world, of man's place in nature. Undazzled by New York's brilliance, he found it only "a splendid desert," where people rushed madly about or drifted aimlessly, sought desperately to gratify superheated desires or were so listless that they had no desires to gratify.

On his *Innocents Abroad* journey, coming along near the ruins of Ain Mellehah, over hot and dusty Roman-built roads, he fell to brooding on human destiny, while the gray lizards glided among the rocks or lay and sunned themselves:

Where prosperity has reigned and fallen; where glory has flamed and gone out; where beauty has dwelt and passed away; where gladness was and sorrow is; where the pomp of life has been, and silence and death brood in its high places, there this reptile makes his home and mocks at human vanity. His coat is the color of aspirations that came to naught, of lives that are buried. If he could speak, he would say, Build temples: I will lord it in their ruins; build palaces: I will inhabit them; erect empires: I will inherit them; bury your beautiful: I will watch the worms at their work; and you, who stand here and moralize over me: I will crawl over your corpse at the last.

This dusty rhetoric is reminiscent of the copybook; but these are gruesome words to be written by a young man recording what purports to be a pleasure trip. The passage ends, as many Mark Twain passages end, in thoughts of death and corpses.

His preoccupation with death is in evidence as early as the Sandwich Islands letters, where figures of speech associated with death abound. In a description of gala Honolulu on Saturday afternoon there enters a heathen from the South Seas, "tattooed till he looks like the customary unfortunate from Reese River who has been blown up in a mine." Minister Harris, the island politician, had a "long, cadaverous countenance" upon which an attempted smile was "as shocking as a facetious leer on the face of a corpse." The tiny cabin on the *Boomerang* was "rather larger than a hearse," while its two bunks were like two coffins. Describing the beauty of the coffin of the dead Hawaiian princess, Mark Twain wrote: "It produces a sort of ecstasy in me to look at it, and holds me like a mesmeric fascination." A part of that fascination lay in his appreciation for the beauty of the woods employed; but a part was derived from his reflections on the final use for this beauty. The preoccupation with death was here intensified, perhaps, by the inevitable contrast between the transiency and seeming triviality of human life and the perpetual loveliness of nature in this beflowered land.

The sight and the stench and the horror of death pervade, too, the *Travels with Mr. Brown*. On a night railway journey Mark Twain noticed how dismal the passengers looked, "doubled up in uncomfortable attitudes . . . in the dim, funeral light—like so many corpses . . . of people who had died of care and weariness." In *The Innocents Abroad*, imagery drawn from the realms of death underlies his accounts of contact with life. The dreary bedrooms of Europe were "tomblike"; the romantic gondola of Venice was a "hearse"; and the *Quaker City* excursion itself was a "Grand Holy Land Funeral Procession"—without a corpse. The horrors of the Capuchin Convent are painted in detail: underground vaults decorated with human bones—grinning skulls, knotted vertebrae, elaborate designs formed of kneecaps and toenails. A dried-up monk lay in an alcove; two lusterless tufts of hair stuck to the skull; "the crisp dead eyes were deep in the sockets . . . the lips had shriveled away from the yellow teeth; and brought down . . . through the circling years and petrified there was a weird laugh—the most dreadful that one can imagine."

From such permanent ghastliness, overthrowing life itself, Mark Twain turned again to the small, fleering annoyances which pass with the day and yet destroy the beauty of the day. At a street-side lunchroom in Naples, the cook took a roll of sausage meat, dropped it in the dirt, picked it up, polished it on his trousers, spat on his hands, and began to apportion the meat into cakes. With one accord, the Americans "all passed out." Other coarsenesses and vulgarities appear, as in Mark Twain's account of his Turkish bath.

Death-imagery is everywhere in *A Tramp Abroad*. Nicodemus Dodge came back to life from the "deep grave" of Mark Twain's memory, where he had lain "buried and forgotten" for twenty-five years. Whenever Mark Twain saw a pile of gravel near a German railway station, it was always "heaped as trimly . . . as a new grave." The invalids staying at Interlaken he spoke of facetiously as "departed spirits . . . preserved from decomposition" by their pet diets. A moraine looked like an endless grave of fine sand; a Swiss woman's huge feet, propped upon a seat in a train, he described as "coffin-clad" and again as "undertaker furniture"; the miniature theater of a Punch and Judy show resembled "a man's coffin stood on end"; the old-fashioned towing industry was then "on its death-bed." A scholar who must part with his beloved library at auction would spend the night before the sale "sitting before his books as one who watches by his beloved dead and prints the features on his memory for a solace in the aftertime of empty desolation."

The death-parade continues through the pages of *Following the Equator*. A man in the train had "teeth which made his mouth look like a neglected churchyard"; at Darjeeling the cabs were "open coffins, in which you sit"; the city of Adelaide had languished in a "death-trance" for two years; then "came the resurrection . . . and the corpse got up and walked." Driving towards a Hindu betrothal ceremony at midnight, he could imagine that he was passing through a city of the dead: the streets were still; native sleepers lay about on the ground, wrapped in blankets; their attitude and their rigidity counterfeited death; on each side were small open booths counterfeiting sepulchers; "with counterfeit corpses motionless in the flicker of the counterfeit deathlamps," the whole scene resembled a "death-watch."

Many of his lines are rank and bitter with pessimism. Early in *Following the Equator,* he told how eagerly he had watched the vast outline of Diamond Head near Honolulu from the deck of a ship anchored offshore, impatient for the morning to come so that he could land. When the morning came, "it brought disappointment, of course"; there was cholera in Honolulu, and the passengers were not allowed to go ashore. "Thus suddenly did my dream of twenty-nine years go to ruin," the dream of revisiting the Sandwich Islands which he had loved so much. But the use of the phrase "of course" reveals the pessimist.

Dark things hide at the heart of nature and sometimes show themselves, to the dismay of mankind. He learned of a leper colony on the island of Molokai; and he felt the "great pity of it all" that the leprosy did not come of sins these lepers had committed, but of sins "committed by their ancestors, who *escaped* the curse of leprosy!" One would not expect to find in such a place a custom worthy of being borrowed, but this leper settlement had one, and he found it "inexpressibly . . . beautiful. When death sets open the prison door of life there, the band salutes the freed soul with a burst of glad music!"

"When death sets open the prison door of life"— There, I believe, is the secret of Mark Twain's preoccupation with death. The moralist within him grew angry with men who were not what they should be; the determinist within him grew angry with forces that made it impossible for men to be what they should be. Rage at the "damned human race" flared at sight of the meannesses, the inexplicable perversities exhibited by that race. Pity for the weak, the sick, and the poor welled within him, pity intensified by his sensibility until extreme pity became itself a sort of rage. Pity and rage thus wrestled for his spirit. Through them, the sensitivity of the artist possessed him; because of them, the serenity of the artist eluded him. But always, through his tragic bewilderment, he held somehow to the idea of death as the final release. One of his maxims maintains that "each person is born to one possession which outvalues all his others—his last breath." And another maxim stands as the condensation of all his endless reflections: "Pity is for the living; envy is for the dead."

When the extremity of his feeling did not rouse him to rage, it sometimes carried him over into the excessive sentimentality which I call patheticism. The humanitarian Mark Twain visited the blind asylum in New York and, after one look, refrained from looking directly at its inmates. "Their dreadful eyes shock [one] once, and after that he looks . . . no more." He was surprised at their ability and cheerfulness, but he called Nature to account for so sorely afflicting them and making them fearfully homely besides, a thing which "the sex hold in proper horror." In *Travels with Mr. Brown* he recorded:

It was the saddest place I ever got into. . . . I felt so sorry for those girls. They could not see the sun, or the moon, or the ocean, the green trees, or the flowers, the gilded clouds or the rainbow—they could not even see the faces they loved. It were better to be dead and buried.

This passage places the overemphasis of patheticism upon the fate of the girls. They were young, presumably healthy, and shared each other's misfortune. They might enjoy music, friendship, or even a good joke. While he was present, they were talking and knitting and "seemed perfectly jolly and contented." Yet to Mark Twain, the perfectionist, "it were better to be dead and buried" than to live life on these terms. He saw the blindness only, disregarding many sources of enjoyment open to the girls; and the overwriting makes the passage fall short of its mark.

During the single night he spent in the station house, the house guests included "two flash girls" of sixteen and seventeen, arrested "for stopping gentlemen in the street in pursuance of their profession." They both cried—not because they were ashamed of being arrested, but because they dreaded the discomforts of jail. "I felt sorry for those poor girls," he wrote, "and thought it was a pity that the merciful snow had not frozen them into a peaceful rest and forgetfulness of life and its weary troubles." Thus it becomes a matter of record that to him theirs actually was a fate worse than death. His view of life, in that early year of 1867, took no account of the human spirit which holds to life tenaciously as a thing to be treasured, precious in the mere fact of living, of being alive.

Certain passages show a lugubrious reveling in the grisly details of misfortune which is the essence of patheticism. In *A Tramp Abroad* he inventoried the items of ghastly human debris yielded up by an Alpine glacier: portions of three human skulls; a human jaw, with fine white teeth; a hand, with the fingers intact, the ring finger still showing a stain of blood; a left foot, the flesh white and fresh. A hoary-haired Mont Blanc guide suddenly cried out, "This is Balmat's hand, I remember it so well!" The guide bent down, kissed the hand reverently, and then clasped his own hand about it in farewell. To Mark Twain, there was "something weirdly pathetic about the picture of that white-haired veteran greeting with his loving hand-shake this friend who had been dead forty years":

When these hands had met last, they were alike in the softness and freshness of youth; now, one was brown and wrinkled and horny with age, while the other was still as young and fair and blemishless as if those forty years had come and gone in a single moment.

The same sort of gruesome relish occurs in a passage which draws out the "sharpest pang" connected with the story of eleven persons who perished in a blizzard on Mont Blanc. They had wandered about, blinded by the snowstorm, until fatigue vanquished them and they lay down "to die by inches, *unaware that five steps more would have brought them into the true path*. They were so near to life and safety as that."[1] An accusation of the injustice of fate, of the malevolence of the Supreme Powers, is implicit in his statement that here the rule failed which ordinarily assures swift death to the victims of the Alps. And it should be noted that this book was not written in his later years; it was written in 1878.

As early as *The Innocents Abroad*, patheticism appears as a blemish in his description of an ancient tear-jug found at Pisa, a vessel fashioned "to receive the tears wept for some lost idol of a household":

[1] The italics are Mark Twain's.

It spoke to us . . . with a pathos . . . with its tale of a vacant chair, a familiar footstep missed from the threshold, a pleasant voice gone . . . a vanished
form! a tale which is always so new to us, so startling, so terrible, so be-
numbing to the senses, and behold how . . . old it is! No shrewdly worded
history could have brought the myths and shadows of that old dreamy
age before us clothed with human flesh and warmed with human sympathies so vividly as did this poor little unsentient vessel of pottery.

This is the sort of nineteenth-century "gush" that Mark Twain himself mercilessly caricatured on occasion, but nothing in this passage
or its context smacks of burlesque. Reading it over when it got cold,
however, he must have recognized its excessive sentimentality; for
later in *A Tramp Abroad* he headed a chapter written in burlesque
vein as "My Precious, Priceless Tear-jug," labeled himself as a devotee of "brick-a-brackery" and a "true ceramiker" and declared:
"I am proud to know that I lose my reason as immediately in the
presence of a rare jug . . . as if I had just emptied the jug." Nevertheless, fresh patheticism invades the later book in the passages on the
glacier and the blizzard, both of which he represents as unfair vic-
tories of Nature over man.

In *Following the Equator*, he injected the same sort of patheticism into his serious account of the wreck of the *Duncan Dunbar*, a
ship bringing back to Sydney a group of wives and daughters who
had been visiting in England. Anxious hearts at home were count-
ing the hours; those on board the ship were expecting soon to be in
the arms of loved ones: "they put away their sea-going clothes and
put on clothes meeter for the meeting . . . their loveliest, these poor
brides of the grave." He labored the fact that the *Duncan Dunbar*
went down "in sight of home." This book, of course, was written
after the tragic death of his daughter Susy; but passages from earlier
books have the same tenor. The unpleasant effect of the phrase
"meeter for the meeting" indicates the kind of stylistic error Mark
Twain scrupulously avoided when he was not temporarily spellbound by his own sentimental rhetoric.

One of the most ironic things about life is that it is often our
good intentions that bring us to disaster. Mark Twain was sure it
was the sympathy felt by the captain of the *Duncan Dunbar* for the
homesick eagerness of his women passengers which led him to try
in the dark the dangerous entry of Sydney Harbor. Result—the loss

of his own life and all lives on board. And when the dice are loaded so that a man's human sympathies bring only disaster and death, what chance has the "damned human race"? Thus Mark Twain's pessimism was reinforced not only by his determinism, but by his patheticism as well.

CHAPTER 12

Ugliness as Reality, Beauty as Dream

IN recent years criticism has lightly by-passed Mark Twain's travel books. Mr. DeVoto makes brief mention of his "set pieces of description," finding in them only the aftermath of his reading in the McGuffey series. But it is in the travel books particularly that Mark Twain's thought-patterns and mind-sets are revealed; for that reason, if no other, these books become required reading for anyone who seeks to understand him.

On his Nicaraguan journey of 1866 the touring party took the route to Virgin Bay. The first thing the ladies noticed was a "dear, dear little baby—oh, see the darling!" Mark Twain looked, but what he saw was only a "vile, distempered, mud-colored native brat, making dirt-pies in front of an isolated cabin." As his travels took him back and forth across the face of the earth, the spectacle of life was constantly presented to his gaze; but the passages in his work which deal with humanity en masse generally reflect a strong distaste. Again and again he laid his emphasis on life's ugliness.

In the Faubourg St. Antoine the visitor sees little narrow streets lined with dirty children, greasy women, and filthy dens housing rag stores. Up most of these streets live the *lorettes* of Paris. Any Syrian village is a hive of mudhuts the height of a man. If one rides through it at noonday, he will first meet a melancholy dog; then a naked boy who begs for bucksheesh; then a woman with her face heavily veiled and her bust completely exposed; finally he will come to "sore-eyed children . . . in all stages of mutilation and decay; and sitting humbly in the dust, and all fringed with filthy rags, is a poor devil whose arms and legs are gnarled and twisted like grape vines." Civita Vecchia is the "finest nest of dirt, vermin, and ignorance," with its alleys "carpeted with deceased cats and decayed rags . . . soaked in dishwater, and the people sit around on stools and enjoy it."

In Magdala the streets reeked with uncleanliness, the houses were graced with "spirited Syrian frescoes of camel dung," and vermin-tortured vagabonds infested the place, swarming about the visitors: "How they showed their scars and sores, and piteously pointed to their maimed and crooked limbs, and begged. . . . we paid the bucksheesh out to sore-eyed children and brown, buxom girls with repulsively tattooed lips and chins." In Jerusalem, Mark Twain found "rags, wretchedness, poverty, and dirt. . . . Lepers, cripples, the blind, and the idiotic assail you on every hand." One cannot know the horror of leprosy until he has looked upon it in Damascus: "Bones all twisted out of shape, great knots protruding from face and body, joints decaying and dropping away—horrible!"

Leaving Milan by rail, he noted that the scenery consisted of "fields and farmhouses outside the car and a monster-headed dwarf and a mustached woman inside it"—not show people, for "deformity and female beards are too common in Italy to attract attention." If one wants a few dwarfs as a curiosity, he should go to Genoa; if he wishes dwarfs "by the gross," he should go to Milan; but if he would see "the very heart and home of cripples and human monsters," he must go to Constantinople:

A beggar in Naples who can show a foot which has all run into one horrible toe, with one shapeless nail on it, has a fortune—but such an exhibition . . . would not provoke any notice in Constantinople . . . among the rare monsters that throng the bridges of the Golden Horn. . . . How could he stand against the three-legged woman, and the man with his eye in his cheek? . . . Where would he hide himself when the dwarf with . . . no upper lip and his under-jaw gone, came down in his majesty? . . . The truly gifted flourish only in the byways of Pera and Stamboul.

That three-legged woman lay on the bridge, with her stock in trade so disposed as to command the most striking effect. . . . there was a man further along who had no eyes, and whose face was the color of a fly-blown beefsteak, and wrinkled and twisted like a lava-flow. . . . In Stamboul was a man with a prodigious head . . . legs eight inches long, and feet like snow-shoes. He traveled on those feet and his hands. . . . Ah, a begger has to have exceedingly good points to make a living in Constantinople.

There is no moralizing here, no pity offered. Mark Twain has chosen and presented all this ugliness as a part of the spectacle of life; but,

since the response it elicits is negative rather than positive, in presenting it he is once more engaging in what is in essence a moralistic
rather than an aesthetic activity. For, although the ugliness portrayed
is not in itself the cause of any real pain in the observer, it produces
a shrinking so extreme as to be painful; and towards it the observer
assumes what amounts to a practical and moral attitude of avoidance.
Crime, idiocy, ugliness, and disease—all are elements which elicit
negative responses; and Mark Twain's obvious absorption with these
elements illustrates his failure to fit them back into their place in the
vast pattern and scheme of life. In brief, in such passages he sees life
steadily, but he fails to see it whole.

In the mosque of St. Sophia he noticed that the balustrades were
battered and dirty; the perspective was marred by a web of ropes
hanging down from the dome, and squatting about on all sides were
ragged Turks. Dirt, dust, dinginess, and gloom abounded: "everywhere were signs of a hoary antiquity, but with nothing touching or
beautiful about it." Here he concerned himself with surfaces only;
the passage conveys no sense of the contemplative mood which
might have found something beautiful in this ancient church.

In contrast appears another description, facetiously written, in
which his sense of humor came to his rescue. St. Mark's, too, he found
ugly; but he was reflective about that ugliness; he fitted it into his
scheme and pattern of the world; he adapted himself to it. Consequently, it held a charm for him. In the vicinity of St. Mark's, he had
a feeling of utter calm because he saw it as "a grand harmonious
whole of soothing, entrancing, soul-satisfying ugliness." To him,
St. Mark's was just about perfect:

To me it soon grew to be so nobly, so augustly ugly, that it was difficult
to stay away from it, even for a little while. Every time its squat domes
disappeared from my view, I had a despondent feeling; whenever they
reappeared, I felt an honest rapture.

Written humorously, the passage nevertheless illustrates the power
of humor as the great reconciler of man's difficulties, even as the
quality that best fits man to live in harmony with his surroundings.
But it was just this use of humor, as I have already said, of which
Mark Twain frequently could not avail himself.

Ordinarily, the fascination of the ugly impaled him like a moth on the point of a pin, where he squirmed in pain, unable to pull away. He underscored his desire to portray the ugliness of life in a passage objecting that the privileges of literature have been "sharply curtailed" in contrast to those allowed to art:

Fielding and Smollett could portray the beastliness of their day in the beastliest language; we have plenty of foul subjects to deal with in our day, but we are not allowed to approach them very near, even with . . . guarded forms of speech. But not so with Art. . . .

In every gallery in Europe there are hideous pictures of blood, carnage, oozing brains, putrefaction—pictures portraying intolerable suffering—pictures alive with every conceivable horror, wrought out in dreadful detail—and similar pictures are being put on the canvas every day. . . . But suppose a literary artist ventured to go into a painstaking and elaborate description of one of these grisly things—the critics would skin him alive. . . . Art retains her privileges, Literature has lost hers.

The power those hideous pictures exerted over him is revealed in the lines of his description. But he did contrive to present "grisly things" wrought out in dreadful detail, in spite of the critics. Visiting the morgue in Paris, he stood before a grating and looked into a room hung with water-soaked garments, "flecked and stained with red; a hat that was crushed and bloody"; and before him,

On a slanting stone lay a drowned man, naked, swollen, purple; clasping the fragment of a broken bush with a grip which death had . . . petrified. . . . A stream of water trickled ceaselessly over the hideous face. . . . We wondered if anybody could love that repulsive object or grieve for its loss. . . . wondered if, some forty years ago, when the mother of that ghastly thing was dangling it upon her knee, and kissing it and petting it and displaying it with satisfied pride to the passerby, a prophetic vision of this dread ending ever flitted through her brain.

Here is a spectacle of nature, if not of life; for death is natural. But Mark Twain failed to arrive at that contemplative mood of sadness and large peace which enfolds the aesthetic response to such an experience. Instead, the passage conveys a sense of repulsion, non acceptance—a wonder that such things can be and a horror at beholding them.

Dirt, deformity, moral decay, and death—these are the specters that lurk in the pages of Mark Twain's travel books. The degree of repulsion which he felt for horrible sights was matched by the degree of their fascination. "It is hard to forget repulsive things," he wrote. Within the Cathedral of Milan he saw a piece of sculpture from the hand of Phidias. He noted that the sculptor had copied nature with faultless accuracy. The passage appears in *The Innocents Abroad*:

The figure was that of a man without a skin; with every vein, artery, muscle, every fiber and tendon and tissue . . . represented. . . . It looked natural, because somehow it looked as if it were in pain. . . . It was a hideous thing, and yet there was a fascination about it somewhere. I am very sorry that I saw it, because I shall always see it now. . . . I shall dream that it is resting its corded arms on the bed's head and looking down on me with its dead eyes. I shall dream that it is stretched between the sheets with me and touching me with its exposed muscles and its stringy cold legs.

Again, it is surprising to have these lines from the pen of a young man fresh from triumphs in lecturing and writing, then on a pleasure excursion. The most striking sentence is the one which states, "It looked natural, because somehow it looked as if it were in pain." Pain—the lot of mankind; and here, as usual with Mark Twain, it is the ugliness of pain which he emphasizes, exhibiting no recognition of its inherent dignity. That dignity he would be able to glimpse briefly now and then; but its fullest realization would come to him many years later and a continent away from the place at which he stared at this hideous thing which looked natural to him only because "somehow it looked as if it were in pain." Pain and ugliness were to him, even this early, the realities of life.

At some points Mark Twain's thought coincides with the thought of writers we commonly call "romantic"; at others, he departs from them abruptly. To Rousseau, Nature was a benevolent guide and the source of genuine spirituality. His belief in the noble aspects of primitive life led him to the strange new doctrine that men are born good. Wordsworth, eagerly adopting Rousseau's beliefs in the uplifting power of Nature, the essential goodness of the human heart, and the contaminating influences of society, became the chief spokesman for those who held that man needs to live simply, close to the soil, communing directly with Nature. How far Mark Twain stood from such a doctrine will appear in the section dealing with his fiction, in a discussion of his treatment of rural and village life; how far he stood from belief in the essential goodness of human nature has already been demonstrated. To Robert Burns, singing the praises of rustic simplicity,

An honest man's the noblest work of God.

Mark Twain's objection would likely be the insurmountable difficulty of finding an honest man. The true romantic is carried away by a sense of wonder, by a zest for life. As Shelley expressed it,

The mystery and majesty of Earth.
The joy, the exultation . . . .

The man of romantic temper cries out for a world which he has not yet found, but which he feels to exist somewhere or at least to be possible. This bright new world he seeks first in revolt, in freedom; but finally in faith. In brief, the great romanticists, knowing that man lives by faith more than by reason, produced a literature of aspiration, of idealization, and of faith in the spirit and the essential dignity of mankind. It is in the matter of aspiration that Mark Twain departs farthest from what is commonly called romanticism. With a strong faith in the ultimate regeneration of mankind, Byron and Shelley urged a revolution to be brought about by love.[1] Mark Twain could rail against the existing order as rebelliously as they, but he lacked Byron's belief in the coming brotherhood of man and Shelley's belief in man's perfectibility.

He shared, however, in the dream aspect of the romantic temperament and in the view which glimpses beauty as the ideal, far off and forgot, remote in time or space or both. For Thomas Campbell,

'Tis distance lends enchantment to the view.

Mark Twain worked Campbell's line into his description of the Lake Como district in *The Innocents Abroad;* he had already succumbed to the magic of distance. For him, "a far countree" and "long, long ago" were always phrases of powerful appeal. He could shroud beauty in what E. C. Stedman called "the Tennysonian golden mist";

[1] I have derived this summary of romanticism from Addison Hibbard, ed., "The Romantics," *Writers of the Western World,* 391–402.

but, unlike Tennyson, he could rarely turn away from the dream beauty to find beauty close at hand. He could enjoy the picturesque aspects of Nature, her lakes, her mountains, and her rivers under moonlight; but to him Nature was frequently malign rather than benevolent. Mark Twain was an extreme manifestation of such romantic qualities as he possessed; but the true romantic temper, imbued with aspiration in spite of shunning the present actuality, is not merely escapist.

The pictorial aspect of the Sandwich Islands was one of their chief charms for him. Writing almost thirty years after his visit there, he recalled the memories his mind held of Hawaii and added: "And pictures—pictures—pictures—an enchanting procession of them!" His first view of Honolulu, described in *Letters from the Sandwich Islands,* was as a picture framed by mountain and sea. The striking feature of his description of a lone palm tree is its likeness to a picture, the palm seen rearing its graceful crest "as in an ebony frame," with its slender stem a clean, black line and its projecting fronds "all sharply cut against the smooth gray background." The complete effect is that of an etching. Leaving Kealakekua by schooner, he sailed all day along the shore, running parallel with a long mountain that rose from the sea and "slanted up . . . like a vast picture, framed in between ocean and clouds. It was marked and lined and tinted like a map." In the Sandwich Islands, he was already seeing natural beauties as pictures of themselves, as maplike reproductions.

Standing in an ancient temple built of rough blocks of lava, he thought

of fettered victims, writhing and shrieking under the knife; of . . . dusky forms straining forward out of the gloom, with eager and ferocious faces lit up with the weird light of sacrificial fires; of the vague background of ghostly trees; of the mournful sea washing the dim shore; of the dark pyramid of Diamond Head standing sentinel over the dismal scene, and the peaceful moon looking calmly down upon it through rifts in the drifting clouds!

How could that distant moon look so calmly down upon such scenes? Contrasts were everywhere in the islands, and not the least of these was the contrast between the loveliness of the land itself and the essential unloveliness of its people. The natives were an indolent lot. Such vitality as they exhibited consisted mainly of excessive sexual activity, of racing the mistreated horses, of pampering the disgusting pet dogs, and of swindling the unwary tourist. To turn away from all this ugliness to the beauty of the landscape must have given him a strange feeling that this beauty was unreal, an illusion of the mind and the eye. To think of these beautiful scenes as pictures, framed and hanging pictures, had the effect of setting them apart, perhaps, from the revolting aspects of island life. Certain passages carry the beautiful scenes even farther away from reality than the imagination achieves by viewing them as pictures; in these passages Mark Twain looked upon the landscape as scenes tinged with dream or as enchanted bits of fairyland. "How calmly the dim city sleeps yonder in the plain! How soft the shadows lie upon the stately mountains that border the dream-haunted Manoa Valley!"

The scenes which he set in fairyland savor more of magic, of unreality, than his dream descriptions. Sometimes he combined the fairyland element and the dream quality in a single description. On the ride to Kilauea, "Portions of that little journey bloomed with beauty. . . . The rich verdant hue of these fairy parks was relieved and varied by the splendid carmine tassels of the *ohia* tree. Nothing was lacking but the fairies themselves."

His mind had a primitive quality that would have distinguished him in the old myth-making days when men told tales of giants and of dwarfs. His imagination led him towards the magnification or diminution of objects, usually in some form of comparison. Mr. Brooks asserts that Mark Twain's imagination was "gigantesque" and that this "natural tendency towards a magnification or a minification of things human is one of the ear-marks of the satirist." He comments further that Mark Twain's eye, "in later life, was always looking through the small end or the large end of a telescope." His diminishing and magnifying of "things human," particularly as a device useful for the writing of fiction, was a later development; but the imaginative faculty itself was by no means confined to his later life. It appears as early as 1861, in a letter written home from Carson City. He described to his mother the flat, sandy desert in which Carson is situated and the mountains that surround it on all sides:

. . . such prodigious mountains that when you gaze at them awhile, and begin to conceive of their grandeur—and next to feel their vastness expanding your soul—and ultimately find yourself growing and swelling and spreading into a giant—I say when this point is reached, you look disdainfully down upon the insignificant village of Carson, and in that instant you are seized with a burning desire to stretch forth your hand, put the city in your pocket, and walk off with it.

The minification process enters one of the early Washoe sketches in a striking figure, presented earlier, which pictures the seals playing on the rocks as "writhing and squirming like exaggerated maggots."

Amid the passages describing the magical beauty of the Sandwich Islands, examples of his magnifying and diminishing powers appear constantly—evidence that his imagination was stirred to new vitality. In his description of Kilauea as seen from aloft by night, he pictured the floor of the crater as illuminated for more than a mile, with twinkling fires in remote corners seen through curtains of hanging mists. The effect was one of great distance, and Mark Twain imagined he was looking down on a continent:

Here was room for the imagination to work! You could imagine those lights the width of a continent away—and that hidden under the intervening darkness were hills, and winding rivers, and weary wastes of plain and desert—and even then the tremendous vista stretched on, and on, and on!

The crater floor is here magnified to the size of a continent; but in the next paragraph the imaginative process is reversed: diminution is applied and the same crater is likened to a map. Mark Twain observed that part of the vast floor was "ringed and streaked and striped with a thousand branching streams of liquid and gorgeously brilliant fire! It looked like a colossal railroad map of the State of Massachusetts done in chain lightning on a midnight sky." Among other early instances of diminution is a passage describing Hawaii as "a little land" which had "the complete machinery, in its minutest details, of a vast and imposing empire, done in miniature." Tall palms, topped with clusters of coconuts, reminded him of "colossal ragged parasols, with bunches of magnified grapes under them."

In the *Travels with Mr. Brown*, the strangeness of the Nicaraguan landscape stimulated his imagination, and his pen began to drop pictures. The unfamiliar scenes gave him a sense of unreality—unknown birds and flowers and trees; calabash trees with strange gourdlike fruit; queer knots on trees, said to be ants' nests; and, along the shore,

huge alligators lay and sunned themselves and slept; birds with gaudy feathers and villainous hooked bills . . . startled one suddenly out of his . . . dimly-defined notion that that sort of bird only lived in menageries; parrots flew by us—the idea of a parrot flying seemed funny enough— flying abroad, instead of swinging in a tin ring; and stooping and nipping that ring with its beak between its feet, and thus displaying itself in most unseemly attitude—flying, silently cleaving the air—and saying never a word!

Strangeness imbued the landscape, as well as the animal life of this queer land. Many scenes impressed Mark Twain with their pictorial effect. As the boat sped through an "unpeopled paradise," it seemed to him that an "exquisite panorama unfolded itself. . . . The changing vistas of the river ever renewed the intoxicating picture." Other Nicaraguan scenes share the dreamlike quality. But, contrasted with his "unpeopled paradise," he presents a "peopled paradise," the town of Greytown, which "does not amount to much. It is composed of two hundred old frame houses and some nice vacant lots. . . . The population is 800, and is mixed. . . . the cows march through the public thoroughfares with a freedom which pen cannot describe."

Years after this Nicaraguan journey, he wrote in his *Notebook* while traveling in India: "And this is India! Tropical, beautiful . . . 'Where every prospect pleases and only man is vile.' " Although he had not then endured the worst of his personal tragedies, he had lived through many disappointing experiences, the common lot of mankind. The passage in the preceding paragraph, however, the passage describing a beautiful scene as an "unpeopled paradise," was written on New Year's Day in 1867. From the beginning, most of Mark Twain's paradises were unpeopled. His descriptions of beauty are customarily reserved for nature, excluding humankind; his descriptions of ugliness customarily present humanity.

A painting by Albert Bierstadt, "The Domes of the Yosemite," may serve to illustrate a trend of thought in Mark Twain which can be traced in the Sandwich Islands letters and on through the later travel books—his tendency to prefer the picture or the dream to the reality. He found Bierstadt's canvas "considerably more beautiful

SAMUEL LANGHORNE CLEMENS
Engraved by Florian from a photograph by Falk and Company.
Sydney, October, 1895

From Harper's New Monthly Magazine, *May, 1896*

than the original"; for the "dreamy lights and shadows that play about . . . the great dome" were to him infinitely more lovely than "the bald, glaring expanse of rocks" which marks the actual scene. It was Mark Twain's practice to describe ugliness as if he stood close to it, his eye on the object, putting in minutely elaborated details, one after another; but beauty for him must be far off, vague, and indistinct. When he stood close to beauty, it became only sticks and stones; it lost its magic. His opinion that pictures are generally better than their originals was merely a minor expression of his general conception of beauty as unreal.

His reaction to Kilauea in the Sandwich Islands again shows his tendency to hold the picture, the dream, or the scene produced by the imagination as always better than the reality. Later in *The Innocents Abroad* he declared that "Oriental scenes look best in steel engravings"; and, reminded of the less-than-dainty Oriental women he had seen, he felt that one looking at the famous picture of the Queen of Sheba might well say, "You look fine, madam, but your feet are not clean, and you smell like a camel." His later acquaintance with Kilauea repaired the damage wrought to his imagined scene; but in *The Innocents Abroad* the injuries were permanent: the picture, the dream, and the image all continued to surpass the reality itself.

"See Naples and die." To see Naples in the early dawn from the heights of Vesuvius was to see "a picture of wonderful beauty." Distance made the dingy buildings look white; they piled themselves up from the blue ocean, rank on rank, till the castle of St. Elmo topped the white pyramid, giving the picture symmetry:

The frame of the picture was charming, itself. In front, the smooth sea— a vast mosaic of many colors; the lofty island swimming in a dreamy haze in the distance. . . . But do not go within the walls. . . . That takes away . . . the romance. The people are filthy in their habits, and this makes filthy streets . . . and disagreeable sights and smells.

Here, again, it is the people who destroy the beauty of the natural scene. And night is the only time to see Galilee. "Gennesaret under these lustrous stars has nothing repulsive about it" and "no boundaries but the heavens"; but in the broad light of day it is only a "little acre of rocks and sand." In the daytime the fetters of reality chain the spirit of man, and disillusionment is the result.

His impression of Venice, the City of the Sea, fluctuated between the city of dreams and the actuality. His first sight of it was of "towers and domes and steeples drowsing in a golden mist of sunset." But a closer view disclosed Venice sitting there "among her stagnant lagoons, forlorn and beggared," completely shorn of the glamour of old romance. The famed gondola and the gorgeous gondolier turned out to be a rusty old canoe and "a mangy, barefooted gutter-snipe" who propelled the thing through dismal ditches:

But I was too hasty.... under the mellow moonlight the Venice of poetry and romance stood revealed.... It was a beautiful picture—very soft and dreamy and beautiful.... In the glare of day, there is little poetry about Venice, but under the charitable moon her stained palaces are white again ... and ... her fourteen centuries of greatness fling their glories about her.

Mark Twain recalled a tale told of Mohammed: When the Prophet reached a high point near Damascus and looked down upon the city, it seemed to him an earthly paradise; he turned away without entering its gates, for he said man could enter but one paradise and he preferred the one above. Mark Twain agreed with Mohammed that

Damascus *is* beautiful from the mountain.... right in the midst of the desert is spread a billowy expanse of green foliage; and nestling in its heart sits the great white city, like an island of pearls and opals gleaming out of a sea of emeralds. This is the picture you see spread far below you, with distance to soften it ... and about it a drowsing air of repose to spiritualize it and make it seem rather a beautiful estray from the mysterious world we visit in dreams than a substantial tenant of our coarse, dull globe.... There is no need to go inside the walls.

For he knew that inside the walls the customary dirt and wickedness which defile every "peopled paradise" would only be repeated.

Nain, near Endor, with its community well drawing together groups of dusky Arabs, was "a grand Oriental picture" which he had admired "a thousand times in soft, rich steel engravings:"

But in the engraving there was no ... dirt; no rags; no fleas; ... no sore eyes; no feasting flies; no besotted ignorance in the countenances; ... no disagreeable jabbering ... no stench of camels; no suggestion that a couple of tons of powder placed under the party and touched off would heighten the effect and give to the scene a genuine interest and a charm which it would always be pleasant to recall.

Here a note of humor is injected into the familiar fretting tone of the writer's disappointment at finding what a reality is like. Is this a Mark Twain exulting in rending the veil of sham, as he is so frequently pictured? Or is it a Mark Twain standing aghast at what he has uncovered, wishing the veil could be restored, for his own happiness and that of the world?

He found the height of the beautiful in a wonderful garden near Genoa, a "mimic land of enchantment" where the visitor wanders among miniature medieval castles and toy palaces, stumbles upon a diminutive marble temple, and comes suddenly upon a sight which fairly opens "the gates of fairy-land." He looks through a pane of yellow glass and through a bright gateway he catches "a glimpse of the faintest, softest, richest picture that ever graced [a] dream," a sweep of sea, with a great mountain in the background:

The ocean is gold, the city is gold, the meadow, the mountain, the sky— everything is golden—rich, and mellow, and dreamy as a vision of Paradise. No artist could put upon canvas its entrancing beauty; and yet, without the yellow glass . . . that cast it into enchanted distance and shut out . . . all unattractive features, it was not a picture to fall into ecstasies over. Such is life, and the trail of the serpent is over us all.

Slightly paraphrasing Thomas Moore in the closing sentence, Mark Twain here virtually summed up his own life view. Without the yellow glass to cast the scene "into enchanted distance" and shut out its unbeautiful realities, it was far from faultless. But "such is life, and the trail of the serpent is over us all." Yes, such is life. And must one, then, go looking through a glass stained yellow rather than face reality? Must one always seek an escape into an artificial dreamland? The glamour of unreality tinged the beautiful; the ugly was always real—sharply, starkly, definitely real—to Mark Twain. But his mind was unable to reconcile the beautiful and the ugly, the good and the evil, as actual and inevitable parts of the same world. He felt that the one must be held apart and kept immaculate, unspotted by the other.

His rude awakening, after looking at his golden city through his pane of yellow glass, came when he was forced to go back to tiresome old Tabor—nothing but some old gray ruins. But even there, if the magic of the moonlight could but summon from their graves the forgotten Crusaders that had perished on that plain and send them sweeping down again "splendid with plumes and banners and glittering lances, I could stay here an age to see the phantom pageant. But the magic of the moonlight is a vanity and a fraud."

With such a mind-set, such habitual thought-patterns, it is small wonder that Mark Twain continued to evaluate beauty in terms of the dream. He could respond to the imagined spectacle of Crusaders marching on that plain with plumes and banners flying; but the day-by-day battle of dull man struggling through a humdrum existence, on that same plain and elsewhere, awakened in him no comparable response—not because he failed to sense sharply the bitter reality of that struggle, but simply because he failed to recognize the high heroism, the beauty, even, hidden somewhere in it. The dream-beauty passages in his travel books are so frequent as almost to defy cataloguing, but I have attempted the task; the resulting compilation is far too extensive to be set down here.[2] The city of Messina, viewed from afar, "milk-like, and starred and spangled all over with gas-lights, was a fairy spectacle." At the distance of a few miles, even the Pyramids looked "soft and filmy":

They swam in a rich haze that took from them all suggestions of unfeeling stone, and made them seem only the airy nothings of a dream—structures which might blossom into tiers of vague arches . . . and then melt deliciously away and blend with the tremulous atmosphere.

But when the foot of the great Pyramid was reached, this "fairy vision" had disappeared and in its place was "a corrugated, unsightly mountain of stone." From the top of the Pyramid, the Nile valley was seen spread below, "asleep in an enchanted atmosphere. There was no sound, no motion. Above the date-plumes in the middle distance, swelled a domed . . . mass, glimmering through a tinted, exquisite mist . . . and at our feet the bland impassible Sphinx looked out upon the picture from her throne." Elsewhere, he referred to

2 Passages not presented here through which the reader may further explore Mark Twain's use of the dream, the picture, fairyland, or escape into dream occur in *Letters from the Sandwich Islands*, 74-75, 76, 149, 206-207; *Travels with Mr. Brown*, 36, 46, 49-50, 143, 239, 250; *Innocents Abroad*, I, 80, 150; II, 45, 202, 244-45; *A Tramp Abroad*, I, 188, 254; II, 48; *Following the Equator*, I, 37, 76, 81, 204, 263, 264, 295; II, 8, 9, 10, 16, 60, 81, 145, 173, 180, 256, 304, 361.

the Sphinx as "the stony dreamer." Everywhere, his descriptions of scenery are studded with magic moonlight, enchantment, fairyland —every facet of unreality—and always and above all, the dream.

The diminution motif, too, grows apace and becomes another medium for viewing life in unreal aspects. Inside St. Peter's, the scale was so vast that he saw the people scattered about as "human pygmies" and "insects." Workmen were busy up in the gallery, and one of them swung loose at the end of a long rope; he was only a spider and his rope was a thread. From the mountain above Damascus, Mark Twain watched the roads below, dotted with "creeping mites" that he knew were camel trains and journeying men. Here, again, space does not permit more than a sampling of this diminishing power of his imagination as displayed in the travel books.[3] As an artistic device for attaining detachment from the subject matter, it became an extremely useful tool to him in the writing of his fiction.

The passages presented above are from *The Innocents Abroad*. In *A Tramp Abroad* he wandered even deeper into the dream world which for him constituted beauty. From Heidelberg Castle he gazed out over "the wide Rhine plain, which stretches away, softly and richly tinted, grows . . . dreamily indistinct, and finally melts imperceptibly into the remote horizon. I have never enjoyed a view which had such a serene and satisfying charm . . . as this one gives." He urged visitors to come to the Black Forest when the low afternoon sun sheds its light so as to produce "the weirdest effect, and the most enchanting":

. . . no single ray is able to pierce its way in, then, but the diffused light takes color from moss and foliage, and pervades the place like a faint, green-tinted mist, the theatrical fire of fairyland. The suggestion of mystery and the supernatural which haunts the forest . . . is intensified by this unearthly glow.

Near Schwarenbach, he looked down upon an exquisitely beautiful valley in which distance did not obliterate the details but made them "little, and mellow, and dainty, like landscapes and towns seen through the wrong end of a spy-glass," so that he "seemed to look

---

[3] Additional passages employing the diminishing process will be found in *Letters from the Sandwich Islands*, 40, 208; *Innocents Abroad*, II, 374; *A Tramp Abroad*, I, 265, 269; II, 123, 168; *Following the Equator*, II, 205.

down into fairyland." It is obvious that the imaginative life of Mark Twain was becoming more and more tinged with dream.

He continued to entertain himself by viewing things out of their natural proportions, thrown thus into an effect of unreality. He had fine opportunities for enjoying such effects in the Alps, where "little atomy Swiss homes" clung precariously. He looked down upon a ledge that seemed merely "a green-baize bench," with black and white sheep clustered about it, resembling "over-sized worms." Life viewed in miniature was a play world, a toy world. From the summit of Rigi-Kulm, he looked sheer down, almost a perpendicular mile, into a valley where he saw "a little world in unique circumstantiality of detail . . . all reduced to the smallest of scales and as sharply worked out . . . as a steel engraving":

The numerous toy villages, with tiny spires projecting out of them, were just as the children might have left them when done with play the day before; . . . the microscopic steamers glided along . . . taking a mighty time to cover the distance between ports which seemed only a yard apart; and the isthmus which separated two lakes looked as if one might stretch out on it and lie with both elbows in the water, yet we knew invisible wagons were toiling across it. . . . This beautiful miniature world had exactly the appearance of those "relief maps" which reproduce nature precisely . . . graduated to a reduced scale.

The imagination infusing these lines was later to flower into such fiction as "The Great Dark" and *The Mysterious Stranger*. From Weggis, the mountains loomed big and grand; but the villages at their feet were "so reduced . . . and lay so flat against the ground that the exactest simile . . . is to compare them to ant-deposits over-shadowed by the huge bulk of a cathedral." The mind that directed the pen through these lines later created Philip Traum, the Mysterious Stranger who, figuratively, leaned earthward with his elbows on the clouds, watching the trivialities of the paltry race of men just, as Mark Twain said in that book, "as a naturalist might be amused and interested by a collection of ants." Thus it is apparent that certain passages in the travel books look forward to the later fiction. So far as its imaginative texture is concerned, Mark Twain's work is remarkably close knit.

From the Sandwich Islands letters on, then, he described the natural setting for mankind as dream, fairyland, enchantment, a play world, a toy world, a thing like a relief map. And the farther removed from reality the ideas called up by a scene, the more beautiful that scene was considered by Mark Twain. In his last travel book, *Following the Equator,* passages displaying these characteristic patterns are especially numerous. Harsh reality in natural scenes is constantly discounted in favor of dreamy, unreal effects. In India, particularly, he found his long-ago dreams of the country "rising in a sort of vague . . . moonlight above the horizon of . . . opaque consciousness." The sense of dream that gripped him in this strange land continued to grow. The Ganges plain seemed "to stretch away and away and away, dimming and softening, to the uttermost bounds of nowhere." Any Indian city was a curiosity, but Jeypore (Jaipur) was especially curious, with its quaint little balconies: "One cannot look down . . . the chief street and persuade himself that these are real houses, and that it is all out-of-doors—the impression that it is an unreality, a picture, a scene in a theatre, is the only one that will take hold." He said repeatedly that he enjoyed India most of all the countries visited on the equator journey, and one reason for his preference is made clear in such lines.

Passages shaded by the beautiful unreality of the dream scenery are accompanied in *Following the Equator* by others in which the reality of things is denounced because it falls so far below the ideal furnished by the imagination. He related an experience previously suffered at Niagara Falls: he had had to visit Niagara fifteen times before he succeeded in getting his imaginary Falls scaled down to the actuality. When he first approached Niagara, it was with his face "lifted toward the sky"; for he thought he was going to see an Atlantic Ocean pouring down "over cloud-vexed Himalayan heights, a sea-green wall of water . . . six miles high, and so, when the toy reality came suddenly into view—that beruffled little wet apron hanging out to dry—the shock was too much for me, and I fell with a dull thud." Thus he knew what he had to do with the Taj Mahal: he must erase the images his mind had built up and keep visiting the Taj until an accurate impression occupied the old space. The Taj of his imagination was, of course, some thirty-five or forty times finer than the reality, "and therefore . . . more valuable than the reality." He decided that he ought never to hunt up a reality, but stay away from it and thus preserve undamaged "my own private mighty Niagara tumbling out of the vault of heaven, and my own ineffable Taj built of tinted mists upon jeweled arches of rainbows supported by colonnades of moonlight."

This foolery is delightful. Here Mark Twain makes comic capital of his own disappointment, employing one of his favorite devices of the humorist's technique—a gentle raillery leveled at his own weaknesses. But the serious tone of his dream passages elsewhere and the rage which frequently mingles with accounts of his disappointments may together serve as evidence that generally his dream-attitude is a further indication of his failure to accept the whole of life. As such, it is important not only for the form which much of his fiction assumed, but also for the welfare and happiness of the man himself. He always expected too much of life, too much of himself, and too much of mankind. Essentially a perfectionist, he was too bitterly disappointed to be able to make ready adjustments when life and mankind failed to measure up to his expectations. Thus his shrinking from hard reality is not confined to his descriptive writing; it lies deep in his life view, whence it dictates his reluctance to grant the mixed nature of life, the inevitable mingling of good and evil which is the very stuff of life.

India, which pervaded even his memories of it with a sense of dream—"an unreality, a picture, a scene in a theater"—remained for him the high light of following the equator. Even a year later, when he thought of India, he seemed to have a kaleidoscope at his eye:

... and I hear the clash of the glass bits as the splendid figures change, and fall apart, and flash into new forms, figure after figure, and with the birth of each new form I feel my skin crinkle and my nerve-web tingle with a new thrill of wonder and delight. These remembered pictures float past me in a sequence of contrasts; following the same order always, and always whirling by and disappearing with the swiftness of a dream.

His inclination to engage in dream fancies, to parade dream figures through his mind, was not the last resort of a tired old man, wrecked by personal disasters; the tendency had grown in him steadily, from the early travel books on. But when he turned aside from scenes of dreamlike quality, or tired of the engaging mental exercise of magnifying or diminishing objects in his imagination, when he took a good straight look at life for what it is, pessimism was often the result, disappointment almost invariably.

The unreality of the kaleidoscope through which life is seen by the old globe-trotter in *Following the Equator* is thus added to the bit of yellow glass through which the young traveler peered in *The Innocents Abroad*. Both play their part among the unreal aspects of beauty as the dream, the picture, and the magic fairy world which colored and shaded Mark Twain's vision of life. The critic Roger Fry maintains that "nothing is more contrary to the essential aesthetic faculty than the dream" and that the best art is always removed from dream life and concerned with reality. Mark Twain's preoccupation with the dream motif is a manifestation of that part of his complex personality which was essentially escapist.

G. Ezra Dane has said that in the Sandwich Islands Mark Twain first discovered beauty. It should be added that in the Sandwich Islands he also discovered the dream. His first passages embodying the dream as his expression of beauty were written in the Islands; and, perhaps as a result of the dream, his first passages embodying an unmistakable desire to escape from life, to withdraw from the swift current and drift lazily in the shallows, were also written in Hawaii.

In youth and age, obsessed as he always was with a sense of responsibility for his fellow creatures, he made human nature his proper study. But the island natives baffled him. By every standard he knew, they were a worthless lot; and yet he could not deny that they were "the happiest creatures the sun shines on." As he watched them, it seemed that their happiness must result from a complete lack of responsibility. They enjoyed an "unfettered liberty" particularly enviable to Mark Twain, who felt his own obligations keenly. Sometimes a complete withdrawal from the world of "civilization," even a complete submergence in the indolent native life, did not seem too high a price for such happiness—too high a price for escape. He described Kailua as "a little collection of native grass houses reposing under tall cocoa-nut trees" and exhorted his readers:

Ye weary ones that are sick of the . . . bewildering turmoil of the great world, and sigh for a land where ye may fold your tired hands and slumber your lives peacefully away, pack up your carpet sacks and go to Kailua!

Looking back on the islands from "the bewildering turmoil" of the world, he felt that a lifetime spent there would not be too long. The islands as an indolent paradise, safe from reality, safe from life itself, hung in the back of his mind ever after his visit there in 1866. In an article of 1873 he said:

If I could have my way about it, I would go back there and remain for the rest of my days. It is paradise for an indolent man . . . he can sun himself all day long under the palm trees, and be no more troubled by his conscience than a butterfly would.

When you are in that blessed retreat, you are safe from the turmoil of life; you drowse your days away in a long deep dream of peace; the past is a forgotten thing, the present is heaven, the future you leave to take care of itself. You are . . . millions of miles from the world; . . . the wide universe is but a foreign land to you and barren of interest. . .

Here he offered a most insidious propaganda, the propaganda of escape. Instead of a robust meeting of life, the passage extols a fleeing away from the variety of existence. The potential magnitude of man is disregarded; the fact that developing mankind cannot remain in a primitive state, however indolent or innocent, is ignored. Despite the variety of his own life, Mark Twain frequently, as here, exhibited a leaning toward what Melville labeled in *Mardi* as the only real infidelity—that is, for "a live man to vote himself dead."[4] Ending a New York lecture on the Sandwich Islands in 1877, Mark Twain restated his escapist mood:

The land I have tried to tell you about . . . is a dreamy, beautiful, charming land. I wish I could make you comprehend how beautiful it is. It is a land that seems ever so vague and fairy-like when one reads about it in books. It is . . . the land of indolence and dreams, where the air is drowsy and lulls the spirit to repose and peace, and to forgetfulness of labor and turmoil and weariness and anxiety of life.

All this amounts to a withdrawal from life itself. Dreams and fairyland are set over against reality, against the fact that the fullness of life must include a measure of "labor and turmoil and weariness and anxiety." Does it seem strange to apply the term "escapist" to Mark Twain—Mark Twain, the hard-bitten, hard-hitting, hard-driving realist? We are following the record which he himself set down in his writings.

In *A Tramp Abroad,* as in earlier books, he recorded again and again his desire to escape from the rush and worry of the world. In

4 *Mardi*, chapter XIII.

the soft gloaming of the Kandersteg valley, there were no sounds but the dulled noise of the torrent "and the occasional tinkling of a distant bell. The spirit of the place was a sense of deep, pervading peace; one might dream his life tranquilly away there, and not miss it or mind it when it was gone." But for true felicity, Mark Twain wrote in *A Tramp Abroad*, one must go down a river on a raft. The raft goes slipping silently along, between green and fragrant banks; the birds sweep back and forth across the river, singing; and one is content. Germany is always beautiful in the summertime; but nobody has enjoyed "the utmost possibilities of this soft and peaceful beauty unless he has voyaged down the Neckar on a raft":

> The motion of the raft is . . . gentle, and gliding, and smooth, and noiseless; it calms down all feverish activities, it soothes to sleep all nervous . . . impatience; under its restful influence all the troubles and vexations and sorrows that harass the mind vanish away, and existence becomes a dream . . . a deep and tranquil ecstasy.

There is evidence, however, that this whole charming journey down the Neckar River by raft took place only in the mind of Mark Twain. The systematic itinerary kept by Joseph Twichell, his fellow voyager, shows that the two "tramps" made the Neckar trip by rail and boat.[5] This praise of rafting, although not couched in Huck's dialect, nevertheless arises from the mind of Huck Finn—a literary souvenir left from a book which Mark Twain had shelved for the time being.

Following the equator through the "Island Wilderness" of the Pacific—the "very home of . . . dreams and mystery," he said that the loneliness, the beauty, and the repose of the place held a charm "for the bruised spirit of men who have fought and failed in the struggle for life in the great world." Out on the Indian Ocean there was nothing but the level blue sea; no mail, no newspapers, no telegrams—

> . . . the world is far, far away; it has ceased to exist for you . . . with all its businesses and ambitions, its prosperities and disasters, its exultations and despairs, its joys and griefs and cares and worries . . . they are a storm which has passed and left a deep calm behind. . . . If I had my way I would sail on forever and never go to live on the solid ground again.

Never to live on solid ground again—what a desirable consummation

[5] *Mark Twain's Letters*, I, 336–37.

of dream that would be! Never to be burdened with businesses and ambitions, prosperities and responsibilities! And at this point in the book some lines from Kipling appear:

> *The Injian Ocean sets an' smiles,*
> *So sof', so bright, so bloomin' blue;*

Here the responsibility of trying to uplift the great mass of humanity, the annoyance when "the damned human race" fails to respond, the bitter anger at malevolent primary forces and frustrating circumstances, the deep pain aroused by watching the sufferings of a struggling mankind—all are dissolved and melted away in a pervading sense of dream. It were better not to attempt a confrontation of hard fact or a harsh glaring reality, without benefit of veil or dream or tinted yellow glass. Better to keep your wondrous Niagara Falls, your ineffable Taj Mahal, as dream-stuff in your head than to have them shrink into puny proportions or fade into commonplace prettiness at the first test of reality. What wonder, then, that Mark Twain often attempted to view life through a veil of illusions? He gave in *Following the Equator* a new warning to his readers: "Don't part with your illusions. When they are gone, you may still exist, but you have ceased to live."

CHAPTER 13

The Twofold Aspect of Life

POSSESSOR of a keen conscience that rode him night and day, Mark Twain was amazed to encounter people who seemed to have no consciences at all. When they were happy as well as conscience free, he envied them. As I have said, the Sandwich Islands natives perplexed him. These dark-skinned people presented to him a grave moral problem:

... they have exploded one of our most ancient and trusted maxims. It ... turns out to be a swindling humbug. Be virtuous and you will be happy. The Kanakas are not virtuous—neither men, women, nor children—and yet they are the happiest creatures the sun shines on.... Theirs is a state of placid happiness. All they want is unfettered liberty to eat, drink, sleep, sing, dance, swindle, lie, and pray.

In an early islands letter he contrasted the present state of the natives with their condition before they were subjected to the influence of the missionaries. Then they had been simple children of nature, "yielding momentarily to sin when sorely tempted," but always able to cleanse their hearts by making sacrifices to their heathen idols. This felicity, however, existed before the missionaries had come to make the poor natives "permanently miserable by telling them how beautiful and how blissful a place heaven is, and how nearly impossible it is to get there." His pity for the benighted natives in their original state is heavily ironic: "How sad it is to think of the multitudes who have gone to their graves in this beautiful island and never knew there was a hell!" The chief charm of this island paradise for Mark Twain appears in his statement that in this place a man is "no more troubled by his conscience than a butterfly" would be. The natives' utter freedom from conscience was a constant marvel to him. He felt it in their indifference to volcanic terrors:

> . . . they ate, drank, bought, sold, planted, builded, apparently indifferent to . . . the bellowing and unearthly mutterings coming up from a burning deep . . . the upward curling of ten thousand columns of smoke. . . . All these moving phenomena were regarded by them as the fall of a shower or the running of a brook; while to others they were as the tokens of a burning world, the departing heavens, and a coming judge.

That Mark Twain was among those "others" is revealed in his description of the crater of Kilauea by night:

> . . . I turned to see the effect on the . . . company. . . . In the strong light every countenance glowed like red-hot iron. . . . The place below looked like the infernal regions and these men like half-cooked devils just come up on a furlough. . . . the floor of the abyss . . . was the idea of eternity made tangible—and . . . visible to the naked eye!

The coloration of Calvinistic thought marks this passage, as well as a humorous line appearing a few paragraphs down: "The smell of sulphur is strong, but not unpleasant to a sinner." The degree to which the background of Calvinistic orthodoxy had taken hold on his mind as he stood and watched this great preview of the wrath to come, may be judged from the fact that Biblical images still thronged his mind on the homeward journey. He looked back on a column of cloud towering into the air above the crater, dyed with a crimson luster so that it "glowed like a muffled torch": "And I was sure that I now had a vivid conception of what the majestic 'pillar of fire' was like." The thought-pattern of orthodoxy appears again in his account of a short cut home from Diamond Head: "not as wide, perhaps, as the broad road that leads to destruction, but nearly as dangerous to travel, and apparently leading in the same general direction."

One thing brought him a recurrent bewilderment which runs through the travel books. As a moralist, he had grounded his life on the assumption of a moral order, on the idea of a universe to be controlled in accordance with conceptions of right and wrong. These conceptions were rigid and absolute: if Providence were just, the virtuous would be rewarded, the sinful would be punished. But in *The Innocents Abroad*, the Portuguese populations of the Azores upset his calculations. Men and women, they pulled harrows in the fields; the good Catholic inhabitant crossed himself and prayed God "to shield him from all blasphemous desire to know more than his father did before him"; the people all lied, cheated, and were "desperately ignorant." They were little better "than the donkeys they eat and sleep with"; and the Azoreans as a whole "are unclean, are ravaged by vermin, and are truly happy."

The upset of the moral order was revealed to him even more clearly in old Italian towns where the people exhibited extreme ignorance, superstition, degradation, poverty, indolence, and "everlasting worthlessness." They had nothing to do but "eat and sleep and sleep and eat"; like "the other animals," they took no thought of the world's concerns, or of any tomorrow: "They were not respectable people—they were not worthy people . . . but in their breasts, all their lives long, resteth a peace that passeth understanding! How can men, calling themselves men, consent to be so degraded and so happy?" This condemnation is qualified by a tinge of envy. The passage reveals the same desire to escape from the world and be rid of its problems which was the keynote of many passages presented in Chapter 12. But here it is the reversal of the expected moral order which is emphasized by Mark Twain. These people make no gestures towards self-improvement, either in economic progress or in moral advancement; yet they have secured life's best gift, happiness. Why, then, the struggle?

In *A Tramp Abroad* he related a somewhat shady adventure of his own and ended his account with a significant remark: "The most permanent lessons in morals are those which come, not of booky teaching, but of experience." Years later, in elucidating what he called "my favorite theory of the difference between theoretical morals and practical morals," he pointed out that theoretical morals are those one gets at his mother's knee, or from reading good books, or from hearing the precepts of the pulpit. He gets them into his head, but not into his heart. On the other hand, practical morals are those which a man "earns and learns" for himself:

As by the fires of experience, so by commission of crime, you learn real morals. Commit all the crimes, familiarize yourself with all sins, take them in rotation (there are only two or three thousand of them), stick to it, commit two or three every day, and by-and-by . . . you will be proof against all sins and morally perfect. You will be vaccinated against every possible commission of them. This is the only way.

Thus, in a mixture of exaggerated humor and grim seriousness, he subscribed to the theory which such a writer as George Bernard Shaw teaches with earnest conviction: that the experiment of being wicked may produce the same beneficial result as the experiment of being good—that is, the development of character.[1]

After *A Tramp Abroad*, almost twenty years elapsed before the publication of the next travel book, *Following the Equator*. The moralist was not so active as in the earlier books; still, he was alive and preaching the same doctrine. Mark Twain presented the figure of the Indian crow as an example of a sinner who has committed all the crimes in the decalogue. The "hardest lot that wears feathers," the crow never arrived at what he is by any careless process; he is a work of art, and "art is long," says Mark Twain. A product of the immemorial ages, he has been reincarnated more times than Shiva and has kept within himself a sample of each incarnation. In the course of his "sublime march toward ultimate perfection,"

. . . he has been a gambler, a low comedian, a dissolute priest, a fussy woman, a blackguard, a scoffer, a liar, a thief, a spy, an informer, a trading politician, a swindler, a professional hypocrite, a patriot for cash, a reformer, a lecturer, a lawyer, a conspirator, a rebel, a royalist, a democrat, a practicer and propagator of irreverence, a meddler, an intruder, a busybody, an infidel, and a wallower in sin for the mere love of it. The strange result, the incredible result, of this patient accumulation of all damnable traits is that he does not know what care is, he does not know what sorrow is, he does not know what remorse is; his life is one long thundering ecstasy of happiness, and he will go to his death untroubled.

The particular felicity of the Indian crow, it appears, is that he does not possess a troublesome conscience. The upset of a rational moral order is thus reflected in the crow, incarnate sin, whom Mark Twain lifts to a "thundering ecstasy."

Other passages present sin as fitting to youthful happiness. When a young bride of India peeps out from the curtains of her palanquin, she commits a sin according to her beliefs; but she exposes her face "with that pure delight which the young and happy take

[1] Henderson, *Mark Twain*, 189.

in sin for sin's own sake." If the follower of the Hindu religion bathes in the Well of Long Life, he emerges young, full of eagerness, and ready "to commit sins now with a fresh, new vivacity."

Such passages are the direct antithesis of orthodox moralism. Under a cloak of humor, Mark Twain appears close to the view of Hawthorne, who saw that human sin is not only inevitable but may even serve as an agent for the regeneration of the human soul through widened experience and resultant pain. In such lines Mark Twain seems to have arrived at an acceptance of the coexistence of good and evil in human nature, a view at variance with his customary one, limited to the extremes of black and white that paint the canvas of the moralist.

Most of these more tolerant passages occur in *Following the Equator*. In this book he was concerned with larger issues of life, emphasized again and again, although scrutinized within the compass of small incidents. In earlier books, while not admitting the moral tolerance of the *Equator* passages, he nevertheless sometimes recognized the mingling of the good and the bad in human existence. Even in the Sandwich Islands letters, rare passages exhibit his awareness that to touch life at many different points, some of them unpleasant, may have its recompense in the enrichment of personality and the added intensity of enjoyment. Relating an experience in which his party got lost near Diamond Head one night and was rescued by a chance Kanaka, he concluded thus:

The moon . . . flooded mountain and valley and ocean with silvery light, and I was not sorry we had lately been in trouble, because the consciousness of being safe again raised our spirits and made us more capable of enjoying the beautiful scene than we would have been otherwise. I never breathed such a soft delicious atmosphere before.

This implies a realization that life lived at a dead level is unsatisfying, that occasional unhappiness serves by contrast to pique the value of happiness, that man's emotional life is constructed on a principle of polarity, that when the opposing elements of good and evil are brought into play man's entire nature is given a fuller expression in the balanced design of life.

Of like nature was an experience met aboard the little *Boomerang*. Mark Twain's small cabin was dark and stuffy. Lying there, he felt large rats gallop over him, and he turned his head to find huge cockroaches perched on his pillow—"fellows with long, quivering antennae and fiery malignant eyes." He dressed and went on deck. "It was compensation for all my sufferings to . . . step suddenly out of the sepulchral gloom of the cabin and stand under the strong light of the moon—in the center . . . of a glittering sea of liquid silver." Here an intensity is added to a pleasurable experience that follows a painful one, just as in the preceding passage safety seems the sweeter after danger. Instead of an active resentment against an ugly and hostile world, instead of the shrinking refusal to accept experience which his lines in praise of a withdrawal from the world convey, here he recorded a mood of sheer joy in meeting diverse experiences, a reaching out of the human spirit to grasp whatever is offered. Such passages are comparatively rare, for a mood of this kind could not hold in Mark Twain. But if he had never felt it at all, *Adventures of Huckleberry Finn* would never have been written. He dimly approaches here a recognition of the fact that a fully developed personality is the recompense for living through all sorts of vicissitudes and complexities.

Literature communicates not only a writer's actual ideas, but also his states of mind, sometimes exceedingly complex. In the Sandwich Islands letters Mark Twain seems to have been groping towards an acceptance of what may be called the twofold nature of life—the fact that good and evil are necessary poles in human experience and that one is not to be had without the other. The beauty of the islands and the extreme contrasts he encountered there brought him nearer to this ultimate acceptance than he would ever be again, so far as the travel books are concerned, until in his old age he wrote down what he saw in India, a land even more notable for contrasts. But in the islands his realization of the twofold aspect of life was never strong enough to enable him to phrase it more directly than in the passages just quoted. It is strongly expressed in symbol, however, in his description of the country near Kilauea. As the route neared "the palace of the dread goddess Pele," the topography presented evidence of primal commotion:

We came upon a long dreary desert of black, swollen, twisted, corrugated billows of lava. . . . There had been terrible commotion here once, when these dead waves were seething fire; but now all was motionless and silent—it was a petrified sea! . . . The invincible *ohia* struggled for a footing even in this desert waste, and achieved it—towering above the billows here and there, with trunks flattened like spears of grass in the crevices.

This is a symbolic awareness that beauty can survive and flourish amidst ugliness as powerful and fierce as the ugliness of black, distorted volcanic rock; a recognition that beauty can adjust itself to unfavorable surroundings. In these lines Mark Twain reaches out towards something that just eludes him, listens for a whisper that he cannot quite catch. He left the Sandwich Islands without having made the object of his quest a permanent possession.

In *Mr. Brown*, few are the passages recording an amelioration of life's ills, or a sense of the mixed nature of life. Only rarely is there a mood of acceptance that tempers the habitual impatience, softens the customary rage. The realization, when it comes, follows a particularly unpleasant experience; the law of compensation which makes for balance in life is thus fulfilled. After a ride in a chair coach, he found the sleeping car an utter delight. "It was worth the forty hours I had gone without sleep to feel the luxury of lying down between clean sheets and stretching out at full length—and drawing up and stretching out again—and turning over and fetching another celestial stretch." Here the bitter and the sweet are so nicely balanced that the bitter only lends a special tang to the sweet. Rarely, his vision probed the darkest souls of mankind and found even there something to commend; after his night in the station house, he remembered his "late fellow-lodgers" as a "pretty good sort . . . though a little under the weather as to respectability. But even the worst . . . freely offered to divide her gin with me."

The most fully articulated conception of the twofold aspect of life in the *Mr. Brown* series, however, appears just after a tirade on the New York weather:

And yet . . . this uncertain climate has its pleasant features. All life demands change, variety, contrast—else there is small zest to it. Here you have rain, snow, bleakness; but after it is all gone, what an imperial green all vegetation puts on! It is worth a winter of suffering to see the rich coloring. . . . And perhaps you know how sick one gets of the eternal fair weather of San Francisco, and how he longs for lightning, thunder, and tempest! how he feels as if he wanted to tear the glaring sun out of the sky, and blot the firmament with a purple pall, and cleanse it down from zenith to horizon with shafts of fire!

Although in the last lines his rage and impatience follow the old pattern, becoming so extreme that he wants to tear the glaring sun from the sky, in this passage he recognizes—again symbolically—the value of storm and pain, the value of fire as an agent for "cleansing down" the sky or the heart of a man.

Possibly as an outgrowth of his occasional acceptance of the mixed nature of life, he came to recognize the value of perspective. In the two earliest travel books this recognition appears only in connection with his oft-repeated view that distance lends enchantment. In *The Innocents Abroad*, however, the function of perspective is specifically noted: the effect of Galilee is dreary, because its "rusty mounds of barrenness" can never "shake the glare from their harsh outlines and fade . . . into vague perspective"; and of all lands for dismal scenery, Palestine is the "prince," for there "every feature is distinct, there is no perspective." These lines merely express his tendency to view the distinct, the near-at-hand, or the *reality* as ugliness, and the vague, the far-away, or the *unreality* as beauty; but, having grasped the value of perspective in a spatial sense, he began to recognize a perspective of time and to apply it to his own literary work:

When one is in Rome, all the domes are alike; but . . . away twelve miles, the city fades . . . and leaves St. Peter's swelling above the level plain. . . . When one is traveling . . . the daily incidents seem all alike; but when he has placed them all two months and two thousand miles behind him, those that were worthy of being remembered are prominent, and those that were really insignificant have vanished.

He came to realize that time intervening between the observation and the recording lends a quality to writing that can be gained in no other way. He noted that it is easy for writers to say, "I thought so and so as I looked upon such and such a scene," when the truth is that "they thought all these fine things afterward. One's first thought is not likely to be strictly accurate, yet it is no crime to think it and none to write it down, subject to modification by later experience."

The perspective lent by time is recognized as an asset to man's happiness—in life, as well as in literature—in his reflection that soon the fatigue of his travels will be forgotten—the heat, the thirst, and the clamoring beggars; and the memories that are left will become at last "all beautiful." He described the mental state which a few years later would become the groundwork for his idyllic book about Tom Sawyer, a book which in some respects is not idyllic at all:

School-boy days are no happier than the days of after life, but we look back upon them regretfully because we have forgotten our punishments at school, and how we grieved when our marbles were lost and our kites destroyed—because we have forgotten all the sorrows and privations of that canonized epoch and remember only its orchard robberies, its wood-en-sword pageants, and its fishing holidays.

Thus he knew that eventually all the experiences of the traveler's day would be "an enchanted memory . . . which money could not buy from us." The knowledge that all the basic incongruities, all the paradoxical perversities of life, will be reconciled if they are but viewed from a sufficient distance, if they are but fitted into their minute place in the vast scheme of things, seems just within his grasp.

In a passage on the hermit-priests of Mars Saba, he explicitly recorded a recognition that a full life must include pain and sorrow as well as joy. The priests of that monastery have been inside its walls for thirty years, and in that time "they have seen no human tears, no human smiles; they have known no human joys, no wholesome human sorrows. . . . They are dead men who walk." Whatever the rigors of such a life, at least it offers peace and security—that withdrawal from the "bewildering turmoil of life" which he extolled so highly in earlier passages. These lines express a belief stated so specifically nowhere else in all his work.

In *A Tramp Abroad* he again expressed—in symbol—a profound truth of human existence. He wrote that the way through Gemmi Pass moved into a barren desolation: on every hand rose gigantic masses of rock, battered by frosts; great fragments, split off, lay about; soiled snow marred the edges of the path. It seemed that there was nothing but death and desolation in those hideous places; but—

In the most forlorn . . . and dismal one of all . . . where the winds blew bitterest and the general aspect was mournfulest and dreariest, and furthest from any suggestion of cheer or hope, I found a solitary wee forget-me-not flourishing away . . . holding its bright blue star up with the . . . gallantest air in the world, the only . . . smiling thing in all that grisly desert. She seemed to say, "Cheer up!—as long as we are here, let us make the best of it." I . . . plucked her up and sent her . . . to a friend who would respect her for the fight she had made, all by her small self, to make a whole vast despondent Alpine desolation stop breaking its heart over the unalterable, and hold up its head and look at the bright side of things for once.

Here Mark Twain attributes to the "despondent Alpine desolation" exactly the mood most common to himself—that of "breaking its heart over the unalterable." The passage is significant for its equation of ice and snow with desolation and loneliness; in his fiction, too, ice and snow appear as the symbols of despair. But here the chief significance lies in another symbolism: like the red ohia flower which had earlier flourished in Hawaii in a heat-maddened tangle of volcanic rock, this bright blue flower standing in an icy desert becomes a symbol of hope and high courage, a sign that something there is worth making a fight for.

Only by the use of symbols could Mark Twain make this feeling clear. The possibilities of life, the dignities latent in human struggle, the courage and the faith, he expressed best by means of symbols. Perhaps his impressions of them were not clear enough to find an utterance more direct than this. But his use of metaphor here makes it express his individual emotion and at the same time charges it with universal significance; and that is the way of the artist, who, as J. Middleton Murry has said, must seek to "carry the articulation of the material world into the world of the spirit," must attempt, in fact, to define the indefinable.

In *Following the Equator*, Mark Twain spoke of India as the "Land of Splendor and Desolation." The mixed nature of life was there emphasized in a way that could not be overlooked. He found there a surface atmosphere of bright color, accompanied by an undercurrent of the sinister—a combination which aroused in him sensations which he described as a mixture of "deadly fright and unimaginable joy," adding: "I believe that this combination makes the perfection of human delight."

What would be the incongruous in other lands is the commonplace in India. There, a confessed Thug will fall at the feet of his mother before going to the scaffold, exhibiting reverence and gratefulness; and she will place her hands on his head and bid him die like a man, on her part exhibiting compassion and fortitude and self-respect; within them is no sense of disgrace, no thought of dishonor.

"The incongruities of our human nature seem to reach their limit here." The good Jain is careful not to crush out the life from an insect; all life in India is sacred, except human life. "India is a hard country to understand," wrote Mark Twain. What is it that gives such a land its power over people?

Part of that power lies in the religious faith which moves the daily life of the natives. At a Jain temple in Bombay the explanations to visitors were made by a "Mr. Gandhi," a recent delegate to the Chicago Congress of Religions. He spoke in masterly English, but when the details of his explanation had faded, Mark Twain was left with "a dim idea of a religious belief clothed in subtle intellectual forms, lofty and clean, barren of fleshly grossnesses," a faith which was nevertheless somehow connected with a crude image, a small sitting idol that had "the pinkish look of a wax doll." India was inexplicable in many ways.

Mark Twain's journey led on to Benares, where religion is the very business of life. In this strange land, one is forced to recognize the power of faith: it is faith that impels the widow to consecrate her body on the burning pyre of the suttee, serene in the belief that by this act she unites her soul to her husband's. It is faith that brings pilgrims to bathe in the waters of the Ganges, sustained by the belief that they will be cleansed of sin by these holy waters. It is wonderful, the power of a faith like that, a faith moving millions to make journeys beset with misery. "It is done in love, or it is done in fear," he wrote. "I do not know which it is. No matter what the impulse is, the act born of it is beyond imagination marvelous to our kind of people, the cold whites." It is faith that moves the natives to wash their mouths out with the Ganges water and drink it, paying no heed to the foul gush from a sewer pouring into it, or to a "random corpse" slopping around in it. "The memory of that sight will always stay by me, but not by request." Out of his feeling for the people of India and, no doubt, marveling at himself, he coined a new maxim: "True irreverence is disrespect for another man's god." A man could only stand in wonder before such faith as this.

Under the spell which India laid upon him, he was willing to admit that the human race is making progress. Discussing the idea that white people are "merely modified Thugs," he continued:

Still, we have made some progress—microscopic—and certainly nothing to be proud of—still, it is progress: we no longer take pleasure in slaughtering or burning helpless men. We have reached a little altitude where we may look down upon the Indian Thugs with a complacent shudder; and we may even hope for a day, many centuries hence, when our posterity will look down upon us in the same way.

Although not exactly a glorification of mankind, the passage expresses a concession on the part of Mark Twain.

Other passages in *Following the Equator* indicate his awareness of the benefits hidden in some unpleasurable aspects of life. One aphorism admonishes: "Let us be grateful to Adam our benefactor. He cut us out of the 'blessing' of idleness and won for us the 'curse' of labor." A recognition of work as a source of happiness is implicit here—a far cry from the tone of the Sandwich Islands letters, which praise a state of idleness as a paradise. Even a recognition of man as an agent capable of developing a character for himself is explicit in another aphorism: "Make it a point to do something every day that you don't want to do. This is the golden rule for acquiring the habit of doing your duty without pain." In contrast with his usual contemptuous view of humanity-in-bulk, he bestowed his approval on the brown people of India: "They are kindly people, the natives. The face and the bearing that indicate a surly spirit and a bad heart seemed to me . . . rare among the Indians." A recognition of life as something that can be satisfying appears in his description of six "Old Settlers" of Australia. Contrary to his usual view of old age as a time of disappointment and bitterness, he saw these men as aging outwardly, but as remaining "young and cheerful" within:

. . . those lovely old boys did so enjoy living their heroic youth over. . . . they had seen so much . . . and had suffered so much; and built so strongly and well, and laid the foundations of their commonwealth so deep, in liberty and tolerance; and had lived to see the structure rise to such state and dignity and hear themselves so praised for their honorable work.

Thus, when compared with the earlier travel books, *Following the Equator* reveals how much Mark Twain had gained in depth of insight, in vision of life.

The equator book also shows a gain in his sense of the value of perspective, this time a different perspective, connected somehow with life itself. He observed that Mauritius is pretty, but it lacks perspective. The island is a garden and a park combined, and it affects one's emotions only as parks and gardens affect them: "The surfaces of one's spiritual deeps are pleasantly played upon, the deeps themselves are not reached, not stirred. Spaciousness, remote altitudes, the sense of mystery which haunts . . . mountain domes . . . these are the things which exalt the spirit and move it to see visions and dream dreams." Here his old longing for the dream world which to him signified beauty is once more apparent. To repeat, in *Following the Equator* the dream passages are so numerous as almost to defy cataloguing; his experience with the Taj Mahal was only another indication of his preference for the dream above the reality, a preference which appears as rather damaging evidence that he was, partially at least, an escapist. It is the chapter on the Taj Mahal that bears his warning to his readers: "Don't part with your illusions. When they are gone you may still exist, but you have ceased to live." Such ideas were vestiges of the mind-set customary to him through the years. And yet it was in India, it appears, that Mark Twain was made most fully aware of the latent dignity of human life.

In India, itself the "Land of Giant Illusions," he apparently came to realize that when reality is met and grappled with, something inexplicably true and fine may rise up to replace those lost illusions. He achieved that recognition by progressing through thought-patterns habitual to him—and familiar to the reader of these pages—and then by going beyond his stereotyped attitudes to something new, something inclusive and significant. At first acquaintance, according to Mark Twain, India appears extremely beautiful, with its brilliantly costumed brown natives and its dream-tinted palaces of palest pink. But on a long drive through the outskirts of Benares, one realizes that the country is only "a vision of dusty sterility, decaying temples, crumbling tombs, broken mud walls, shabby huts. The whole region seems to ache with age and penury. It must take ten thousand years of want to produce such an aspect." Not only does the whole region seem to ache, but an Indian river at low water suggests a skinned human body, with water channels for muscles and sandbars for "archipelagoes of fat and flesh." The passage strikes a note on the ugliness of human pain, a note by no means new in Mark Twain. But the progress through India continues, and a new note at last is heard:

Out in the country . . . the day begins early. One sees a plain, perfectly flat, dust-colored . . . stretching limitlessly away on every side in the dim gray light, striped everywhere with hard-beaten narrow paths . . . and along all the paths are slender women and . . . lanky naked men moving to their work. . . .

All day long one has this monotony of dust-colored dead levels and scattering bunches of trees and mud villages. You soon realize that India is not beautiful; still there is an enchantment about it that does not pall. You cannot tell just what it is that makes the spell, perhaps, but . . . you know . . . that it is . . . a haunting sense of the myriads of human lives that have blossomed, and withered, and perished here, repeating and repeating and repeating, century after century and age after age, the barren and meaningless process; it is this sense that gives to this forlorn, uncomely land power to speak to the spirit.

In brief, it is the dignity of human pain which Mark Twain felt gave to that unlovely land its power to speak to the spirit of mankind. The deserts and the icy wastes of the world have no such power, for man has not peopled them; "with nothing to tell of man and his vanities, his fleeting glories and his miseries, they have nothing wherewith to spiritualize their ugliness and veil it with a charm." But the mud villages of India, with their ugly sun-baked walls shutting in men and cattle and vermin, have a power able to "spiritualize their ugliness" with a haunting sense of the dignity of human pain, the sense of suffering shed upon them by the human lives that have blossomed and withered and perished there.

Mark Twain in no sense idealized India. But he did recognize there the twofold aspect of human life, the inextricable mingling of good and evil in human nature—there, at last, recognized in humanity-in-bulk. Nowhere else could murder be committed with such "cold business-like depravity"; but even a Thug could exhibit reverence and tenderness and gratitude. On one hand was the selfish arrogance of the native princes; on the other, the self-sacrifice that made the suttee possible. On one hand was the caste system, including everybody from the Brahmins to the untouchables—a system repugnant to Mark Twain's democratic heart; on the other was the amazing religious faith before which he stood in humble wonder, and it, too, included everybody. The land itself he saw as an allegory of Nature's powers of re-creation. The great brown tide of human life is periodically sucked up by famine and by plague; but Nature spills out from her deep reservoirs "a continuously repeated and re-plenished multitude of naked men." The whole process he stamped as "barren and meaningless"; nevertheless, he realized that the ebb and flow of human life gave even an ugly land a power to "speak to the spirit."

In the Sandwich Islands he had early found beauty; but it was a surface beauty of appearances—a beauty of mere picture and dream, a hocus-pocus of magic world and fairyland, a beauty that had no essential dignity in it. In *The Innocents Abroad* he had portrayed a distant beauty which vanished when one drew close to it; but more than anything else he had there delineated the ugliness of life—an ugliness horrible, repulsive, yet recorded with a painstaking partic-ularity of detail. In *Following the Equator*—at least in India—he found both beauty and ugliness. The ugliness was permanent, he felt; but he soon discovered the beauty to be, once more, mere dream-stuff, surface stuff, like "a picture painted on water." But out of the ugli-ness there arose a beauty and a dignity that were lasting, because they had their roots in the permanent ugliness. This beauty and this dig-nity grew out of the recurring cycles of human suffering, out of the spiritualizing qualities of human pain. Thus, arising from the same source, the beauty and the ugliness were intermingled and inextric-able, both parts of one world, man's world. This much he glimpsed, certainly, and recorded in his book.

This new insight, however, was not rooted deeply enough to crowd out altogether his old prepossessions. In this same book he headed his chapter dealing with the settlement of Australia by con-victs with a significant sentence which contains the essence of what is perhaps his greatest defect as a literary artist. The sentence crys-tallizes his basic failure to sense the latent dignity of mankind. It is this sweeping statement: "Everything human is pathetic."

CHAPTER 14

Life As Broad Spectacle

ALTHOUGH Mark Twain constantly chronicled as an interested observer the spectacle furnished by life, it was not always that he recorded it as a zestful observer. Long ago, St. John of the Cross said that a man can take greater comfort in his fellow creatures if he detaches himself from them; he can have no joy in them if he looks upon them as his own. That way, responsibility lies. In Mark Twain's early days in Hawaii, before he had begun to feel sufficiently well acquainted with the natives to want to reform them, he reveled in the pageantry of the island life about him. His letter describing "Saturday in Honolulu" paints the full glory of a festive afternoon among the islanders. He admired the native girls in their robes of rainbow hues as they cantered up and down the streets on their horses, making, he said, "a gay and graceful and exhilarating spectacle."

In his *Travels with Mr. Brown,* he occasionally turned away from the fantastic beauty of the landscape to watch the animate scene. At a church service in Key West, a "decaying town," some of the men were "unquestionably Southern bloods . . . slim, spruce, long-haired young fellows, in broadcloth, black kids, whalebone canes, ruffled shirts, and funny little cravats an inch wide, made of flaming yellow silk ribbon." Back home again, one does not need a map to tell him when he crosses the boundary of a state; he knows by the appearance of the passengers as they come on board a train: "If they had Ohio or Pennsylvania . . . or Illinois written on their foreheads, one could not detect their abiding place much easier."

As a spectator of the procession of life in New York, he watched great crowds troop over a new iron bridge above Broadway and Fulton Street, merely to test a novelty. A washerwoman came along with three hundred pounds of laundry on her back, eyeing the bridge. Mark Twain wondered "if that old scalliwag really meditates lugging that clothing-store up that tiresome stairway now, when the street below is comparatively free from vehicles?" Sure enough, the woman tugged and sweated till she reached the top, then "cast a critical eye up Broadway, went down on the other side, toiled up again, crossed over to her original point . . . and went off about her business. There is a great deal of human nature in people."

In *The Innocents Abroad*, in holiday moods neither marred by rage nor tinged by the desire to reform his fellows, Mark Twain could sometimes enjoy the spectacle furnished him by humanity-at-large. In the Bois de Boulogne of Paris, he saw thousands of vehicles traveling up and down in a scene of gaiety. There were hacks containing families; there were "conspicuous little open carriages with celebrated ladies of questionable repute in them"; there were Dukes and Duchesses abroad, with gorgeous footmen; there were "blue and silver, and green and gold, and pink and black, and all sorts . . . of stunning and startling liveries out."

Taken as a whole, *A Tramp Abroad* does not contain so much dirt, crime, and decay as does *The Innocents Abroad*. Europe revisited yielded less material for his impatience and rage. He praised the careful industry and "beautiful order" exhibited in Germany. Even in the poorest quarters of Frankfurt, "the little children . . . were nearly always nice enough to take into a body's lap." An 1878 letter to Howells, written from Frankfurt in the early stages of the *Tramp* tour, reveals the chief reason for this tolerant attitude:

Ah, I have such a deep, grateful, unutterable sense of being "out of it all." I think I foretaste some of the advantages of being dead. Some of the joy of it . . . .
What a paradise this is! What clean clothes, what good faces, what tranquil contentment, what prosperity, what genuine freedom, what superb government. And I am so happy, for I am responsible for none of it.

There he strikes the keynote of the mood: "I am so happy, for I am responsible for none of it." His frequent rages, as I have already said, seem to have arisen from some obscure sense of guilt; he felt himself somehow responsible, simply because he was a part of the social structure permitting the wrongs he raged at. He was as aware as

Thoreau or Albert Schweitzer that responsibility must be, in the final analysis, individual—not civic, not national, but individual.

Other passages in *A Tramp Abroad* show that his sense of non-responsibility granted him other relaxed moods. A forbearance towards the failings of others appears in his picture of a callow sophisticate who had been particularly condescending about Mark Twain's writing and who "had all the look of an American person who would be likely to begin his signature with an initial and spell his middle name out." Exhibiting a tolerance that is, in him, simply amazing, Mark Twain commented: "what little indignation he excited in me soon passed and left nothing behind it but compassion. One cannot keep up a grudge against a vacuum."

His enjoyment of the spectacle of life displayed in the grounds of Heidelberg Castle is evident in his account of afternoons spent there:

> ... one could sit ... and pretend to sip at his foamy beaker of beer while he inspected the crowd. . . . I only pretended to sip. . . . Sometimes so many people came that every seat was occupied, every table filled. And never a rough in the assemblage—all nicely dressed fathers and mothers . . . and children; and plenty of university students and glittering officers; with here and there a gray professor, or a peaceful old lady with her knitting. . . . Everybody had his glass of beer before him, or his cup of coffee, or his bottle of wine . . . ; young ladies chatted, or fanned themselves, or wrought at their . . . embroidering; the students fed sugar to their dogs, or discussed duels, or illustrated new fencing tricks with their little canes; and everywhere was comfort and enjoyment; and everywhere peace and good-will to men.

As a mere spectator here, he reveled in an uninvolved mood in which his enjoyment became an aesthetic one; and yet, even here, his satisfaction was deepened by his knowledge that anybody could have "a seat in that place and plenty of music, any afternoon, for about eight cents, or a family ticket for the season for two dollars." Even here, he was still concerned with the welfare of the common people.

In *Following the Equator*, his last sustained travel writing, the first volume is filled with perfunctory travel talk; but in the second, the magic of the Orient throws its spell over the page. India not only stirred his spiritual depths, an effect which was investigated in the preceding chapter, but also afforded him the keenest aesthetic en-

joyment. There is the great city of Bombay, "a bewitching place
... the Arabian nights come again!" Across the street from the hotel,
under some great trees, sits a turbaned juggler with his snakes; and
all day long the bright costumes flock by: "It does not seem as if one
could ever get tired of watching this moving show, this shining and
shifting spectacle." In the great bazaar, there is "a sea of rich-colored
turbans and draperies"; and the ceaseless movement of carriages and
the constant yells of native footmen increase "the general sense of
swiftness and energy and confusion and pow-wow." The Parsee
women form "perfect flower-beds of brilliant color, a fascinating
spectacle." The typical workingman wears only a loincloth; his skin
is a deep, dark-brown satin, his rounded muscles knobbing it "as if
it had eggs under it." The typical working woman is slender and
graceful in her single garment, with fanciful bunches of jewelry on
her ankles and arms; she has a large, shiny water jar on her head, and
one of her naked arms curves up and holds it there. She steps with
easy grace and dignity, her curved arm and her brazen jar becoming
mere adjuncts to her charm—"our working-women cannot begin
with her as a road decoration." And everywhere on every hand is
"color, bewitching color, enchanting color." For this is India,

... the land of dreams and romance, of fabulous wealth and fabulous
poverty, of splendor and rags ... of tigers and elephants, the cobra and
the jungle ... birthplace of human speech, cradle of the human race ...
the one sole country under the sun that is endowed with an imperishable
interest ... the one land that *all* men desire to see, and having seen once
... would not give that glimpse for the shows of all the rest of the globe
combined.

At a village well, picturesque groups flocked to and fro, laughing and chattering; once "brawny men were deluging their bronze
bodies with the limpid water, and making a refreshing and enticing
show of it." At a railway station there would be a "perennially
ravishing show, the ebb and flow and whirl of gaudy natives ...
always surging up and down" so that one was likely to lose himself
in the ecstasy of watching them and be left by his train. Elsewhere,
a long station-wait was "a dull thing and tedious"; but in India one
had always "the monster crowd of jeweled natives, the stir, the
bustle, the confusion, the shifting splendors of the costumes. ... the

delight of it, the charm of it are beyond speech," and a two-hour wait was over too soon. Along the banks of the muddy Ganges there was

...a world of activity and turmoil and noise, partly religious, partly commercial; for the Mohammedans were there to curse and sell, and the Hindus to buy and pray. . . . At last came a procession of naked holy people marching by and chanting, and I wrenched myself away.

On a holiday he spent in Jeypore, the terraces and roofs were packed with natives, making "solid masses of splendid color . . . up and up, against the blue sky, and the Indian sun turning them all to beds of fire and flame . . . each crowd was an explosion of brilliant color." It is the aesthetic appeal of such scenes that makes them entrancing to the literary artist. But it was always the people themselves, apparently, that were the most challenging sight, whether he approved of them or not. And he did approve of the people of India. He summed them up as "much the most *interesting* people in the world— and the nearest to being incomprehensible." Standing in his box at the circus of life, he watched with unflagging interest while these brown-skinned actors played scene after scene.

Out in the country he saw villages built of matting, standing about three hundred yards apart among the bamboo; villages, villages, dozens in sight all the time: "a mighty City, hundreds of miles long. . . . I have seen no such city as this before." And there was always in view a multitude of naked men and boys: "We fly through it mile after mile, but it is always there, on both sides and ahead." A drive along a country road was "India in motion," a satisfying confusion of strange human life and curious animal life and outlandish vehicles. At Darjeeling, he selected a back window from which to view Mount Everest; but after two hours of Everest's magnificence he "changed from the back to the front of the house and spent the rest of the morning there, watching the swarthy strange tribes flock by from their far homes in the Himalayas . . . a strange and striking pageant." Earlier, he had written from Melbourne, Australia: "The things which interest us when we travel are, first, the people; next, the novelties; and finally, the history of the places and countries visited." In the early Sandwich Islands letters, the beauties and wonders of the country overshadow the people; but in later travel books, the interest in people consistently stands above all else.

Mark Twain and Lewis at Quarry Farm

As he moved his gaze along the panorama of humanity, occasionally his glance was halted by a specimen that seemed to deserve more detailed scrutiny. As early as the Islands letters, his interest in human behavior resulted in brief character sketches, which appear as interpolations among scenic descriptions and generalized observations of island life. There was the native judge of the Kau district who was a specialist in financial and moral matters. He considered that if he committed adultery it was the same as if the government committed the offense; hence, as he considered that all fines for adultery properly belonged to himself as head of the government, "whenever he had collected a good deal of money from other . . . revenues, he used to set to work and keep on convicting himself of adultery until he had absorbed all the money on hand." Mark Twain's presentation of the native judge contains no moralizing; this specimen is simply recorded, with some zest, as an example of human oddity. The island letters offer, too, Mrs. Captain Jollopson of the nautical vocabulary. She had just "hove on her dress and cleared for the market" and was "laying off and on before the Post Office" when a ship-keeper came "round the corner three sheets in the wind," failed to "sheer off and shorten sail," and consequently struck her "a little abaft the beam." The gusto with which these people are described indicates the author's enjoyment of them. No impatience, no moralism, filters through these brief sketches; they are marked by the serene tone of the writer in command of his material. Apart from such sketches, *Letters from the Sandwich Islands* points towards the novel through Mr. Brown, the first character Mark Twain equipped with definite personality, mannerisms, and vocabulary and moved through an entire series of letters.

Scattered through the *Travels with Mr. Brown* are literary snapshots of other fascinating subjects. There is Captain Ned Wakeman (fictionized as "Captain Waxman" from the second letter on), that "stormy-voiced old salt . . . as rough as a bear . . . and yet as kind-hearted and tender as a woman" whom Mark Twain later used as Captain Ned Blakeley in *Roughing It*, as Hurricane Jones in the "Idle Excursion" notes, and as Captain Stormfield in *Captain Stormfield's Visit to Heaven*. In the Mr. Brown letters, old man Finn enters print for the first time in his role of town drunkard for Hannibal: "Jimmy Finn had always kept the town in a sweat," and when he died, it almost died, too, "from utter inanition." As character sketches these passages naturally deal with individuals, but Mark Twain treats one group with marked success. Compared with his earlier work, this group drawing shows an advance in technique and an even deeper difference: the attitude has changed to one of detachment.

The group drawing in question presents the bootblacks of New York, those skeptics of the sidewalk who are already casting their ragged shadows along the road that Huck Finn will one day come walking, swinging his dead cat.

Sometimes, down about the City Hall Park, it does seem to me that every little ragamuffin in New York has bought a brush and a foot-box and gone in the boot-blacking business. "Blackin', sir, blackin'!" "Shine, sir?—nice shine, sir, only five cents!" So they assail a man at every step. . . . If you give one of them a job, half a dozen of them will crowd around and sit on the ground to see it done and criticize it; and to blackguard each other in a slang that no Christian can understand . . . and speak familiarly and disrespectfully of the gentlemen of the City Government and abuse their stupidity . . . and even find fault with . . . the general conduct of the National Government. I notice that they usually speak of great personages as "old" Seward, "old" Johnson, etc. It is because these free-souled young blackguards scorn to be respectful to anything or anybody. . . .

I saw a sign on a house . . . yesterday, which read "Boot-Black-Brigade Chapel" . . . I went in, and found a preacher earnestly exhorting about two hundred of the rattiest lot of little outlaws that any city can produce. Most of the time they listened pretty intently, but critically—always critically, for behold, the bootblack is nothing if not critical. Part of what the preacher said they seemed to receive . . . under mild protest —but when he said that Lazarus was brought to life after he had been dead three days, there was a pretty general telegraphing of incredulity from eye to eye . . . and one boy with a shock head and rags all over to match nudged his neighbor, and said in a coarse whisper, "I don't go that, Bill, do you?—'cause he'd stink, wouldn't he?"

A spirit of camaraderie existed, apparently, between the bootblacks and our traveling correspondent. One of them warned him against a certain streetwalker spoken of as "that curly girl." Lawless, the bootblacks certainly are, but they are not condemned by their recorder; they are simply accepted as they are—even enjoyed for being so completely what they are. No moralizing is directed towards them by Mark Twain. In fact, he has grave doubts about the success of the moral aspirations held on their behalf by the enthusiast who preaches and prays for them. It is significant that, concerning the nature of boys, he generally seems ready to accept them just as they are, without any condemnation.

Mr. Brown accompanied Mark Twain to Europe; but when the *Quaker City* letters were revised for book publication as *The Innocents Abroad,* part of Brown became Blucher, part became Jack, and the coarsest part of him was expurgated entirely.[1] Although large segments of the human race are generally viewed in this book with distaste, sometimes with a feeling that veers close to hate, individuals are enjoyed and presented without animus in thumbnail sketches exhibiting Mark Twain's delight in the eccentricities of humankind. The Oracle, the "Poet Lariat," the Interrogation Point, the "Fergusons"—generic name for all guides—all these persons are studied, understood, and depicted with care. Such sketches constitute an approach to the novelist's art. Even in a brief account of an occasion on which Napoleon III and the Sultan of Turkey reviewed troops in Paris, Mark Twain gets underneath the externals to underlying human nature in his lines on the Emperor:

Napoleon, in military uniform—a long-bodied, short-legged man, fiercely mustached, old, wrinkled, with eyes half closed, and *such* a deep, crafty, scheming expression about them! Napoleon, bowing ever so gently to the loud plaudits, and watching everything and everybody with his cat-eyes from under his depressed hat-brim, as if to discover any sign that those cheers were not heartfelt and cordial.

In such passages, brilliantly done, the embryo novelist's relish in human nature shines through the traveler's report of the military parade. Leading even more directly to the novel are those characterizations which are maintained throughout the book: Dan, Mark Twain's roommate; Blucher, from "the Far West"; Jack, a young man determined to wring the utmost from his experiences; and the Doctor, whose look of "inspired idiocy" proved such an effective foil to the Fergusons.

---

[1] Introduction, *Travels with Mr. Brown*, 6. *The Innocents Abroad* is by no means simply a reprinting of the letters written for the *Alta California*. Mark Twain edited the letters, rewriting some, eliminating others entirely. His account of France was expanded, and about half of the Italian chapters were new. See DeLancey Ferguson, *Mark Twain: Man and Legend*, 136.

It was early in the *Tramp Abroad* tour, it should be remembered, that Mark Twain celebrated in an exultant letter to Howells his new-found feeling of freedom to enjoy the scene about him: "And I am so happy, for I am responsible for none of it." Freed of the weight of guilt-inducing responsibility, he was able to free his imagination to the point where he could achieve the aesthetic attitude, looking on the people about him as part of the spectacle of life, writing about them from a distance sufficient to insure detachment. This mood lasted long enough to produce some excellent bits of writing. Perhaps it is no accident that *A Tramp Abroad*, despite its dead weight of burlesque, contains the two best among all the character sketches which form interludes in the travel books.

The second-best characterization is that of Nicodemus Dodge, "a loose-jointed . . . tow-headed, jeans-clad, countrified cub" from the back country of Missouri. His prototype was Jim Wolfe of Hannibal, but his dialect foreshadows that of Huck Finn: he has seen people who could "lay over" him in writing, but in ciphering he "ain't no slouch." The high point of character drawing for all the travel books, however, appears in the sketch of Jim Baker and his "Bluejay Yarn." Its subject matter arises from imaginative fantasy, akin to ancient mythical and bestiary material about "animals which talk, and kobolds, and enchanted folk." But its narrator is a realistic embodiment of the California frontier, a miner whose patient, explanatory mind, in Bernard DeVoto's phrase, "actually works before our eyes," whose speech is "so cunningly caught that its rhythms produce complete conviction." Mark Twain's harmonious blending of the material of fantasy and the framework of realism has not only a competent technique but also an artistic value.

Jim Baker's bluejay yarn was brought to Mark Twain's mind in the woods near Heidelberg, but it arose from his memories of Jim Gillis and the Tuolumne hills. Nicodemus Dodge came back to him on a walk in the country near Oppenau, but Dodge's origin lay in the sharp perception Mark Twain had given to his type in the years spent in Missouri. These two character portraits are more successful than others appearing in the travel books not only because of the greater freedom of imagination which plays about them, but also because they had the immeasurable advantage of having lain long in the seedbed of Mark Twain's mind. The greater part of the travel books consists of material written up day by day under the exigencies of sight-seeing, or elaborated later from brief jottings. On aesthetic grounds the process by which Jim Baker and Nicodemus Dodge were finally arrived at is far superior to the travel-note method. Time and a liberated imagination operated together to give Mark Twain the perspective, the aesthetic distance, necessary for artistic creation.

In *Following the Equator*, he encountered an "imitation dude," wearing a pomatum cake on his head and smoking "the most extraordinary cigarettes—made of some kind of manure, apparently." This fellow ardently imitated the Prince of Wales:

He was living in a dude dream-land where all his squalid shams were genuine, and himself a sincerity. It . . . mollified spite to see him so enjoy his imitation languors, and arts, and airs, and refinements. . . . He began to pose as the Prince and work his dreams and languors for exhibition.

This person met in a travel book embodies one of the favorite themes of Mark Twain's fiction—the insidious effects of living within a dream.

His servants in India are deftly exhibited. Manuel was first, Manuel of the deferential stoop, the gentle and timid black eyes, who stood before his employers and bowed "in the pathetic Indian way." Of different caliber indeed was Satan, who answered to that name because his own was so Indian and so unpronounceable. Satan flew about in a manner that contrasted greatly with the "slumbrous way" of Manuel:

All my heart . . . all my admiration, went out spontaneously to this frisky little forked black thing, this compact and compressed incarnation of energy and force and promptness . . . this smart, smily, engaging, shiny-eyed little devil, feruled on his upper end by a gleaming fire-coal of a fez with a red-hot tassel dangling from it.

But in an evil hour Satan got drunk once too often and had to be dismissed to please the women of the party. Mark Twain lamented, "I would rather have lost a hundred angels than that one poor lovely devil." Satan's successor, the grave Sahadat, was competent and satisfactory—"But where he was, it seemed always Sunday."

Thus, as Mark Twain journeyed about the world, in infrequent moods of detachment he recorded persons, not from the point of view of the moralist-reformer, but from the point of view of the spectator, the people themselves being presented as part of the broad spectacle of life. The space given to people in the travel books is indicated in *Following the Equator* in the introduction to his chapter on Hobart: "Necessarily, the human interest is the first interest in the log-book of any country."

CHAPTER 15

Mark Twain's Style

ACCORDING to Bernard DeVoto, it was Ford Madox Ford who first had the courage to list the style of Mark Twain among the great styles of literature in English. That style is here examined principally in the travel books because in them Mark Twain speaks in his own person, with no necessity for adapting himself to the exigencies of characterization or of dialect, as is often the case in his fiction. Factors affecting his style have already been discussed in preceding chapters; it is pertinent at this point to present a more minute analysis than was possible in the discussions which have emphasized the successes and failures of his insight. "When the writer speaks in his own person," says J. Middleton Murry, "... you look first to his turn of thought, then to his turn of phrase." It is now time to examine Mark Twain's turn of phrase.

Style is the aspect of writing which he considered most closely in the writings of others and with which he concerned himself most frequently in his own work. In a letter to Howells in 1875 he commented on his own style:

... how awkwardly I do jumble words together; and how often I do use three words where one would answer—a thing I am always trying to guard against. I shall become as slovenly a writer as Charles Francis Adams if I don't look out. (That is just in jest; because ... I do not seriously fear getting so bad as that. I never shall drop so far toward his and Bret Harte's level as to catch myself saying "It must have been wiser to have believed that he might have accomplished it if he could have felt that he would have been supported by those who should have &c. &c. &c.")

In his essay "Howells," he praised his friend as excelling in "certain great qualities—clearness, compression, verbal exactness, and unforced and seemingly unconscious felicity of phrasing," as well as for his mastery of "the right word . . . cadenced and undulating rhythm . . . and architectural felicities of construction." Compactness, simplicity, and vigor of expression are the elements he praised in a book discussed in *Roughing It*. The "pemmican sentences" of Thomas Fuller delighted him: "Old Fuller . . . boils an elaborate thought down and compresses it into a single crisp and meaty sentence. It is a wonderful faculty." In his essay on "Fenimore Cooper's Literary Offenses," he presents his "nineteen rules governing literary art," which cover the matter of style. "As to the Adjective," says Pudd'nhead Wilson, "when in doubt, strike it out." It was style that he stressed in his letter to his daughter Susy, praising her literary superiorities: ". . . clearness of statement, directness, felicity of expression, photographic ability in setting forth an incident—style, good style—no barnacles on it in the way of unnecessary, retarding words (the shipman scrapes off the barnacles when he wants his racer to go her best gait and straight to the buoy)." Mark Twain came to be proud of his own style. He commended a "just and laudatory" biographical sketch that had set his head "to swelling—I will not deny it. For it contained praises of the very thing which I most loved to hear praised—the good quality of my English." In his book *Christian Science*, he said:

No one can write perfect English and keep it up through a stretch of ten chapters. It has never been done. It was approached in the "well of English undefiled"; it has been approached in Mrs. Eddy's Annex to that Book; . . . I have even approached it myself; but none of us has made port.

Van Wyck Brooks, commenting on what he calls Mark Twain's "lifelong preoccupation with grammar," points to "signs of the young schoolboy who has begun to take pride in his compositions and has become suddenly aware of words." It is true that Mark Twain did lay considerable stress on what he called "that elusive and shifty grain of gold, the right word." He once remarked that the difference between the almost right word and the right word is "the difference between the lightning-bug and the lightning." In "Some Rambling Notes of an Idle Excursion," he expended several paragraphs in his search for a figure to describe the peculiar white of the

Bermuda houses, built of blocks of white coral: "the whitest white you can conceive of, and the blindingest . . . and, besides, there is a dainty, indefinable something . . . about its look." He felt immense satisfaction when he discovered that this particular white "is exactly the white of the icing of a cake, and has the same unemphasized and scarcely perceptible polish." But the diligent search for the exact word is simply a manifestation of the artist's love for his tools.

Among rhetorical ornaments Mark Twain had an especial love for the metaphor and the simile, both of which he made strikingly vivid. The world of nature was the storehouse from which he drew his imagery. In the Sandwich Islands, Molokai "lay like a homely sway-back whale on the water," and Kealakekua Bay was "a little curve like the last kink of a snail shell." Later, St. Mark's Cathedral, propped on its row of "low thick-legged columns, its back knobbed with domes . . . seemed like a vast warty bug, taking a meditative walk." Mountains in the distance showed "rounded velvety backs [that] made one want to stroke them, as one would the sleek back of a cat." The city of Athens, flooded with moonlight, seemed "like some living creature wrapped in peaceful slumber."

The vegetable kingdom, winds, storms, and geographical and topographical features form the bases for figures both humorous and serious. The thrill of an intellectual discovery "swells a man's breast with pride above that which any other experience can bring"; that is, "to discover a great thought—an intellectual nugget, right under the dust of a field that many a brain-plow had gone over before." This last figure is a notable example of Mark Twain's faculty for expressing abstract ideas in concrete terms, always one of the distinguishing features of his style. Nicodemus Dodge wore an old slouch hat whose rim "hung limp and ragged about his eyes like a bug-eaten cabbage leaf." In India, clumps of natives, "not still, but moving, swaying, drifting, eddying, a delirious display of . . . all shades of color, delicate, lovely, pale, soft, strong, stunning, vivid, brilliant," were like "a storm of sweetpea blossoms passing on the wings of the hurricane." Yes, he loved words, this frontier humorist.

In the Sandwich Islands "the red sun looked . . . through the tall, clean stems of the cocoa-nut trees, like a blooming whisky bloat through the bars of a city prison." But by the time of *A Tramp Abroad*, the humorous figures are more carefully wrought, though exaggeration still appears in good measure:

Some German words are so long that they have a perspective. . . . These things are not words, they are alphabetical processions. . . . one can open a German newspaper any time and see them marching majestically across the page—and if he has any imagination he can see the banners and hear the music, too. They impart a martial thrill to the meekest subject.

Unusual figures everywhere surprise the reader. The average Hindu was a slave to "two million gods and twenty million priests . . . and other sacred bacilli." In Hobart, the tidy houses had a human aspect: even the "modestest cottage" looked "combed and brushed." The huge ruin of Heidelberg Castle, with its empty windows and moldering towers, was "the Lear of inanimate nature—deserted, discrowned, beaten by the storms, but royal still, and beautiful." Quaint phrasings distinguish some lines, as in his mention of a hill, rising without preparatory slopes, as an "instantaneous hill"; or his remark that a certain rich woman "had never moistened the selvedge edge of her soul with a less plebeian tipple than champagne." Other passages convey a curious sense of movement, as in his description of a journey up the Himalayas: "receding down, down . . . was a shaven confusion of hilltops, with ribbony roads and paths squirming and snaking cream-yellow all over them." His description of the struggles of the moon in trying to top the Alpine peaks, those "sky-piercing fingers" of bare rock, embodies force strongly suggested:

While the moon was behind one of those sharp fingers, its shadow was flung athwart the vacant heaven—a long, slanting, clean-cut, dark ray—with a streaming and energetic suggestion of *force* about it, such as the ascending jet of water from a powerful fire-engine affords.

Mark Twain at times used something akin to Baudelaire's synesthesia, presenting visual effects in terms of sound, where no sound would naturally occur. The same moon that tried in vain to top the Alps "would show the glittering arch of her upper third, occasionally, and scrape it along behind the comblike row" of pinnacles. In a passage which recounts the gold strike in Australia, a "roaring avalanche" of people swept out of Melbourne and left it

. . . desolate, Sunday-like, paralyzed . . . all signs of life departed, all sounds stilled save the rasping of the cloud-shadows as they scraped across the vacant streets.

As in the humorous sketches, so in the travel books, images derived from the elements of fire and water outnumber the rest. The water figures display careful elaboration. In *Travels with Mr. Brown*, Mark Twain described "gleaming cataracts of vines pouring sheer down a hundred and fifty feet . . . wonderful waterfalls of green leaves as deftly overlapping each other as the scales of a fish." Later, he pictured trees in terms of water: "What a soaring, strenuous, gushing fountain-spray of delicate greenery a bunch of bamboo is! . . . vegetable geysers grace the view, their spoutings refined to steam by distance." People, too, he described in water imagery: crowds at a railway station in India passed each other "in opposing floods," while inside the station "tides of rainbow-costumed natives . . . washed up to the long trains and flowed into them . . . followed at once by the next wash, the next wave." And we come again to "the awful German language":

One is washed about in it . . . in the most helpless way; and when at last he thinks he has captured a rule which offers firm ground to take a rest on amid the general rage and turmoil of the ten parts of speech, he turns over the page and reads, "Let the pupil make careful note of the following exceptions." . . . So overboard he goes again to hunt for another Ararat and find another quicksand.

The great number of water images in Mark Twain's work may be explained by the fact that he spent his impressionable years in sight of the mighty Mississippi, but to explain the even greater number of his fire figures is not so simple. Fire had taken early hold on his imagination. In the *Autobiography* he tells of a fire which burned up the Hannibal jail and the drunken tramp inside it under circumstances which horrified him. Little Sam had brought the tramp a box of "lucifer matches" so that he might ease his confinement by smoking; but the tramp started a fire with the matches and lost his life in the flames. Mark Twain wrote that the death of this tramp "lay upon my conscience a hundred nights afterward and filled them with hideous dreams—dreams in which I saw his appealing face as I had seen it . . . pressed against the window bars, with the red hell glowing behind him." The sights and sounds connected with that fire made a lasting impression upon small, remorseful Sam Clemens. By the time of his early days in the West, however, he could view a fire as a splendid spectacle, exclaiming "Superb! magnificent! beautiful!" even when it was the burning of his own timber claim that furnished the thrilling sight. His aesthetic enjoyment of the beauty of fire was in part, no doubt, the result of his intense love for the color red.

At any rate, images based on fire and light far outnumber all others in his work. Plants and trees are described in terms of fire: in the Australian hills he saw a tree whose "mass sphered itself above the naked straight stem like an explosion of misty smoke." Another tree had "a lovely upright tassel . . . red and glowing as a fire-coal." The Blue Mountains were "a softly luminous blue, a smoldering blue, as if vaguely lit by fires within." The average man anywhere is ignorant of all countries except his own, knowing of others only one or two facts which "rise like torches in his mind, lighting up an inch or two of it and leaving the rest all dark." The city of Benares is "a religious Vesuvius," and in its bowels theological forces have been "rumbling, thundering, and quaking, boiling, and . . . flaming and smoking for ages." People, their costumes, and their attributes are described in fire imagery. Jeff Davis was "an extinguished sun" who had gone out "as meekly as a farthing candle." And through the dim haze of years Mark Twain in imagination could still see the lips of Feringhea, the deadly Thug, uncover his teeth and could still catch "the incandescent glimmer of his smile."

The diamonds of South Africa were "smooth and limpid, and in the sunlight they vomited fire." Upon the likeness of gems to fire, Mark Twain based one of his most famous descriptions, the "ice-storm" which Paine considered as a high-water mark of his style. He described an ice-covered tree with the sun upon it. At time for the sunrise, the tree stands waiting, a "white ghost," bare and dead:

. . . at last the sun fires a sudden sheaf of rays into the ghostly tree and turns it into a white splendor of glittering diamonds. . . . The sun climbs higher, and still higher, flooding the tree . . . turning it into a glory of white fire; then in a moment, without warning, comes the great miracle . . . ; a gust of wind sets every branch and twig to swaying, and in an instant turns the whole white tree into a spouting and spraying explosion of flashing gems of every conceivable color; and there it stands and sways this way and that, flash! flash! flash! a dancing and glancing world of rubies, emeralds, diamonds, sapphires, the most radiant spectacle, the most blinding spectacle, the . . . most intoxicating vision of fire and color and intolerable . . . splendor that ever any eye has rested upon in this world.

Particularly suggestive of deliberate artifice are those figures which describe fire in terms of water, or water in terms of fire, or mingle fire imagery and water imagery. At Heidelberg he liked to see the evening sunlight "suddenly strike the leafy declivity at the Castle's base and dash up it and drench it as with a luminous spray." In combining such images, or in conveying a sense of the sound made by "the rasping of cloud-shadows as they scraped across" deserted streets, Mark Twain perhaps experienced what Mr. Murry terms "the arduous joy of compelling words to accept a strange context and a new significance."

In the travel books his descriptions show a style more wordy, less compact, than in any other part of his work save his gaudy Western burlesques. His figures exhibit a conscious artistry to a degree that now and then spoils a passage by putting too much gilt on the lily. Certainly, his descriptive prose is carefully done, couched in a conscious mannered rhythm that calls attention to itself through its succession of adjectives linked with the conjunction *and*. The complex sentence, though employed often enough to avoid monotony, is comparatively rare; the characteristic Mark Twain sentence is the compound sentence. Joseph Warren Beach's description of Ernest Hemingway's style may with some propriety be applied to the style of Mark Twain, except that many of Twain's sentences are long, while most of Hemingway's are "short and simple":

And most of the rest are strings of simple statements held together with *ands*. The rarest thing with him is the statement modified by subordinate clauses indicating . . . intrusive refinements of thought, which only serve to clutter things up and blur the simple . . . sequence. . . . It is the great leveling democracy of the *and*.

The simplicity of sentence pattern in Mark Twain's work resulted, perhaps, from a desire recently attributed to Hemingway, the desire for "a deliberate directness of utterance that permits no involution of thought."[1] Mark Twain's intention, as he said in his 1889 letter to Andrew Lang, was to write so that he would be understood by the common people. He shared this intent with Abraham Lincoln.

[1] J. W. Linn and H. W. Taylor, *A Foreword to Fiction*, 112.

The exactness, clarity, and simplicity of Mark Twain's style are the qualities of good prose wherever it is found; but for individual similarities the style most rewarding in comparison with Mark Twain's seems to be Lincoln's. In a recent article, Roy P. Basler lists the following Lincolnian characteristics: in diction, concrete rather than abstract words, current idiom rather than "authoritarian nicety," reiteration of key words, repetition of sound effects, alliteration, and assonance; in imagery, "an instinct for analogy and metaphor," with antithesis everywhere; in sentence structure, balance and grammatical parallelism; a poetical cadence sometimes elaborrated on a basic pattern of parallel thought, the cadenced prose arising from balanced rhythms with caesurae arranged in a way suggestive of the King James Bible. Most of this applies with equal force to the prose of Mark Twain. Commenting upon Lincoln's repetitive pattern in both diction and sentence structure, Mr. Basler remarks: "These devices were the result of Lincoln's deliberate seeking for an emphasis and simplicity which would prove effective with the common man." Mark Twain's use of parallelism, like Lincoln's, gives a complex idea an almost deceptive simplicity. In Twain's ironic "War Prayer" of 1905, the distinctive features of the style are grammatical parallelism, repetition of key words and sound effects, and alliteration:

O Lord our Father, our young patriots . . . go forth to battle. . . . With them—in spirit—we also go forth from the sweet peace of our beloved firesides to smite the foe.

O Lord our God, help us to tear their soldiers to bloody shreds with our shells; help us to cover their smiling fields with the pale forms of their patriot dead; help us to drown the thunder of the guns with the [screams of] the wounded, writhing in pain; help us to lay waste their humble homes with a hurricane of fire; help us to wring the hearts of their unoffending widows with unavailing grief; help us to turn them out roofless with their little children to wander unfriended through wastes of their desolated land in rags and hunger and thirst, sport of the sun-flames of summer and the icy winds of winter, broken in spirit, worn with travail, imploring Thee for the refuge of the grave and denied it—for our sakes, who adore Thee, Lord, blast their hopes, blight their lives, protract their bitter pilgrimage . . . water their way with their tears, stain the white snow with the blood of their wounded feet! We ask of one who is the Spirit of love and who is the ever-faithful refuge and friend of all that are sore beset, and seek His aid with humble and contrite hearts. . . . Amen.

But figures of speech, sentence structure, prose rhythms—all these may be considered the minor qualities of style. The major aspects are not so easily pointed out and labeled, yet they reveal the organic nature of the style. For, as Buffon succinctly phrased it, "the style is the man himself"; and style considered thus will depend upon the writer's individual way of thinking and feeling.

A travel book is expected to be largely "personal" writing and is under no obligation to achieve a definite form, as is a novel or a poem; therefore, in the travel book the style of the author may be expected to bloom in utter freedom. But, although no definite form is demanded, the reader has a right to expect a certain coherence of ideas—leading, perhaps, to an emergent sense of the quality of the land perceived by the traveler. All descriptive writing must rest upon sensuous perceptions, and the writer who can store up vivid sensory images has a distinct advantage in the creation of descriptive prose. Descriptive writing as embodied in a travel book, Mr. Murry points out, may be conducted on several planes: (1) the sensuous perceptions of the writer may be merely presented; (2) the sensuous perceptions may have certain emotional accompaniments; (3) the emotional responses may be so sustained and systematized that they embody attitudes held by the writer; and (4) these characteristic attitudes may lead to a contemplative activity, a reflection which indicates the writer's realization of the dominant quality pervading the visited land. When the last stage is attained, the travel book will possess a universality which makes it a true "criticism of life," although it neither asserts nor defines. It will display an understanding of the peoples of the lands through which the writer journeys, an understanding which will lift it above mere surface impressions, mere reporting. As Mr. Murry maintains, "The great writer does not really come to conclusions about life; he discerns a quality in it."

Possessing more than ordinary sensibility, Mark Twain had great capacity for storing up the sensuous perceptions which are the chief resource of the descriptive writer. All his travel books contain passages on the first and elementary level, the mere accumulation of detail, which may be photographic in its visual effects but nevertheless fails to reveal any essential quality of the place described. Here is an example from *The Innocents Abroad;* the lines, describing Fayal in the Azores, are so devoid of individual life that they might have been lifted from a prospectus:

> The town has eight thousand to ten thousand inhabitants. Its snow-white houses nestle cozily in a sea of fresh green vegetation, and no village could look prettier. . . . It sits in the lap of an amphitheater of hills three hundred to seven hundred feet high and carefully cultivated clear to their summits. . . . Every farm . . . is cut up into little square inclosures by stone walls. . . . These hundreds of green squares, marked by their black lava walls, make the hills look like vast checker-boards.

Mixed with the statistics, there is here an abundance of figurative language, but no distinction in the style. This is merely routine travel talk in which Mark Twain ticks off descriptive bits like items in an inventory.

On the second descriptive level, some emotional element in the writer's mind enters the description. In a second passage taken from *The Innocents Abroad,* Mark Twain appears to have felt a certain quality in what he saw and to have tried to fix that quality for the reader. He describes the ascent of Vesuvius over a rough trail leading across an old lava flow:

> . . . a wilderness of furious whirlpools, of miniature mountains rent asunder—of gnarled and knotted, wrinkled and twisted masses of blackness that mimicked branching roots . . . and all . . . this turbulent panorama, all this stormy . . . waste of blackness, with its thrilling suggestiveness of life, of action, of boiling, surging, furious motion, was petrified!—all stricken dead and cold in the instant of its maddest rioting!—fettered, paralyzed, and left to glower at heaven in impotent rage forevermore!

Colored with an emotion absent from the first quotation, this passage is decked with some of his favorite images; still the passage is not successful as style. For the source of good style, as Mr. Murry points out, must be a decisive original emotion in the author which challenges him to communicate the same emotion to the reader. Whatever emotion Mark Twain experienced was, apparently, shifting and chaotic. Its chaotic nature is revealed by his use of the "miniature" and the "panorama," customary in his descriptions of far-off beauty, but employed here to describe close-at-hand black ugliness and fettered rage. There is a plethora of adjectives, and the last lines become mere rhetoric, a verbal exaggeration of an emotion which dissolved away in the mere act of expression. Lacking the clarity and precision and vividness of emotion which would render the description true for the reader, Mark Twain attempted to raise it to a more powerful stage; he pumped it up with words. As a result, the passage overshoots its mark.

On the same level of sensuous perception with emotional accompaniment, but more successful stylistically, is a third passage from *The Innocents Abroad* in which he describes a night storm at sea:

There was no thunder, no noise but [that of] the pounding bows of the ship, the keen whistling of the gale through the cordage, and the rush of the seething waters. But the vessel climbed aloft . . . then paused an instant that seemed a century, and plunged headlong down again, as from a precipice. The sheeted sprays drenched the decks like rain . . . darkness was everywhere. At long intervals a flash of lightning clove it with a quivering line of fire that revealed a heaving world of water where was nothing before, kindled the dusky cordage to glittering silver, and lit up the faces of the men with a ghastly luster! . . . Some thought the vessel could not live through the night, and it seemed less dreadful to stand out in the midst of the wild tempest and *see* the peril . . . than to be shut up in the sepulchral cabins, under the dim lamps, and imagine the horrors that were abroad on the ocean. And once out . . . where they could hear the shriek of the winds, and face the driving spray . . . they were prisoners to a fierce fascination they could not resist, and so remained. It was a wild night—and a very, very long one.

Here the emotion was a true one; Mark Twain was among those held prisoner on deck by the "fierce fascination" of the scene, and the particularity of his emotion renders the description true for the reader. Images of sound here reinforce visual details, but neither class of images could insure success if the original emotion had not been keenly felt by the writer; for sound images may become merely phonographic, as visual images may be merely photographic. In the latter part of the description, the effort at communication has compelled the writer to select language drawn from a body of emotions already systematized into an attitude: Mark Twain's preoccupation with death. This preoccupation is revealed in the figurative language:

the ghastly luster on the men's faces, the sepulchral cabins, the ship that might not "live through the night."

The descriptions presented thus far have been of a relatively simple nature. They show Mark Twain responding directly to separate impressions; although his sensuous perceptions have been sensitively acute, his emotions have remained episodic. But on the third level of descriptive writing, impressions of a certain type have a peculiar weight and significance for the writer because the emotions accompanying them arise from predispositions connected with his "mode of experience," to employ Mr. Murry's phrase. These emotions reinforce each other, as they accumulate in the writer's consciousness, until they are systematized into a body of emotional content which may be labeled an attitude. This psychological fact explains the striking similarity of Mark Twain's passages describing the beauty of scenes encountered in his travels. His attitude towards beauty, his habitual thought-pattern concerning beauty, led him to evaluate it over and over in terms of the dream because for him beauty was far off, somehow not real. These lines from *Following the Equator* will recall similar passages quoted earlier as examples of Mark Twain's reaction to beauty in nature. This, then, is the African veldt:

... it was ecstasy to ... gaze out over the ... solitudes of the velvet plains ... softest and loveliest of all in the remote distances, where dim island-hills seemed afloat, as in a sea—a sea made of dream-stuff flushed with colors faint and rich.

Mark Twain possessed, too, an attitude crystallized from his predispositions concerning ugliness, a body of emotions lying deep in his consciousness which rose to the surface for his use in describing the ugliness of life. Ugliness was very real to him. As I have said, most of his passages describing beauty have to do with landscapes, most of the ugliness with human-kind. Beauty is always so vague, so far away, that its very distance stamps it as unattainable. But where there is ugliness to portray, his close scrutiny is reflected in his recording of details. Describing the drowned man who lay, "naked, swollen, purple," on a stone in the Paris morgue, he stood close enough to picture the stream of water trickling "ceaselessly over the hideous face," and the dead hand that clutched a bit of broken bush. His obvious absorption with ugliness reveals his failure to see life whole. He can only glimpse the beauty; but his descriptions of ugliness detail a particularity of emotion, definite, real, and fascinating.

Another accumulation of emotions arising out of his mode of experience is embodied in his moralizing attitude. In such passages as his horrified description of the Parisian cancan, emotions which have received the endorsement of an attitude lend coherence to the sensuous perceptions. In a writer of maturity and power, such attitudes may attain the dignity of convictions. Mark Twain's moralistic passages seem imbued with conviction; but their final worth must depend upon the comprehensiveness of the attitude embodied in that conviction. The cancan passage begins, "I placed my hands before my face for very shame," details the procedure of the dance, accents the "vicious kick" that ends it, and concludes:

This is the Can-Can. The idea of it is to dance as wildly, as noisily, as furiously as you can; expose youself as much as possible if you are a woman; and kick as high as you can, no matter which sex you belong to. There is no word of exaggeration in this. . . . I suppose French morality is not of that strait-laced description which is shocked at trifles.

Hiding his face for shame was, of course, a humorous exaggeration, humorously intended; but the passage above was soberly written, seriously intended. In such lines the writer's purpose seems to be not merely to make the reader see, but to make him think and feel in a certain way. The complex emotional leanings which constituted Mark Twain's attitude of moralism are here functioning; but the style is inadequate, since it does not compel in the reader an emotion similar to the writer's. It reveals instead a limited, personal, less than significant experience; it falls short of the highest achievement in style, which Mr. Murry defines as the "complete fusion of the personal and the universal."

Only on the fourth and highest level does style attain that complete fusion. This level is reached when the writer's attitudes lead him into a reflection which crystallizes in certain passages his realization of the dominant quality pervading the universe of man's existence. In order for a writer to enter the first rank, his capacity for sensuous experience should be practically unlimited; but this in itself is not enough. For, as Mr. Murry observes, "the apprehension of the quality of life as a whole, the power to discern the universal in the particular, and to make the particular a symbol of the universal, which is the distinctive mark of the great writer . . . is derived not from sensuous perceptions but from emotional contemplation." In other words, the wisdom, the understanding of the writer, must reveal itself through what he writes.

In the travel books Mark Twain reaches this level only rarely. One example, already quoted, occurs in *A Tramp Abroad* in his account of finding the solitary forget-me-not amid desolate ice and snow. In this passage he reaches out, beyond his custom, for a metaphor possessing universal significance—the blue flower, a symbol of hope and courage fighting to conquer despair. By such use of metaphor a quality perceived on one plane of existence is transferred to define a quality recognized on another plane of existence. The blue flower thus enables Mark Twain to carry the articulation of the sensuous, material world on into the world of the spirit; and the object employed as metaphor becomes at once the cause and the symbol of the emotion. Baudelaire wrote that, in certain states of the soul, "the profound significance of life is revealed completely in the spectacle, however commonplace, that is before one's eyes; it becomes the symbol of this significance." And the greater the writer, the more continuous does the comprehensive condition of the soul become. With Mark Twain, this comprehensive condition was more intermittent than continuous; among the travel books, it was more continuous in *Following the Equator* than in any other.

Criticism has generally looked upon this book with small favor. Speaking of the agonizing personal calamities under which Mark Twain wrote it, Bernard DeVoto has labeled it the dullest of his books. DeLancey Ferguson sees it as the work of a weary man, full of bitter wisdom. Mark Twain *was* old, bitter, and weary when he wrote the book, shortly after the death of his daughter Susy; yet it was the writing, the love of writing, that saved him. While the book was underway, he wrote to Howells that he was indifferent to nearly everything but work:

Indeed I am a mud image, and it will puzzle me to know what is in me that writes, and has comedy-fancies and finds pleasure in phrasing them. It is a law of our natures, of course, or it wouldn't happen; the thing in me forgets the presence of the mud image and goes its own way, unconscious of it and apparently of no kinship with it. I have finished my book, but I go on as if the end were indefinitely away.

To me, *Following the Equator* has a spiritual quality that the other travel books lack. In an 1899 letter to Howells, reserved for more detailed discussion in connection with Mark Twain's fiction, Twain singled out as the most potent factor in Howells' ability to write vitally and forcefully the sense of the dignity in human life which Howells possessed. Although the first volume of the *Equator* book is dull enough, in the second volume—at least in the extensive sections on India—Mark Twain showed that he, too, sensed the eternal dignity of the human spirit, the quality which he later recognized as rendering vital the work of Howells. Discussing the way a writer tries to hide his true feelings—"the secret sigh behind the public smile, the private What-in-hell-did-I-come-for!"—he confided to Howells that this concealment was his own aim while writing the *Equator* book: "I wrote my last book—in hell; but I let on, the best I could, that it was an excursion through heaven." When a writer can transcend illness and age and personal grief to make his work embody qualities of universal significance beyond the scope of ordinary travel-writing, he has at last attained a literary maturity. He has even attained what may be fairly labeled a great style. Mark Twain's belated recognition of the beauty which underlies the boredom and the horror of human existence, impermanent though it was, permeates the style of the second volume and gives to it a fullness and a vitality which the other travel books lack.

Even the lines in which he fell back into his old habit of viewing beauty as unreality have a personal immediacy not evident elsewhere. For instance, in the passage in which he spoke of remembering India with the sense of having a kaleidoscope at his eye, he said: "... I hear the clash of the glass bits as the splendid figures change, and fall apart, and flash into new forms, figure after figure, and with the birth of each new form I feel my skin crinkle and my nerve-web tingle with a new thrill of wonder and delight." The immediate response of crinkling skin and tingling nerve-web seems to show that he was much closer to this beauty than in passages in which he saw beauty through a dream mist, far off.

Paradoxically, in some passages dealing with India even the dream descriptions achieve a sort of reality—enough of reality that human beings become a part of the dream scenes described. Mark Twain wrote that on a long drive through the open country of India, there were always

... barefoot natives gliding by like spirits, without sound of footfall, and others in the distance dissolving away and vanishing like the creatures of dreams. Now and then a string of stately camels passed by ... and they were velvet-shod by nature, and made no noise. Indeed, there were no noises of any sort in this paradise ... [save] one, for a moment: a file of native convicts passed along ... and we caught the soft clink of their chains.

Here, even the clink of convicts' chains could be "soft," soft enough not to destroy, for the erstwhile fuming humanitarian, the loveliness of this paradise. The style presents a perfect harmony between the writer's temper, the chosen land of his journeying, and his language. Other passages reveal a style in which every word seems relevant to the originating emotion and the rhythm of the lines is appropriate to that emotion, as in his description of the compound at Jeypore:

The inn cow poked about the compound and emphasized the secluded and country air of the place, and there was a dog of no particular breed, who was always present ... and always asleep, always stretched out baking in the sun and adding to the deep tranquillity and reposefulness of the place, when the crows were away on business. White-draperied servants were coming and going all the time, but they seemed only spirits, for their feet were bare and made no sound. Down the lane a piece lived an elephant in the shade of a noble tree, and rocked and rocked, and reached about with his trunk, begging of his brown mistress or fumbling the children playing at his feet. And there were camels about, but they go on velvet feet, and were proper to the silence and serenity of the surroundings.

The dominant mood of serenity is emphasized here by the absence of sound: the crows that were not there; the dog that was always asleep; the noiseless, bare feet of the servants; the padded, velvet feet of the camels. The passage demonstrates the repose of a writer in full mastery of his style, compelling language to conform to his mode of experience, giving it the stamp of individuality which makes it almost impossible to mistake this passage for the work of any other writer.

To sum up the style of Mark Twain, his stylistic excellence arises from simplicity, long rhythms, idiomatic phrasing, colloquial ease, vivid vocabulary, and an imagery in intimate accord with the senses. Against the assertions of criticism, Mr. DeVoto reminds us, "it should be remembered that such a style is not developed inattentively, nor are infants born with one by God's providence." Mark Twain's artistic conscience is reflected in his intense care for the exact word and in his ability, usually, to give an effect of complete naturalness and unself-consciousness—the art that seems no art—although in the travel books there is sometimes a mannered rhythm which lets the careful craftsmanship show through. His stylistic weaknesses appear to arise not from carelessness or indifference, but sometimes from the larger structural failure contingent upon a clash of unreconciled ideas and sometimes from the smaller but more immediate obstacle of his indignation. Since style depends not only upon the temperament of a writer but also upon the nature of his theme, the content of the travel books has been examined. Here the struggle between form and content does not impair the form as much as it does elsewhere, because the travel books fall naturally into a simple chronological or topical order; but in the matter of content, it is in the travel books especially that Mark Twain's failure to accept life as a whole is revealed in his tendency to view all beauty as unreal, as dream, while he sees in the ugliness of life a sharp reality.

Although the earlier travel books contain passages of intermittent brilliance and many descriptions made consistent by Mark Twain's attitudes, most of these show him responding separately to every stimulus. His moralistic attitudes, not reinforced by and often at variance with the aesthetic depths of his nature, produced mere surface reactions. Only in the *Equator* book are his attitudes crystallized into an underlying realization of the dominant quality of the life he travels through. At rest in a conception that is satisfying to him, at last the artist writes out of his complete being. The other travel books are episodic in effect rather than philosophic. Only *Following the Equator* gives the reader a sense of the universal significance emerging from the multitude of Mark Twain's vivid perceptions—that universality which makes of such a travel book a true criticism of life.

Mark Twain has been a strong influence in literature because he was an innovator. The liberating effect on other writers of such innovations as Twain's use of the vernacular and his early "revolt from the village" (an element of his subject matter to be discussed later in connection with his fiction) can hardly be overstated. Ernest Hemingway's praise of *Huckleberry Finn* as "the best book we've had" has already been cited; William Faulkner acclaimed Mark Twain as "the first truly American writer" and continued: "all of us since are his heirs, we descended from him." Thus two American Nobel Prize winners have put themselves on record. Among his other American heirs and descendants may be mentioned Jack London, O. Henry, Ring Lardner, Theodore Dreiser, Booth Tarkington, Sherwood Anderson, Sinclair Lewis, John Steinbeck, and J. D. Salinger. The chief vehicle of his influence has been *Huckleberry Finn*.

Indeed, it seems not too much to say today that his use of the vernacular and his deliberate colloquial ease have exerted an influence that has spilled over into world literature. In its remarkable simplicity, clarity, and flexibility Mark Twain's style, described by Bernard DeVoto as "so lucid that it seems effortless," led DeVoto to maintain that Twain "had a greater effect than any other writer on the evolution of American prose."

BOOK IV

The Reminiscences

CHAPTER 16

Looking Backward

M ARK TWAIN's books of personal reminiscences include *Roughing It, Life on the Mississippi*, and the *Autobiography*, of which there is now a third volume, culled from the Mark Twain Papers and arranged and edited by Bernard DeVoto under the title *Mark Twain in Eruption*. Together, the travel books and the reminiscences make up half of Mark Twain's published works. It is not necessary to deal with the reminiscenses in detail in this volume, for they have been thoroughly analyzed and discussed in other places. Still, no study of Mark Twain would be complete without some mention of these reminiscent books and the manner of their writing.

Roughing It, the first of them, exists in embryo in Chapter XII of *The Innocents Abroad*, in the suggestion of the enjoyment to be found in a trip across the continent by stagecoach, while one lies on the mail sacks and dreamily smokes his pipe. Encouraged by the sale of *The Innocents Abroad*, its publisher, Elisha Bliss, proposed a book to relate Mark Twain's experiences in the Far West, beginning with the cross-country stage trip. On July 15, 1870, Mark Twain wrote to Orion Clemens that he had begun the book that day. His memory of the stage journey was faulty, and he implored Orion, "Jot down a foolscap page of items for me." Orion complied. On September 4, Mark Twain wrote to Bliss that he was at work on the book and added: "*The Innocents Abroad* will have to get up early to beat it."

Then misfortune struck the undertaking. Mrs. Clemens's father had died in August; she herself became ill; her first child was prematurely born in November, 1870; and in March her husband wrote to Orion that he was "still nursing Livy night and day." He was working on *Roughing It*, but the work moved slowly. Nevertheless, he was able to inject a large zest into his writing, as these lines show:

The stage whirled along at a spanking gait, the breeze flapping curtains in a most exhilarating way; . . . the pattering of the horses' hoofs, the cracking of the driver's whip, and his "Hi-yi! g'lang!" were music; . . . and as we lay and smoked the pipe of peace . . . we felt that there was only one complete and satisfying happiness in the world, and we had found it. . . . Ham and eggs, and after these a pipe—an old, rank, delicious pipe—ham and eggs and scenery, a "down grade," a flying coach, a fragrant pipe and a contented heart—these make happiness. It is what all the ages have struggled for.

Livy's health improved with time, and Mark Twain wrote to Bliss: "I am writing with a red-hot interest. . . . Nothing grieves me now; nothing . . . bothers me or gets my attention. I don't think of anything but the book, and don't have an hour's unhappiness. . . . It will be a starchy book." Always, he could drown his troubles in writing as some men drown them in drink. To Orion, he disclosed some of the difficulties of the professional writer: ". . . right in the first chapter, I have got to alter the whole style of one of my characters and rewrite him clear through to where I am now. It is no fool of a job . . . but the book will be greatly bettered by it." The only character who appears early enough to fit the role and seems a likely candidate is the driver of the stagecoach, who lasts through several chapters and struts before worshiping hostlers as a person of "insufferable dignity."[1]

The impact of the frontier West is recorded in this book. In 1868 Mark Twain had written to Mrs. A. W. Fairbanks:

There is nothing that makes me prouder than to be regarded by intelligent people as "authentic." A name I have coveted so long—and secured at last! *I* don't care anything about being humorous, or poetical, or eloquent, or anything of that kind—the end and aim of my ambition is to be authentic—is to be considered authentic.

[1] DeLancey Ferguson believes (*Man and Legend,* 157) that Mark Twain had begun the book by ridiculing his brother Orion and "had thought better of it." His tendency to make fun of the ineffectual Orion did crop up at various times; it is unlikely, however, that this was one of the times. On the very day he began *Roughing It,* he had been forced to appeal to Orion for help, and his sense of justice was keen. Furthermore, he had enjoyed basking in Orion's official glory during the period reflected in this book. Although he learned soon after his arrival in the West that there was no salary provided for an assistant secretary of the Territory, nevertheless in the Nevada Directory of 1861 one reads: "Orion Clemens, Secretary of State. Sam'l L. Clemens, Assistant Secretary of State." (Mack, *Mark Twain in Nevada,* 77).

In the epic sweep and vigor of *Roughing It,* he captured what must be an authentic reproduction of that Western life. The fresh wild humor of the West produced the tales of the tree-climbing buffalo, the gold-bearing flour sack, and the remarkable Mexican plug. There are also character sketches done in the frontier vernacular, with every intonation, every gesture and pause, indicated by Mark Twain. Among them stand the anecdote of Jim Blaine and "Grandfather's Old Ram"; the tale of Dick Baker (a literary alias for Dick Stoker) and his strangely sagacious cat, Tom Quartz; and the inimitable story of Buck Fanshaw's funeral. The prototype for Buck Fanshaw was the colorful Tom Peaseley, fire chief *extraordinaire* of Virginia City and owner of The Sazerac, famous saloon on C Street.[2] This book exhibits Mark Twain's facility in limning a character in a few lines; we feel we know the frontier woman on the stagecoach who represents herself as "kind o' offish and partic'lar for a gal that's raised in the woods . . . but when people comes along which is my equals . . . I'm a pretty sociable heifer after all."

But the bulk of the two volumes is given over to the saga of the gold rush, to the fabulous Comstock lode which, said Mark Twain, "stretched its opulent length straight through the town of Virginia City, Nevada, a magnet for young men from all over the nation." In these pages Mark Twain showed how much he had progressed technically since the day-by-day travel reporting of *The Innocents Abroad.* Looking back across the four years which separated him from the time depicted in *Roughing It,* he gained a perspective which lent his work a finer finish than the earlier book had possessed. He described the inhabitants of the Sacramento Valley of California as men who reveled in "gold, whisky, fights, and fandangoes, and were unspeakably happy"; but they hated aristocrats, having "a particular and malignant animosity toward what they called a 'b'iled shirt.' "

In spite of his statement that these people were happy, he shows his constant awareness of the tragedy that stood always behind these scenes of carefree, riotous living. In a passage celebrating the Western exuberance, he views the California of those days as a cross-section of gold-mad masculinity:

It was a driving, vigorous, restless population . . . the *only* population of the kind that the world has ever seen gathered together. . . . For, observe,

[2] Mack, *Mark Twain in Nevada,* 198.

it was an assemblage of two hundred thousand young men—not simpering, dainty, kid-gloved weaklings, but stalwart, muscular, dauntless young braves. . . . none but erect, bright-eyed, quick-moving, strong-handed young giants. . . . And where are they now? Scattered to the ends of the earth—or prematurely aged and decrepit—or shot or stabbed in street affrays—or dead of disappointed hopes and broken hearts . . . victims devoted upon the altar of the golden calf—the noblest holocaust that ever wafted its sacrificial incense heavenward.

These victims sacrificed to "the golden calf" were sometimes pocket miners, who haunted the ghost towns. Grassy slopes that had once held a flourishing city might now hold a single log cabin, sheltering a handful of miners who had seen the town "pass away like a dream. With it their hopes had died, and their zest for life." Like Tennyson's "Lotos-Eaters," having eaten of the yellow dust, they "had resigned themselves to their exile, and ceased to . . . turn longing eyes toward their early homes. . . . they stood . . . in a living grave."

Mark Twain himself inevitably fell a victim to the contagion and was "smitten with the silver fever." Much of his later fiction deals with the insidious effects of dreams of wealth to come; in *Roughing It* he showed himself experiencing such dreams. He and three companions rushed eagerly into the Humboldt region: "We were stark mad with excitement . . . smothered under mountains of prospective wealth . . . but our credit was not good at the grocer's. . . . It was a beggar's revel." Later, he pictured his roseate dreams when he believed that he and his partner Cal Higbie had struck it rich in their "blind lead." He dreamed all day and lay awake all night —for each new splendor "that burst out of my visions of the future . . . jerked me to a sitting posture just as if an electric battery had been applied to me"—while he planned a mansion in San Francisco.

The myth-making power of his imagination is in evidence in this book. The jackass rabbit is first discovered sitting quietly among the sagebrush, "thinking about his sins," but soon he breaks into a long lope, and finally "straightens himself out like a yard-stick every spring he makes, and scatters miles behind him." The slim gray coyote is a creature of myth, "a living, breathing allegory of Want." He goes "swinging gently off on that deceitful trot of his," smiling "a fraudulent smile over his shoulder," a smile calculated to fill the smug and hopeful town dog pursuing him with "encouragement and worldly ambition"; but the town dog soon learns what a swindle "that long, calm, soft-footed trot is." When the coyote tires of the game, "there is a rushing sound, and the sudden splitting of a long crack in the atmosphere, and behold that dog is solitary and alone in the midst of a vast solitude!" With its aftermath of the crestfallen town dog, shorn of all ambition to hunt coyotes, his tail hanging "at half-mast," the entire passage has the savor of an old beast fable.

The diminishing power of Mark Twain's imagination, seen over and over in the travel books and destined to play a great role in his fiction, appears occasionally in *Roughing It*, as in his description of the sagebrush as a "monarch of the forest in miniature ... a gnarled ... live oak tree reduced to a little shrub two feet high, with its rough bark, its foliage, its twisted boughs, all complete":

Often, on lazy afternoons ... I have lain on the ground with my face under a sage-bush, and entertained myself with fancying that the gnats among its foliage were lilliputian birds, and that the ants marching and countermarching about its base were lilliputian flocks and herds, and myself some vast loafer from Brobdingnag waiting to catch a little citizen and eat him.

Here in the year 1870 is seen functioning the gigantesque imagination which produced *The Mysterious Stranger* in the late nineties.

Roughing It gives unforgettable pictures of early Nevada, furnishing an astute and amazing commentary on the people, the government, and the industries. Mark Twain himself said he intended the book as a personal narrative, plus information concerning "an interesting episode in the history of the Far West, about which no books have been written by persons who were on the ground ... and saw ... with their own eyes ... the rise, growth, and culmination of the silver-mining fever in Nevada." Commenting upon the informal, spontaneous manner of the telling, the author of a *History of Nevada* recently remarked: "*Roughing It* may seem to the uninformed to be a loosely written, anecdotal narrative. But such is not the case. When the history of the era is known, the continuity of the book is obvious."[3]

This book, too, presents its gallery of the "damned human race." Mark Twain depicted the "half-civilized station-keepers and hostlers" who fawned disgustingly on the swaggering stage driver, all applauding his one joke, "coarse, profane, witless." Cooped up in a

bid., 49.

dingy tavern by an overflow of the Carson River, he felt repugnance for the ruffians likewise confined there, hating their swearing, drinking, card playing, and fighting. But his strongest language he reserved for white people who abuse the "kindly-disposed, well-meaning Chinese": "Only the scum of the population do it . . . they, and naturally . . . the policemen and politicians . . . for these are the dust-licking pimps and slaves of the scum, there as well as elsewhere in America." The passage holds the fury of his early Western sketches.

In general, however, *Roughing It* reveals a control over his material which argues a technical advance. His adequacy appears in lines describing a gun battle in Carson City in which "Harris" and an unnamed stranger "rebuked and explained to" each other with six-shooters. "When the pistols were emptied . . . Mr. Harris rode by with a polite nod, homeward bound, with a bullet through one of his lungs, and several through his hips; and from them issued little rivulets of blood that coursed down the horse's sides and made the animal look quite picturesque." The surface attitude is one of amused and callous detachment, contrasting vividly with the grisly realism of the blood running from the man's wounds down the sides of his horse. Condemnation of such affrays is implicit in the passage, but its tone is far distant from the vehement, exaggerated humor he had earlier employed as his medium of denunciation. He was arriving at satiric indirection.

In *Roughing It*, he dramatized many episodes that seemed to him a little tame, touched up others, and invented others outright when the narrative demanded it. He fictionized himself, too, and his own adventures; his picture of himself in a penniless state, after leaving the San Francisco *Morning Call*, is a case in point. As Paine observed, the book is "true in its aspects, rather than in its details. The greater artist disregards the truth of detail to render more strikingly a . . . condition, to produce an atmosphere, to reconstruct a vanished time." Viewed in this light, *Roughing It* has a startling vividness. Akin to a picaresque novel, it stands as a link between Mark Twain's Western sketches and early travel books on the one hand, and on the other his first published fiction, *The Gilded Age*, which was to appear a year later.[4]

[4] He had originally intended to make a book of his Sandwich Islands letters, but, failing that, he used about one-third of them to fill out *Roughing It*. The interested reader can collate the two texts, noting the revisions, the omission of old material, and the addition of new.

Mark Twain, a saddened humorist

In *Life on the Mississippi,* as earlier in *Roughing It,* he caught the fading glory of a vanished day. Howells had requested a story for the *Atlantic Monthly* of January, 1875. Mark Twain was about to "give it up" when he took a long walk with Joe Twichell and told him about "old Mississippi days of steamboating glory and grandeur as I saw them (during 5 years) from the pilot house. He said 'What a virgin subject to hurl into a magazine!' I hadn't thought of that before," Mark Twain wrote to Howells. "Would you like a series of papers . . . ?" The first glowing chapters of *Life on the Mississippi*—twenty of them—thus appeared in the *Atlantic* as "Old Times on the Mississippi." What was then the first chapter describes Sam Clemens's home town of Hannibal as a little river village "drowsing in the sunshine of a summer's morning," with idle clerks asleep in the sun, sows and pigs "loafing along the sidewalk," and the "fragrant town drunkard asleep in the shadow" of skids on the wharf—with, just beyond, "the great Mississippi, the majestic, the magnificent Mississippi, rolling its mile-wide tide along, shining in the sun." Then a Negro drayman, "famous for his . . . prodigious voice, lifts up the cry, 'S-t-e-a-m-boat a-comin'!' and the scene changes!" The dead little town wakes to a brief hour of bustling life, after which, with the departure of the boat, it sinks back into lethargy. But here, as in many incidents in *Roughing It,* Mark Twain is fictionizing; for Hannibal in that day was not so dead-alive as he paints it. His effect is to dramatize the permanent ambition held by all the small boys—including Sam Clemens—to be steamboatmen.

The first part of the book details the duties of a pilot and the difficulties of "learning the river," twelve hundred miles of it, a subject which Mark Twain claimed he was "the only man alive" fitted to handle. He explained to Howells that he had been obliged to expend time and space in "working up an atmosphere" to fit the special conditions of the river; otherwise, "every reader would be applying his own or sea experiences, and *that* shirt wouldn't fit."

In 1882, seven years after the publication of "Old Times on the Mississippi," his publishers decided to bring out the series in book form. He then made a trip along the river in search of new material to finish out the book. The first part presents material which had lain in his mind for years; the second part is, in general, merely good travel reporting. Even so, the style of each part is appropriate to its content: the first part deals with the romance of the river in the flush times, and he presented it in the idyllic light in which his memories enveloped it. The second part is a realistic picture of the river as it then was, stripped of its glamour, a barren stretch of almost empty water where it was a sensation to see two boats at once. The railroads had almost destroyed the river traffic. "The romance of boating is gone now," Mark Twain lamented. "In Hannibal the steam-boatman is no longer a god. The youth don't talk river slang any more." In a sense, the second part of *Life on the Mississippi* is fact; the first part, fiction. Held in the suspending glow of Mark Twain's imagination, the river emerged freed from its unlovely aspects—the sordid commercialism of its trade, as well as the prostitutes, pimps, and thugs who had infested it in actual life.

Nevertheless, it was the river which had sharpened his perception of the "damned human race." Speaking of his apprenticeship as a cub pilot, he wrote:

. . . in that brief, sharp schooling, I got personally and familiarly acquainted with about all the different types of human nature . . . to be found in fiction, biography, or history. . . . When I find a well-drawn character in fiction or biography, I generally take a warm personal interest in him, for the reason that I have known him before—met him on the river.

The Mississippi was, as A. P. Hudson has said, the "tawny and slippery avenue upon which . . . most of the people lived, along which they hauled and haggled, sold and stole most of their goods and chattels, up and down which they wandered and fought and gambled and made love and took their pleasure. It was the Midway of the longest and greatest World's Fair our country has boasted. . . . Every barge . . . was a floating booth; every steamboat, a showboat." Up and down this Giant Midway, Mark Twain daily plied his pilot's trade, observing the great barges, the keelboats, the broadhorns that floated from the upper river down to New Orleans and were laboriously poled back by hand. Interesting specimens of humanity were to be found in this commerce; it gave employment to what Mark Twain described as

. . . hordes of rough and hardy men; rude, uneducated, brave, suffering terrific hardships with sailor-like stoicism; heavy drinkers, coarse frolickers in moral sties like . . . Natchez-under-the-hill; . . . heavy fighters, reckless fellows . . . elephantinely jolly, foul-witted, profane, prodigal of their money, bankrupt at the end of the trip, fond of barbaric finery, prodigious braggarts; yet, in the main, honest, trustworthy, faithful to promises and duty, and often picturesquely magnanimous.

The Mississippi was also the highway of humor. Our American folk myths have been mainly humorous ones, products of the tall tales of the frontier, embodied in such exaggerated figures as Davy Crockett, Mike Fink, and Paul Bunyan. Mark Twain, with his ear and eye alert for oddities in speech or character, was inevitably attracted to the "half-horse, half-alligator" river boasters, emerging from the river mud to swagger upon barges or to engage in gorgeous rows at "Natchy-under-the-hill," where blows often fell merely because one roisterer must finally fail to top the boasts of another. The heyday of the broadhorn boys and steamboat bullies was vanishing in Mark Twain's youth, but he recalled it as part of the romance of the river. By way of illustrating keelboat talk and raft life, he inserted in his Mississippi manuscript a chapter of *Huckleberry Finn* which has never been restored to its proper context and still stands as the third chapter in *Life on the Mississippi*. He transcribed the talk of two braggarts, threatening to lick each other. One jumped into the air and cracked his heels together and shouted out:

"Whoo-oop! I'm the old original iron-jawed, brass-mouthed, copper-bellied corpse-maker from the wilds of Arkansaw! Look at me! . . . Sired by a hurricane, dam'd by an earthquake . . . I split the everlasting rocks with my glance. . . . Who-oop! Stand back and give me room according to my strength! Blood's my natural drink. . . . Cast your eye on me, gentlemen, and lay low . . . for I'm 'bout to turn myself loose!"

Then the man that had started the row tilted his old slouch hat over his right eye; then he bent stooping forward with his . . . south end sticking out and his fists . . . in front of him, swelling himself up and breathing hard. Then he jumped up and cracked his heels together three times . . . and he began to shout like this:

"Whoo-oop! bow your neck and spread, for the kingdom of sorrow's a-coming! . . . I'm a child of sin, *don't* let me get a start! Smoked glass, here, for all! Don't attempt to look at me with the naked eye, gentlemen! . . . I scratch my head with the lightning and purr myself to sleep with the thunder! . . . I put my hand on the sun's face and make it night in the earth; I bite a piece out of the moon. . . . Whoo-oop! bow your neck and spread, for the Pet Child of Calamity's a-coming!"

The Corpse-Maker's parentage recalls that of the semi-deities of mythology, and the Child of Calamity's attainments might stamp him a god himself. No passage in Mark Twain's work better illustrates the gigantic scope, the primitive power, the elemental quality of his imagination. Yet he is simply following the tradition of the Mississippi. He here restores a sense of legend, a flavor of forgotten myths.[5]

In the second part of the book, lamenting a vanished past, he denounced the "unholy train" as it came tearing along, ripping the "sacred solitude" of the river "to rags and tatters with its devil's war-whoop." He pictured the boom town of St. Paul on the upper river—St. Paul,

... giant young chief of the North, marching with seven-league stride in the van of progress ... carving his beneficent way with the tomahawk of commercial enterprise, sounding the war-whoop of Christian culture, tearing off the reeking scalp of slothful superstition ... ever in his front stretch arid lawlessness, ignorance, crime, despair; ever in his wake bloom the jail, the gallows, and the pulpit.

The phrase "tearing off the reeking scalp" recalls the gory satires of his Washoe days, particularly the "Empire City Massacre." His fitting out "Christian culture" with a war whoop discloses the satiric eye with which he viewed this civilization of commercial enterprise. He was apparently out of sympathy with the "progress" along the upper Mississippi: "How solemn and beautiful is the thought that the earliest pioneer of civilization . . . is never the steamboat, never the railroad, never the newspaper, never the Sabbath-school, never the missionary—but always whiskey! 'Westward the Jug of Empire takes its way.' " That, he wrote, was the history of St. Paul. A Canadian, one Pierre Parrant, "uncorked his jug, and began to sell whiskey to the Indians. The result is before us."

The second half contains some excellent character studies— Uncle Mumford, for instance—and some rather dull narratives interpolated to fill out the book. But much of it is devoted to social criticism leveled against the South. Howells once spoke of Mark Twain as the most desouthernized Southerner he had ever known. Having cast aside what he considered the romantic shams of the Old

[5] Constance Rourke, *American Humour*, 219–20.

South—her mint-magnolia-and-moonlight traditions—Mark Twain denounced Sir Walter Scott because of the baleful influence cast by Scott's "medieval chivalry-silliness." Southern architecture, Southern education, Southern society, Southern sports, and Southern literature—all were drooping under the malignant blight of "the Sir Walter disease." Contrasting the good influence of Cervantes, through *Don Quixote,* with the pernicious influence of Scott, through *Ivanhoe,* he showed his belief in the lasting power of a book.

Even in the relatively glamorous first part, there are passages of stark realism in which he presented the species commonly known as "river rats." At flood time, on crazy rail fences sticking up out of the water, there sit "jeans-clad, chills-racked, yellow-faced male miserables roosting on the top rail . . . grinding tobacco and discharging the result at floating chips." Twice a year they are rousted from their wretched homes, by the December rise out of the Ohio and the June rise out of the Mississippi. They live in flatboats until the river subsides and allows them to return to their log-cabins and their chills, "chills being a merciful provision of an all-wise Providence to enable them to take exercise without exertion." The colored folk of the "migrating negro region" are treated realistically, but with more sympathy than is accorded the white river rats. The childlike qualities of the Negroes are exhibited: they pull out when the desire to travel seizes them, taking along their little assortment of household goods, "consisting of a rusty gun, a crippled looking-glass, a venerable arm-chair, and six or eight base-born and spiritless yellow curs, attached to the family by strings. . . . Sometimes a child is forgotten and left on the bank; but never a dog."

Life on the Mississippi, like *Roughing It,* is important because it records a period of American life now gone forever. But, beyond that, it is important as the agent which perhaps inspired Twain to finish the river story of *Huckleberry Finn,* on which he worked at intervals from 1876 to 1883. Passages in the Mississippi book present scenes effectively developed in *Huckleberry Finn*; the descriptions of the river at dawn, with the songs of invisible birds floating over it, parallel similar descriptions couched in Huck's expressive vernacular. *Life on the Mississippi* may be called the biography of a river; in it, as Carl Van Doren has said, Mark Twain reduced the river to its own language.

A part of the *Autobiography* was written as early as 1870; as

"The Tennessee Land," it now stands as the first section in the book. Other parts were added from time to time, but not until 1897 did he express a definite intention to write his autobiography. In Florence, in 1904, he hit upon a plan of dictating it to a secretary, a plan which he recommended to Howells. But Howells, realizing their temperamental differences, replied: "You are dramatic and unconscious; you count the thing more than yourself; I am cursed with consciousness to the core, and can't say myself out; I am always saying myself *in*, and setting myself above all that I say, as of more worth. . . . I'd like . . . to read your autobiography. You always rather bewildered me by your veracity. . . . but . . . even *you* won't tell the black heart's truth." Mark Twain insisted that an autobiography is the truest of all books, "for while it inevitably consists mainly of . . . shirking of the truth, partial revealments of the truth . . . the remorseless truth *is* there, between the lines, where the author is raking dust upon it." He had hit upon the right way:

Start it at no particular time of your life; wander at your free will all over your life; talk only about the thing which interests you for the moment; drop it the moment its interest threatens to pale, and turn your talk upon the new and more interesting thing that has intruded itself into your mind meantime.

Actually, this was what he had been doing all along. Thereafter, he followed the plan with wild abandon, interpolating into his manuscript personal letters and even headlines from the daily papers. Sometimes his interest in the project waned; sometimes this stream-of-consciousness writing filled him with fresh enthusiasm. In the latter mood, he predicted that his autobiography would become a model for all future autobiographies because of its form and method. Since it was both diary and autobiography, "you have the vivid thing of the present to make a contrast with memories of like things in the past." Thus in his old age, as in his early Washoe sketches, he was indulging himself in a deliberate chaos, achieving a disorder in a completely foreseen, even planned and ordered, way.

In January, 1906, Albert Bigelow Paine began to write Mark Twain's authorized biography. Mark Twain resumed his dictations, dictating to a stenographer with Paine present to ask him questions. Paine gradually came to realize that "these marvelous reminiscences . . . were . . . built largely—sometimes wholly—from an imagination that, with age, had dominated memory. . . . Those vividly real personalities that he marched . . . before us were the most convincing creatures in the world, the most entertaining, the most . . . humorous, or wicked, or tragic; but, alas, they often disagreed in their performance, and even in their characters, with the documents in the next room. . . . His gift of dramatization had been exercised too long to be discarded now." Such considerations must always operate to make any autobiographical interpretation of Mark Twain not only inadequate, but also untrustworthy.

Despite the hodgepodge collection of subjects, in extensive portions of the *Autobiography* the style of Mark Twain flashes and glows. Nowhere does his prose show to better advantage in its inimitable mingling of studied effect and colloquial ease. Much of the material had been received as zestful experience during his boyhood, tinged with vivid emotion, and at the time of writing recollected in tranquillity. In the travel books he frequently reported material he had not had time to assimilate; but this book is something lived, not something reported from tourist car or steamer deck. Everything is brought into focus, as if he looked far down a tube of distance and time. The passages devoted to the home life in Hartford, when his children were small, have charm and vitality. In the section "Early Days," describing the farm of his Uncle John Quarles, the style is notable for its concrete realization of mood. The living prose grows from deep-hidden roots. A complete liaison with the senses was always a feature of Mark Twain's style; but in the passages dealing with Florida, Missouri, there is an Indian-summer mellowness that blends thought and style with remarkable richness.

His reminiscence takes us out into the country four miles from Florida, to the Quarles farm; down to the swings behind the house where children, white and black, played together; on down to the Negro quarters beyond the orchard, where lived an aged Negress whom the children believed to be a thousand years old, a person who had talked with Moses; on down the dusty road where snakes lay and sunned themselves. The scene moves inside the farmhouse on winter nights; we see the fireplace, the apples roasting and sizzling on the hearth, the lazy cat spread out basking, the drowsy dogs blinking, the small children "romping in the background twilight"; the flickering firelight casts shadows over the walls and into a corner where a cradle sits, "out of service, but waiting, with confidence." All in all, it was "a heavenly place for a boy, that farm." The life which the child Sam Clemens had led there was full of charm; and so were the memories the man Mark Twain held of it. His prose expresses nostalgia through sensory awareness:

I can call back the solemn twilight and mystery of the deep woods, the earthy smells, the faint odors of the wild flowers, the sheen of rain-washed foliage, the rattling clatter of drops when the wind shook the trees, the far-off hammering of woodpeckers and the muffled drumming of wood pheasants in the remoteness of the forest, the snapshot glimpses of disturbed wild creatures scurrying through the grass—I can call it all back and make it as real as it ever was, and as blessed. I can call back the prairie, and its loneliness and peace, and a vast hawk hanging motionless in the sky, with his wings spread wide and the blue . . . showing through the fringe of their end feathers. I can see the woods in their autumn dress, the oaks purple, the hickories washed with gold, the maples and the sumachs luminous with crimson fires, and I can hear the rustle made by the fallen leaves as we plowed through them. I can see the blue clusters of wild grapes hanging among the foliage . . . and I can remember the taste of them and the smell. . . . I can feel the thumping rain, upon my head, of hickory nuts and walnuts when we were out in the frosty dawn to scramble for them with the pigs, and the gusts of wind loosed them and sent them down. . . . I know the taste of maple sap . . . and how to boil down the juice, and how to hook the sugar after it is made, also how much better hooked sugar tastes than any that is honestly come by, let bigots say what they will. I know how a prize watermelon looks when it is sunning its fat rotundity among pumpkin vines and "simblins"; I know how . . . inviting it looks when it is cooling itself in a tub of water under the bed, waiting; . . . I know the crackling sound it makes when the carving knife enters its end, and I can see the split fly along in front of the blade as the knife cleaves its way . . . ; I can see its halves fall apart and display the rich red meat and the black seeds, and the heart standing up, a luxury fit for the elect.

The reminiscence moves on and on. There is an unhurried certainty, a ripe plenitude about it, that makes reading it a satisfying experience. This rich sensuousness contrasts markedly with the thin texture of his travel descriptions in which he found imaginative release chiefly in looking at dreamy landscapes, or in looking into water or glass, where scenes were imaged as mere pictures of themselves. Bernard DeVoto has said that in the travel books, *Roughing It*, and *Life on the Mississippi*, Mark Twain developed a kind of personal commentary "unique in our literature" and that the *Autobiography* is the same thing in kind, but it is "shaped and colored by the deeper impulse . . . which gets free expression only in his fiction."

Many lines in the prose of his old age are distinguished by their rhythmic flow and exactness of expression, others by their power of ridicule. For, to the last, he kept burning the bright, pure flame of his animosity. An example in the *Eruption* volume, "The Hunting of the Cow," deals with the highly publicized exploits of President Theodore Roosevelt in hunting what he and certain "White House domestics . . . all under wages to the great hunter" alleged to be a bear. But Mark Twain insists "the circumstantial evidence that it was a cow is overwhelming":

. . . it even left a cow track behind, which is what a cow would do . . . in a frenzy of fright, with a President of the United States and a squadron of bellowing dogs chasing after her; when her strength was exhausted . . . she stopped in an open spot, fifty feet wide, and humbly faced the President of the United States with the tears running down her cheeks, and said to him . . . : "Have pity, sir, and spare me. . . . I have no weapon but my helplessness, you are a walking arsenal . . . have pity, sir—there is no heroism in killing an exhausted cow." . . . [But] there it is—he hugged the guides after the kill. It is the President all over; he is still only fourteen years old after living half a century; he takes a boy's delight in showing off. . . . A grown person would have milked the cow and let her go; but no, nothing would do this lad but he must kill her and be a hero. . . .

Whatever Hercules does is to him remarkable . . . .

Written when Mark Twain was almost seventy-two years old, this passage shows that much of his power of scornful derision remained to him. The tenor of the thing is not so much rage, however, as an irritated pity for one who, in spite of his exalted position, is only a specimen of the flimsy human race. But in the *Autobiography*, as elsewhere, the stumbling block of his rage sometimes becomes an obstacle insurmountable for the style. Mr. DeVoto discloses that in editing *Mark Twain in Eruption* he left out some passages completely, "because the exaggeration gets so far into phantasy that it becomes a trivial rage," and that he had to work over the text of at least one passage, "trying to reduce its vindictiveness." Mark Twain's tempers and rages, engendered by his view of his "damned" and "mangy" race, thus affected his writing to the last.

BOOK V

The Fiction

CHAPTER 17

Revolt from the Village

ARK TWAIN's novels exhibit his conception of the relation of the individual to society as embodied in village
society, a theme which carries on his preoccupation with
the great masses of common men. In *The American Novel,* Carl Van
Doren says that American fiction up to about 1915 had been accustomed to celebrate the American village as the natural home of the
virtues and that, though certain writers might now and then have
"laid disrespectful hands upon the farm . . . even these hesitated to
touch the village." He notes that, prior to the date he sets for the
Revolt from the Village, E. W. Howe, in *The Story of a Country
Town,* had shown that a village might become a stagnant backwater;
Clarence Darrow, in *Farmington,* had insisted that one village, at
least, had had its simple bliss alloyed with restless longing; and Mark
Twain in *The Man That Corrupted Hadleyburg* "had put it bitterly on record that villages too complacent about their honesty might
. . . become a hospitable soil for meanness." Nevertheless, Mr. Van
Doren insists that the village in its filth and apathy, its dead-alive
existence, its repression of ambitious spirits—the literary treatment
that "brought a new tone into American fiction"—was first used by
Edgar Lee Masters in 1915, followed in quick succession by Sherwood Anderson, Zona Gale, and Sinclair Lewis.

Mark Twain wrote *The Man That Corrupted Hadleyburg* in
1898; but twenty-five years earlier, in Hartford in 1873, he had written the book which began his appraisal of the American village.[1]
That book was *The Gilded Age.* Its first chapter presents Obedstown, in east Tennessee, a village caught in a lassitude that extended
to the gaunt hounds sleeping before the doors and the cat that began
to drink from a pail of water, but, overtaxed by this exertion, stopped

[1] Mr. DeVoto makes this point in *Mark Twain's America,* 294–95.

to rest. The inhabitants of the fifteen houses of Obedstown, dressed in homespun jeans, with dilapidated straw hats resting on lice-infested hair, chewed tobacco listlessly and listened "reflectively" to the news brought in by the mail carrier; but fatigue soon mastered them, and "they climbed up and occupied the top rail of the fence, hump-shouldered and grave, like a company of buzzards assembled for supper and listening for the death-rattle." Too apathetic to be actually cruel, they still condemned anyone who dared to depart from the traditional way of village life. They sneered at Si Higgins for his "hell's mint o' whoop-jamboree notions" and at his high-toned wife for "plarsterin' " her shack in the mode of Kaintuck:

"What's plarsterin'?"
"I dono. Hit's what *he* calls it. Old Mam Higgins, she tole me. She say she warn't gwyne to hang out in no sich a dern hole like a hog. Says it's mud, or some sich kind o' nastness that sticks on 'n' kivers up everything. Plarsterin', Si calls it."

So much for the apathy of village life as depicted by Mark Twain in 1873. And what of the repression of ambition?

The contagion of dry rot that pervaded Obedstown was recognized by its leading citizen, Squire Hawkins. Resolving to go where he could have more incentive, he told himself: "A man will just rot, here. My house . . . everything around me . . . shows that I am becoming one of these cattle." A few minutes later he said to his wife, "I am going to Missouri. I won't stay in this dead country and decay with it." Much of their past life in Obedstown is packed into Mrs. Hawkins' answer:

"We *will* go to Missouri. You are out of your place here, among these groping dumb creatures. We will find a higher place, where you can walk with your own kind, and be understood when you speak—not stared at as if you were talking some foreign tongue. . . . I would rather my body should starve and die than your mind should hunger and wither away in this lonely land."

Upon their arrival in Missouri, they fitted themselves into another village, Murpheysburg. Mark Twain presented the second group of villagers as uncouth, uncultivated, and unindustrious, but as worthy of respect in some ways. "Their patriotism was . . . of the old-fashioned pattern. . . . They still cursed Benedict Arnold as if he were a personal friend who had broken faith but a week gone by." A balance is thus held between the good and bad points of these Missouri villagers; but through them a strong light is thrown into the nooks and crannies of the village mind. Upon the first inkling that Laura was not the child of Mr. and Mrs. Hawkins, the unthinking cruelty of human nature came uppermost; here, the cruelty was motivated by village curiosity:

The gossips were soon at work. . . . They supplied all the missing information themselves, they filled up all the blanks. The town soon teemed with histories of Laura's origin . . . no two versions precisely alike, but all elaborate, exhaustive, mysterious, and interesting, and all agreeing in one vital particular—to wit, that there was a suspicious cloud about her birth, not to say a disreputable one.

In this way the village records its antagonistic suspicion of anything it does not understand. The proud girl, encountering cold looks and averted eyes, was hurt, astonished, and incredulous. Finally she discussed the question of her birth with her foster mother. The two decided to forget the secret of Laura's parentage and to live together in peace and happiness. Things might have adjusted themselves

. . . if the village gossips could have quieted down. But they could not quiet down and they did not. Day after day they called at the house, ostensibly upon visits of condolence, and they pumped away. . . . They meant no harm—they only wanted to know. Villagers always want to know.

Under this ceaseless persecution Laura, high strung and sensitive, grew morbid. In their consuming desire "to know," villagers take no account of the damage they do. Laura tried to console herself by disdaining them: "Animals! What are their opinions to me? Let them talk. . . . nobody I care for . . . is changed toward me, I fancy." But there Laura was wrong; for Ned Thurston, the young man she meant, was a villager of the villagers. A friend, who "naturally came and told her all about it," heard him say he would not call on Laura any more:

". . . it's not because I don't want to and it's not because *I* think it is any matter who her father was . . . it's only on account of this talk, talk, talk.

I think she is a fine girl in every way . . . but you know how it is when a girl once gets talked about—it's up with her—the world won't ever let her alone, after that."

Thurston, in bondage to the village, thus sacrificed both himself and the girl he loved rather than fly in the face of village opinion. Laura scorned him: "Poor crawling thing, let him go." But all the same, "she cried a little."

The Gilded Age, Mark Twain's first published novel, was written in collaboration with his Hartford neighbor, Charles Dudley Warner. In a letter which puts the division of labor on record, Mark Twain said that he himself "wrote the first eleven chapters, every word and every line." In that part of the book, the Tennessee village of Obedstown and the Missouri village of Murpheysburg are presented, and the visionary Colonel Sellers, who welcomes the Hawkins family to Missouri, is introduced. Sellers is the synthesis of all the get-rick-quick, dreaming speculators produced by the Gilded Age. He is at the same time warm-hearted, generous, likable, and pathetic. He is not a crook. He is sincerely and honestly convinced that his schemes are for the public good, as well as for his own. He contrasts with Senator Dilworthy, who only pretends to consider the public good.

After a financial collapse, Colonel Sellers moves his family to the village of Hawkeye, where Washington Hawkins, the son of Squire Hawkins, soon follows to seek a new job. Warner introduced the railroad graft, with its fortunes made in the selling of town lots; but, when Washington Hawkins goes to the nation's capital as secretary to Senator Dilworthy, Mark Twain again takes up the pen. Having served in Washington briefly as a secretary himself, perhaps he felt qualified to handle the doings of the capital. Here the story rises to its greatest heights, satirically. To his secretarial experience Mark Twain had added his intimate knowledge of the Western Nob Hill society, reflected in one of his early sketches in which the mythical Duchess of Goat Island rented "a quart of diamonds" to wear to a ball. The glitter of that greedy world is here mingled with governmental graft, open bribery, and black corruption. Mark Twain wrote that upon arriving in the city and approaching the Capitol, the visitor sees on his left "a sail here and there and a lunatic asylum on shore; . . . on a distant elevation, you see a squat yellow temple.

... the Monument to the Father of his country towers out of the mud—sacred soil is the customary term. It has the aspect of a factory chimney with the top broken off. . . . Beyond the Treasury is a fine large white barn. . . . The President lives there." But once inside the Capitol, there is felt the real touch of the Gilded Age:

And one of the . . . most startling things you find out is that every individual . . . in the city of Washington almost . . . and certainly every separate and distinct individual in the public employment, from the highest bureau chief, clear down to the maid who scrubs Department halls . . . and the darky boy who purifies the Department spittoons—represents Political Influence. Unless you can get the ear of a Senator, or a Congressman, or a Chief of a Bureau or Department, and persuade him to use his "influence" in your behalf, you cannot get . . . employment. . . . Mere merit, fitness, and capability are useless baggage to you without "influence." . . . It would be an odd circumstance to see a girl get employment . . . in one of the great public cribs without any political grandee to back her, but merely because she was worthy, and competent, and a good citizen of a free country that "treats all persons alike." . . . If you are a member of Congress . . . and one of your constituents who doesn't know anything and does not want to go into the bother of learning something . . . comes besieging you for help . . . you . . . take him to a Department and say, "Here, give this person something . . . "—and the thing is done. . . . There is something good and motherly about Washington, the grand old benevolent National Asylum for the Helpless.

Hawkins was dazzled by the company frequenting the Capitol. "And more, this world of enchantment teemed with speculation . . . and that, indeed, was Washington Hawkins's native air." Though villagers, Washington and Sellers can dream with the best.

Colonel Sellers becomes interested in the railroad scheme, selects a desolate spot known as Stone's Landing, and changes it—on paper —into the thriving little metropolis of Napoleon. He plots on the tablecloth the route the railroad is to take, through successive villages whose names have an anticipatory flavor of Sinclair Lewis's place names. The road is to run through Slouchberg, Doodleville, Brimstone, Belshazzar, Catfish, Babylon, Bloody Run, Hail Columbia, Hark-from-the-Tomb, thence to Napoleon, then to Hallelujah, and finally to Corruptionville. This route calls for many bridges, a fact which commends it to the Colonel's impractical mind: "Rail-

road . . . wades right along on stilts. Seventeen bridges in three miles
and a half. . . . perfect trestle-work of bridges for seventy-two miles."

The tie-up among speculators, lobbyists, and Washington politicians is minutely detailed. The original appropriation of two hundred thousand dollars is spent in paying off House committees and
Senate committees and lobbyists, with "a high moral Congressman
or Senator here and there—the high moral ones cost more, because
they give tone to a measure." Senator Dilworthy invites Laura to go
to Washington as a lobbyist in the cause of selling to the government
a huge unprofitable tract owned by the Hawkins family. This tract
is known in the story as "the Tennessee Land." Laura is honest with
herself; she does not pretend, Dilworthy fashion, to be working in
a noble cause. Instead, looking at the villagers of Hawkeye, she
thinks: "I do long to know whether I am only simply a large-sized
pygmy among these pygmies here, who tumble so easily when one
strikes them, or whether I am really——" She does not complete her
thought.

Occasionally it is brought home to the reader that this tale of
The Gilded Age has its roots in the village. Mark Twain shows
Washington's ladies to be mainly transplanted villagers set down in
an alien soil. Among the first women to call on Laura were the Hon.
Mrs. Patrique Oreillé (pronounced "O-re*lay*") and Miss Bridget
(pronounced "Breezhay") Oreillé. They suffused the air with suf-
focating perfumes; "they were hung with jewels—chiefly diamonds.
It would have been plain to any eye that it had cost something to up-
holster these women." Mark Twain makes the reader understand
that they glittered when they walked. Their husband and father,
Pat O'Riley, had begun as a lowly immigrant from Cork; he had
been hod carrier, rum-shop keeper, then ward heeler, liquor dealer,
and finally "bosom friend of the great and good William M. Weed
himself, who had stolen twenty million dollars from the city, and
was a man so . . . honored, so adored, indeed, that when the sheriff
went to his office to arrest him as a felon, the sheriff blushed and
apologized." Mark Twain presents the complete pattern of the
ward-heel system in which candidates are picked according to their
boot-licking service to the party rulers. But the fault rests with the
people themselves:

The publicans and their retainers rule the ward meetings (for everybody else hates the worry of politics and stays at home); the delegates from the ward meeting . . . make up a list of candidates . . . and then the great meek public come forward at the proper time and make unhampered choice and bless Heaven that they live in a free land where no form of despotism can ever intrude.

Mark Twain knew that a little democracy is a dangerous thing because it gives the illusion of reality. Apparently, he viewed the American commonwealth in the Gilded Age as the sort of government Charles Beard once described as a government for the benefit of knaves at the expense of fools. Pat O'Riley had risen by the ward-heel ladder until he was elevated enough to contract for a courthouse and furnish the nails at three thousand dollars a keg. "By and by the newspapers came out with exposures and called Weed and O'Riley 'thieves'—whereupon the people rose as one man (voting repeatedly) and elected the two gentlemen to their proper theater of action, the New York legislature."

Other callers of Laura's had similar lowly beginnings. The Hon. Mrs. Oliver Higgins, wife of a delegate from a western territory, was among them. But this element was important in Washington society; for official position, no matter how obtained, entitled a man and his family to a place in the social sun:

Great wealth gave a man a still higher and nobler place . . . than did official position. If this wealth had been acquired by conspicuous ingenuity, with just a pleasant little spice of illegality about it, all the better.

Oliver Higgins bears a striking resemblance to Tom Peaseley, owner of The Sazerac, colorful saloon of Virginia City, Nevada.[2] Higgins had kept a saloon in the West, had sold the best whisky in "the principal village of his wilderness," and therefore,

. . . of course, was recognized as the first man of his commonwealth and

2 Tom Peaseley was fire chief of Virginia City, Nevada, and served as sheriff of Storey County between 1862 and 1864. He was sergeant-at-arms of the Nevada State Senate in 1865. He killed at least two "parties"—"Sugar-foot Jack" and a man named Barnhart; he himself was killed by Barnhart's bullets. "Every public occasion found Tom Peaseley on the committee of arrangements," and The Sazerac was one of "two important places where almost everything in the Territory was settled"— the other being the Magnolia Saloon in Carson City, kept by Pete Hopkins (Mack, *Mark Twain in Nevada*, 194–97).

its fittest representative. He was a man of paramount influence at home, for he . . . was chief of the fire department, he had an admirable command of profane language, and he had killed several 'parties.' His . . . watch-chain weighed a pound; . . . he wore a diamond cluster-pin. . . . He had always been regarded as the most elegant gentleman in his territory, and it was conceded by all that no man thereabouts was anywhere near his equal in the telling of an obscene story, except the venerable white-haired governor himself. . . . The appropriation which he had engineered through Congress for the maintenance of the Indians in his territory would have made all those savages rich if it had ever got to them.

Mark Twain devoted several chapters to the inside workings of Congress concerning the bill which was to purchase the Tennessee Land from the Hawkins family. The university to be established upon it was to be open to the Negro race; for the hypocritical Senator Dilworthy claimed a firm principle of conduct: he would never push a private interest if it were not justified and ennobled by some larger public good. In intricate detail Mark Twain showed the logrolling, the back-scratching, the nose-counting. Twenty-five years after the publication of *The Gilded Age*, he wrote to Howells from London, "If I were not a hermit, I would go to the House every day and see those people scuffle and blether about the brotherhood of the human race." It is the scuffle and blether of the human race that he presents in this book in the chapters dealing with the United States government.

There is a dramatic intensity in the all-night struggle over the land bill. In one of Mark Twain's chapters, Sellers says: "I think Congress always tries to do as near right as it can, according to its lights." But in the same chapter, when Washington Hawkins suggests that the Colonel should be in Congress himself,

The gladness died out of the Colonel's face, and he laid his hand upon Washington's shoulder and said gravely:

"I have always been a friend of your family, Washington, and I think I have always tried to do right as between man and man. . . . Now I don't think there has ever been anything in my conduct that should make you feel justified in saying a thing like that."

Sellers turned and walked from the room, leaving Washington abashed and bewildered.

Finally Mr. Noble, member of the state legislature of Dilworthy's home state of Happy-Land-of-Canaan, was approached in the city of Saint's Rest, the state capital, by the Senator, who recognized in Noble a political enemy merely because Noble was "straight." When Noble walked into the House bearing seven thousand dollars which he said Dilworthy had given him to buy his vote, Congress roundly denounced Noble as "a shameless person" who by his own confession had received a bribe and now had "maliciously brought disrespect upon a Senator of the United States." Meanwhile, Congress upheld Dilworthy as a public-spirited Christian gentleman.

But *The Gilded Age* is not only a satire on democracy in the United States: it is also a study of the evil effects of dreams of wealth. When Mark Twain and Warner were challenged by their wives to write a novel better than those the women were currently reading and accepted the challenge in the best James Fenimore Cooper tradition, Mark Twain already had, according to Paine, "the beginning of a story in his mind." It is this story he tells in *The Gilded Age*, the story of the Tennessee Land, the dream of future wealth which poisons the existence of the Hawkins family. In the *Autobiography* he told of the actual Tennessee Land and the high hopes his father held of the fortune it would bring to his children:

Thus with the very kindest intentions . . . he laid the heavy curse of prospective wealth upon our shoulders. . . . the land . . . furnished me a field for Sellers and a book. . . . I was the only member of the family that ever profited by it. . . . it influenced our lives . . . during more than a generation. . . . It put our energies to sleep and made visionaries of us—dreamers and indolent. We were always going to be rich next year—no occasion to work. . . . The man who has not experienced it cannot imagine the curse of it.

Perhaps the writing of the recently completed *Roughing It,* with its miners running gold mad, had recalled to him the baleful influence of the Tennessee Land. Autobiographical traces are strong in *The Gilded Age,* as Paine pointed out: Washington Hawkins is Orion Clemens; Squire Hawkins is John Marshall Clemens, Mark Twain's father; and Colonel Sellers is James Lampton, a cousin of his mother's.

Colonel Sellers embodies the hopefulness of all visionaries who perpetually await riches in some immediate tomorrow. Upon Washington Hawkins' first visit to the Sellers mansion in Hawkeye, the family sat with their only warmth coming from a lighted candle which shone through the isinglass door of a dilapidated stove. His lips blue with cold, Washington was spellbound into believing in the Colonel's plans for cobweb fortunes, spun with words. For each new speculation, the Colonel's stock phrase was "There's millions in it—millions." Mark Twain's first installment of the book ends with the dinner in the Sellers home at which Washington drops in, an uninvited guest, to share "an abundance of clear, fresh water, and a basin of raw turnips—nothing more." Although on this occasion Colonel Sellers outdid himself in verbal grandeurs, his wife was obviously distressed. The Colonel and Washington are, apparently, as happy in dreaming of wealth as they would be in its actual possession. But when Warner takes up the pen, the Gilded Age is not content with mere dreams. Warner's characters are not so easily satisfied.

Laura, the victim of circumstances beyond her control, is driven to desperation and kills Colonel Selby, the smooth-talking villain who has tricked her into a fake marriage. She is tried for his murder and acquitted. Mark Twain described a morning in early spring, just after Laura's acquittal, as a time

... when one's spirit is subdued and sad, one knows not why; when the past seems a storm-past desolation, life a vanity and a burden, and the future but a way to death. It is a time when one ... dreams of flight to peaceful islands in the remote solitudes of the sea, or folds his hands and says, What is the use of struggling and toiling and worrying any more? Let us give it all up.

This 1873 passage is weighted with the same sense of futility, the same desire for escape, which we have already seen in many passages from the travel books and which criticism has associated mainly with Mark Twain's later years. After an abortive attempt at lecturing, Laura had a tragic end. Alone in her hotel room she sat, her face in her hands, longing for her lost innocence, longing for death. Part of her prayer was answered: she died of heart disease, in that room.[3]

Mark Twain and Warner finished this novel in two months. They worked, as Mark Twain later said, "in the superstition that

[3] The passage which describes the dead figure of Laura, sitting by a table, seems to echo Hawthorne's famous chapter describing the dead Judge Pyncheon as he sits alone through varying shades of sunlight and twilight and moonlight.

we were writing one coherent yarn, when . . . we were writing two *incoherent* ones." The difference in the two men is nowhere more apparent than in the fate which they mete out to their characters. Warner's more conventional story of Philip Sterling and Ruth Bolton is the typical American story which still appears constantly in magazines—that of the young man who "makes good" after all sorts of struggles and disappointments, marries the boss's daughter, and wins the final accolade of financial success. Mark Twain wrote the chapter in which Philip strikes the vein of coal and assures his fortune; but Warner had committed Philip to this success from the start. And what of the characters which Mark Twain presented to the reader in the first eleven chapters? What destiny does their creator decree for them, this man of thirty-seven, happily married three years, already the successful and prosperous author of three unusually popular books? Squire Hawkins dies in poverty, his dream unrealized, murmuring to his children, "Never lose sight of the Tennessee Land! . . . wealth that is boundless!" Laura, victim of circumstance, always yearning for something beyond her reach, dies tragically alone, her character besmirched, her name coupled with "murderess" in the mouths of the mob. Washington Hawkins, creature of dreams and visions, is white haired at thirty, with lined face and shattered spirit, his spirit broken on the wheel of speculation. He lives to curse the Tennessee Land:

". . . it has cursed every hour of my life. . . . I depended on it all through my boyhood. . . . I have chased it . . . as children chase butterflies. We might all have been prosperous now; we might all have been happy, all these heart-breaking years, if we had . . . gone contentedly to work and built up our own weal by our own toil and sweat. . . . Instead of that, we have suffered more than the damned themselves suffer!"

Washington pulls up at the last with a resolution to begin his life over again, but we have little faith in his power to redeem himself. Colonel Sellers, unable to learn by any experience, however tragic, ends as he began, in an empty dream of the future. He will take up the study of law; he will practice first in Hawkeye, then successively in Jefferson, St. Louis, New York, "and wind up on the *Su*preme bench. Beriah Sellers, Chief Justice of the *Su*preme Court of the United States, sir! A made man. . . . That's the way *I* block it out, sir—and it's as clear . . . as the rosy morn!" To Mark Twain, Sellers was not the comical creature that many readers have found him. To Mark Twain, James Lampton himself was not funny:

The real Colonel Sellers . . . was a pathetic and beautiful spirit. . . . James Lampton floated all his days in a tinted mist of magnificent dreams, and died . . . without seeing one of them realized. . . . I saw him last . . . when . . . he was become old and white-headed, but he . . . was all there yet . . . the happy light in his eye, the abounding hope in his heart, the persuasive tongue, the miracle-breeding imagination—they were all there; and . . . he was polishing up his Aladdin's lamp and flashing the secret riches of the world before me.

Neither was Colonel Sellers to Mark Twain the farcical figure he became on the stage when John T. Raymond acted the title role in the play *Colonel Sellers*, arranged in collaboration by Mark Twain and a California dramatist, Gilbert S. Densmore. The *Autobiography* reveals Mark Twain's dissatisfaction with the actor:

. . . Raymond's audiences used to come near to dying with laughter over the turnip-eating scene; but . . . in the hands of a great actor that piteous scene would have dimmed any manly spectator's eyes with tears, and racked his ribs apart with laughter at the same time. But Raymond was great in humorous portrayal only. . . . in all things else he was a pygmy of the pygmies. . . . The real Colonel Sellers was never on the stage. Only half of him was there. Raymond could not play the other half of him; it was above his level.

The Gilded Age is an important book in the study of Mark Twain. It embodies his desire to satirize the contemporary life about him. He was later to achieve, by the practice of various literary devices, a satiric indirection; but in this first published fiction the satire, such as it is, could scarcely be more direct, more pointed.[4] Commenting upon the novelists of the time, Mr. DeVoto has said that among them Mark Twain alone "concerns himself with the national muck"; in him alone exist "the boom towns, the railroad builders, the Dilworthies, the lobbyists, the gallicized Irish, society swelling to a gimcrack pretension with the manure of empire under its finger nails, the monster fungus of the gilded age."

[4] Contemporary readers of *The Gilded Age* easily recognized in it a *roman à clef*. The model for Senator Dilworthy was Samuel C. Pomeroy of Kansas, who had recently been involved in flagrant vote-buying (Ferguson, *Mark Twain: Man and Legend*, 170).

The book is important, too, because it foreshadows better books to be written later by Mark Twain. The chapter in which Uncle Dan'l gets his first sight of a steamboat anticipates the exploration of Negro psychology which Mark Twain later undertook in *Pudd'n-head Wilson*. Stricken to the marrow with fear of the terrible shape of a steamboat as it belches out fire and smoke in the darkness, Uncle Dan'l takes it to be "de Almighty . . . a-tiltin' along in a chariot of fire," thus revealing the Negro's conception of a God of physical appearance and reaching-out proclivities. Loyal to the Hawkins children, Uncle Dan'l falls on his knees and tries to reason with the Almighty. His prayer is skilfully arranged to indicate the rising and falling inflections, the oratorical climaxes of the old Negro:

"O Lord, we's ben mighty wicked, an' we knows dat we 'zerve to go to de bad place, but good Lord, deah Lord, we ain't ready yit, we ain't ready— let dese po' chil'en hab one mo' chance, jes' one mo' chance. . . . Good Lord, good deah Lord, . . . dese chil'en don't b'long heah, dey's f'm Obedstown whah dey don't know nuffin, an' you knows, yo' own sef, dat dey ain't 'sponsible."

This closeness of the Negro to his God, Mark Twain expressed repeatedly. He understood that to the black race of the time Heaven was just a few miles away at any given moment; during his childhood spent among the slaves, he had himself absorbed much of their religion, which contained elements of fear and horror; the horror they had brought with them from their dark continent, where any god was a fearsome "voodoo" being.[5] Mr. DeVoto suggests that when Mark Twain's mental development carried him beyond the beliefs of this childlike race, "the only religion that was ever vital to him," he took for granted that he had outgrown all religion and was consequently unable to bring himself to accept any orthodox pattern of it.

The dialect which he produced for Uncle Dan'l is a notable advance over the literary versions of colored speech that had appeared mainly, as Mr. DeVoto observes, in the pages of Edgar Allan Poe and Harriet Beecher Stowe. While working on *Tom Sawyer*, Mark Twain wrote out a story told him by the Negro cook of Livy's sister, Mrs. Sue Crane. He held closely to the speech and manner of

[5] DeVoto, *Mark Twain's America*, 67.

old Auntie Cord, "without departing too far from literary requirements"; and Howells, praising the dialect as "the realest kind of
black talk," published the piece as "A True Story" in the *Atlantic
Monthly*. Mark Twain requested Howells to send the proof sheets
to him for correction, explaining:

I amend dialect stuff by talking and talking and *talking* it till it sounds
right—and I had difficulty with this negro talk because a negro sometimes (rarely) says "goin' " and sometimes "gwyne," and they make just
such discrepancies in other words—and when you come to reproduce
them on paper they look as if the variation resulted from the writer's
carelessness. But I want to work at the proofs and get the dialect as nearly right as possible.

No doubt many who read that dialect charged Mark Twain with
carelessness, when just the reverse was true. Here, once again, the
record refutes the accepted legend that he was either negligent
about revision or shunned it altogether. To test his early facility in
this dialect, one has only to read "A True Story," particularly the
page which presents the Negro dance held in the kitchen.

Life on the Mississippi is forecast in an early chapter of *The
Gilded Age*, a chapter containing details of steamboating, leadsmen's
calls, and a race between the *Boreas* and the *Amaranth* in which the
Amaranth is blown up. The explosion, presented as the fruit of
rivalry between the two crews, results in twenty-two known dead,
ninety-six missing, and thirty-nine injured. Foolhardy risks had
been taken during the race. "A jury of inquest . . . returned the inevitable American verdict which has been so familiar to our ears all
the days of our lives—'NOBODY TO BLAME.' " The obtuseness
of the human race is here indicted by Mark Twain.

Late in the novel he introduced another village, "the miserable
hamlet of Cattleville," in a scene which foreshadows the showing-
off scene later re-enacted in *Tom Sawyer*. The spirit of this scene he
had first caught in his 1856 letter to Annie Taylor, a letter describing
a religious convention of insects, discussed earlier in connection with
Mark Twain's humor. Here, Senator Dilworthy, campaigning for
re-election, goes to Cattleville to let his constituents "look upon him."
Having heard that the Senator will visit the Cattleville Sunday
school, villagers, farmers, and ranchmen gather their families to
church to see the great man. The minister, the Sunday school super-

intendent, the town dignitaries—all have their turn at showing off before the guest and the congregation. The Senator eulogizes the Sunday school in a story about a poor little boy who grew up into a great man: *"That man stands before you! All that he is, he owes to the Sunday-school."* The modest Senator, too, is showing off. In *Mark Twain at Work*, Mr. DeVoto notes Mark Twain's habit of rehearsing his best scenes in slighter studies before incorporating them into his books. Walter Blair believes that this practice was to Mark Twain what extensive revision is to other writers; it was, says Mr. Blair, "his way of perfecting his technique."

Finally, *The Gilded Age* is important for a quality that has already been mentioned. In the unhappy fate Mark Twain allotted to his chief characters—and Colonel Sellers is the most pathetic of them all—the book belies the theory that his bitter view of life was the result of his personal disasters suffered in the late eighteen nineties. The idea of death as a welcome release from life forms the closing sentence of the second chapter. The Hawkinses, having adopted the orphaned boy Clay, visit his mother's grave with him for the last time. They plant roses upon it and then leave "the dead to the long sleep that heals all heartaches and ends all sorrows." The mechanics of writing cannot keep out of this passage the depth of its author's personal conception, revealing in its simple statement.

But these villages of *The Gilded Age*—Obedstown and Murpheysburg and Hawkeye and that other overgrown village of Washington, D. C.—were merely the first of a long line of villages constructed by his pen. He next erected St. Petersburg, the locale of *Tom Sawyer*. This, of all his villages, most nearly resembles Hannibal. Upon completing *Tom Sawyer* in 1875, he wrote to Howells: "It is not a boy's book, at all. It will only be read by adults. It is only written for adults." But Howells insisted, "I think you ought to treat it implicitly as a boy's story. . . . if you should put it forth as a study of boy character from the grown-up point of view, you give the wrong key to it." Mark Twain agreed and began to cut the satire out of it, writing to Howells: "I finally concluded to cut the Sunday school speech down to the first two sentences, leaving no suggestion of satire, since the book is to be for boys and girls." He presumably referred to the speech made by Judge Thatcher in the showing-off scene. The Judge unequivocally links the memories of "the precious Sunday-school privileges of boyhood" and the memorizing of two

MARK TWAIN

thousand verses of scripture with the production of "great and good men."

Despite the pruning, there are many suggestions of satire left. The Revolt from the Village—somewhat softened by nostalgia for Hannibal—is carried on in this book, although the predominance of the boys' story reduces its importance. The entire community of the "poor little shabby village of St. Petersburg" is given body in the chapter "Showing Off at Sunday School," where the children's vying with each other for public notice reflects, in the manner of the Western sketches, a childish world patterned after the grown-up one they know; village cowardice prevents the villagers from bringing Injun Joe to trial; village repression of ambition, of the sort revealed in *The Gilded Age,* appears here in the person of Mr. Dobbins, the village schoolmaster who, disappointed in his desire to be a doctor, takes out his frustration on his students; village vacillation is reflected in the changing attitudes exhibited towards Muff Potter, himself a type of apathetic elderly village drunk; village instability is seen in the revival, at which everyone gets religion "temporarily"; village sentimentality is embodied in the "sappy women" who go "wail around the governor and implore him to be a merciful ass and trample his duty under foot" by issuing a pardon for Injun Joe; village juvenility is presented through the men in their reaction to the discovery of the buried treasure, an event "glorified until the reason of many of the citizens tottered under . . . the unhealthy excitement" and every old house for miles around was ransacked for treasure—"and not by boys, but men." Other unlovely aspects of the village appear: the ill-mannered choir that titters and whispers during the service contributes its part to complete the community that is Mark Twain's St. Petersburg.

In *Huckleberry Finn* the raft ties up at various riverside villages where Mark Twain's early renditions of Main Street are presented: the "little one-horse town" of Pokeville, where the king gets religion; then the little one-horse Arkansas town of Bricksville, a cluster of unpainted "shackly" houses, with gardens growing "jimpson-weeds and sunflowers, and ash-piles, and old curled-up boots and shoes, and pieces of bottles, and rags, and played-out tinware"—a village of leaning fences and rooting hogs, with at least "one loafer leaning up against every awning-post" on the single street; finally, the unnamed village of the Wilks family.

In 1891, while Mark Twain was losing a fortune in the Paige typesetting machine, he wrote *The American Claimant* quite frankly as a potboiler. The book is his worst literary failure; yet there are good things in it, as in any Mark Twain work. In *A Connecticut Yankee,* his formula had been to show an American looking at England; in *The American Claimant,* he shows an Englishman looking at America. The young Viscount Berkeley determines to renounce his rank and go to America "where all men are equal and all have an equal chance," in order to try his own mettle without benefit of title. The book displays the disillusionment of the young idealist as he comes to realize the disparity between the American democratic theory he has heard and the reality he experiences. When he applies for a clerkship in Washington, his university training and his obvious fitness for the post count for nothing; he finds that "political backing" is the thing. In depicting the scenes in the dingy boardinghouse where the young lord lives under the name "Howard Tracy," Mark Twain does his best work of the book. The reader realizes that this boardinghouse is another version of the village. As Barrow, the household philosopher remarks, "this boarding-house is merely the world in little." A fine young man who cannot pay his rent is insulted at table by the landlord, and the boarders all hate Brady because they are ashamed of themselves for not helping him. Other qualities of Mark Twain's genus of villagers appear.

Before he separated the two stories "Those Extraordinary Twins" and *Pudd'nhead Wilson,* the theme of the village was apparently designed as his main narrative. The villagers, exemplified by Aunt Patsy Cooper, Aunt Betsy Hale, and Rowena—the "lightweight heroine" whom Mark Twain described as stupid, irritating, and "nauseatingly sentimental"—were to demonstrate the curiosity, the envy, and the jealousy of the village while showing its reaction to foreigners and to freaks. Much of this remains in "Those Extraordinary Twins." In *Pudd'nhead Wilson,* the revolt continues in the study of Dawson's Landing. These villagers—hostile towards all strangers, towards anything they do not immediately understand—through their petty cruelties to David Wilson deprive him of his deserved success and would warp his life if he allowed them to. Refusing to be embittered, Wilson is a heroic person because his strength of character prevents the cruelty and ignorance of the village from ruining him. He is the individual standing against a society which exerts every pressure to make him conform to the mores of the village; but, holding to his integrity, he refuses to relinquish his spiritual independence.

It is always clear that these small communities, with their ignorance, their stupidity, and their pettiness, are illustrations of a larger humanity. If George Bernard Shaw viewed the United States as a nation of villagers, Mark Twain saw a world of villagers. His villagers are merely "the damned human race." As the boarding-house of *The American Claimant* is "the world in little," so is each village. The narrow confines of village life only serve to bring the inhabitants under a microscopic scrutiny. Obedstown, Murpheysburg, Hawkeye, St. Petersburg, Pokeville, Bricksville, the little un-named town "below the P'int," Dawson's Landing—all these are in Mark Twain's itinerary. Near the end of the line stands Hadleyburg. At the very end stands Eseldorf—translation, "Assville." As his re-volt precedes that of such writers as Edgar Lee Masters, Sherwood Anderson, and Sinclair Lewis, his importance to the trend of our literature since his time is strikingly apparent. The villagers of his last two villages, Hadleyburg and Eseldorf, are no more "damned" and "mangy" than those of Bricksville, if we accept Colonel Sher-burn's analysis of the Bricksville character. But Hadleyburg and Eseldorf are particularly interesting, for different reasons, in the study of Mark Twain as a literary artist.

CHAPTER 18

Moralism versus Determinism

MARK TWAIN's fiction is that part of his work in which, as Bernard DeVoto noted, the artist stands most clearly revealed, in his weakness and his strength. As I have pointed out, two main forces can be discerned, pulling against each other in his mind: on one hand, the idea of the ethical responsibility of the individual man; on the other, an idea which transfers responsibility from the individual to the universal, thus releasing man from all obligation for his own conduct. These two poles of thought in his work have been variously observed. As early as 1912, Paine recognized this ideological conflict when he wrote that once admitting the postulate that existence "is merely a sequence of cause and effect beginning with the primal atom . . . we have a theory that must stand or fall as a whole. We cannot say that man is a creature of circumstance and then leave him free to select his circumstance, even in the minutest fractional degree." And Mr. Wagenknecht wrote in 1935, "If Mark Twain is anything he is a moralist, yet there is no room for morality in his philosophy of life," while he spoke elsewhere of Mark Twain as "a fanatical determinist." Mr. Wagenknecht noticed that in one speech of the Connecticut Yankee the two poles of thought appear to exist simultaneously and that the "Gospel" itself contains an important passage that accords badly with Mark Twain's determinism: "Diligently train your ideas *upward* and *still upward* toward a summit where you will find your chiefest pleasure in conduct which, while contenting you, will . . . confer benefits upon your neighbor and the community." Or, as the laconic Pudd'nhead Wilson phrased it, "Let us endeavor so to live that when we come to die even the undertaker will be sorry." The conflict in Mark Twain's thought, then, has been recognized previously; but I know of no attempt, so far, to analyze the effect of that conflict upon his literary work.

That he himself recognized the conflict that went on inside him is clear. In 1898 he wrote to Twichell, concerning a prisoner held for assassinating the Empress of Austria: "A man is either a free agent or he isn't. If a man is a free agent, this prisoner is responsible for what he has done; but if a man is not a free agent . . . there is no rational way of making this prisoner even partially responsible for it. . . . Logic is logic." In 1904 he roundly scored his friend Twichell for his connection with party politics, because of its deteriorating effect upon "a man's mental and moral make-up." He pleaded with Twichell to "get out of that sewer" and then fumigate himself. But he added a postscript:

I wish I could learn to remember that it is unjust and dishonorable to put blame upon the human race for any of its acts. For it did not make itself, it did not make its nature, it is merely a machine, it is moved wholly by outside influences, it has no hand in creating the outside influences nor in choosing which of them it will welcome or reject . . . ; wherefore, whatever the machine does . . . is the personal act of its Maker, and He, solely, is responsible. I wish I could learn to pity the human race instead of censuring it . . . and I could, if the outside influences of old habit were not so strong upon my machine.

His condemnations arose always from emotional attitudes, not from his reason. At another time he wrote to Twichell, "I know the human race's limitations, and this makes it my duty . . . to be fair to it." Still, he continued to rage. His letters, which he intended for publication, are overflowing with this rage. During the hard-fought Blaine-Cleveland campaign of 1884, he wrote to Howells of those who think one way and vote another: "*Isn't* human nature the most consummate sham and lie that was ever invented? Isn't man a creature to be ashamed of . . . ? Man, 'know thyself'—and then thou wilt despise thyself. . . . Hawley is howling for Blaine, Warner and Clark are eating their daily crow in the paper for him. . . . O Stultification, where is thy sting, O Slave, where is thy hickory!" In an 1892 article, "Concerning the Jews," he discussed race prejudices, adding: "I can stand any society. All that I care to know is that a man is a human being, that is enough for me; he can't be any worse." The following year he complained bitterly to Howells: "I have been reading the morning paper . . . well knowing that I shall find in it the usual depravities and basenesses and hypocrisies and cruelties that make up

Mark Twain and Dorothy Quick
Arriving in New York, July 22, 1907
From a photograph by Geo. G. Bain

civilization, and cause me to put in the rest of the day pleading for the damnation of the human race." In 1905, he wrote to Twichell, who had been arguing the case for "progress," that neither the human heart nor the human brain had undergone any change since the beginning. But a little later, to J. Howard Moore, he wrote that the human brain *had* improved. The morals, alas, had not:

. . . as inheritors of the mentality of our reptile ancestors we have improved the inheritance by a thousand grades; but in the matter of the morals which they left us we have gone backward as many grades. . . . Necessarily we started equipped with their perfect and blemishless morals; now . . . we have no real morals, but only artificial ones—morals created and preserved by the forced suppression of natural and hellish instincts. Yet we are dull enough to be vain of them.

Certainly, we are a sufficiently comical invention, we humans.

He was always alert to spot a conflict between moralism and determinism in some other writer. From Stormfield in 1909, he took Howells to task for an article Howells had written on Poe: "you grant that God and circumstances sinned against Poe, but you also grant that he sinned against himself—a thing which he couldn't do." Seven years earlier, he had pounced on the same flaw in Jonathan Edwards. Finding in *Freedom of the Will* "the glare of a resplendent intellect gone mad," he had "wallowed and reeked with Jonathan in his insane debauch":

. . . the drunk does not come on till the last third. . . . Jonathan seems to hold . . . that the Man (or his Soul or his Will) never *creates* an impulse itself, but is moved to action by an impulse *back* of it. That's sound!

Also, that of . . . things offered it, it infallibly chooses the one which for the moment is most *pleasing* to ITSELF. Perfectly correct! . . .

Up to that point he could have written chapters III and IV of my suppressed "Gospel." But there we seem to separate. He seems to concede the indisputable and unshakable dominion of Motive and Necessity (call them what he may, these are *exterior* forces and not under the man's authority . . .)—then he suddenly flies the logic track and . . . makes the *man* and not these exterior forces responsible to God for the man's thoughts, words, and acts. It is frank insanity. . . .

And so he . . . arrived at this handsome result:

Man is commanded to do so-and-so.

It has been ordained from the beginning of time that some men *shan't* and others *can't*.

These are to be blamed: let them be damned.

I enjoy the Colonel very much, and shall enjoy the rest of him with an obscene delight.

But Mark Twain is in no position to sneer when Jonathan Edwards "flies the logic track." Let us see what Mark Twain himself does in his fiction, taking as an example *The Man That Corrupted Hadleyburg,* praised by Paine as his greatest short story, "wonderfully done": "The mechanism of the story is perfect, the drama of it is . . . supreme in its artistic triumph." It deals with the force of environment, since "temptations were kept out of the way of the young people, so that their honesty could have every chance to harden and solidify." But in another passage this environmental training is shown as powerless to change underlying human nature: ". . . it's been one ever-lasting training and training and training in honesty—honesty shielded, from the cradle, against every possible temptation, and so it's *artificial* honesty, and weak as water when temptation comes. . . ." There is deterministic motivation through the force of circumstances in the guise of "the stranger." Almost half a hundred citizens are affected by his manipulations, and Mark Twain is obviously exhibiting "the damned human race." It is the acquisitive instinct, the greed for wealth, that is involved in this probing of humanity's frailty. The stranger controls the action of the characters by building up a certain set of circumstances to which he knows they will respond as one man: they have no interior motivation, no wills of their own, to save them from the trap which the stranger sets for them, baited by his own knowledge of human greed.

Nevertheless, in spite of his strongly marked deterministic pattern, Mark Twain is unable to eliminate moral judgments from his solution. The characters, thieves and hypocrites as they are, are all held responsible for their acts by way of the derisive condemnation of the audience; and the two old people, the only ones who win the reader's sympathy, likewise hold themselves morally responsible and are so conscience-stricken that they actually die of broken hearts. With such faults of intellection, the wonder is that Mark Twain is able to make the story as powerful as he does. And it has power. But for the thoughtful reader there is a mischief in it that keeps it from being altogether satisfying to him, though he may not stop to analyze why. The stranger who devises almost-laboratory conditions for the testing of human behavior in Hadleyburg coincides well with Mark Twain's theme of determinism; but the switch to an implied theme of divine justice—the great theme of the judgment of God as it operates through the consciences of Mr. and Mrs. Richards—makes any unity of effect impossible. The unholy glee with which "the house" chants its sardonic joy at the unmasking of the "Nineteeners" echoes through what is in itself an adolescent voice of judgment, confusing and perplexing the reader. There is no continuity of motivation, no steadiness of emotional effect, no philosophical unity to the story. In it the moralist gives an out-of-bounds blow to the determinist, and Hadleyburg settles itself on a philosophic quicksand.

The mind of Mark Twain was a workshop in which two creatures were constantly busy, a creature of hope and a creature of despair. Despite their enforced intimacy, they were not on good terms; their natures were far too different. Sometimes one would cow the other into temporary submission so that he could finish a piece of work—hurriedly, perhaps; but often one—that is, whichever began first—would be challenged by the other, who would insist on doing a part of the job his way. There were always two Mark Twains, the Moralist *versus* the Determinist. We have noted what these two workmen made of *The Man That Corrupted Hadleyburg*. There the clash between moralism and determinism is discerned more readily than in the longer fiction, since the narrow scope brings the opposing ideas into closer juxtaposition. But the ideological conflict that is basic in the Hadleyburg tale appears again and again. It appears briefly even in *The Prince and the Pauper*, which grew out of his reading *The Prince and the Page*, by Charlotte M. Yonge. In the Yonge story a nobleman lives for years disguised as a blind beggar. Mark Twain decided that he would not only disguise a prince as a beggar, but also a beggar as a prince. He chose Edward VI, small son of Henry VIII, as his subject and began to study the period from books and maps.[1] He wrote about half of the story in 1877 and completed it in 1880.

So far as structure is concerned, this book is perhaps his finest achievement. He wrote to Howells, "It begins at 9 A.M., Jan. 27, 1547 . . . and goes on for three weeks—till the . . . coronation grandeurs in Westminster Abbey, Feb. 20." The narrow compass and the contrast formula both laid restraints upon him; add the fact that

[1] Paine, *Biography*, II, 597–98.

the period of the action was far enough away to allow him aesthetic distance and the further fact that the chief characters are boys, and the extraordinary unity which he achieved in *The Prince and the Pauper* stands explained. In a recent article, A. L. Vogelbeck notes that it was the first work on which critics mainly agreed that Mark Twain displayed "notable abilities as a serious writer and literary artist." For *The Prince and the Pauper* complied with literary conventions of the time, while *Tom Sawyer* and later *Huckleberry Finn*, lying outside the tradition of correctness and imitation, puzzled and disturbed the critics.

This book was Mark Twain's first full-length study of the power of determining environment and circumstance. The transformation of beggar into prince and vice versa was effected by a mere change of clothes. The significance of clothes in the work of Mark Twain rests upon some such explanation as this: since the world judges by outward appearance, the clothes one wears become a part of the exterior determining circumstances which decide what everyone will be. His original intention had been to center attention upon the real prince, accounting for the "mildness which distinguished Edward VI's reign from those that preceded and followed it" by having him experience at first hand the hardships of his subjects. But, as the story progressed, Mark Twain gave most of his attention to the pressure of environment upon the moral fiber of the small bogus prince, Tom Canty of Offal Court. Even the humanitarian's zeal for reform could not overcome the pessimistic determinist's interest in the weaknesses of human nature. Tom lapses from a sturdy rebellion in which he denounces servants for troubling him "with offices that harass the spirit and shame the soul, they misbecoming any but a doll, that hath nor brains nor hands to help itself withal," into a slothful enjoyment of the splendors that surround him. Finally he sinks into a corrupt resignation in which, when his mother recognizes him in one of his public appearances, he says, "I do not know you, woman!" Here the conflict between moralism and determinism appears: Tom, brought to this shameful state by circumstances beyond his control, was assailed so strongly by his conscience that his shame "withered his stolen royalty. His grandeurs were stricken valueless; they seemed to fall away from him like rotten rags."

This incident occurred upon the very day that restoration was made to the rightful prince. One wonders what would have happened to Tom Canty if his masquerade had been prolonged. Mark Twain realized the importance of both environment and heredity, but *The Prince and the Pauper* shows environment as the stronger force. If heredity had triumphed, the real prince might have returned to his palace unchanged. This tale of rags and robes uncovers Mark Twain's characteristic thought-patterns. Although he had planned the story to show the broadening and mellowing of the prince, his chief emphasis falls upon the deterioration which has begun in the other boy. Human nature's frailty always engrossed him.

A by-product of this story of sixteenth-century England was "1601: A Fireside Conversation in the Time of Queen Elizabeth," which has been called "the most famous piece of pornography in American literature." While Mark Twain was reading ancient books "with the purpose of saturating myself with archaic English to a degree which would enable me to do plausible imitations of it," in one of them he came across a conversation which impressed him with the indelicacies of speech permissible "among ladies and gentlemen in that ancient time. . . . I was immediately full of a desire to practice my archaics and contrive one of these stirring conversations out of my own head." The result was "1601," which Mark Twain and Joe Twichell read together, rolling on the grass with laughter. It presents Queen Elizabeth, Shakespeare, Ben Jonson, Walter Raleigh, young Beaumont—persons who, as Mark Twain said, "hadn't a thing to recommend them except their incomparable brains"—engaged in a spirited conversation recorded by the Queen's aged cupbearer, who records it in the line of duty, though in scorn and indignation. The piece is marked by its bawdiness. Mr. Wagenknecht finds in it the flavor of Swift's obscenities: "the writer will show the human race what filthy creatures they are." This fireside bawdry displays vitality and imagination, certainly, but does not necessarily indicate the suppression of genius which Mr. Brooks sees in it.

A Connecticut Yankee in King Arthur's Court was begun in 1886 and published in 1889. An 1883 entry in the *Notebook* gives probably the first germ of the story:

Dream of being a knight errant in armor in the Middle Ages. Have the notions and habits of thought of the present day mixed with the necessities of that. No pocket in the armor. Can't scratch. Cold in the head—can't blow. . . . Iron gets redhot in the sun—leaks in the rain . . . and freezes me solid in the winter. . . . Can't dress or undress myself. Always getting struck by lightning. Fall down and can't get up.

After George W. Cable had put a copy of Malory's *Morte d'Arthur* into Mark Twain's hands, it was inevitable that he would write the *Yankee*. He prepared for the work, as he had for *The Prince and the Pauper*, by an intensive study of the period. He brought the modern age and the time of "nineteenth of June, 528," into a juxtaposition which contrasts the two civilizations. Howells viewed the book as Mark Twain's "highest achievement in the way of a greatly imagined and symmetrically developed romance. Of all the fanciful schemes in fiction, it pleases me most." Modern critics, however, are not so enthusiastic. Mr. DeVoto labels it a "chaos" because of its mingling of burlesque and serious material. But most critics now agree that *A Connecticut Yankee* was written to point up the injustices both of Victoria's England and of Mark Twain's America. There are hits in it at high tariffs, the practices of contemporary corporations, the spoils system in political appointments, and profiteering under the "pork-barrel laws." The Yankee argues with Dowley, the blacksmith, that high wages are not preferable to low wages unless they can buy more. The competitive examinations as held at King Arthur's court convey an objection to the practice of using favoritism rather than merit as a basis for rewards and appointments in Mark Twain's own time. A *Notebook* entry, made while he was writing the *Yankee*, reads: "The Victoria Cross—who gets it? Intrepid commoners? Do not deceive yourself. Examine the V. C. records."

The satire on injustices of his own day is important, refuting as it does the original charge of criticism that he took refuge in the sixth century because he lacked the courage to speak out concerning his own. Perhaps even more important for the understanding of Mark Twain is the fact that this book reveals, once more, the basic conflict that constantly went on inside him. Early in the story The Boss says: "Inherited ideas are a curious thing . . . and the man who should have proposed to divert them by reason and argument would have had a long contract on his hands." But listen to the soliloquy of The Boss a few chapters farther on:

Training—training is everything; training is all there is *to* a person. We

speak of nature; . . . what we call by that misleading name is merely
heredity and training. We have no thoughts of our own . . . they are
transmitted to us, trained into us. All that is original in us . . . can be
covered up . . . by the point of a cambric needle, all the rest being . . .
inherited from . . . the Adam-clan of grasshopper or monkey from whom
our race has been so . . . unprofitably developed. And as for me, all that
I think about in this pathetic drift between the eternities is to . . . save that
one microscopic atom in me that is truly *me*: the rest may land in Sheol
for all I care.

Here, the argument is that all ideas of the individual are determined
by something other than himself; but the crux of the passage lies in
the praise of the distinctive *"me,"* the essence of individuality and
personality that The Boss apparently hopes to keep unchanged inside him. This inner core of *me*, assuredly, is the soul—the thing that
corresponds to conscience in other passages in Mark Twain's work.
Which is it to be, then? external determinism, or inward moral force?
  While he was working on the *Yankee*, he was involved with
the Paige typesetting machine which ultimately cost him a fortune.
In January of 1889, however, his letters show him confident that
success lies in the machine. Nevertheless, the riotous burlesque which
appears in the *Yankee* is laid upon a groundwork of pessimism. The
thoughtful reader finds a deal of symbolism in the book. It is plain
that Mark Twain makes the two villains of Arthur's England the
Catholic church and the monarchy. Accordingly, America, having
no established church and no monarchy, should be exempt from the
wrongs he pictures. But he apparently uses church and monarchy
merely as vehicles to carry the sins and injustices perpetrated in general by the "damned human race." At the time he was writing the
scenes dealing with slavery and burnings, with Morgan le Fay's
dungeons, he was recording in his *Notebook*:

There are in Connecticut, at this moment, and in all countries, children
and disagreeable relatives chained in cellars, all sores, welts, worms, and
vermin.—Cases come to light every little while—two recent cases in our
state. This is to suggest that the thing in man which makes him cruel to a
slave is in him *permanently* and will not be rooted out for a million years.

The enchantment that sees swine as ladies and gentlemen introduces
the argument that swine are the only "valuable nobility," but when

Sandy kisses the swine and bespeaks them "reverently," the Yankee is "ashamed of her, ashamed of the human race."

The principal symbolism, however, lies in the constant duel between The Boss, with his machine-age progress, and Merlin, the incarnation of ancient superstition. Criticism usually equates the Yankee with Mark Twain himself, in his boastful attitude about nineteenth-century progress. But Mark Twain fully understood the Yankee's deficiencies. In discussing the character with Dan Beard, the prospective illustrator, he said: "You know, this Yankee of mine has neither the refinement nor the weakness of a college education; he is a perfect ignoramus; he is boss of a machine shop; he can build a locomotive or a Colt's revolver, he can put up and run a telegraph line, but he's an ignoramus, nevertheless."

Although the ignoramus Yankee gets the better of the contest for a while, the outcome of the book shows that so-called "progress" has no real chance against superstition; but, beyond that, it shows that if real progress is to be made, another sort of advancement must keep pace with technical advancement. "Did you think you had educated the superstition out of these people?" Clarence asks; and The Boss replies, "I certainly did think it." The Boss and Clarence direct their last fight against England from the cave of Merlin, the very stronghold of superstition. The picked boys grow pale when the march on their cave begins, although they finally rally. Even within the cave, with its modern marvels of electric switches and controlled explosives, superstition is present. For Merlin is there, disguised as an old woman, come to do the cooking. And Merlin has the last word: "Ye were conquerors; ye are conquered! . . . He sleepeth now—and shall sleep thirteen centuries. I am Merlin!" The scene ends with Superstition making the magical passes in the air that put Progress to sleep for centuries, while The Boss's followers are left to die in "a trap of our own making." The pestilence which destroys everyone except The Boss comes of using the death-dealing invention of modern Progress, a monster that destroys its Frankenstein inventors by diseases bred of decaying human flesh. Instead of the popular interpretation as solely a celebration of American progress, the book may conceivably be viewed as a fictional working out of the idea that a too-quick civilization breeds disaster. In brief, civilization must be organic. It must come from within the people themselves; it cannot be imposed upon them from without.

This same theme had been treated by Mark Twain several years earlier, in 1878, in a short story called "The Great Revolution in Pitcairn." The people on Pitcairn's Island are living peacefully and tranquilly far from the world when an American Yankee, "a *doubtful acquisition*," settles there. Butterworth Stavely is a palpable villain from the start. Disrupting the life of the island completely, he introduces many "improvements" and winds up as emperor. The islanders illustrate, for a time, the theme of outside motivation later used in Hadleyburg; they follow this Yankee like blind sheep, yielding themselves to be molded by his consuming desire for personal power. Finally some spirit within them, some lingering vestige of self-respect, prompts his overthrow. The people rise against him and revert rapidly to their former ways, upon which he reproaches them, in Hitleresque oratory, for "ingratitude." In *A Connecticut Yankee*, The Boss is much less villainous, much closer to being a hero. But The Boss, too, is a dictator; and it is not safe to assume that Mark Twain was unaware of that fact.

The question of mechanical progress *versus* cultural progress is treated explicitly, though ironically, in *The American Claimant*. Viscount Berkeley, as "Howard Tracy," learns of American ways not only in dialectics with Barrow, the boardinghouse philosopher, but also by observation. Struggling to make democratic theory and practice coincide, Tracy finds that the American measuring-stick is material prosperity. Barrow takes him to the Mechanics Club, a meeting place for the male vestals—clerks and mechanics—who keep the flame glowing at the forge of America's industrialism. There, a patent-office clerk answers a college professor's speech on the results of culture. The clerk admits that culture has made some progress in America but insists, proudly, that "material progress has been immeasurably vaster." He goes on, rhapsodically chanting statistics in praise of this same material progress. Mark Twain's irony is thick in these lines; but for those who would take the praise at its face value,[2] I refer once more to his letter answering Twichell's claim for "the steady progress . . . of righteousness." Mark Twain agreed that the nineteenth century had made progress, "colossal progress"; but—in what?

---

[2] Van Wyck Brooks writes (*The Ordeal of Mark Twain*, 146) that Mark Twain "had fully accepted the illusion of his contemporaries that the progress of machinery was identical with the progress of humanity."

Materialities. Prodigious acquisitions . . . which add to the comfort of many and make life harder for as many more. But the . . . materialities were not invented in the interest of righteousness. . . . In Europe and America today there is a vast change (due to them) in ideals—do you admire it? . . . Money is the supreme ideal. . . . Money-lust has always existed, but not . . . a craze, a madness, until your time and mine. This lust has rotted these nations; it has made them hard, sordid, ungentle, dishonest, oppressive.

Mr. Brooks rightly says that Mark Twain's birthright was "of our age rather than his own." He holds that the "whole tendency of Mark Twain's spirit ran precisely counter to the spirit of his age," in moral, religious, political, and economic aspects. He adds, however, that Mark Twain expressed such ideas only in letters and conversations, withholding them from his literary work from the time of his vigorous early writing to the time when he was "too old and too secure to fear public opinion," when he revenged himself for past repressions in *The Man That Corrupted Hadleyburg*: "Not till then . . . did he ever again, openly and on a large scale, attack the spiritual integrity of industrial America." Nevertheless, the patent-clerk's speech in *The American Claimant*, with its ironic praise of material progress, is an attack on the spiritual quality of industrial America. The fact that such attacks appear in his later work in veiled form, instead of the direct open attack he made so early in *The Gilded Age*, testifies only that he had taught himself something about satiric indirection. A literary artist is not a pamphleteer.

Edmund Clarence Stedman, looking over a manuscript copy of *A Connecticut Yankee* in 1889, was more discerning than some readers of our own day. He wrote to Mark Twain: "Some blasted fool will surely jump up and say that Cervantes polished off chivalry centuries ago, etc. After a time he'll discover, perhaps, that you are going at the *still existing* radical principles or fallacies which made 'chivalry' possible once, and servility and flunkeyism and tyranny possible now." Actually, Mark Twain was going at human nature—as he saw it. Before he attempted *A Connecticut Yankee* and *The American Claimant*, he had learned something of the indirect attack by writing *Huckleberry Finn*. The *Yankee*, however, is marred by his failure to resolve his old dilemma of moralism and determinism, as well as by the burlesque which he shoveled in on all sides to make his sermon more palatable to the common man. The *Claimant* is marred by hasty writing and by the fact that he tried to do too much: there are sermons in the boardinghouse scenes against America as a nation of villagers; in the Mechanics Club scene a sermon against materialism; and sermons throughout against the deteriorating effect of dreams of wealth.

We come now to what is perhaps the most effective treatment of determinism Mark Twain ever wrote, the book *Pudd'nhead Wilson.* As early as 1869 he had written a sketch on the original Siamese twins, presenting them as enlisted on opposite sides in the Civil War and as taking each other prisoner at Seven Pines.[3] He had the frontier's interest in freaks, it is true; but he had also a serious interest in the marvel of dual personality. He gave a novel twist to this grotesque material by probing its moral possibilities: Eng liked liquor, Chang was a teetotaler; but Chang was made drunk on liquor swallowed by Eng, though Chang's principles remained untouched. Years later, he saw a pictured Italian freak, and in 1892 he began an "extravaganza" about it, naming the story "Those Extraordinary Twins."

But as he wrote, the idea of the dual personality began to recede in his mind before the ever present lure of determinism. The two personalities joined in one body were not suitable to his theme of compulsion by outside influences. When he was planning *The Prince and the Pauper,* according to Paine, the "old device of changelings in the cradle ... presented itself to him, but it could not provide the situations he had in mind." But that same device, in spite of its hoary age, in spite of its hackneyed treatment, was a "natural" for the theme of determinism. He accordingly adopted it. He dragged into the story of the Siamese twins the second story of Roxy and the two babies. He prefaced the published version of "Those Extraordinary Twins" with some remarks on the troubles sometimes encountered by a man not "born with the novel-writing gift." He knew from experience that such a man "merely has some people in his mind, and an incident or two, also a locality. He knows these people, he knows the selected locality, and he trusts that he can plunge those people into those incidents with interesting results." But in this case, because of the sway which the deterministic motif held over the mind of Mark Twain, the late-comers gradually usurped control of the story:

[3] Ferguson, *Mark Twain, Man and Legend,* 251.

Among them a stranger named Pudd'nhead Wilson, and a woman named Roxana; and presently the doings of these two pushed up into prominence a young fellow named Tom Driscoll. . . . Before the book was half finished those three were taking things almost entirely into their own hands and working the tale as a private venture of their own.

It was "a most embarrassing circumstance," he said, when the tale "changed itself from a farce to a tragedy" in the process of writing. At that point he realized that he had two stories instead of one and separated them by what he called "a kind of literary Caesarean operation." In July, 1893, he wrote to his publisher:

The whole story is centered on the murder and the trial; from the first chapter the movement is straight ahead without divergence or side play to the murder and the trial; everything that is done or said or that happens is a preparation for those events. Therefore, 3 people stand up high, from beginning to end, and only 3—Pudd'nhead, "Tom" Driscoll, and his nigger mother, Roxana.

This emphasis on murder and trial high-lights the fingerprints; yet Mark Twain unquestionably was using the story to illustrate his deterministic philosophy.

But there is an intricate slant to the handling of determinism in this story that has been generally overlooked: he works out two kinds of determinism in his use of the two boys, a determinism contrasted and complex. The true Tom Driscoll, white and aristocratic by birth, illustrates the influence of environment and training; he thinks himself a Negro and so becomes a Negro in actions, manner, speech, and even in thought. The pseudo Tom Driscoll, the real son of Roxy, illustrates a conflicting theory of Mark Twain's that a man's inborn nature is "rock" and yields in no way to training. Among the Pudd'nhead Wilson maxims used as chapter headings stands one which maintains: "Training is everything. The peach was once a bitter almond; cauliflower is nothing but cabbage with a college education." That is all very well for the so-called Valet de Chambre, all white and an aristocrat to boot, who is in speech and thought a slave because he has been reared a slave. He shows that it is training, not innate quality, which makes the free man or the slave, thus illustrating Mark Twain's conviction that human nature is essentially the same. But what of the so-called Tom Driscoll, false and colored? He is thirty-one parts white, only one thirty-second Negro; but, according to his mother Roxy, that one thirty-second is his soul. It is his essence, determining what he is by its innate quality so that training and environment are powerless to change it. It is what the Yankee called "the one microscopic atom in me that is truly *me*." It is impregnable; and Tom's essential difference from the white boy shows that human nature is not the same, after all. Tom's inner core remains unchanged; and this fact is underscored by Wilson's comment on the infatuated love of Judge Driscoll and his wife for Tom: "A devil born to a young couple is measurably recognizable by them as a devil before long, but a devil adopted by an old couple is an angel to them, and remains so."

The locale of this story is Dawson's Landing, a village that—unlike Obedstown and Hawkeye and Pokeville and Bricksville—was attractive to look at. It was a collection of white cottages, almost concealed by climbing roses, morning-glories, and honeysuckle, with neat white fences, and sometimes on the ledge outside the window boxes a cat—"stretched at full length, asleep and blissful, with her furry belly to the sun and a paw curved over her nose." But this rose-scented garden spot had the black canker of slavery eating at its heart.

Roxy spoke as if she were a black Negro, though she had a fair complexion, soft brown hair, and brown eyes. Her movements were marked by dignity and grace; her face was expressive, "shapely, intelligent, and . . . even beautiful": "Only one-sixteenth of her was black, and that sixteenth did not show." But she was a slave, and salable. Her child, thirty-one parts white, had blue eyes and flaxen curls; but he, too, "was a slave, and by a fiction of law and custom a negro."

Roxy and her son are the problem of race made flesh, the problem intensified and made acute by the preponderance of white blood, which gives these unfortunates the appearance of white persons but leaves them Negroes still. Roxy talks her nigger talk and bandies wit with coal-black Jasper, who warns her, "I's gwine to come a-court'n' you bimeby, Roxy." She laughingly retorts, "*You* is, you black mudcat! Yah—yah—yah! I got somep'n' better to do den 'sociat'n' wid niggers as black as you is." But we are let into her secret thoughts, now and then. When she reproaches her son for his cruelty to her, she sobs: "You . . . wouldn't ever let me forget I's a nigger." Roxy is conscious most of the time that she is colored; that fact, with all its implications, is seldom out of her mind. In the scene in which she forces the false Tom to get on his knees to her, she taunts him: "Fine nice young white gen'l'man kneelin' down to a nigger wench! I's wanted to see dat jes' once befo' I's called. Now, Gabr'el, blow de hawn, I's ready."

There are echoes of Calvinism in the book. Roxy justifies her switch of the children in their cradles partly on the Biblical grounds of election and selection: ". . . de Lord . . . do jis' as he's a mineter. He s'lect out anybody dat suit him, en put another one in his place, en make de fust one happy forever en leave t'other one to burn wid Satan." Consequently, Roxy tries her hand at arranging destinies. But in spite of his advantages, her son fails to develop into a man because his innate quality prevents it. His natural viciousness is shown by his sadism directed at "Chambers," as well as by his treatment of Roxy. But she scorns him, in her turn, when he refuses to fight a duel of honor. She glowers at him "with measureless contempt" in her face, fairly spitting out her words:

"En you refuse' to fight a man dat kicked you . . . ! En you ain't got no mo' feelin' den to come en tell me, dat fetched sich a po' low-down ornery rabbit into de worl'! Pah! it makes me sick! It's de nigger in you, dat's what it is. Thirty-one parts o' you is white, en on'y one part nigger, en dat po' little one part is yo' *soul*. 'Tain't wuth savin'; 'tain't wuth totin' out on a shovel en throwin' in de gutter."

The scene is melodrama, yet it compels the reader's belief. Immediately after, Roxy mumbles to herself: "Ain't nigger enough in him to show in his finger nails, en dat takes mighty little—yit dey's enough to paint his soul. . . . Yessir, enough to paint a whole thimbleful of 'em." Mark Twain's knowledge of the Negro permits her mood to alter, her temper to change in flashes as a child's does; and soon she sends out the sort of wholehearted laughter which God has granted only to "the happy angels in heaven and the bruised and broken black slave on earth."

The effect on Tom of his discovery of his Negro blood is shown in his bitter thinking: "Why were niggers *and* whites made? What crime did the uncreated first nigger commit that the curse of birth was decreed for him? And why is this awful difference made between white and black?" For four pages, Mark Twain elaborates the psychological changes which take place in Tom as he tries to get his bearings:

> If he met a friend, . . . the "nigger" in him asserted its humility, and he blushed and was abashed. . . . He found the "nigger" in him involuntarily giving the road . . . to the white rowdy and loafer. . . . The "nigger" in him went shrinking and skulking here and there and yonder. . . . He presently came to have a hunted sense and a hunted look.

The effect upon the true Tom Driscoll of the disclosure that he is white is not presented with the emotional gradations which Mark Twain gives to the "nigger." Judging from this proportion, one would say that the theme of innate depravity embodied in the colored man engrossed him even more than the theme of determining circumstances embodied in the white. The true Tom Driscoll is shown as the victim of a tragedy not of his own making. He could neither read nor write, and

> . . . his speech was the basest dialect of the negro quarter. His gait, his attitude, his gestures, his bearing, his laugh—all were vulgar—all were vulgar and uncouth. . . . Money and fine clothes could not mend these defects . . . ; they only made them the more glaring and the more pathetic.

The boy moves, shambling and pitiful, between two worlds, belonging to neither. For Mark Twain, like Hawthorne, knew there are some wrongs that can never be righted.

Unquestionably his most lifelike female character, Roxy is, in Mr. DeVoto's phrase, unique and formidable. And Mark Twain's calm, courageous handling of the theme of miscegenation, almost nonexistent in Victorian novels, is a part of the moving force of the book. He presents this theme simply, matter-of-factly, as a commonplace of the time. Gone is the embarrassment which hobbles him elsewhere when he approaches the subject of sex; missing, too, is the heat, the anger, with which he might have been expected to treat this evidence of the baseness in human nature.

Pudd'nhead Wilson is one of three characters named by De-Voto as Mark Twain's only heroes, the others being Nigger Jim and Joan of Arc. But Mark Twain stands too close to Pudd'nhead Wilson, a character perhaps too much like himself. He is unable to render his hero true and whole, even in his best scenes. Victorian melodrama pervades the courtroom when Wilson holds the stage with studied pauses, his eye on the wall clock, the murder weapon in his hand:

"Upon this haft stands the assassin's natal autograph, written in blood. . . . There is but one man in the whole earth whose hand can duplicate that crimson sign . . . and please God we will produce that man in this room before the clock strikes noon!"

Finally Wilson says dramatically: "The murderer . . . sits in among you. Valet de Chambre, negro and slave . . . make upon the window the finger-prints that will hang you!" We miss here the wonderful objectivity of like passages in *Huckleberry Finn*, with everything keyed down for reporting through Huck's lips.

Mark Twain pointed out to his publisher that the fingerprints were "virgin ground—absolutely *fresh*, and mighty curious and interesting to everybody." But, despite his interest in novelties, his deepest interest was assuredly the subject of determinism as presented through the racial problem. Perhaps the claptrap of courtroom melodrama and the "fresh" lure of fingerprints were merely snares by which he meant to catch the reader, a course comparable to his practice—recorded by himself—of hiding the core of his moral lessons in humorous burlesques.

There is, of course, additional melodrama in the scenes in which the Negroes figure—for example, Tom on his knees before Roxy. Nevertheless, such scenes have the ring of truth; for the Negro is at his best in roles of high emotionalism. Certainly, in depicting the pre–Civil War Negroes—untaught and generally childlike—any analysis of their character must be built on emotional reaction rather than on intellectual estimate. Viewing the world of the blacks, Mark Twain stands at a distance which gives him the proper perspective. It is not his world. As an observer, he can see it rounded and whole. Mr. Wagenknecht has said that no white man ever dealt more justly with the Negro race than Mark Twain did in this book, where all the racial faults are "so mercilessly revealed, yet so tenderly and understandingly, so utterly without any sense of racial superiority."

Indirect evidence that he viewed all human nature as cut from one piece appears here in his bestowal of the name "Tom" on the false heir. For years, he had been naming likable characters Tom;

the early Quintus Curtius Snodgrass letters—unauthenticated, but perhaps his—praised Tom Morgan of the Baton Rouge Fencibles— "plain, honest, warmhearted *Tom*." But here Tom Driscoll sinks to the lowest possible level when he sells his own mother "down the river to Orleans." One shrinks from imagining how Mark Twain would handle a white man guilty of a comparable offense. Yet no rage, no recrimination, is directed against Tom. In the courtroom scene, the reader even has sympathy for him as he sits under Wilson's accusation: "Tom turned his ashen face imploringly toward the speaker, made some impotent movement with his white lips, then slid limp and lifeless to the floor." Mr. DeVoto commends Mark Twain for adhering "to the artistic necessities of his structure" in the tough-minded ending in which Tom himself is sold down the river. In this book, at least, Mark Twain was true to his own tenets of determinism.[4]

He was a sensitive creative artist, and he needed the human race as the material for his art. But frequently, when he looked at that race, his ideas fell off into mere rages in which a sympathetic conception of humanity became impossible. Instead of being neutral, dispassionate, and objective, he became scornful and contemptuous; and he was led into shattering outbursts of hatred against human evil in which the whole idea—if there had been a literary idea—came to naught. His rage and disgust, however, were rarely on account of his own troubles. He told Paine:

Once Twichell heard me cussing the human race, and he said, "Why, Mark, you are the last person in the world to do that—one selected and set apart as you are." I said, "Joe, . . . I am not cussing altogether about my own little troubles. Anyone can stand his own misfortunes; but when I read in the papers all about the rascalities and outrages going on

---

[4] He used his tenets of determinism with devastating effect in his bitterly ironic "Defence of General Funston," commemorating the deed in which Funston and his followers, after being fed and sheltered by the Filipino leader Aguinaldo, murdered the guard and kidnaped Aguinaldo. Funston, Mark Twain argued, was not to blame for what he did; he was only following his natural bent, as George Washington had done. Funston's "It took as naturally to moral slag as Washington's took to moral gold, but only It was to blame, not Funston. . . . it would be in the last degree unfair to hold Funston to blame for the outcome of his infirmity; as clearly unfair as it would be to blame him because his conscience leaked out through one of his pores when he was little—a thing which he could not help, and he couldn't have raised it, anyway. . . . If blame there was, and guilt, and treachery, and baseness, they are not Funston's, but only Its."

I realize what a creature the human animal is. Don't you care more about the wretchedness of others than anything that happens to you?" Joe said he did, and shut up.

As a moralist, he raged at men because they are what they are; as a determinist, he raged at the primary forces or environing circumstances that make men what they are. Speaking of Mark Twain's "tendency to rage, violence," Mr. Wagenknecht writes that his temper was "his Achilles heel, the place where the lime leaf clung." Wagenknecht applies this statement to the life of the man, seeing his rage as a contributing cause for his pessimism. But this same tendency becomes "his Achilles heel" when his writings are considered according to the requirements for literary art.

For it is there that one of his chief weaknesses as an artist lies, a weakness especially apparent when he approaches tragic material. His experience of life had compelled his attention to problems essentially tragic. He noted the American contrast between the lives of the rich and of the poor, between the professed creeds of democracy and religion and the practiced ones. The tragedy of war he had briefly witnessed; the tragedy of slavery he had known at first hand. But, as Mr. DeVoto remarks apropos of *Joan of Arc*, "he was uncomfortable in the demands of tragedy, formalizing whatever could not be sentimentalized." And this brings us once more to the question of his patheticism. The sentimentality with which he handles "The Californian's Tale" becomes almost maudlin. His very tenderness carries him into an extravagance which breaks the bounds of artistic restraint. Instead of the reserve with which reflective perception grounds its emotions upon deep truths of human life, he aims at the short cut of vivid intensity, and sometimes the effect is neither vivid nor intense. He had, in fact, two Achilles heels where his art was concerned—pity and rage, rage and pity—and he was always torn between the two moods. He carried within his soul the intolerable burden of pity, and frequently his rage was only a mechanism set up in self-defense.

The German critic Friedrich Schönemann finds in the temperament of Mark Twain an example of the theory of romantic irony. It is true enough that he had the age-old conflict of head-and-heart; yet his particular conflict seems to have reversed what we ordinarily mean by those terms. For it was in his emotions, his keen conscience, that he most severely condemned mankind, while in calmer moods his intellect and his reason tended to sway him away from such narrow and bitter thinking. But the spirit of his stern and uncompromising conscience generally triumphed; and mankind remained for him to the end only "the damned human race."

CHAPTER 19

Acceptance versus Rejection

IN attempting an elucidation of what appears to be Mark Twain's greatest weakness as a literary artist, there must be considered the two extremes with which the true artist has nothing to do: on one hand, there is a blithe, easy, blind optimism; on the other, a pessimism which amounts to the chaos of despair. Both of these worlds escape into exaggeration. The great writer shuns both and selects for his medium the broad middle-ground where the two fields overlap. Viewing man as a social being, he recognizes the mixed nature of life, the blending of good and evil in mankind. F. O. Matthiessen considers, with special reference to the writing of tragedy, that the author must not only "have accepted the co-existence of good and evil in man's nature, he must also possess the power to envisage some reconciliation between such opposites, and the control to hold an inexorable balance." And any literature, if it is to gain our assent to its significance and truth, must reflect the same acceptance and the same control. Failing this balanced control, this artistic tension between life forces, any conflicts the writer may picture must fail to give the illusion of human reality upon which great art depends.

Mark Twain, the uncompromising idealist, was rarely able to bridge the gulf between the ideal and the actual by this inclusive acceptance of fact. I have spoken earlier of his mind as a homeland of extremes. His friends usually appeared to him as robed in spotless white, while the great unknown mass of "the damned human race" he beheld, apparently, as garbed in hell's own black. It was only rarely that he was aware of people whose moral garments had a tinge of gray—that great majority who are such curious mixtures of heroism and cowardice, of gentleness and cruelty, of selfishness and generosity. The strongly lighted black-and-white extremes of his life view made him frequently incapable of attaining that "norm," the absence of which criticism has deplored in his work. He possessed, therefore, only at times a mental synthesis of life forces that could act as a frame of reference within which his characters might be allowed to struggle towards their human destinies—with many failings, yet somehow glorious.

When John Keats defined the tragic attitude as "the love of good and ill," he must have had in mind the sort of broad comprehension and courageous acceptance which Hawthorne later possessed. Mr. Matthiessen has referred to an "enchanted wholeness" in the mind of Hawthorne. In that mind, it seems, good and evil are both enclosed as within a magic circle; for Hawthorne, in his penetration of moral obliquity, seems sometimes to have an odd sort of affection for evil, simply because it is a part of every man. Mark Twain's knowledge of moral obliquity was a match for Hawthorne's; but there the likeness ends. For Mark Twain, whose experience of living, whose very sense of being alive, should have given him a sympathy far beyond that of Hawthorne (who felt himself lacking in these respects)—Mark Twain could enter that magic circle only at times. Often, he was disenchanted and thrust outside it; or he was working inside a circle partial and incomplete because he could not close the arc by an acceptance of the inevitable evil that accompanies the good of life. He therefore could not forge an artistic unity comparable to that of life itself—life as we know it.

The writer must reflect the world as he sees it. It can hardly be useful to him to demand that mankind be perfect; it will be more useful so to handle his materials that somehow beauty may be found. He need not have a beautiful world to deal with if he is able, as T. S. Eliot has said, "to see beneath both beauty and ugliness; to see the boredom, and the horror, and the glory." He must not flinch from the boredom and the horror; but he must manage somehow to make the glory apparent to his fellows, as bored and as horror-struck as he.

Mark Twain's is a mind in rebellion, a mind that flinches from what it sees and cannot accept it—cannot bear to look upon that chasm between the real and the ideal which opens before his horrified eyes. Consequently, his mind refuses to attempt the synthesis necessary for bringing the two aspects of life together within his consciousness, thus circumscribing and controlling his material and giving it what we think of as artistic form. This is, I believe, the reason that he could never write "a play that would play," in spite of what Howells called his "unequaled dramatic authority." For in a drama, beyond all other forms of literary art, there must be some sort of unity wrought out of diverse elements, a struggle in which is reached some solution forced as a momentary truce with life.

Textbooks, defining plot as that element which imparts form to the action, maintain that in a well-plotted play the events must be clearly related to each other in a chain of cause and effect; inevitability must arise from the sense that the character of the particular hero would allow of no other conclusion; and thus a structural entity, a feeling of completeness, is established. Among Mark Twain's most cherished ideas were his concepts of the inexorability of the cause-and-effect chain and the inevitability of every happening to every man. Yet he could never write "a play that would play." But there is another element necessary to drama: an appropriate conclusiveness derived from the sense of *alleviation* that must arise in the minds of the audience as the play moves to its end. The alleviation may come from a feeling that life has done its worst to the principals, leading to a sense of stoical calm; or it may arise from the sense that the characters' sufferings were brought about by weaknesses within themselves and thus their fate is preferable to the overthrow of the moral order which must ensue if they escape unpunished, undestroyed; or, as Mr. Matthiessen suggests, it may grow from recognition by the characters themselves of the justice of their fate, a recognition through which they participate "in the purgatorial movement, the movement towards regeneration." It is this sense of alleviation that Mark Twain, writing in bitterness, was frequently unable to inject into his material.

His moralism is itself an indication of his failure to see life whole. The moralizer tends to over simplify—to see life only in terms of black and white. He displays a partial, incomplete knowledge of man and reality through his overmastering urge to set the stage of life for those he would reform, furnishing it with certain selected props, arbitrarily excluding large areas of human activity and experience—as Mark Twain excludes sex, generally, from his fiction.

All of this amounts to an "artificial training" of the sort he himself condemns in *The Man That Corrupted Hadleyburg*, a tale which points to the futility of the prayer not to be led into temptation when it is only by resisting temptation that men grow strong. Mark Twain, however, just after the assassination of President Mc-

Kinley, urges in a letter to Twichell that newspapers should not print "inflaming details" of such crimes because reading them will cause rickety-minded men "who envy the criminal his vast notoriety" to imitate his act. Nothing will check lynchings and assassinations, he says, except absolute silence: "How are you going to manage that? By gagging every witness . . . ; by abolishing all newspapers; . . . and by exterminating God's most elegant invention, the Human Race."

The same reasoning, I believe, lay beneath his careful exclusion of the subject of sex from his fiction. Believing humanity to be a form of the Bandar-Log in imitativeness, he felt that characterless creatures with susceptible minds might be too easily inflamed by "sexy" reading. His abandonment of the subject of drunkenness has already been mentioned. In the Rabelaisianism of his conversations and letters, he hand-picked his audience, a thing he could not do in writing fiction for the general public. The moralist thus lacks tolerance with human weakness. He cannot admit that "man still must err, while he doth strive." But the greatest art has always recognized the twofold nature of life and has utilized its doubleness in beautiful ways.[1]

Mark Twain pondered long on the sins native to the human heart. He was obsessed with Satan above all other figures of Christian theology. On the river in 1858 he wrote to Orion Clemens that "the Arch-Fiend's terrible energy" is "the grandest thing in 'Paradise Lost.'" His works contain "Sold to Satan," "A Humane Word from Satan," the Satan analogy in "Is Shakespeare Dead?" and finally *The Mysterious Stranger*. He is fascinated by Satan as a literary possibility, but he utilizes Satan only as a tool for his habitual condemnation of the human race. In "Concerning the Jews" he writes that he has no prejudice against Satan:

A person who has for untold centuries maintained the imposing position of spiritual head of four-fifths of the human race, and political head of the whole of it, must be granted the possession of executive abilities of the loftiest order. In his large presence the other popes and politicians shrink to midges for the microscope. . . . I would rather see him and shake him by the tail than any other member of the European Concert.

It is clear that he is striking through Satan at the "European Concert"

[1] Philo Buck, *The Golden Thread*, 495.

in particular and at the human race in general. His most artistic use of Satan is in *The Mysterious Stranger;* but even there the real force of young Satan is to high-light the cruelty of the villagers, since he seems merciful as compared with them. As a moralist, Mark Twain too often fails to sense the eternal paradox of man, the great truth that out of the conflict of good and evil there emerges the greatest of human achievements, man's ethical character.

As I have said, his sympathy was deep and intense, though it was not broad. In proportion to the strength of his personal feeling, his literary effects are often marked by intensity and power. In proportion to his lack of breadth, his work suffers from a narrowness, a lack of comprehension of the incentives and aspirations open to mankind. Observing that intensity in literature usually implies something of narrowness, C. T. Winchester pointed out that often "a symmetrical, broadly perceptive, tolerant character is deficient in the personal force necessary to produce decided literary effect; while . . . those men whose personality seems most pronounced and strenuous, who have scored the deepest mark in the literature of their time, are often men whose limitations are most . . . marked." This criticism seems particularly applicable to Mark Twain. Only the very greatest writers can be said to possess, to a high degree, both intensity and breadth. Although Mark Twain's writing in general is stamped by intensity rather than by breadth, *Huckleberry Finn* unquestionably possesses both qualities.

He could have done larger justice to his art had he realized, as did Howells, that since "injustice is the most ridiculous thing in the world," it follows that indignation with it must feel its own absurdity. But such a mood was impossible for Mark Twain, still so vibrantly sensitive, so intensely sympathetic in the deep and narrow sense. Impossible for him, generally, was the long view which Emerson held—that there is an "amelioration" which, though it cannot be glimpsed in a short span of years, will appear over a long period. Mark Twain was too impatient for Emerson's point of view. And though he continued to read Suetonius and Saint-Simon and other writers who added to his conception of mankind as contemptible, he felt a need also for the other sort. He claimed that Howells' books were the novels he enjoyed most. Certainly, the friendship of the two men must be considered; but, beyond that, the bland type of "realism" employed by Howells—who insisted on seeing "the more smiling aspects of life" as "the more American"—filled a need in Mark Twain. His love for Browning may be explained by Browning's zest for life, found in such poems as "Rabbi Ben Ezra": "Grow old along with me, The best is yet to be." And Kipling's emphasis on human values perhaps made him necessary to Mark Twain, who very well knew that Kipling's work left something to be desired from the artistic point of view—"he is just about my level."

Mark Twain's life view automatically closed to him many lines of literary incentive. His strongest motive—the moralistic urge to reform mankind—was often rendered impotent by the strangle hold of his determinism. When his work falls off into burlesque or sheer improvisation, when the "book gets tired" and he must let it rest until its interest in itself revives, when the "tank gets empty" and he has to let it fill up again—it is because he has not entered upon his work with the wholeness of conception which would circumscribe his material and confine it in channels where it can be controlled. Instead, ideas are allowed to diffuse themselves in every direction, like escaping steam, till the impulse to write grows thinner and thinner and gradually fades out altogether.

The philosophic nihilism of *What Is Man?* (in which the chief idea is that man cannot be blamed for his worthlessness, since the malevolent intelligence which created the universe controls his actions) contrasts sharply with Twain's rage at mankind. When the lava boils up within him, he longs "for a pen warmed up in hell." But as early as 1878 he was enough the conscious artist to realize that such moods were fatal to his art. From Rome he wrote to Howells:

I wish I *could* give those sharp satires on European life which you mention, but of course a man can't write successful satire except he be in a calm, judicial good humour. . . . In truth, I don't ever seem to be in a good enough humour with anything to satirize it. No, I want to stand up before it and curse it and foam at the mouth, or take a club and pound it to rags and pulp.

"In tales like *The Stolen White Elephant*," says Mr. Brooks, "he delights in the general smash-up of a world that does not seem to him to be worth saving." And Mr. Brooks is right. Mark Twain views the debacle with a wry satisfaction. The dialectical determinism of *What Is Man?* contrasts in mood with the scornful derision of *The Man That Corrupted Hadleyburg*, but in neither does the game of life appear to be worth the candle. And this lack of the proper measure of all things human often prevented his attaining an ideal norm which could have implemented his satire.

Mr. Brooks speaks of Mark Twain's "inborn Calvinistic will-to-despise human nature." But, as Carl Van Doren noted, he could not lay his hatred of the race wholly upon his fellows—"his hatred came home and condemned him, too." Frequently, in that sorry companionship he pitied men more than he hated them. "Everything human is pathetic," he wrote. But he expended his pity for the wrong things. Instead of pitying man for his failure to develop his latent capacities, Mark Twain pitied him because he possesses no latent capacities. Thus is all power of growth denied to the human race. Futility and worthlessness of man—indifference or malevolence of the cosmic powers—"It is like the sky," he once said; "you can't break through anywhere."

But in his books about boys—and this partly explains their greatness—he accepts the whole of life because he accepts the whole of boy nature, good and bad. In Hannibal he had seen both aspects of life. In Hannibal he had witnessed scenes of brutal violence, of absolute terror, of superstitious fear; and, because it remained for him both a summer idyl and a dark ground of horror, Hannibal was always the most fruitful setting for his work. The boy's world that he remembered had been full of charm; and yet his submerged consciousness recognized the dangers that had lurked beneath that surface of charm. Tom Sawyer's St. Petersburg, lying between the forest and the river, seems filled with a slow golden peace. It *seems* so. Jackson's Island was his Shangri La; but it was not a safe island, for life is not safe. Out of his steady apprehension of the terror of life, he wrote into the book that embodies his village idyl, as Mr. DeVoto has noticed, grave-robbing, revenge, murder, robbery, drowning, starvation, witchcraft and demonology, the malevolence of Injun Joe, and the fear of death that grips Tom and Becky lost in the cave and awaiting death in the dark. But after their emergence from the cave, the sun shines again and life goes on, much as before. And there is nowhere the suggestion that that life is not worth the living. Although inartistic in its minor effects—in the momentary impact of its melodramatic scenes, for instance—the book is ultimately satisfying because it has the artistic tension between life forces, the equilibrium necessary for art.

At Quarry Farm, in a small study shaped like a pilothouse, Mark Twain busied himself in the summer of 1874 with *Tom Sawyer*. Paine believed that he had begun the story in 1872 as a play; but perhaps this play was only an attempt to dramatize the story after it was written. In working among the Mark Twain Papers, DeVoto discovered some sheets labeled by Paine as "Boy's Manuscript," actually an early form of *Tom Sawyer*. Mr. DeVoto believes that this manuscript, in diary form, was written as early as 1870, which means that *Tom Sawyer*, rather than *The Gilded Age*, was Mark Twain's first attempt at fiction. In *Mark Twain at Work*, Mr. De-Voto has published the unfinished manuscript, and its relationship to *Tom Sawyer* is unmistakable, though the characters wear different names in the diary.

Mark Twain and Olivia Langdon were married on February 2, 1870. For months before and after that date his letters—to his mother, his sister, and his friends—were full of Livy, Livy, Livy. Setting the date of the "Boy's Manuscript" about 1870 suggests to me that the boy's diary may have been begun as a sort of playful, whimsical love letter to Olivia. The subject matter of the diary adds weight to this speculation.[2] But whatever the impulse that led him to set forth, when he was once started on that road of boyhood reminiscence the result was inevitable.

Constance Rourke wrote of Mark Twain that "he was never the conscious artist, always the improviser," and both Mr. DeVoto and Mr. Wagenknecht have recorded their agreement. Recent

---

[2] On the *Quaker City* excursion Mark Twain met Olivia's brother, Charley Langdon, fell in love with her picture in Charley's stateroom, and cultivated Charley's acquaintance thereafter. Billy Rogers writes in his diary, "I've got acquainted with her brother Tom, and I expect he tells her about me. I'm always hanging around him." Boasting of Livy's charm to his mother, Mark Twain wrote: "Her father and mother and brother embrace and pet her constantly, precisely as if she were a *sweetheart*." The diary reads: "How awful it is to meet her father and mother! They seem like kings and queens to me. And her brother Tom—I can hardly understand how it can be—but he can hug and kiss her whenever he wants to." Paine relates an amusing incident in which, as Mark Twain was leaving the Langdon home after a visit, an accident occurred and he fell out of a light wagon to the cobbled street. Mark Twain feigned injury and was carried into the house; Olivia was especially attentive, and his visit was prolonged two weeks. Billy Rogers confides to his diary: ". . . a man . . . nearly ran over me with his wagon. I wished he had, because then I would have been crippled and they would have carried me into her house all bloody and busted up, and she would have cried, and I would have . . . had to stay there till I got well, which I wish I never would get well." (*Mark Twain at Work*, 26.) All these passages occur in the first few pages of the manuscript.

study, however, has departed from this view—specifically, Walter Blair's analysis of *Tom Sawyer*. Mr. DeVoto holds, "Structurally, *Tom Sawyer* is a better job than most of Mark's fiction"; but he objects to "psychological anachronisms" in the boys and to the elastic time element which allows the Missouri summer to last far too long. Mr. Blair argues that if the book is viewed as Mark Twain's answer to the sentimental "Sunday school books" of the time, it takes on a new meaning which explains its structure; and even the time scheme may be defended as "a device contributing to developments important in the novel."

As the story opens, Tom is caught stealing jam, but he evades punishment by deceiving Aunt Polly. He plays hooky, attempts more deceit, and is exposed by Sid; he dashes out, threatening revenge. Later he meets a strange boy whom he hates at sight because of his neat clothes, licks the stranger, and then chases him home. By the end of the first chapter, Mr. Blair points out, in the hands of the moral writers Tom would stand committed as a Bad Boy. Tom continues on his unhallowed way, while Mark Twain chronicles him with gusto and even commends his chicanery in the whitewashing coup. Mark Twain summarizes Tom: "He was not the Model Boy of the village. He knew the model boy very well though—and loathed him."

Sid stands for the regulation Good Boy of the sentimentalized tales. Early in the book Mark Twain describes Huck Finn, the "juvenile pariah of the village," the envy of all the other boys because of his "gaudy outcast condition," who doubtless would appear in the moralized literature as a sort of Super Bad Boy:

Huckleberry came and went, at his own free will. . . . he did not have to go to school or to church . . . ; he could go fishing or swimming when and where he chose. . . . he never had to wash, nor put on clean clothes; he could swear wonderfully. In a word, everything that goes to make life precious, that boy had. So thought every harassed, hampered, respectable boy in St. Petersburg.

Mr. Blair suggests that Mark Twain held the additional motive of showing his readers that boyish pranks are a natural means of development. Although he saw the adult world in a different light, he could grant that a real boy was not simply good or bad, but a mixture of virtue and mischief. "If *Tom Sawyer* is regarded as a working out . . . of this notion of a boy's maturing," says Mr. Blair, "the book will reveal . . . a structure . . . quite well adapted to its purpose." Under a patterning of action which shows a boy developing, Mr. Blair finds four units of narrative: the story of Tom and Becky; the Jackson's Island episode; the story of Tom and Muff Potter; and the Injun Joe story. In the boy-and-girl story, Tom begins with a fickle desertion of Amy and winds up by taking Becky's punishment at school and later manfully guarding her in the cave. The Jackson's Island episode begins with Tom's childish revolt against Aunt Polly, which spurs him to run away, and ends with his concern for his aunt's uneasiness about him. The Muff Potter story begins with the superstitious trip of Tom and Huck to the graveyard and ends with Tom's defiance of superstition in testifying for Muff Potter. In the Injun Joe story, which begins with a boyish search for buried treasure, the development is concerned more with Huck than with Tom: Huck conquers his fear of Injun Joe to rescue the Widow Douglas from the dangerous renegade. Of the thirty-five chapters, only four are not in some way concerned with one of these narrative units, and of these four, one is the first and necessarily expository chapter.

Considered thus, the structural pattern refutes Mr. Van Doren's objection that the book is "overloaded with matters brought in . . . when no necessity calls for them," as well as Mr. DeVoto's objection that Tom has "no nebulous, inarticulate vision of growing up," no notion of "the strengths, the perceptions, and the failures that will eventually make a man." Having traced Tom through a number of situations in which his actions grow less and less irresponsible and more and more mature, Mr. Blair directs attention to Mark Twain's conclusion of the book as an indication that he himself was fully aware of this structural pattern: "So endeth this chronicle. It being strictly the history of a *boy*, it must stop here; the story could not go much further without becoming the history of a *man*."

When the Welshman said that Huck had "good spots" in him, the Widow Douglas agreed: "That's the Lord's mark. He don't leave it off. . . . Puts it somewhere on every creature that comes from his hands." That Mark Twain viewed the life of his village as rounded and whole is revealed in such passages. Mr. DeVoto explains the hold Hannibal had over his imagination on the ground that "when he invoked Hannibal he found there not only the idyll of boyhood but anxiety, violence, supernatural horror, and an uncrystallized but enveloping dread."[3] Perhaps this means simply that Mark Twain had recognized in Hannibal the twofold aspect of life.

His view of Hannibal as twofold explains the artistry he achieves in his fiction grounded there. Bringing the boy-world into a proper focus, he gains the same sort of perspective he attains in viewing the world of the blacks. The wholeness of these two worlds is attested by his recognition that boys can lie and that slaves can feel sexual desire; that developing boys can be mixtures of good and bad, and that the blacks—as embodied in Roxy—can be malicious and vengeful, loyal and loving, thieving and tipsy, self-sacrificing and courageous. Through this perspective, he is enabled to discern the forces of good and evil held in the tension that art demands. The result is that even the pettiness of the village Sunday school in *Tom Sawyer* is handled with a detachment which robs it of his customary scorn. The book has the permanency of a beautiful fairy tale. The golden haze of Tom Sawyer's summer enshrouds it; and Mark Twain was right when he said of it, "*Tom Sawyer* is simply a hymn, put into prose to give it a worldly air."

Tom and Huck may themselves be viewed as symbols of the two aspects of life. Tom Sawyer has a home and a loving, overwatchful aunt who doses him with painkiller; he swipes doughnuts and plays hooky and goes in swimming; he is stirred by an ambition to appear as a hero in Sunday school; he is thrilled by his imaginary adventures. On the whole, Tom's is mostly an idyllic existence. In contrast appears Huck Finn. Huck fears his father and apparently never knew his mother; a homeless waif, he sleeps on doorsteps or in hogsheads; he is troubled by no ambition and steers clear of Sunday school; his life is as aimless as a bit of drift on the Mississippi. And yet Mark Twain finds Huck and Huck's life infinitely worth while. Huck himself nowhere suggests that his life is not satisfactory.

But Huck Finn wears a moral garment definitely tinged with gray. In the book which he relates, he lies to everybody who threatens Jim's safety or his own. Life is precious to him; freedom is precious to him. And it is no wonder that he lies. Young as he is, he has known a deal of violence. He escapes his drunken father by staging a mock murder—his own; he notes that the Grangerfords carry their guns to church and watches their feud end in the murder of boys; he sees the drunken, blackguarding Boggs and is at hand when

[3] Introduction, *Mark Twain in Eruption, xviii.*

the blackguarding is ended by Sherburn's bullet; he associates daily with the king and the duke, two creatures who emerge from the slime of the river, as amoral as gnomes. But Huck has a code of his own and sticks to it in defiance of hell itself. He is frequently troubled by his conscience. Huck's conscience appears at times to be much keener than that of the romantic Tom Sawyer.[4] Tom makes a great show of adhering to the letter of the law, while Huck cuts through to the essentials of the spirit.

Although Huck's adventures were popular with readers from the first, contemporary critics preferred *The Prince and the Pauper*, as did Mark Twain's own family. There was, however, as Mr. De-Voto has noted, an occasional recognition. Barrett Wendell of Harvard, in *A Literary History of America* (1900), devoted only a few lines to Mark Twain in a book of five hundred pages; but he mentioned "a book which . . . one is disposed for all its eccentricity to call the most admirable work of literary art as yet produced on this continent . . . that Odyssean story . . . to which Mark Twain gave the grotesque name of 'Huckleberry Finn.' "[5]

Out of the countless lines praising the book, I have selected this passage because the "eccentricity" which Wendell noted is an element important for the understanding of the story. Huck Finn is not a "normal" boy; he has not had a normal bringing up, and his life has prepared him to be surprised at nothing. Commenting upon Mark Twain's technique in making use of the eccentricity of Huck, John Erskine said that Mark Twain skilfully "manipulated his material . . . so that the most outrageous melodrama could present itself as matter of fact, through the medium of Huckleberry's temperament, and even while we are rearranging the values and discerning what the boy was blind to, we . . . concede that he is true to life"—

---

[4] Still, I cannot agree with Mr. DeVoto's statement (*Mark Twain at Work*, 21) that Mark Twain denies us "the entire struggle of fear, pity, and horror" which precedes Tom's testifying for Muff Potter, "in order to give us the simple melodrama of the revelation." Although not so detailed as is Huck's later battle with his conscience, an analysis of Tom's struggle appears. Tom wakes the morning after the murder, "gloomy and sad"; when Potter is accused, "Tom's fearful secret and gnawing conscience disturbed his sleep" for a week; he carried small offerings to Potter in the jail and thus "helped to ease his conscience"; during his vacation the secret of the murder was "a very cancer for permanency and pain"; he hung about the jail and when he found Potter hopeless and resigned, he "went home miserable, and his dreams that night were full of horrors"; finally his "harassed conscience" hounded him to the lawyer's house, where he told his story.

[5] DeVoto, *Mark Twain's America*, 300.

for the sort of life his has been. The romanticist, narrator of the unusual adventures of Huck and Jim; the realist, portrayer of the daily round of life in small towns along the river; and the satirist, critic of the narrowness and meanness of human nature—in this story Mark Twain is "all three kinds of storyteller at once"; and the way he blends the realistic, the satiric, and the romantic elements has produced a thing that is art—a book, in John Erskine's phrase, "so close to the life of the people that it can hold any reader, and yet so subtle in its art that the craftsman tries to find out how it was done."

It is no secret that Mark Twain had difficulty in writing Huckleberry Finn. He described it to Howells as "a book I have worked at, by fits and starts, during the past five or six years." Actually, it was seven years; yet the finished whole seems easy, simple, natural. Huck, the unifying thread tying everything together, gains in stature by having no taller rivals near him—only the river tramps who impose on his generosity and the hunted Negro whom he befriends.

In spite of its episodic nature, the book falls naturally into three thematic units. In the first sixteen chapters the theme has to do with what is of and from St. Petersburg: Huck, Tom, Nigger Jim, and Pap. The second thematic unit includes the most strongly satiric, the most powerful part of the book, bringing Huck and Jim into contact with the outside world. In the cross-section of the South through which they journey, Huck witnesses the Grangerford-Shepherdson feud, the chicanery of the king and the duke, the killing of Boggs, Colonel Sherburn's quelling of the mob, and finally the village funeral. The characters of the king and the duke add to the thematic unity of this section. The third thematic unit is short, a sort of coda to the rest, covering the period at the Phelps farm in which Tom re-enters the story. It repeats the romanticized motif of the first part, bringing the book full circle before its close.

The art of characterization is the one most important to a novelist, and Mark Twain's characters are his greatest literary achievement. Something of his method in characterization may be learned from a passage he wrote in 1907:

Every man is in his own person the whole human race, with not a detail lacking. I am the whole human race without a detail lacking; I have studied the human race with diligence and strong interest all these years

Mark Twain in a familiar pose

in my own person; in myself I find in big or little proportion every quality and every defect that is findable in the mass of the race.

This suggests that when he had need of a certain trait, his habit was to dig for it within himself, to isolate and study it, then to enlarge it to the proportion proper to the character in question. This suggestion is borne out by a marginal note in one of his books: "If Byron—if any man—draws 50 characters, they are all himself—50 shades, 50 moods, of his own character, And when the man draws them well, why do they stir my admiration? Because they are me—I recognize myself."

A careful study of *Huckleberry Finn* shows that it is the characters and their interrelationship which determine the arrangement and structure of the book. The three thematic sections subdivide into little units notable for the contrast they offer each other. The first three chapters continue, naturally enough, the vein of *Tom Sawyer*, to which this book becomes a sort of sequel. Everything is colored by the excitement of Tom's imaginary adventures; he insists on doing all things according to the books he has read, from having his Gang sign in blood their oaths of allegiance to capturing and holding people for ransom. Ben Rogers, a Gang member, wants to know what being "ransomed" means, and Tom replies:

"I don't know. But that's what they do. I've seen it in books; and of course that's what we've got to do."
"But how can we do it if we don't know what it is?"
"Why, blame it all, we've *got* to do it. Don't I tell you it's in the books? Do you want to go to doing different from what's in the books and get things all muddled up?"

And here, in a simple argument among boys, Mark Twain sets the pattern for this, his greatest story, as a satire on institutionalism. The three figures, Tom, Huck, and Jim, represent three gradations of thought and three levels of civilization. Tom, pretending so intensely that it becomes so, says we can't do it except as in the books. Is this what civilization really is—merely a pretense according to a set pattern? Tom is on the highest level, in the sense of being most civilized; but he represents a mawkish, romantic, artificial civilization. Compared with him, Nigger Jim and Huck are primitives; and the closer Mark Twain gets to primitivism, the better his writing becomes. He shows us the African in Jim, imbuing him with a dark knowledge that lies in his blood and his nerve ends. Huck Finn stands between these two; he is the "natural man," suggesting Walt Whitman's dream of the great American who should be simple and free. Both Tom and Jim are in bondage to institutionalism.[6] Tom can't do anything against the rules of his books; Jim can't do anything against the rules of his taboos, his voodoo fears and charms and superstitions. Only Huck is free of institutions. Tom and Jim are always sure they are right, since each has his institution to consult and to follow; but Huck is tormented by doubts. When he is with Tom, he is willing to join Tom in following the books; when he is with Jim, he is careful not to break Jim's taboos, especially after the incident of the rattlesnake skin. But when Huck is alone, because he has no rules to go by he is guided by the voice within himself. He listens to what goes on inside him. He is free to probe within his own heart, where is to be found whatever bit of divinity man has—what we know as his soul.

If *Tom Sawyer* is accepted as a satire against the moralizing Sunday school tales, *Huckleberry Finn* has a much broader field as a satire against institutionalism in general. The institution of slavery is basic in this book, just as it is in *Pudd'nhead Wilson*. In *A Connecticut Yankee*, Mark Twain fulminates against church and state. In *Joan of Arc* he attacks the oppressions of formal religion and formal law. In *Hadleyburg* he frowns upon the institutionalism by which young people are trained in hypocrisy and the forms of empty "honor." Indeed, he sees the village itself as an institution—the tight little institution of the mores of the folk, which dictates the condemnation of all outlanders and innovators.

Within each of the thematic units in *Huckleberry Finn* there is a subtle variation of character and atmosphere. After the idyllic, romantic atmosphere which permeates the first three chapters, in the next four the story veers sharply from the mood of *Tom Sawyer*, and Pap takes the stage, drunken and disreputable, feeling himself the victim of sundry social ills. Into this satiric portrait went Mark Twain's years of observation of mountain whites, piney-woods people, and river rats. Pap is completely revealed through his oration on

---

[6] I am indebted to Professor Floyd Stovall, formerly of North Texas State Teachers College and now of the University of North Carolina, for the suggestion that *Huckleberry Finn* is a satire on institutionalism, as well as for some suggestions pertaining to the structure of the book.

the "guv'ment." This unit ends when Huck flees because he fears his father will kill him in a fit of delirium tremens.

After so much violence, Jackson's Island gives him a feeling of peace. He explores the island, and just as he begins to feel lonely he discovers Jim, a Negro who has run away from home because his owner is planning to sell him "down to Orleans"—the Negro's equivalent of hell. Thereafter the runaway slave and the outcast waif share the island and comfort each other. This small unit of four chapters, the interlude on Jackson's Island, ends once more in the threat of violence and fear. Men are approaching the island to search for Jim.

Mark Twain's prefatory note warns the reader that seven different dialects are used in the book; the shadings among them are so fine that not every reader can perceive them, and he does not want readers to think that "all these characters were trying to talk alike and not succeeding." His sensitivity to speech enabled him to say, "The shadings have not been done in haphazard fashion, or by guesswork, but painstakingly." But the artistry of such shadings in dialect fades before his skill in employing the vernacular of Huck Finn for a book-length narrative. Huck has a strong, vivid, natural imagination—not an artificial one, such as Tom's, or a superstitious one, such as Jim's. He describes, with memorable effect, a summer storm which he and Jim watched from the security of their cave on the island:

. . . it looked all blue-black outside, and lovely; and the rain would thrash along by so thick that the trees off a little ways looked dim and spider-webby; and here would come a blast of wind that would bend the trees down and turn up the pale underside of the leaves; and then a perfect ripper of a gust would follow along and set the branches to tossing their arms as if they was just wild; and next, when it was just about the bluest and blackest—*fst*! it was as bright as glory, and you'd have a little glimpse of tree-tops a-plunging about a way off yonder in the storm, hundreds of yards further than you could see before; dark as sin again in a second, and now you'd hear the thunder let go with an awful crash, and then go rumbling, grumbling, tumbling, down the sky towards the under side of the world, like rolling empty barrels down stairs—where it's long stairs and they bounce a good deal, you know.

Mark Twain's elemental imagination lends vigor and freshness to many passages. As Huck and Jim lie on their backs at night looking up at the stars, while the raft slips silently down the river, they argue

341

about whether the stars "was made or only just happened": "Jim said the moon could 'a' *laid* them; well, that looked kind of reasonable . . . because I've seen a frog lay most as many." Huck describes Pap as having hair that was "long and tangled and greasy, and hung down, and you could see his eyes shining through like he was behind vines," while his face was white—"not like another man's white, but a white to make a body sick . . . a fish-belly white." At the parlor funeral of Peter Wilks, "the undertaker he slid around in his black gloves with his softy soothering ways, . . . making no more sound than a cat. . . . He was the softest, glidingest, stealthiest man I ever see." When the old king got a sudden shock, he "squshed down like a bluff bank that the river has cut under, it took him so sudden." Huck's language is equal to any effect demanded of it.

Part of the power of this book lies in Mark Twain's drawing of the character of Nigger Jim. From the time Jim first appears, a "big nigger" silhouetted in the kitchen door with the light behind him, he is a figure of dignity. In the famous syllogism in which Jim argues that since a Frenchman is a man, he should talk like a man, Mark Twain shows Jim's slow, purposeful reasoning. But in other moods Jim's spirit opens out to a wider horizon. Like Huck, he senses the beauty of the river. In his interpretation of a dream, Jim lets "the big, clear river" symbolize "the free States"—in other words, freedom. If "The Enchanted Village" might serve as a subtitle for *Tom Sawyer*, so "The Road to Freedom" might serve the same purpose for *Huckleberry Finn*. Jim has two big scenes in the book. One occurs when he relates the tragic moment of his discovery that his little girl was "plumb deef en dumb, Huck, plumb deef en dumb." His second big scene comes when he risks capture to help the doctor care for the wounded Tom Sawyer.

Whatever may be said of Tom Sawyer, Huck Finn is a developing character. Much of his development is due to his association with Jim and his increasing respect for the black man. In *Tom Sawyer*, Huck apologized to Tom for eating with a Negro, the Rogers' Uncle Jake, who had given him food: "A body's got to do things when he's awful hungry he wouldn't . . . do as a steady thing." When he first finds Jim on the island, he is glad simply because he wants companionship; but as the two share the peace of the place, Huck comes to regard Jim as a human being rather than a faithful dog. When he hears there is a reward for Jim, the money offers no temptation to him; but under attack by his conscience, he fears he may have done wrong in helping a slave to escape. His traditions and environment pull him one way; what he feels in his heart pulls him the other way. Finally, he goes so far as to write a note to Miss Watson, Jim's owner, telling her where Jim is to be found. At first, he feels better for writing the note:

... thinking how near I come to being lost and going to hell. ... [Then I] got to thinking over our trip down the river; and I see Jim before me all the time: in the day and in the night-time, . . . and we a-floating along, talking and singing and laughing. But somehow I couldn't seem to strike no places to harden me against him, but only the other kind . . . and then I happened to look around and see that paper.

It was a close place. I took it up and held it in my hand. I was a-trembling, because I'd got to decide, forever, betwixt two things, and I knowed it. I studied a minute, sort of holding my breath, and then says to myself:

"All right, then, I'll *go* to hell"—and tore it up.

A part of Huck's development came when he apologized to Jim for fooling him about a dream. Jim very properly resented Huck's deceit, and Huck was abashed before Jim's stately indignation. When Huck waked in the night to find Jim mourning for his children—'Po' little 'Lizabeth! po' little Johnny!'"—a new realization was borne in upon the boy: "I do believe he cared just as much for his people as white folks does for their'n. It don't seem natural, but I reckon it's so." Although the doctor and others seemed amazed at Jim's risking capture to aid the wounded Tom, Huck felt no surprise at all: "I knowed he was white inside."

The beautiful stretches of the river had power over Huck's spirit, as is shown in his own words: "It was kind of solemn, drifting down the big, still river . . . looking up at the stars, and we didn't ever feel like talking loud, and it warn't often we laughed." He has learned to read early in the story, and he reads at the Grangerford home; of *Pilgrim's Progress*, his verdict is, "The statements was interesting, but tough." He feels that somebody should write a poetical tribute to the dead Emmeline Grangerford, "so I tried to sweat out a verse or two myself, but I couldn't seem to make it go somehow." Such a sentiment would have seemed out of character for Huck in the beginning, but not now. He describes Colonel Grangerford as an aristocrat, and his own sensitive nature responds to the Colonel's fine-wire temperament: "everybody was always good-mannered where he was."

The first thematic unit ends with the smashing of the raft by a steamboat. This incident also ended the writing of *Huckleberry Finn* for an indefinite period. Mark Twain had written thus far in the summer of 1876; he apparently had no further plan, and when the raft was smashed, he stopped working on the book for a time. Two years after he had shelved *Huckleberry Finn*, he wrote the 1878 letter to Howells, explaining that he felt unable to write successful satire because to do so calls for "calm, judicial good humor." His trip down the river in 1882 to get material for *Life on the Mississippi* naturally was related to the other river story in his mind. Somehow, after this trip, he arrived at the design which made the book a masterpiece. All the meannesses of Mark Twain's "damned human race" are seen through the eyes and presented through the lips of Huck Finn. Mark Twain was enabled, at last, to attain the calm detachment with which satire should be presented.

The second thematic unit begins when Huck stops at the Grangerford mansion after the wreck of the raft. The Grangerford-Shepherdson feud is one of the most tragic things in the book, but nothing is told with greater restraint. This restraint is art; but Mark Twain, as John Erskine observed, makes it seem the work of nature. Beginning his account of the climax of the feud, Huck says, "I don't want to talk much about the next day." All that blood and dying was nauseating to the boy, and "it would make him sick again" if he should tell about the killings. He tries not to remember the details, because those memories spoil his sleep at night. To measure Mark Twain's growth in artistry, one has only to compare this restraint with the early sketches in which the reformer purposefully emphasized blood and violence for their shock value in directing attention to situations he deplored. Now, to get back to the raft and to Jim is, for Huck, like going home; and his soul expands in the healing peace of the quiet river: "We said there warn't no home like a raft.... Other places do seem so cramped up and smothery."

After the episode of the feud, the king and the duke board the raft and begin to dominate the lives of Huck and Jim. The loafers of Bricksville, Arkansas, lean and whittle; around noon, they all laugh and look glad, for old man Boggs comes riding into town drunk and begins to blackguard Colonel Sherburn. Finally Sherburn's outraged honor demands that he stop this blackguarding with a bullet, and Boggs dies in a little drugstore, with a heavy Bible on his chest.

All these wrongs are condemned through the mere fact of their presentation. With the exception of one scene, Mark Twain is invisible, inaudible, lost in the artistry of Huck's particular kind of communication. In that scene Colonel Sherburn appears on his veranda to pour his withering scorn down upon the mob and send them scurrying like whipped curs. "I know you clear through. I was born and raised in the South, and I've lived in the North." It is Mark Twain speaking:

So I know the average all around. The average man's a coward. . . . Your mistake is that you didn't bring a man with you; that's one mistake, and the other is that you didn't come in the dark and fetch your masks. . . . The pitifulest thing out is a mob. . . . But a mob without any *man* at the head of it is *beneath* pitifulness. Now the thing for *you* to do is to droop your tails and go home and crawl in a hole.

Mark Twain's voice rings out, clear and unmistakable, in the hit at militarism: "an army is—a mob; they don't fight with courage that's born in them, but with courage that's borrowed from their mass." If a "Colonel" had talked like that, would Huck have reported him like that? No matter; the force of the book is so strong at this point that the illusion is not shattered; but the utter objectivity of the scene immediately preceding ranks it far above this one.

There, we see the innate cruelty of the dead-alive loafers. "There couldn't anything wake them up all over, and make them happy all over, like . . . putting turpentine on a stray dog and setting fire to him, or tying a tin pan to his tail and see him run himself to death." Then old Boggs rides in "on the waw-path," a pitiful figure who "throwed his hat down in the mud and rode over it, and . . . went a-raging down the street again, with his gray hair a-flying" while the loafers, at first "listening and laughing and going on," are quickly sobered by the ultimatum of Colonel Sherburn. "Everybody that seen the shooting was telling how it happened," and one "long, lanky man, with long hair and a big white fur stovepipe hat" enacted the scene in its entirety. Huck's comment is, "The people that had seen the thing said he done it perfect." And Mr. DeVoto adds that the long lanky man records this society "with an unemotional certainty beside which either Mr. Lewis's anger or Mr. Anderson's misery" seem merely hysterical. Those who understand Mark Twain can only guess how much of that calm detachment, that "unemotional certainty," was sheer artistry, a triumph of technique.

With each of these scenes, Huck's character develops as his experience is widened. He perceives the manly qualities of Jim and scales correctly the duke and the king; he knows that the duke is not so low as the king, and yet he is tolerant of the "poor old king" when he sees him in "a little low doggery, very tight, and a lot of loafers bullyragging him for sport." When Huck finds himself stranded on the *Walter Scott* with some murderers, his sympathy, broad and beautiful, makes him realize "how dreadful it was, even for murderers, to be in such a fix. I says to myself, there ain't no telling but I might come to be a murderer myself yet, and then how would I like it?" In his last glimpse of the king and the duke, tarred and feathered so that they "just looked like a couple of monstrous big soldier-plumes," he was "sorry for them poor pitiful rascals," and it made him sick to see it: "Human beings *can* be awful cruel to one another."

There is an occasional hint of determinism in *Huckleberry Finn*. Early in the story Huck backslides under the power of environment while living with Pap: ". . . I was used to being where I was, and liked it." If fear of his drunken father had not driven him forth, Mark Twain seems to say, Huck might have become another Pap. When his conscience troubles him over not giving up the runaway slave, he excuses himself on the ground of early environment and its effects:

. . . I knowed very well I had done wrong, and I see it warn't no use for me to try to learn to do right; a body that don't get *started* right when he's little ain't got no show—when the pinch comes there ain't nothing to back him up. . . . Then I . . . says to myself, hold on; s'pose you'd a done right and give Jim up, would you felt better than what you do now? No, I says, I'd feel bad—I'd feel just the same way I do now. Well, then, says I, what's the use you learning to do right when it's troublesome to do right and ain't no trouble to do wrong, and the wages is the same?

Huck's questioning of himself recalls Ernest Hemingway's definition of morality, which appears early in *Death in the Afternoon*: "I know only that what is moral is what you feel good after." Unquestionably, Mark Twain and Hemingway are akin in their preoccupation with death and in the care and skill with which they write the idiom of their people; but it seems to me that Hemingway's nearest approach to the earlier writer lies in the moral tests his characters apply inwardly. Having no moral code to go by, they test an action by the way they feel after it.[7]

Huck usually looks into his own heart for guidance. He "goes to studying things out" whenever he feels himself "in a tight place." He learns from experience, but his environment determines him only as his experiences develop what is within. Moral intuition is the basis on which his character rests. But if a man is not responsible to God or to society, and Mark Twain's determinism holds that he is not, why should he be responsible to himself? The inner voice of conscience, the voice of God, always holds him morally responsible. In this way *Huckleberry Finn* is a wise book, as all great books are wise.

In the final thematic unit, the story lags for most readers. Tom re-enters the plot to free Jim according to all the time-worn devices of literature, thus resuming his perpetual game of make-believe. Tom's imagined adventures are merely cheap after the real ones which Huck and Jim have experienced together. Is this anticlimax altogether accidental? Was Mark Twain perhaps comparing the genuine experience of life with the fanciful, secondhand one? If the book is viewed as a satire on institutionalism, Tom's silly insistence on "going by the books" has more point. Or, remembering Jim's use of the "big, clear river" to symbolize freedom, is there an even deeper symbolism here? the fact that, living in a civilization, we can keep our freedom only by conforming to its patterns?

Of all Mark Twain's books, *Personal Recollections of Joan of Arc* received his most careful attention. On his seventy-third birthday he wrote:

---

[7] Joseph Warren Beach said, "In certain ways, contemporary American fiction opens with Ernest Hemingway." In the first chapter of *Green Hills of Africa*, Hemingway himself said: "All modern American literature comes from one book by Mark Twain called *Huckleberry Finn*. . . . it's the best book we've had. All American writing comes from that. There was nothing before. There has been nothing as good since."

I like the Joan of Arc best of all my books; and it *is* the best; I know it perfectly well. And besides, it furnished me seven times the pleasure afforded me by any of the others: 12 years of preparation and 2 years of writing. The others needed no preparation, and got none.

To Henry H. Rogers, his financial adviser, he confided: "Possibly the book may not sell, but that is nothing—it was written for love." Like many other books by Mark Twain, it brings out disagreement among the critics. To Mr. Brooks it is "a literary chromo," and Mr. De-Voto condemns it as "mediocre" because it turns medieval France into a Missouri village. Mr. DeVoto praises only the qualities of the prose, its "color and warmth, its nervous and subtle strength, the delicacy and assurance of its effects." On the other hand, Edgar Lee Masters, in a book generally condemnatory of Mark Twain's literary craftsmanship, sees in it "great, indisputable beauty": "This book is the most finished, the most sustained and consistent to the end of anything that Twain did, excepting only *The Mysterious Stranger*."[8]

It was finished after the failure of his publishing company, but at a time when he was most hopeful for the typesetting machine and before the personal tragedies of his late years. Yet the Sieur Louis de Conte, Mark Twain's mouthpiece, has a decidedly pessimistic view. He looks back upon his youth as a time when he "foolishly thought life valuable"; he sees the human race as "worse than other animals"; he keeps repeating "we were young" as explaining Noel's ability to believe there is good in human nature.

Still, the fifteenth century carries its own perspective and helps to exclude Mark Twain's characteristic rages, even when he writes of Joan's sufferings and death at the stake. Man, he says, is only "a pitiful animal." Joan and the peasants of Domremy were simple and good; "they had never known anybody but people." The innate nobility of the common people is stressed in one passage, with continued emphasis on Joan herself as a commoner. One of the best things in all Mark Twain's fiction is the way in which the Paladin rises above his natural cowardice and dies bravely, defending the person of Joan of Arc. And Mark Twain expresses amazement,

---

8 *Mark Twain: A Portrait*, 180–81. Despite his minimizing of Mark Twain's literary achievement in general, Masters insists that "the conclusion of *The Mysterious Stranger* is one of the most superb pieces of writing in American literature" (*ibid.*, 232).

through the lips of Louis de Conte, at Joan's ability to transcend the limitations of weak human nature during the trials, her long struggle without hope. With Nigger Jim and Pudd'nhead Wilson, this young girl with her slight body and her spirit of steel becomes the third of his heroic figures.

But *Joan of Arc* falls far short of the objectivity of *Huckleberry Finn*. Huck wins his battle with his "yaller dog" conscience and continues, Mr. DeVoto observes, to vindicate "the realities of friendship, loyalty, and courage." DeVoto doubts that Mark Twain could have asserted them except in the belief of a boy. Perhaps it was, in part, the comparatively keen consciences of the young that attracted him. Like Hawthorne, he accepted the dramatic reality of the issues of conscience; Huck's conscience becomes the battleground for the chief struggle of the book. Although not dissatisfied with life, Huck is sometimes briefly pessimistic, as when he predicts that his Pap has likely "got [the money] all away from Judge Thatcher and drunk it up." But this prediction does not leave him despondent—he is ready to accept life as it comes. And Mr. DeVoto insists that "if the book makes a statement through Nigger Jim that human life is tragic, it also asserts through Huck that human life is noble . . . noble enough for the likes of us. . . . It is not a book of despair but rather of realistic acceptance."

It is chiefly in his boy-books, however, that Mark Twain was able to achieve this "realistic acceptance," this synthesis of both aspects of life. The joint charge of Brooks and DeVoto that he was imprisoned in his boyhood is thus seen to have supporting evidence. But the reason for that apparent imprisonment is also plain: Mark Twain was artist enough to know—or to sense, unconsciously, if you will—that such a synthesis, such a realistic acceptance, is demanded by the very nature of art. And so he turned again and again to the boy-world, the place where he could best achieve that synthesis and achieve it honestly. For he was honest; and he could rarely bring himself to an acceptance of human nature as exemplified in adults. While working on *Tom Sawyer*, he wrote to Howells that he had decided not to take Tom into manhood, for "he would just lie like all the one-horse men in literature and the reader would conceive a hearty contempt for him." This, in the face of the countless lies Huck will tell throughout his story! Why could Mark Twain accept human nature only in boy nature?

From *Huckleberry Finn* onward, his doubts about life's worth seem to be growing, but only gradually is the artist within him overcome. It is significant that the Connecticut Yankee collects an army of fifty-two boys to help him inaugurate the New Deal in Camelot.[9] But that fine enterprise comes off rather badly, as we have seen in the preceding chapter.

Twenty-one years after his 1878 letter to Howells confessing that his moods of rage prevented his writing good satire, he sent Howells another letter in which he shows that he is conscious of the connection between a writer's art and his attitude toward life and mankind. He is living abroad, in Vienna, and he is eager to read Howells' serial, "Their Silver Wedding Journey." He writes:

I am waiting for the April *Harper* . . . waiting and strongly interested. You are old enough to be a weary man, with paling interests, but you do not show it. You do your work in the same old delicate . . . and forceful and searching and perfect way. I don't know how you can—but I suspect. I suspect that to you there is still dignity in human life, and that Man is not a joke—a poor joke—the poorest that was ever contrived. Since I wrote my Bible (last year) . . . Man is not to me the respect-worthy person he was before; and so I have lost my pride in him, and can't write gaily nor praisefully about him any more. . . . I mean to go on writing, for that is my best amusement, but I shan't print much. . . .

He dates his "Bible" from "last year," or 1898; but parts of it had been written out years before, and it expresses ideas which had had an early beginning. Explicitly, in this letter he expresses his consciousness that the best work can be done only by a writer who senses the "dignity in human life"; implicitly—note the last lines—he shows his realization of an author's obligation to offer some moral inspiration, some incentive, to his readers. Mr. Brooks suggests that it was an "artistic sense . . . that led him to suppress, and indeed to leave incomplete" so many works of a satiric nature. With this letter before us, we can see that his artistic sense was actively functioning. Occasionally he was saddened at recognizing something in his friends which he himself lacked. In 1905 he wrote that Aldrich "was here

---

[9] An interviewer once asked Franklin D. Roosevelt, then president of the United States, how he had happened to hit upon the phrase "The New Deal" which he applied to his official program. President Roosevelt answered that he had borrowed the phrase from Mark Twain's *Connecticut Yankee*. See "Mark Twain's New Deal," *Saturday Review of Literature*, Vol. X, No. 22 (December 16, 1933), 352.

half an hour ago, like a breeze from over the fields, with the fragrance still upon his spirit. I am tired of waiting for that man to grow old." And he called Howells a "shameless old fictitious butterfly," flitting around: "But . . . I wouldn't brush a flake of powder from his wings for anything. I only say it in envy of his indestructible youth."

But it was not a simple question of mere aging; for Mark Twain was always enrolled among youthful-seeming men. He realized, quite well, what it was that these men had and he lacked. He realized, too, what it means to be a writer in this dreary world where readers beg writers for the alms of courage and faith. Not only had he thought earnestly about the relations between life and literature; he had also realized that the chief function of a writer should be to encourage the aspirations of the human race.

CHAPTER 20

The Microscope and the Dream

THE book called *The Mysterious Stranger* presents Mark Twain's final expression of the village and its inhabitants. Bernard DeVoto believes that this book resulted from the personal disasters which engulfed Mark Twain in the late eighteen nineties. His publishing firm failed; the Paige typesetting machine wrecked his fortune in its debacle; his youngest daughter, Jean, was discovered to be afflicted with epilepsy; his eldest daughter, Susy, closest to him in talent and spirit, died of meningitis; and Livy, after Susy's death, was an invalid the last eight years of her life. "The gods had turned against their darling," says Mr. DeVoto in *Mark Twain at Work;* and he believes that the tragic writings which include "The Great Dark" and *The Mysterious Stranger* constituted an attempt by Mark Twain to reintegrate his writing talent, almost destroyed by these disasters, and to still the accusing voice of his conscience by proving to himself that he was not to be blamed.

Mark Twain was always among the most autobiographical of writers. Yet, studying the record, it seems impossible to escape the conclusion that *The Mysterious Stranger* must some day have been written, substantially as he wrote it, with or without his personal calamities. As a matter of fact, the earliest hint of the story appears in a "Mr. Brown" letter of June 2, 1867. There Mark Twain reports an Apocryphal New Testament, seen in a New York library. In Chapter 15, according to Mark Twain, the boy Jesus plays with other boys; he makes clay animals that come to life and "clay birds which he causes to fly." Believing Jesus to be a sorcerer, the parents of the other boys forbid them to play with him. In Chapter 16, Joseph is seen to be unskillful at his carpenter's trade; young Jesus assists him by touching the ill-shapen articles, thus giving them the proper dimensions. In Chapter 19, Jesus is charged with causing the death of various boys who have displeased him. Mark Twain summed up the activities of this apocryphal lad:

The young Savior's resentments were so frequent . . . that Joseph finally grew concerned about the matter and gave it his personal attention:

"16. Then said Joseph unto Mary, henceforth we will not allow him to go out of the house, for every one who displeases him is killed."

His society was pleasant, but attended by serious drawbacks.

Remembering Mark Twain's view of life, even in his happiest years, remembering too the fascination which the figure of Satan had always held for him, it seems inevitable that he would write *The Mysterious Stranger*. In the writing of *Huckleberry Finn*, he had already experimented with beauty tinged with strangeness and horror. A passage in *A Tramp Abroad*, which he wrote while *Huckleberry Finn* lay unfinished, anticipates an important bit in the presentation of young Satan as the Stranger. The passage describes the "prismatic colors" of clouds over the Alps, clouds resembling "gossamer webs" of a "lovely phantom fabric, . . . a fabric dainty enough to clothe an angel with." Soon he realized that the continuous movement of those delicate opaline colors reminded him of "what one sees in a soap-bubble that is drifting along." Both the Apocryphal account of the boy Jesus and the description of a soap-bubble as fit clothing for an angel were to furnish details for the earthly visits of Satan in *The Mysterious Stranger*.

The essence of tragedy in this book lies not in any malevolence against mankind exhibited by the Superior Powers in the person of young Satan, for there is little, although it appears. The chief tragedy lies in the utter indifference towards mankind which Satan exhibits. And this idea appears in Mark Twain's writings dating from his halcyon days. On August 12, 1883, a time of great personal happiness, he wrote in his *Notebook*: "I think we are only the microscopic trichina concealed in the blood of some vast creature's veins, and it is that vast creature God concerns himself about and not us." In the notes of 1885–86, just before the time of *A Connecticut Yankee*, he wrote:

Special Providence! That phrase nauseates me—with its implied importance of mankind and triviality of God. In my opinion these myriads of globes are merely the blood corpuscles ebbing and flowing through the arteries of God and we but the animalculae that infest them . . . and God does not know we are there and would not care if He did.

Later, he recorded in *Following the Equator* a "large dream" in which he dreamed "that the visible universe is the physical person of God," with vast worlds as the blood corpuscles of His veins, and all living creatures are the microbes that infest the corpuscles. These passages are curiously reminiscent of the theories of Robert Fludd, as well as those of eighteenth-century Deists whom Mark Twain probably never read. The notes seem more closely connected with "3,000 Years Among the Microbes" than with any of his other fiction; yet they are linked, too, with *The Mysterious Stranger*. A note of August, 1897, labeled by Paine as probably for *The Mysterious Stranger*, reads:

He had but one term for that large body which has such a fine opinion of itself—"the little stinking human race, with its little stinking kings and popes and bishops and prostitutes and peddlers."
He said: "The globe is a living creature, and the little stinking human race and the other animals are the vermin that infest it—the microbes."

A definite forecast of the *Stranger* appears in a *Notebook* entry of September, 1898:

Story of little Satan Jr., who came to Hannibal, went to school, was popular and greatly liked by those who knew his secret. The others were jealous and the girls didn't like him because he smelled of brimstone.
He was always doing miracles . . .

The note suggests that his first idea was to use Tom and Huck as Satan's associates; later he changed Hannibal to Eseldorf, in the Austria of 1590, and made the scene far off and forgot in both time and space, thus lending perspective to the story. He prepared the reader for the Stranger through Felix Brandt's ghostly tales; but the strangest thing was that Felix himself had seen angels: "They had no wings, and wore clothes, and talked . . . and acted just like any natural person, and you would never know them for angels except for the wonderful things they did."
One fine May morning when the boy Theodor, the narrator,

was on a hilltop with his friends Nikolaus and Seppi, a handsome youth came strolling along, "easy and graceful and unembarrassed, not slouchy and awkward and diffident like other boys." He sat down and talked to the boys in a simple, gentle way, winning their friendship at once. As he talked, he made a tiny squirrel out of clay, and it ran up a tree; he made a mouse-sized dog that barked at the squirrel, and birds that flew away singing. At last Theodor asked who he was. " 'An angel,' he said, quite simply, and set another bird free and clapped his hands and made it fly away." Then he formed tiny men and women from clay; they went to work, cleared a small space, and began to build a little castle. The three boys made horses and cannon and halberdiers, but dropped the figures and broke them in the astonishment of learning that their visitor's name was "Satan." Young Satan mended them with a touch, as the boy Jesus had mended Joseph's ill-formed work in the passage copied in Mark Twain's *Notebook* in 1867. Satan explained that only his uncle, for whom he was named, had been affected by the Fall; the rest of the family were still untouched by sin. At that moment two of the tiny workmen began to quarrel "in buzzing bumblebee voices" and fell to fighting. Momentarily annoyed,

Satan reached out his hand and crushed the life out of them with his fingers, threw them away, wiped the red from his fingers on his handkerchief, and went on talking . . . : "We cannot do wrong; neither have we any disposition to do it, for we do not know what it is."

The boys were shocked and grieved at "the wanton murder he had committed," but he talked on, switching his young listeners quickly from horror to beauty:

somehow . . . charming us in spite of the pitiful scene that was now under our eyes, for the wives of the little dead men had found the crushed . . . bodies and were crying over them . . . and a priest was kneeling there . . . praying; and . . . pitying friends were massed about them . . . a scene which Satan paid no attention to until the small noise of the weeping and praying began to annoy him, then he . . . took the heavy board seat out of our swing and brought it down and mashed all those people . . . just as if they had been flies.

But he soon enchanted the boys again "with that fatal music of his voice. . . . He made us drunk with the joy of being with him."

This fluctuation of mood between beauty and horror continues. The boys were always expecting beautiful things to happen when they were in Satan's presence. He told them of "the daily life in heaven" and also "of the damned writhing in hell." The vision of hell was so horrible, with condemned persons shrieking in their anguish, that the boys could hardly bear it; but Satan was "as bland about it as if it had been so many imitation rats in an artificial fire."

Whenever Satan's conversation turned to the human race, one would think he was talking "about bricks or manure or any other thing that . . . hadn't feelings." Presently he had the tiny castle finished, and it was beautifully done. He offered to create a miniature storm and earthquake around it, as entertainment, but warned the boys to stand back out of danger. They wanted to warn the tiny people, too, but "he said never mind them; they were of no consequence, and we could make more, some time . . . if we needed them." The tone of contemptuous indifference is only slightly more exaggerated than that of Mark Twain's Western sketch of 1864, "The Case of Smith vs. Jones," in which the ignorant, lying witnesses are shown in a sorry light, with a witness box in a corner "where more can be had when they are wanted." This time, however, Mark Twain's sympathy seems to be with the creatures in the box—here, the castle. A small cloud settled over the castle, and the little people flocked inside for shelter, but lightning blazed out and set it on fire. They "came flying out, shrieking, but Satan brushed them back, paying no attention to our begging and crying and imploring." Then an earthquake rent the ground, and the castle toppled into the chasm, which "closed upon it, with all that innocent life, not one of the . . . poor creatures escaping. . . . 'Don't cry,' Satan said; 'they were of no value. . . . we can make plenty more.'"

The boys wondered how he could be so callous to the tiny men he created, so indifferent to the sufferings of the villagers. Theodor asked him "why he made so much difference between men and himself." Satan picked up a creeping wood louse:

"What is the difference between Caesar and this?"

I said, "One cannot compare things which by their nature are not comparable."

"You have answered your own question," he said. ". . . Man is made of dirt. . . . Man is a museum of disease, a home of impurities . . . ;

he begins as dirt and departs as stench. . . . And man has the *Moral Sense*. You understand? He has the *Moral Sense*."

They could not understand his dislike of the Moral Sense, especially when Father Peter explained it to them as "the one thing that lifts man above the beasts." Gradually they came to understand that Satan hated the Moral Sense because it gives man the power "to distinguish between right and wrong, with liberty to choose which he will do . . . and in nine cases out of ten he prefers the wrong." Satan maintained that men are more "brutal" than the beasts: "When a brute inflicts pain he does it innocently. . . . And he does not inflict pain for the pleasure of inflicting it—only man does that." And yet man cannot perceive that "the Moral Sense degrades him . . . and is a shameful possession."

The microscopic motif enters Satan's illustrations again when he explains that he has no more in common with man than an elephant has with a tiny red spider, not so big as the head of a pin. The elephant "cannot shrink his sympathies to the microscopic size" of the spider's affairs. "No, we cannot love men, but we can be harmlessly indifferent to them; we can also like them, sometimes." Satan declares that because he likes the boys and Father Peter, he is helping the villagers of Eseldorf. He insists that he has wrought well for the villagers,

"though it does not look like it on the surface. . . . What I am doing for the villagers will bear good fruit some day. . . . a child's first act . . . begets an act, that act begets another and so on. . . . You people do not suspect that all of your acts are of one size and importance . . . ; to snatch at an appointed fly is as big with fate for you as is any other appointed act."

He explains that he has arranged for Nicky to try, in twelve days' time, to rescue little Lisa Brandt from drowning; both Lisa and Nicky will drown. Horrified, Theodor pleads for the two children, but Satan is adamant. This early death will save Lisa from a life of pain, shame, and depravity; Nicky, from a living death of forty-six years as "a paralytic log." After Nicky's death his mother keeps blaming herself; Satan explains that people are foolish to blame themselves for anything: "nothing happens that your first act hasn't made inevitable; and so, of your own motion you can't ever alter the scheme." But other parts of the story set moralism against this determinism. Satan himself falls briefly into the contradictions natural to Mark Twain. He protests mere indifference for mankind; yet sometimes his excoriation of the mangy, filthy race belies indifference. Moral condemnation of the villagers issues from the lips of Frau Brandt, sentenced to be burned for blasphemies uttered in grief at Lisa's death; she "would rather live with the professional devils in perdition than with these imitators in the village."

Throughout his life, Mark Twain derided man's belief that he is the favored creature of the universe; and the irony basic in this story appears in the relationship of the boys and Satan. When Satan takes Theodor to China on a tour of inspection, Theodor is "drunk with vanity and gladness." The three boys feel themselves to be the pets of Satan: yet he destroys Nicky and blasts the happiness of the other two by opening their eyes to what human life really is.

To entertain the two surviving boys, Satan shows them "the progress of the human race . . . its development of that product which it calls civilization." Mark Twain passed the ages in review: the boys saw the murder of Abel by Cain; then a long series of wars, murders, massacres; Sodom and Gomorrah; more wars. Christianity finally came into existence, but always there were wars, "hideous drenchings of the earth with blood." Then Satan exhibited the future, showing them "slaughters more terrible, . . . more devastating in their engines of war." Apparently, the chief progress had been, and would continue to be, in instruments for the mutual destruction of men. " 'And what does it all amount to?' said Satan with his evil chuckle. 'You gain nothing; you always come out where you went in.' "

A peculiar mingling of the beautiful and the horrible pervades *The Mysterious Stranger*. Once, departing, Satan dissolved himself and let the boys see him do it:

He stood up and . . . thinned away until he was a soap-bubble, except that he kept his shape. You could see the bushes through him . . . as you see things through a soap-bubble, and all over him played and flashed the delicate iridescent colors of the bubble. . . . You have seen a bubble strike the carpet and lightly bound along two or three times before it bursts. He did that. He sprang—touched the grass—bounded—floated along—touched again—and . . . presently exploded—puff! and in his place was vacancy. It was a strange and beautiful thing to see.

Mark Twain records here his distrust of all institutions. Satan argues that "monarchies, aristocracies, and religions" are institutions that will always remain to oppress and degrade the individual, who is always destined to be a slave of the minorities. A striking illustration is seen in the institution of war, aggressive war:

"I can see a million years ahead, and this rule will never change in so many as half a dozen instances. The loud little handful ... will shout for the war. The pulpit will ... object—at first; the big, dull bulk of the nation will rub its sleepy eyes and try to make out why there should be a war, and will say ... 'It is unjust and dishonorable, and there is no necessity for it.' Then the handful will shout louder. A few fair men ... will argue and reason against the war with speech and pen, and at first will have a hearing ... ; those others will outshout them, and presently the anti-war audiences will thin out. ... Before long you will see this curious thing: the speakers stoned from the platform, and free speech strangled by hordes of furious men who in their secret hearts are still at one with those stoned speakers—as earlier—but do not dare to say so. And now the whole nation—pulpit and all—will take up the war-cry, and ... mob any honest man who ventures to open his mouth. ... Next the statesmen will invent cheap lies, putting the blame upon the nation that is attacked, and every man will be glad of those conscience-soothing falsities, and will ... refuse to examine any refutations of them; and thus he will ... convince himself that the war is just, and will thank God for the better sleep he enjoys after this process of grotesque self-deception."

Can anyone, reading these lines, believe that Mark Twain had in mind the practices of sixteenth-century Austria, rather than the world patterns of his own time?

One of his favorite themes, the distintegrating effect of money, appears here. The money found by Father Peter proves far greater curse than blessing; he is arrested for theft. At his trial the opposing lawyer points to the money on the table and says, "There it lies, the ancient tempter, newly red with the shame of its latest victory—the dishonor of a priest of God."[1]

Satan insures Father Peter's future happiness by causing him to go mad, insisting that the insane priest "is now, and will remain, the one utterly happy person in this empire." When Theodor protests

[1] Mark Twain's fiction reflects his interest in legal procedure. Besides the trial of Father Peter, we have the trial scene which is, naturally, the high point in *Joan of Arc;* murder trials appear in *The Gilded Age, Tom Sawyer, Pudd'nhead Wilson,* and *Tom Sawyer, Detective.*

his method of making Father Peter happy, Satan grows almost angry: "Are you so unobservant as not to have found out that sanity and happiness are an impossible combination? No sane man can be happy, for to him life is real, and he sees what a fearful thing it is." To his remedies of death and delusion, Satan adds a third at the close of the book: one must cling to the idea that life is only a dream.[2]

As manifested in Mark Twain's fiction, his conceptions of good and evil, beauty and ugliness, are closely connected with the philosophy of escape displayed in the travel books. There, ugliness is reality; beauty is dream. But in his late fiction the urge towards escapism enlarges the dream motif until the dream finally engulfs the whole of life, the ugliness as well as the beauty. The difference, however, is of degree rather than of kind. When Mark Twain at last arrives at the nihilism of *The Mysterious Stranger*, he arrives by a path on which his feet have been set since the Sandwich Islands letters of 1866, with their siren song of escape from an active life to an isle of dreams.

The Mark Twain of *The Mysterious Stranger* even affirms, in an elevated form, the creed of that Mark Twain of Western journalism who had insisted that "one can deliver a satire with telling force through the insidious medium of a travesty." Satan tells Theodor that laughter can destroy certain "juvenilities":

"For your race, in its poverty, has unquestionably one really effective weapon—laughter. Power, money, persuasion, supplication, persecution —these can lift at a colossal humbug—push it a little—weaken it a little, century by century; but only laughter can blow it to rags and atoms at a blast. Against the assault of laughter nothing can stand."

Satan continued to take Theodor about the world, showing him wonders reflecting the "triviality of our race. . . . not out of malice . . . it only seemed to amuse and interest him, just as a naturalist might be amused and interested by a collection of ants."

The Mysterious Stranger is Mark Twain's greatest use of the device of diminishing humanity to microscopic proportions. By means of Satan he employs the Olympian detachment of a god and at the same time, by means of Theodor, reports it through the lips of a

[2] It is significant that, among men, young Satan calls himself "Philip Traum," and *traum* means *dream*.

boy. Thus he is twice-removed from the rage-provoking perversities of mankind. After studying early manuscripts of this story, Mr. DeVoto wrote that at first young Satan was "no more than a vehicle for Mark's derision of that God whose vengefulness creates human pain and for his scorn of the ant-like race pain is inflicted on. . . . But he became more than that." Yes, for the artist in Mark Twain would demand more than that—some sense of the alleviation that art requires to give a feeling of conclusiveness, as well as to make the tragic thing tolerable. He would not feel that need in a Socratic debate such as *What Is Man?* but in fiction he would be more alert to the obligations of the artist.

Unfortunately, by the time of *The Mysterious Stranger* he can no longer depend upon his boys for the saving grace. For Theodor confesses:

Naturally there were some who pitied Marget and Ursula for the danger that was gathering about them, but naturally they did not say so; it would not have been safe. . . . We boys wanted to warn them, but . . . when it came to the pinch . . . [we] found that we were not manly enough nor brave enough to do a generous action when there was a chance that it could get us into trouble.

Huck had often protected Nigger Jim at the risk of his own safety. But Mark Twain's boys have now become "like all the one-horse men in literature" and seem bent on earning the reader's contempt. By this time he cannot close the arc of his artistic circle by a realistic acceptance of human nature, even though he is dealing with boy nature; for these boys, through Satan, have had their eyes opened to the futility of human existence. And what does Mark Twain do to give the requisite sense of alleviation? As an artist, he does two things: he first presents the tragedy of life as a spectacle of the human race in miniature, with, as Mr. DeVoto says, "the suffering diminished to the vanishing point since these are just puppets, unreal creatures moving in a shadow-play"; and then he moves the reader on into a sense of dream. For anything can be endured in a dream.[3]

[3] Commenting upon the use of the dream in *The Mysterious Stranger*, Mr. DeVoto says that for Mark Twain the dream had "closed the arc," that in this story the dreadful things alleged against mankind in *What Is Man?* are said again, "but now they are tolerable, conformable, acceptable, for they have been removed far away, over them broods the peace of distant dream" (*Mark Twain at Work*, 129).

These two devices used by Mark Twain for attaining what may be called an *artificial alleviation*—the dream and the diminution—appear over and over in his work, travel and fiction. In his fiction they were probably applied to satisfy his artistic sense; and these devices—like his preoccupation with palliatives for human suffering, with all sorts of external alleviations to be applied in one way or another—were necessary to him only because he could not attain the inner alleviation which comes with an unqualified acceptance of life. For him, art would not come full circle simply because he could not sense the latent grandeur of life, the glory that lies hidden somewhere beneath the boredom and the horror.

In *Tom Sawyer Abroad* (1894), he employed for the first time in fiction his device of diminishing the human race to microscopic proportions, thus achieving a perspective which enabled him to paint injustice without what he called his "foaming at the mouth." The first instance comes when Tom, Huck, and Jim, high in their balloon, look down upon the desert and see a caravan winding across it, like a string of insects. As they watch, tiny robbers swoop down upon the caravan, shooting and killing; when the smoke has "cleared a little," they can see the dead and wounded. There is no comment upon this wrong, only Huck's objective presentation. Later the same device is employed in an example of Nature's cruelty to mankind. Another caravan crawls across the desert "like a thousand granddaddy-long-legses," seen from above; the caravan camps, and the boys watch its people with interest. A sand storm sweeps across it, burying men, women, and camels beneath a level stretch of yellow sand. Huck says they had watched from above until they "had got to feeling real friendly" with the people, so that "this caravan's death went harder with us." The objective handling gives these scenes power.

In *Mark Twain at Work*, Mr. DeVoto has published the incomplete manuscript of "The Great Dark," which he considers "The Mysterious Stranger in embryo" and also a fictional expression of Mark Twain's mood of pessimism resulting from Susy's death and other disasters. The earliest published note indentifiable with "The Great Dark" stands under date of August 10, 1898:

Last night dreamed of a whaling cruise in a drop of water. Not by microscope, but actually. This would mean a reduction of the participants to a minuteness which would make them nearly invisible to God, and He wouldn't be interested in them any longer.

Much earlier, in 1883—one of his happiest years—there is a *Notebook* entry headed "Theme for a Story." This note markedly resembles "The Great Dark":

Life in the interior of an iceberg. Luxuriously furnished from the ship. . . . Children born. . . . Iceberg drifts in a vast circle, year after year. . . . The children born reach marrying age and marry. Others try to make them comprehend life on land . . . but wholly fail. . . .

This must be a woman's diary, beginning abruptly and does not explain how they got there. . . .

She must speak of a young girl who is an idiot and who is now 80 years old. She visits her husband's clear-ice grave . . . and finds him fresh and young, while she is old and gray.

This note contains the suggestions of drifting in an aimless circle at sea, of imprisonment there resulting in an unnatural way of life, of idiocy, of death, of tragedy. And the story "must be a woman's diary, beginning abruptly," which is the way "The Great Dark" begins. Mr. DeVoto believes that in "The Great Dark" Mark Twain was struggling to find the correct form for reducing to art his bitter experiences and also for embodying certain obsessive ideas. Through ten pages in *Mark Twain at Work*, DeVoto traces these ideas, which are here summarized:

Perhaps the earliest idea is that of the great stretch of time which may seem to elapse in a very short dream; then comes the idea of confusing dream with reality. A notebook entry proposes a story in which a man is to nod for a moment over a cigarette, to dream a sequence of events which appears to last for seventeen years, and to wake to such a confusion of reality with the dream that he cannot recognize his wife. Mark Twain attempts sketches dealing with persons—some innocent, some guilty—who are cast down from high places by circumstance. Other sketches deal with surface events in which sailors are marooned in vast wastes of ice.

He combines some of these ideas in the sketch which Mr. DeVoto named "The Great Dark," using a phrase from the story itself. A happy and prosperous man falls asleep just after looking through a powerful microscope at a drop of water in which he watches the movement of minute forms of life. The idea of the microscope, Mr. DeVoto remarks, "immensely deepens the story." The ensuing dream unrolls events in which the man and his family—reduced to microscopic proportions—are on a mysterious ship, sailing through "a perpetual darkness filled with storms of snow and ice. . . . No one knows . . . where they are going or for what purpose . . . but they are in the Great Dark at the edge of the microscope's field, a place of unimaginable desolation, and somewhere far off is the horror of the Great White Glare, which is really the beam cast through the microscope's field by the reflector."

There is a supernatural being on board, the Superintendent of Dreams (he is the God of *What Is Man?* as well as the Satan of *The Mysterious Stranger*), who has power over both the bodies and minds of his passengers. And in the terrifying darkness monsters roam about the ship, threatening the lives of its people. At first there is on board some recollection of waking life—"the world of reality outside both the microscope and the dream"; but gradually this fades, and the Superintendent of Dreams "steadily, vindictively, cultivates in their minds the doubt of reality which becomes the belief in dream."

This story Mark Twain was unable to finish. Mr. DeVoto finds strong autobiographical evidence in the notes which he left for its completion: the wife is maddened with grief over a lost child; and the beloved daughter dies "in exactly the delirium" which Mark Twain's notebooks record of Susy Clemens's fatal illness. Certainly, the autobiographical material is traceable. In "The Great Dark" the eldest daughter's birthday is March 19, the birthday of Susy Clemens, and the height of the husband and father is five feet, eight, exactly Mark Twain's height.

Nevertheless, the keynote of horror, of a life lived under some terrible enchantment, appears as early as 1876 in Mark Twain's letter to Mrs. Fairbanks, already quoted, in which he writes concerning Charley Fairbanks's current happiness:

I rejoice in his gladness. . . . Never mind about that grisly future season when he shall have made a dazzling success and shall sit . . . and look around upon his corpses and mine, and contemplate his daughters and mine in the mad-house, and his sons and mine gone to the devil.

And the *Notebook* shows an entry made before the catastrophes of the late nineties which outlines, in terms of regrettable sentimentality, a new tale of Tom and Huck:

Huck comes back sixty years old . . . and crazy. Thinks he is a boy again and scans always every face for Tom, Becky, etc.

Tom comes at last from sixty years' wandering in the world and attends Huck and together they talk of old times; both are desolate, life has been a failure, all that was . . . beautiful is under the mold. They die together.

The date is 1891; but the note of tragedy and futility is indubitably present.

In "The Great Dark," the unfinished story of the dream-bound ship on the icebound sea for which no chart exists, both the microscope and the dream are fundamental elements, as is Mark Twain's use of ice and snow as the symbols of despair. With time, the word *dream* takes on increasing significance in his work. The curious part played by dreams in his own life is too well known to need recounting here.[4] In 1893 when his only apparent trouble was sporadic worry over his investments, he wrote to his sister-in-law, Sue Crane:

I dreamed I was born and grew up and was a pilot on the Mississippi and a miner and a journalist in Nevada and a pilgrim in the *Quaker City*, and had a wife and children and went to live in a village at Florence—and this dream goes on and on and sometimes seems so real that I almost believe it is real. I wonder if it is? But there is no way to tell, for if one applied tests they would be part of the dream, too, and so would simply aid the deceit. I wish I knew whether it is a dream or real.

And he wrote in his *Autobiography*: "What a wee little part of a person's life are his acts and his words. His real life is led in his head, and is known to none but himself; and his thoughts, not those other things, are his history."

It was not only in his old age that he led a sort of double life. In a book dealing with Mark Twain as a businessman, his great-nephew Samuel C. Webster has shown how his "double personality" affected his middle years. Mr. Webster observes that his book might well have been entitled *Mark Twain vs. Mark Twain* and that, apart from Mark Twain's business life, the title seems to apply also "to the

---

[4] His most notable dream forecast the death of his brother Henry. In 1858, in a dream, he saw Henry lying dead in a metallic casket, supported by two chairs; on Henry's breast was a bouquet of white flowers, with a single red blossom in the center. Mark Twain woke next morning and was dressed and out in the street before he realized that this vision was a dream, its impression was so vivid. In June, 1858, Henry was killed in the explosion of the *Pennsylvania*. When Mark Twain went in to see his brother's body, prepared for burial, Henry lay in a metallic casket like the one of the dream; as Mark Twain stood there, a woman brought in a bouquet and placed it on Henry's breast; it was made of white flowers, with one red rose in the center. See Paine, *Biography*, I, 139–43.

struggles that went on between his conscious and unconscious. . . . What came to him from the inside was as real as what came from the outside." Because of these quirks and facets of personality, the biographical approach to Mark Twain, though valuable, can never be an adequate approach. The *Notebook* poses a query:

How is it that I, who cannot draw or paint, can sometimes shut my eyes and see faces (dark colored always, color of putty) most delicate and perfect miniatures, and can note and admire the details. How is it? They are not familiar faces, they are new—how can I invent them? And what is it that makes perfect images in my dreams? I cannot *form* a face of any kind by deliberate effort of imagination.

After Livy's death, his inability to reproduce faces in his memory became a calamity to him. But in his dreams he saw her so vividly that he sometimes woke feeling it was her death that was the dream.

The curious mingling of dreams and reality which threaded his life is seen, blended with the harmful effects of daydreams, in a number of short stories. In the book *The American Claimant* (1892), Colonel Sellers reappears in the title role. Mark Twain perhaps meant to show an advanced stage in the life of the habitual dreamer, a phantasy life in which the actual world is indistinguishable from the chimeras that throng the brain; but Colonel Sellers himself is here a chimera, an unbelievable figure. Mr. Brooks says that in *The American Claimant* Mark Twain has conducted us into "the penetralia of his soul." Sally Sellers, like her father, is a confirmed dreamer. Love awakens her to reality; but Colonel Sellers is too far gone. As in *The Gilded Age*, he remains steeped in dreams. If Mark Twain wished to inject a dreamlike quality into the character of Sellers in this book, the result, judged by any standards, is a failure.[5]

By 1904, however, in "My Platonic Sweetheart" he was able to produce a story in which the dream world is presented with a clarity

[5] In the *Autobiography* (I, 89–92), Mark Twain recorded his view of the real Colonel Sellers as "a pathetic and beautiful spirit" and his feeling that the character as acted on the stage should be a blend of the farcical and the "piteous." Perhaps he meant to show a grotesquely tragic figure, a warm, generous soul geared to a puerile intellect; but the result is a cruelly ridiculous figure. His handling of Colonel Sellers in *The American Claimant* is fantastic, incoherent, and absurd, but at the same time sinister; the Colonel's schemes include one to resurrect the dead by "materializing" their spirits, another to utilize sewer gas for purposes of illumination. Mark Twain's mocking, sardonic spirit could hardly go beyond this grim and ghoulish humor in showing the essential indignity of the human race. The book, his worst failure, was written in 1891.

and precision which make it believable without destroying its magical effects. The delightful heroine's speech has a Carrollian flavor. Seated somewhere in India, in sight of both Bombay and Windsor Castle, with the Thames winding at her feet, she remarks that England is beautiful "because it is so marginal." For complete artistry, this small dream story is perhaps the most perfect of Mark Twain's short fictional pieces. In it he appears to have attained a mastery over dream in literature, a difficult feat. In one passage he claims to live an actual dream life, independent of the life lived in his body and usually more vivid and interesting. He maintains:

In our dreams—I know it!—we do make the journeys we seem to make; we do see the things we seem to see; the people, the horses, the cats, the dogs, the birds, the whales, are real, not chimeras; . . . and they are immortal and indestructible. They go whither they will. . . . That is where those strange mountains are which slide from under our feet while we walk, and where those vast caverns are whose bewildering avenues close behind us and in front when we are lost, and shut us in.

His favorite themes and fancies shuttle back and forth between the travel books and the fiction in a way which it is fascinating to watch. In *Following the Equator* he describes a river of India in terms of the human body; in "3,000 Years Among the Microbes" he describes the human body in geographic terms. This "Autobiography of a Microbe" presents "the planet Blitzowski"—a tramp inhabited by millions of microbes, one of which, *Bkshp* by name, is the narrator: "Our tramp is mountainous, there are vast oceans in him . . . there are many rivers." Mark Twain constantly satirized the "sublime conceit" of man, that poor creature who believes that he is the darling of God and that the universe was created for his pleasure and comfort. The microbe writes that, in his view, man was created only to provide a home and nourishment for the microbe and the bacillus; "let him do the service he was made for, and keep quiet."[6]

---

[6] Paine, *Biography*, III, Appendix V, 1663–70. The microbe Bkshp is an extremely Twainian character. He examined a drop of his own blood under a microscope and saw a field spotted with white tents and a military review in progress. The soldiers were "so immensely magnified that they looked to be fully a finger-nail high." (Mark Twain speaks of this "atomic race" sometimes as "finger-nailers" and sometimes as "Swinks.") But the female Swinks were seen to be crying; the Swinks were preparing for war. Their little monarch—"the sweetest little thing that ever travestied the human shape, I think"—came out and blessed the passing soldiers; but he didn't fight. He "stayed at home . . . and waited for the swag."

Although Mark Twain's view of the essential meanness of the human race did not alter, his knowledge of how to attain detachment increased with the years; and at the end his use of the diminishing device was especially favored. Besides "3,000 Years Among the Microbes" (1904), he wrote "Letters from the Earth" (1909), purportedly written by an angel visiting the earth, thus achieving the Olympian detachment of *The Mysterious Stranger*. The letters are directed to another angel in Heaven, and their subject is Man, his innate perversity and irrationality.

We come now to the more or less neglected story called *Captain Stormfield's Visit to Heaven*, published in 1908. According to Paine, Mark Twain began the story in 1868 and worked on it intermittently for forty years. It is foreshadowed, however, in a Western sketch of 1863, devoted to Mark Twain's adventures among the spiritualists; he questions one of the "irrepressible Smiths" resident in the spirit world about life in the hereafter. According to this particular Smith,

there are spheres—grades of perfection—he is making pretty good progress—has been promoted a sphere or so . . . he don't know how many spheres there are (but I suppose there must be millions, because if a man goes galloping through them at the rate this old Universalist is doing, he will get through an infinitude of them . . . I am afraid the old man is scouring along rather too fast . . .). . . . I sincerely hope he will continue to progress . . . until he lands on the roof of the highest sphere of all.

In 1878 when Orion Clemens was attempting to write a visit to hell, burlesquing Jules Verne, he had appealed to Mark Twain for literary advice. Mark Twain suggested some of the technical difficulties and gave warning that Orion was "not advanced enough in literature to venture upon a matter" so precarious:

Nine years ago I mapped out my "Journey to Heaven." . . . I gave it a deal of thought. . . . After a year or more I wrote it up. It was not a success. Five years ago I wrote it again . . . but still it wouldn't do. . . . So I thought and thought . . . and at last I struck what I considered to be the right plan! Mind, I have never altered the *ideas* . . . the plan was the difficulty. Now . . . I have tried, all these years, to think of some way of "doing" hell too—and have always had to give it up. Hell, in my book, will not occupy five pages of MS . . . it will be only covert hints.[7]

The plan was to good purpose. This story is, with the exception of *Huckleberry Finn*, Mark Twain's best fictional expression of the twofold aspect of life. This fact may be accounted for in several ways. He works inside the mind of Captain Stormfield, whose prototype, Captain Ned Wakeman, he described elsewhere (under the name of Hurricane Jones) as "only a gray and bearded child . . . an innocent, lovable old infant." As when he works inside the childlike mind of Nigger Jim, or speaks through the lips of the boy Huck Finn, this childish quality in Stormfield at once operates to give the necessary perspective by removing Mark Twain from him. But perhaps even more effective, here, is the device by which Stormfield looks back on the earth from a point far away in the sky, as if he were looking through a telescope; this device reduces everything to microscopic proportions. Aided by these devices, Mark Twain describes Heaven in a way that makes existence there the well-rounded sort of life he was generally unwilling to accept for life on earth.

When Captain Stormfield arrives at Heaven after "whizzing through space" for thirty years and racing a comet at one point, he announces that he is from the earth. The puzzled clerk, using a great magnifying glass, finally identifies the earth as a speck the heavenly clerical staff commonly call "the Wart." Stormfield demands his personal halo, harp, and wings, and rushes off to a cloud bank to join the heavenly choir. But he finds that singing hymns and waving palm branches is a dull and boresome business, stops singing, and "dumps his cargo": "heaven is . . . just the busiest place you ever heard of. There ain't any idle people here after the first day." Having worked hard, the people have good appetites and sleep well. "It's the same here as it is on earth—you've got to earn a thing, square and honest, before you enjoy it."

Heaven is explained to the Captain by Sandy McWilliams, formerly of New Jersey. Sandy makes it clear that sorrow and disappointment, as well as work, are a part of Heaven, so that happiness becomes the sweeter by reason of the contrast. A woman passes, with tears running down her face. Her baby girl had died years before; and, when she came to Heaven herself, she expected to get her

---

[7] Clara Clemens says that he worked out a two-page plot and complete notes for writing *Tom Sawyer, Detective;* she also mentions his plot work on two short stories (*My Father: Mark Twain,* 106, 79). This suggests that his best work was likely to be done, not when he plotted it out on paper—for *Tom Sawyer, Detective* is one of his poorest jobs—but when he gave it a "deal of thought."

baby back again. But in Heaven one can be whatever age one wishes, and this particular baby has elected to grow up. Moreover, she has improved her mind with "deep scientific learning" until a wide gulf now exists between mother and daughter:

> ". . . what will they do—stay unhappy forever in heaven?"
> "No, they'll come together and get adjusted by and by. But not this year, and not next. By and by."

In Heaven, it seems, there is time for the slow amelioration of ills which the impatient Mark Twain could never quite acknowledge on earth. And Heaven need not possess the perfection he seems to have demanded for earth life. His Heaven shows clearly that pain is necessary for human growth and that both pain and growth are a part of the progress which man continues to make in Heaven.

In many short stories he repeated the themes that form the material of his books. Some stories, sentimental and melodramatic in effect, have the conventional climax of an escape from death, back to life. Somehow, these never quite come off. Generally, when he tried to treat tragic subjects without some artificial means of attaining perspective, he failed. The results may be seen in the maudlin sentimentality of "The Californian's Tale," in the melodramatic claptrap of "The London Times of 1904," or in the patheticism of "The Death Disk," in which he had spared neither time nor effort; for he claimed he had worked twelve years on "The Death Disk," though it was "the shortest story I ever wrote." But the mawkish, sentimental coloring of the scene between seven-year-old Abby and her father contrasts with the honest simplicity of the scene between Nigger Jim and his little black daughter, as Jim relates it in *Huckleberry Finn*.

When Mark Twain reverses his theme to write of death as an escape from life, he is usually more convincing because he seems more convinced. Death as a release forms the theme of the little fairy story, "Five Boons of Life." In "About Play Acting" (1898), his review of Adolf Wilbrandt's *The Master of Palmyra*, he wrote:

Death, in person, walks about the stage in every act. . . . To me he was always welcome, he seemed so real. . . . Wherever . . . that black figure . . . passed . . . always its coming made the fussy human pack seem in-

Mark Twain and his daughter Clara playing cards
in their Fifth Avenue home, 1908

finitely pitiful and shabby and hardly worth the attention of either saving or damning.

Although Mr. DeVoto and Mr. Brooks agree that he was "imprisoned in his boyhood," it seems doubtful that he was more imprisoned than any other man who in nostalgic moods returns to the memories of his boy days, settled beneath other superimposed memories like gold in the bed of a stream. As Howells wrote to Mark Twain just after reading *Tom Sawyer*, "I wish *I* had been on that island." Mark Twain himself said that the life of boys had a "peculiar charm" for him and therefore he used it in his fiction; but that same charm is probably felt by many men who write and by many others who do not. As a matter of fact, in actual life the adult Mark Twain consistently preferred girls to boys as companions; and this preference held true after his own daughters were gone from home. He remarked that he didn't associate with boys much—"their ways provoke me a good deal." The "peculiar charm" that boy-life once held for him had long been distilled into a literary technique.

In his use of boys—particularly in his use of Huck Finn—he availed himself of a means of gaining the detachment he found it hard to attain in other ways. When a literary device is recurrent in the work of an author, it is usually because it is the right answer to a technical problem. Nothing could indicate a plainer realization of his own shortcomings than Mark Twain's 1878 letter to Howells, already quoted, in which he expressed his desire to write satire and at the same time announced his inability to do so because of his inclination to stand before his subject and "curse it and foam at the mouth, or take a club and pound it to rags and pulp." When he wrote that letter, he had already finished the first unit of *Huckleberry Finn*, which, on the level of *Tom Sawyer*, has a light satiric touch but only that. When Huck Finn scanned the various levels of Southern life through which Mark Twain had so recently passed on his way down the river, when Huck took up the pen once more and put those scenes on paper in a way which impels the craftsman to try to find out how it was done, Mark Twain must have realized that a part of his own technical problem was solved.

So sensitive that when he was twenty-three his brother Orion wrote that "Sam's organization is such as to feel the utmost extreme of every feeling," he came to the business of writing, rich in the faculty of storing up emotional material, but handicapped in the parallel requisite of recollecting it in tranquillity—the tranquillity that alone can impose form upon it. His practice through the years, as we have seen, enabled him to employ various devices by which he achieved a measure of the serenity that art demands: speaking out his say through the lips of Huck Finn, through the childlike mind of Nigger Jim, through the childlike mind of Captain Stormfield; setting scenes for the handling of satire far off in time and space—the sixth-century England of King Arthur, the fifteenth-century France of Joan of Arc, the sixteenth-century England of Edward VI, the sixteenth-century Austrian village of Eseldorf, or "Assville," the far-off Heaven of Captain Stormfield; diminishing scenes in which human beings are involved to microscopic proportions, as when viewed from a balloon in *Tom Sawyer Abroad*, or glimpsed through the wrong end of a telescope in "The Great Dark," or seen through the Olympian eye of a god in *The Mysterious Stranger;* finally, reducing life to a dream, as in both "The Great Dark" and *The Mysterious Stranger,* where the reality is so mingled with the dream that the dream at last submerges the reality, and the greatest wrongs become tolerable simply because they are not real. As techniques, some of these devices are more successful than others; but the effect of all of them is one and the same—to lend perspective, to lend aesthetic distance, to lend serenity; and these were the very qualities Mark Twain needed most as a literary artist. He developed and used these devices through forty years of practice as a professional writer.

Who is to say whether his use of them was conscious or unconscious? His letters to Howells would indicate that it was conscious, just as he was certainly conscious of devising his early-day "ingenious satires" in burlesque for the express purpose of teaching his moral lessons. His 1899 letter to Howells acknowledges that a writer's value depends upon his ability to recognize the latent dignity in mankind. But, without benefit of his devices, he stood before what he disliked and "pounded it to pulp"; or he enveloped his material in a sentimental glow which destroys the reader's illusion of reality. These defects were inescapable because his view of the world was frequently not rounded and whole, not compounded of the contending forces of good and evil which could have furnished him the necessary artistic tension. Part of his frustration lay in the fact that, after consciously dedicating the main body of his work to the common people, he could not content himself finally with their verdict. "Ah, Helen, . . . you don't understand," he complained to Helen Keller. ". . . Their laughter has submerged me." In 1899 he wrote Howells that he had put the potboiler pen away to do what he had long wanted to do: "write a book which should take account of no one's feelings, delusions; a book which should say my say . . . without a limitation of any sort. . . . It is under way now, and it is a luxury! an intellectual drunk. . . . I believe I can make it tell what I think of Man, and how he is constructed, and what a shabby poor ridiculous thing he is." This book, of course, was *The Mysterious Stranger*.

Man is a pretty horrifying creature to many people when he is stripped to the bone, and Mark Twain had stripped him to the bone. He wrote that "what a man sees in the human race is merely himself in the deep and honest privacy of his own heart. Byron despised the race because he despised himself. I feel as Byron did, and for the same reason." Inevitably recognizing the human evil within himself, he feared it, could not accept it. Neither in his hatred of the race nor in his excoriation of himself was there any catharsis. Sometimes it is as if he used his art as a form of self-torture.

He was not a profound thinker. His reaction to life itself was emotional rather than intellectual, and his criticism of life followed the same pattern. Formal education, perhaps even a planned program of reading, might have aided him to bridge the gaps in his thinking, might have helped him to resolve his philosophical dilemma and thus to achieve philosophic unity in his work. But, on the other hand, formal education might have detracted from the buoyancy and freshness of his writing style. It is often the excellence of the writing itself—its vigor and vividness, its sincerity and emotional drive— which holds the reader's interest sufficiently to mask the weakness of ideas.

Stung by the inexplicable failure of justice, steeped in bitterness, plangent with scorn—all these things Mark Twain was; but he was far from apathetic about anything. Still, if life is futile, writing is futile, too; and the fact that he kept doggedly on perhaps indicates that his pessimism was not complete, after all. It was always hard for him to remember that the human race was not worth saving. Clara Clemens says that he "took for granted that anyone he met must be a nice person."

Hawthorne and Dostoevsky shared the belief that only those

who can suffer intensely are fully alive. On this basis, Mark Twain lived life to the full; for he suffered intensely, and—paradoxically—he was happy, even as he went roaming through the Waste Land. He himself said that he was partly a pessimist, partly an optimist. On January 26, 1910, a few months before his death, he wrote: "I am happy—few are so happy." Living the present moment intensely, he could find enjoyment in his family, his friends, his pipe, his cats, his billiards, his books; but in his view of mankind and the world, he was a pessimist. Since it was this view that he chiefly expressed in his work, it is what counts mainly for literature.

By his use of Nigger Jim and Huckleberry Finn he achieved what literary art demands for permanence because his twofold vision of life in their book gives it a firm aesthetic base; but in "3,000 Years Among the Microbes," in "The Great Dark," and in *The Mysterious Stranger* the limitations of his life view leave the reader defrauded and unsatisfied. His realization of this fact perhaps explains why he left those stories unfinished, save for *The Mysterious Stranger*. And there his practice is better than his theory. For, while denying the goodness of human nature as embodied in some of the villagers, he affirms it in the persons of Marget and Wilhelm Meidling and Father Peter; and among sixty-eight people who threw stones at a dying woman, sixty-two of them, according to Satan's count, felt no desire to do so in their hearts. Recalling Mark Twain's claim that if a man "draws 50 characters, they are all himself," we are ready to believe that somewhere in his heart, under the scornful Philip Traum, otherwise known as "Satan," he was also the tolerant Captain Stormfield and the broadly sympathetic Huck Finn.

When he read *The Mysterious Stranger* to Olivia Clemens, her reaction was that it was "Perfectly horrible—and perfectly beautiful!" Reporting this verdict to Howells, Mark Twain admitted, "Within the due limits of modesty, that is what *I* think." The impingement of horror on beauty pervades every scene in which Satan figures. And the art of Mark Twain is more complex than is generally believed. But, forced as he is to close the arc of his artistic circle by the emptiness of a dream, his last conclusion in *The Mysterious Stranger* is, in Satan's words,

"Life itself is only a vision, a dream. . . . God—man—the world—the sun, the moon, the wilderness of stars—a dream, all a dream. . . . Nothing exists save empty space—and you! . . . The dream-marks are all present, you should have recognized them earlier. . . . there is . . . no universe, no human race. . . . It is all a dream—a grotesque and foolish dream."

The artistic restraint of this story covers profound deeps of despair. The despair is greater in this dreamlike hopelessness than in the anger which rages and foams. But the art is greater, too. And Mark Twain, whom Mr. DeVoto has called "the fallen angel of our literature," perhaps measured and himself understood his greatest artistic defects.

With a dramatic insight that amounted to sheer clairvoyance, he could adopt the view of life appropriate to Huck Finn or to Captain Stormfield; as Mark Twain, it is to be feared, his personal view remained the same. The objectivity and artistic restraint of what John Erskine labeled as "our first and still our best account of Main Street" are explained by the fact that Huck Finn is its narrator. Huck's imaginative response to beauty also makes him valuable. He holds the beauties of the river so close to the printed page that the reader feels he, too, can almost reach up and pluck the stars down from the sky; he, too, can hear the singing of the birds as they fly across the water; he, too, can fairly smell the river.

Generally, however, Mark Twain's experience of life seems to have been far different. He longed for, seems even to have expected from life, a sort of perfection. He was constantly seeing reflections of beauty, flowerlike clusters of stars mirrored in the dark waters of a moonlit river; but when he leaned down to pluck the starry flowers, his fingers closed on a handful of Mississippi mud. The ugliness of life stood at his elbow, maliciously inviting him to look on shabby scenes, urging him on with laughter coarse or sardonic; the beauty of life floated far away, beckoning him to follow. But when he drew near, beauty became a quick-change artist, transforming itself into the familiar ugliness, so that he came to see the beckoning as a mere mockery and began to fling back mockery in return. Only at times was he able to see the glory beneath the boredom and the horror of life. Only at times was he able to sense the dignity that is latent in mankind.

His struggle was not an easy one. He could develop various devices for mitigating the effects of his rage, which he so clearly recognized as a literary blemish. But, although he explicitly recorded his realization that the best work can be done only by a writer who senses the "dignity in human life," he was frequently unable to invent any technical devices to replace this lack within himself. His final literary achievement, under such a handicap, was really very great.

> *Haply—who knows?—somewhere*
> *In Avalon, Isle of Dreams,*
> *In vast contentment at last,*
> *With every grief done away . . .*
> *With that incomparable drawl*
> *He is jesting with Dagonet now.*[8]

[8] "The Last Day at Stormfield," by Bliss Carman, Collier's, Vol. XLV (May 7, 1910), 8.

Bibliography

Extensive bibliographies of material relating to Mark Twain will be found in the works of Ivan Benson, Walter Blair, Bernard DeVoto, and Edward Wagenknecht, all appearing below. The list which I append here includes only the titles of books and articles on which I have actually drawn in the preparation of this book.

PRIMARY SOURCES

The Writings of Mark Twain. Uniform edition. New York, Harper & Brothers, 1899–1910. 25 vols.
   Adventures of Huckleberry Finn
   The Adventures of Tom Sawyer.
   The American Claimant and Other Stories.
   Christian Science.
   A Connecticut Yankee in King Arthur's Court.
   Following the Equator. 2 vols.
   The Gilded Age. 2 vols.
   The Innocents Abroad. 2 vols.
   Life on the Mississippi.
   Literary Essays.
   The Man That Corrupted Hadleyburg and Other Stories.
   Personal Recollections of Joan of Arc. 2 vols.
   The Prince and the Pauper.
   Pudd'nhead Wilson; Those Extraordinary Twins.
   Roughing It. 2 vols.
   Sketches New and Old.
   The $30,000 Bequest and Other Stories.
   Tom Sawyer Abroad; Tom Sawyer, Detective; and Other Stories.
   A Tramp Abroad. 2 vols.
The Adventures of Thomas Jefferson Snodgrass. Edited by Charles Honce. Chicago, P. Covici, Inc., 1928.
The Curious Republic of Gondour and Other Whimsical Sketches. New York, Boni & Liveright, 1919.

"A Defence of General Funston," *North American Review*, Vol. CLXXIV (May, 1902), 613–24.

"Lecture on the Sandwich Islands," *Modern Eloquence*. Edited by Thomas B. Reed. Vol. IV, pp. 253–59. Philadelphia, J. D. Morris & Company, 1901. 15 vols.

Letters from the Sandwich Islands. Edited by G. Ezra Dane. Stanford, California, Stanford University Press, 1938.

The Letters of Mark Twain to Mrs. Fairbanks. Edited by Dixon Wecter. San Marino, California, Huntington Library, 1949.

The Letters of Quintus Curtius Snodgrass. Edited by Ernest E. Leisy. Dallas, University Press in Dallas, Southern Methodist University, 1946. (Not positively authenticated as Mark Twain's.)

Mark Twain's Autobiography. With an Introduction by Albert Bigelow Paine. New York, Harper & Brothers, 1924. 2 vols.

Mark Twain in Eruption. Edited by Bernard DeVoto. New York, Harper & Brothers, 1940.

Mark Twain's Letters. Arranged with Comment by Albert Bigelow Paine. New York, Harper & Brothers, 1917. 2 vols.

Mark Twain's Notebook. Prepared for Publication with Comments by Albert Bigelow Paine. New York, Harper & Brothers, 1935.

Mark Twain's Speeches. Stormfield edition. New York, Harper & Brothers, 1929.

Mark Twain's Travels with Mr. Brown. Edited by Franklin Walker and G. Ezra Dane. New York, Alfred A. Knopf, 1940.

"My Methods of Writing," edited by Cyril Clemens, *Mark Twain Quarterly*, Vol. VIII, No. 3 (Winter-Spring, 1949), 1.

The Mysterious Stranger and Other Stories. New York, Harper & Brothers, 1922.

Sketches of the Sixties. By Bret Harte and Mark Twain. Edited by John Howell. San Francisco, John Howell, 1926.

The Washoe Giant in San Francisco. Edited by Franklin Walker. San Francisco, George Fields, 1938.

What Is Man? and Other Essays. New York, Harper & Brothers, 1917.

The early Western sketches discussed in the text will be found in the two collections, *Sketches of the Sixties* and *The Washoe Giant*.

SUPPLEMENTARY SOURCES

Aldrich, Mrs. Thomas Bailey. *Crowding Memories*. Boston, Houghton Mifflin Company, 1920.

Basler, Roy P. "Abraham Lincoln's Rhetoric," *American Literature*, Vol. XI, No. 2 (May, 1939), 167–82.

Beach, Joseph Warren. *American Fiction, 1920–1940.* New York, The Macmillan Company, 1941.

Bellamy, Gladys C. "Mark Twain's Indebtedness to John Phoenix," *American Literature,* Vol. XIII, No. 1 (March, 1941), 29–43.

Benson, Ivan. *Mark Twain's Western Years.* Stanford, California, Stanford University Press, 1938.

Blair, Walter. *Horse Sense in American Humor.* Chicago, University of Chicago Press, 1942.

———. "Mark Twain, New York Correspondent," *American Literature,* Vol. XI, No. 3 (November, 1939), 247–59.

———. *Native American Humor.* New York, American Book Company, 1937.

———. "On the Structure of *Tom Sawyer,*" *Modern Philology,* Vol. XXXVII, No. 1 (August, 1939), 75–88.

———. "Review of *Mark Twain at Work,*" *American Literature,* Vol. XIV, No. 4 (January, 1943), 447–49.

Brashear, Minnie M. *Mark Twain, Son of Missouri.* Chapel Hill, University of North Carolina Press, 1934.

Brooks, Van Wyck. *The Ordeal of Mark Twain.* Revised edition. New York, E. P. Dutton and Company, 1933.

Buck, Philo. *The Golden Thread.* New York, The Macmillan Company, 1931.

———. *Literary Criticism: A Study of Values in Literature.* New York, Harper & Brothers, 1930.

Clemens, Clara. *My Father: Mark Twain.* New York, Harper & Brothers, 1931.

Croce, Benedetto. *Aesthetic as Science of Expression and General Linguistic.* Translated by Douglas Ainslie. Second edition. London, The Macmillan Company, 1922.

DeVoto, Bernard. *Mark Twain's America.* Boston, Little, Brown & Company, 1932.

———. Introduction, in *Mark Twain in Eruption.* New York, Harper & Brothers, 1940.

———. *Mark Twain at Work.* Cambridge, Harvard University Press, 1942.

Eastman, Max. "Humor and America," *Scribner's,* Vol. C, No. 1 (July, 1936), 9–13.

Erskine, John. *The Delight of Great Books.* Indianapolis, Bobbs-Merrill Company, 1928.

Ferguson, DeLancey. *Mark Twain: Man and Legend.* Indianapolis, Bobbs-Merrill Company, 1943.

————. Review of Walter Blair's *Native American Humor*, *American Literature*, Vol. IX, No. 4 (January, 1938), 483.

Fields, Mrs. James T. "Bret Harte and Mark Twain in the Seventies," *Atlantic Monthly*, Vol. CXXX (September, 1922), 341–48.

Fisher, Henry W. *Abroad with Mark Twain and Eugene Field*. New York, Nicholas L. Brown, 1922.

Frank, Waldo. *Our America*. New York, Boni & Liveright, 1919.

Fry, Roger. "The Artist and Psycho-Analysis," a Paper read to the British Psychological Society, London. Reprinted in *The New Criticism*, edited by Edwin Berry Burgum. New York, Prentice-Hall, Inc., 1930.

Goodwin, C. C. *As I Remember Them*. Salt Lake City, Salt Lake Commercial Club, 1913.

Haweis, H. R. *American Humorists*. Third edition. London, Chatto & Windus, 1890.

Hemingway, Ernest. *Green Hills of Africa*. New York, Charles Scribner's Sons, 1935.

Henderson, Archibald. *Mark Twain*. New York, Frederick A. Stokes, 1910.

Hibbard, Addison, ed. *Writers of the Western World*. Boston, Houghton Mifflin, 1942.

Howells, William Dean. *My Mark Twain: Reminiscences and Criticisms*. New York, Harper & Brothers, 1910.

Hudson, Arthur P. *Humor of the Old Deep South*. New York, The Macmillan Company, 1936.

Jones, Joseph. "Josh Billings: Some Yankee Notions on Humor," University of Texas *Studies in English* (1943), 148–61.

Johnson, Robert Underwood. *Remembered Yesterdays*. Boston, Little, Brown & Company, 1923.

Keller, Helen. *Midstream, My Later Life*. Garden City, Doubleday, Doran & Company, Inc., 1929.

King, Grace. *Memories of a Southern Woman of Letters*. New York, The Macmillan Company, 1932.

Kipling, Rudyard. *From Sea to Sea: Letters of Travel*. Part II, Vol. XVI of *The Writings in Prose and Verse of Rudyard Kipling*. New York, Charles Scribner's Sons, 1899.

Lawton, Mary. *A Lifetime with Mark Twain. The Memories of Katy Leary*, for Thirty Years His Faithful and Devoted Servant. New York, Harcourt, Brace & Company, 1925.

Leacock, Stephen Butler. *Humor: Its Theory and Technique*. New York, Dodd, Mead, & Company, 1935.

———. "Two Humorists," *Yale Review*, Vol. XXIV, No. 1 (September, 1934), 118–29.

Leisy, Ernest E. "Mark Twain and Colonel Sellers," *American Literature*, Vol. XIII, No. 4 (January, 1942), 398–405.

Linn, James Weber, and Houghton Wells Taylor. *A Foreword to Fiction*. New York, D. Appleton-Century Company, 1935.

Lovejoy, A. O. *The Great Chain of Being*. Cambridge, Harvard University Press, 1936.

Lyman, George D. *The Saga of the Comstock Lode*. New York, Charles Scribner's Sons, 1934.

Mack, Effie M. *Mark Twain in Nevada*. New York, Charles Scribner's Sons, 1947.

Macy, John. *The Spirit of American Literature*. Garden City, Doubleday, Page & Company, 1913.

"Mark Twain's New Deal," *Saturday Review of Literature*, Vol. X, No. 22 (December 16, 1933), 352.

"Mark Twain's Private Girls' Club," *The Ladies' Home Journal*, Vol. XXIX (February, 1912), 23, 54.

Masson, Thomas L. *Our American Humorists*. New York, Dodd, Mead & Company, 1931.

Masters, Edgar Lee. *Mark Twain: A Portrait*. New York, Charles Scribner's Sons, 1938.

Matthews, Brander. "Mark Twain and the Art of Writing," *Harper's Magazine*, Vol. CXLI, No. DCCCXLV (October, 1920), 635–43.

Matthiessen, F. O. *American Renaissance: Art and Expression in the Age of Emerson and Whitman*. New York, Oxford University Press, 1941.

Meine, Franklin J., ed. *Tall Tales of the Southwest: An Anthology of Southern and Southwestern Humor, 1830–1860*. New York, Alfred A. Knopf, 1930.

Murry, J. Middleton. *The Problem of Style*. London, Oxford University Press, 1922.

Paine, Albert Bigelow. *Mark Twain: A Biography*. The Personal and Literary Life of Samuel Langhorne Clemens. New York, Harper & Brothers, 1912. 3 vols.

Perry, Bliss. *A Study of Prose Fiction*. Revised edition. New York, Houghton Mifflin Company, 1920.

Rideing, William H. *Many Celebrities and a Few Others*. Garden City, Doubleday, Page & Company, 1912.

———. "Mark Twain in Clubland," *Bookman*, Vol. XXXI, No. 4 (June, 1910), 379–82.

Rourke, Constance. *American Humour: A Study of the National Character*. New York, Harcourt, Brace & Company, 1931.

Santayana, George. "The Nature of Beauty," from *The Sense of Beauty*. New York, Charles Scribner's Sons, 1897.

Schönemann, Freidrich. *Mark Twain als Literarische Persönlichkeit*. Jena, Verlag der Frommanschen Buchhandlung, Walter Biedermann, 1925.

Sherman, Stuart P. "Mark Twain," *Cambridge History of American Literature*. Vol. III. New York, G. P. Putnam's Sons, 1921. 4 vols.

Stewart, George R. "Bret Harte upon Mark Twain in 1866," *American Literature*, Vol. XIII, No. 3 (November, 1941), 263–64.

Taylor, Walter Fuller. *A History of American Letters*. Boston, American Book Company, 1936.

Van Doren, Carl. *The American Novel: 1789–1939*. Revised edition. New York, The Macmillan Company, 1942.

Vogelbeck, A. L. "The Prince and the Pauper: A Study in Critical Standards," *American Literature*, Vol. XIV, No. 1 (March, 1942), 48–54.

Wagenknecht, Edward. *Mark Twain: The Man and His Work*. New Haven, Yale University Press, 1935.

Walker, Franklin. *San Francisco's Literary Frontier*. New York, Alfred A. Knopf, 1939.

Wallace, Elizabeth. *Mark Twain and the Happy Island*. Chicago, A. C. McClurg and Company, 1913.

Webster, Samuel C. *Mark Twain, Business Man*. Boston, Little, Brown & Company, 1946.

Weisinger, Mort. "Listen! Mark Twain Speaking," *Saturday Evening Post*, Vol. 221, No. 1 (July 3, 1948), 12.

Winchester, C. T. *Some Principles of Literary Criticism*. New York, The Macmillan Company, 1928.

Woolf, S. J. "Painting the Portrait of Mark Twain," *Collier's*, Vol. XLV (May 14, 1910), 42–44.

Index

Abélard, Pierre: 173–74
Addison, Joseph: 49
Aguinaldo, Emilio: 323
Aldrich, Thomas Bailey: 9, 57, 350
Aldrich, Mrs. Thomas Bailey: 9
Alger, Horatio: 134
Alps Mountains: 3, 198, 216, 232, 252, 353
Alta California: 150, 164, 167, 245
Ament, Joseph P.: 70
America: 3, 10, 15, 25, 28, 92, 98, 99, 103, 108, 161, 167, 169, 171, 172,
     179, 274, 303, 312, 313, 315 ff.
American: 3, 27, 30, 47, 53, 58, 59, 93, 103, 108, 113, 132, 136 ff., 138,
     161 ff., 167 ff., 175, 190, 195, 240, 277, 279, 287, 293, 297, 300, 303,
     311, 314, 315, 324, 331, 340
Anderson, Sherwood: 287, 304, 346
Angel's Camp (California): 94, 144 ff., 150, 154
Apocryphal New Testament: 352, 353
Aristotle: 139
Arnold, Matthew: 11–12
Atlantic Monthly: 9, 10, 14, 49, 275, 300
Australia: 180, 196, 199, 234, 237, 242, 248, 252, 254
Austria: 306, 354, 359, 372
Azores: 224–25, 258

"Babes in the Wood": 120
Basler, Roy P.: 256
Beach, Joseph Warren: 255, 346
Benchley, Robert: 124 ff.
Benson, Ivan: 78 n., 88 n., 110 n., 153
Biblical references: 6, 43, 48, 73, 75, 84, 87, 102, 106, 109, 119, 129, 130,
     160, 163, 166, 168, 169, 173, 176, 177, 179, 193, 202, 224, 234, 244,
     250, 253, 256, 281, 299, 320, 358

Bierce, Ambrose: 99, 100, 101
Big Tree region (California): 94, 116, 145
Billings, Josh (Henry Wheeler Shaw): 135–36
Bixby, Horace: 4, 75
Blair, Walter: 125n., 127n., 145, 148, 165, 301, 334, 335
Bliss, Elisha: 8, 269, 270
Brashear, Minnie M.: 26, 28, 34, 35, 49n., 62, 69, 71, 72n., 74n., 75, 148
Brooks, Van Wyck: 22ff., 26, 29, 30ff., 40, 41, 53, 103, 136, 153, 155, 176, 177, 311, 349, 371; quoted, 4, 10, 38, 50, 74, 99, 102, 172, 208, 250, 315, 316, 331, 332, 348, 350, 366
Browne, Charles Farrar: see Artemus Ward
Brownell, Ed: 73
Browning, Robert: 46 47, 48, 331
Buck, Philo: 127n., 139n., 140n.
Buffalo (New York) Express: 19, 91, 92
Bunyan, John: 44, 135
Byron, George Gordon, Lord: 58, 132, 206, 373

Cable, George W.: 57, 115, 312
Calaveras County (California): 94, 116
California: 7, 45, 59, 94, 98, 100, 102, 128, 131, 147, 160, 246, 271
Californian: 91, 99, 100, 105, 111, 112, 120, 131, 145, 154
Carlyle, Thomas: 43, 48
Carson City (Nevada): 5, 6, 50, 60, 77, 82, 85, 88, 89, 92, 159, 208, 209, 274, 293
Catholicism: 225, 231, 313
Cervantes: 23, 43, 46, 75, 103, 279, 316
Churchill, Winston: 179
Civil War: 25, 44, 59, 76–77, 317, 322
Clemens, Clara (Mrs. Jacques Samossoud): 15, 21, 38, 41, 369, 373
Clemens, Henry: 76
Clemens, Jane Lampton: 4, 28, 32, 37, 67, 68–70, 92, 152
Clemens, Jean: 7, 14, 50, 51n., 352
Clemens, John Marshall: 28, 52, 69–70
Clemens, Langdon: 62
Clemens, Olivia Langdon: 13, 15ff., 32, 33, 60, 67, 68, 174, 269, 270, 333, 352, 366, 374
Clemens, Orion: 5, 67, 70, 71, 74, 75, 77, 78, 101, 269, 270, 295, 329, 368, 371
Clemens, Samuel L.: see Mark Twain
Clemens, Susy: 10–11, 13, 15, 199, 250, 262, 352, 362, 364
Cleveland (Ohio) Plain Dealer: 74

Comstock Lode region (Nevada): 6, 82, 85, 90, 271
Constantinople: 175, 184, 190, 202
Coon, Ben (Ross Coon): 145–46, 147, 148, 154
Cooper, James Fenimore: 44, 295
Crane, Sue Langdon: 299, 365

Dane, G. Ezra: 219
Derby, George Horatio: *see* John Phoenix
DeQuille, Dan (William Wright): 80, 82, 90
DeVoto, Bernard: 24, 26, 28, 30, 31, 33 ff., 40, 49, 53, 56, 103, 132, 155,
    201, 262, 269, 282, 287, 299, 301, 305, 332, 333, 336n., 337, 344, 352,
    362 ff., 371; quoted, 12, 26, 28, 29, 32, 34, 57, 85, 115n., 153, 246, 249,
    265, 283, 298, 312, 321, 323, 324, 335, 345, 348, 349, 361, 375
Dickens, Charles: 43, 51, 52, 53, 54, 73, 75, 142
Don Quixote: 46, 74, 134, 279
Eastern United States: 7 ff., 12, 50, 53, 83, 99, 105, 112, 147, 153
Edward VI of England: 309, 310, 372
Edwards, Jonathan: 307, 308
Eliot, T. S.: 33, 327
Elizabethans: 6, 10, 19, 122, 311
Emerson, Ralph Waldo: 14, 22, 41, 330
England: 9, 10, 16, 17, 21, 41, 178, 199, 303, 312, 313, 314, 367, 372
English people: 9, 10, 16, 186, 303
Erskine, John: 337, 338, 344, 375
Europe: 14, 19, 42, 45, 50, 57, 58, 112, 162, 167 ff., 176, 178, 180, 195, 204,
    239, 245, 316, 329, 331
Fairbanks, Mrs. A. W.: 7, 46, 61, 116, 270
Fairbanks, Charles: 61, 364
Ferguson, DeLancey: 24, 127, 133, 245n., 262, 270, 298, 317
Fields, Mrs. J. T.: 10, 35, 43
Finn, Jimmy: 70, 243
Fitch, Tom: 115, 122, 174
Florence (Italy): 14, 173, 177, 280, 365
Florida (Missouri): 3, 4, 69, 281
France: 168, 172, 348, 372
French people: 58, 169, 173, 175, 178, 261, 342

Galaxy (New York): 88, 91, 92, 99, 114, 131
German language: 252, 253
Germany: 14, 178, 195, 215, 221, 239
Gillis, Jim: 94, 144, 145, 150, 246
Gillis, Steve: 58, 82, 94

Goat Island (California): 84, 290
Golden Era (California): 82, 83, 91, 93, 99, 100, 151
Goldsmith, Oliver: 43, 74
Goodman, Joseph: 6, 38, 78, 80, 81, 82, 96
Gray, John A.: 71, 74
Greenough, Horatio: 170, 172

Hannibal (Missouri): 4, 28, 29, 31, 32, 49, 50, 52, 53, 67, 69, 75, 103, 141, 155, 246, 253, 275, 276, 301, 302, 332, 335, 336, 354
Hannibal *Courier*: 70, 71
Hannibal *Journal*: 70–71, 74n.
Harper's Magazine: 10, 350
Harris, Joel Chandler: 149, 150
Harte, Bret: 7, 99, 100, 102, 112, 116, 128, 131, 132, 144, 146, 147, 152, 249
Hartford (Connecticut): 8, 10 ff., 46, 281, 287, 290
Hawthorne, Nathaniel: 44, 103, 135, 155, 227, 296, 321, 327, 349, 373
Heidelberg (Germany): 215, 240, 246, 252, 255
Hemingway, Ernest: 255, 346, 347
Henderson, Archibald: 115, 138, 174, 226
Hindus: 178, 196, 227, 242, 252
Holland, George: 92, 93
Holy Land: 8, 101, 168, 176–77, 190, 191, 211, 212, 214, 230
Howells, William Dean: 9, 12 ff., 23, 31, 33, 38, 41, 44, 48, 49, 53, 57, 68, 123, 135, 137, 138, 177, 178, 239, 246, 249, 262, 263, 275, 278, 294, 301, 306, 309, 330, 331, 350, 351, 371, 372, 374; quoted, 7, 10, 11, 13, 15, 18 ff., 52, 59, 116, 280, 307, 312, 328, 349
Humorists, early frontier: 45–46

India: 178, 185, 210, 217, 218, 226, 228, 232, 233, 235 ff., 240–41, 242, 247, 251, 254, 263, 367
Injun Joe: 70, 302, 332
Italy: 135, 167, 171, 195, 198, 202, 205, 211, 213, 225, 317, 331

Jackass Hill (California): 144, 150
James, Henry: 26, 31, 44, 103
Jeypore (Jaipur, India): 217, 242, 264
Joan of Arc: 60, 321, 324, 372
Johnson, Samuel: 14, 49
Jones, Joseph: 136

Kanakas: 99, 162, 180, 223, 227
Keller, Helen: 20, 112, 373

Keokuk (Iowa) *Post*: 73, 159
Kipling, Rudyard: 11, 16, 63, 222, 331

Lampton, James: 295, 298
Lang, Andrew: 59, 113, 115, 255
Leacock, Stephen Butler: 52, 122, 124n., 131n.
Leary, Katy: 6, 7, 13, 18, 22
Lecky, William Edward H.: 43, 62
Lewis, Sinclair: 287, 291, 304, 346
Lincoln, Abraham: 10, 179, 256
London (England): 10, 14, 16, 21, 52, 53
Longfellow, Henry Wadsworth: 14, 22
Low, Governor F. F.: 83, 86, 123, 150

Mack, Effie M.: 78n., 89, 90, 270, 271, 273, 293
Magnolia Saloon (Carson City, Nevada): 85, 293
Malory, Thomas: 43, 46, 312
Masson, Thomas L.: 51, 52
Masters, Edgar Lee: 287, 304, 348
Matthews, Brander, 45, 138
Matthiessen, F. O.: *vii*, 154, 155, 326, 327, 328
Mazeppa: 108, 155
Meine, Franklin J.: 45, 141n.
Menken, Adah Isaacs: 107, 108
Miller, Joaquin: 10, 99
Mississippi River: 4, 7, 29, 41–42, 59, 74, 77, 142, 253, 275, 276, 277, 278, 279, 336, 365, 375
Missouri: 26, 28, 53, 59, 126, 152, 246, 281, 288ff., 334, 348
Murry, J. Middleton: 232, 249, 255, 257, 258 260, 261

Natchez-under-the-Hill: 31, 76, 277
Negroes: 99, 126, 275, 281, 299, 318ff., 322, 338, 341
Nevada: 5, 7, 20, 59, 80, 86, 89, 90, 101, 102, 108, 109, 115, 121, 131, 174, 270, 273, 365
"New Deal" the: 350
New Orleans: 4, 31, 73, 75, 142, 276, 323, 341
New York City: 7, 9, 17, 42, 50, 59, 71, 74, 105, 148, 153, 159, 164ff., 183, 188, 189, 192, 197, 220, 238–39, 244, 293, 297, 352
Niagara Falls: 10, 60, 217, 222
Nicaragua: 164, 201, 209, 210

Overland Monthly: 100

Oxford University: 16, 17

Paige typesetting machine: 14, 18, 302, 313, 352
Paine, Albert Bigelow: 17, 21, 43, 48, 56, 63, 67 n., 74, 78, 85 n., 91, 99,
    112, 115, 142 n., 159, 254, 274, 308, 309, 323, 365, 367, 368; quoted,
    3, 4, 5, 6, 8, 9, 12, 14, 16, 17, 18, 19, 22, 44, 46, 68, 96, 153, 280, 295, 305,
    317, 333, 354
Paine, Tom: 62, 75
Paris (France): 14, 168, 174, 175, 176, 184, 201, 204, 239, 245, 260, 261
Peaseley, Tom: 271, 293
Philadelphia (Pennsylvania): 50, 71, 105, 159
Phoenix, John (George Horatio Derby): 45, 122
Pochmann, Henry A.: 35, 43
Poe, Edgar Allan: 44, 73, 187, 299, 307

Quaker City (ship): 7, 8, 57, 71, 101, 164, 167, 168, 183, 195, 333, 365

Rabelais: 57, 103, 120, 121
Rideing, William H.: 6, 12
Rogers, Henry H.: 60, 348
Romantic movement: 206
Roosevelt, Franklin Delano: 350
Roosevelt, Theodore: 54, 283
Rourke, Constance: 26, 333
Russia: 8, 58, 178

St. Louis (Missouri): 4, 15, 42, 69, 71, 73 ff., 167, 297
Sandwich Islands (Hawaii): 7, 160, 162 ff., 187, 194, 196, 207 ff., 211,
    219–20, 223, 224, 229, 232, 237, 238, 243
San Francisco (California): 7, 11, 28, 50, 58, 82 ff., 126, 130, 131, 144, 145,
    155, 160, 161, 165, 189, 229, 272
San Francisco *Morning Call*: 90–91, 92, 108, 274
Santayana, George: 117, 118, 147
Satan: 179, 320, 329, 330, 353, 354–59, 361, 364, 374
Sazerac, The (Virginia City, Nevada): 271, 293
Schönemann, Friedrich: 103, 324
Shakespeare: 43, 46, 75, 311, 329
Shakespeare: 43, 46, 73, 311, 329
Shaw, George Bernard: 12, 23, 43, 226, 304
South, the: 44, 45, 55, 93, 238, 278, 279, 338, 345
Southwest, the: 10, 19, 23, 27, 28, 45, 50, 55, 59, 141, 145, 152
Stanford, Leland: 86, 123, 150

Stedman, Edmund Clarence: 206, 316
Stewart, William M.: 20, 87, 101
Stoker, Dick: 145, 271
Stormfield: 21, 41, 307
Stovall, Floyd: *viii*, 340
Swift, Jonathan: 23, 103, 273, 311

Taj Mahal: 217, 222, 235
Taylor, Annie: 71, 300
"Tennessee Land": 280, 292, 294, 295, 297
Tennyson, Alfred, Lord: 206–207, 272
Thoreau, Henry David: 101, 167, 240
Thuggee: 185–86, 232, 233–34, 236, 254
Tuolumne region (California): 94, 140, 144, 145, 246
Turner, George: 78, 78n., 87
Twain, Mark, the man: genius, 3, 4, 10, 18, 22, 25, 26, 34, 35, 38, 46; magnetism, 3 ff., 7, 8, 11, 12, 19, 22, 23; personality, 3 ff.; popularity, 3 ff., 8, 10, 14, 15, 16, 21 ff.; childhood and early life, 3–4, 53; appearance, 4 ff., 17, 19, 20, 21, 102; clothes, 4 ff., 8, 9, 17, 21, 57; pilot, 4–5, 59, 74 ff., 78, 275; miner, 5, 6, 77–78; newspaper work, 6, 7, 59, 78, 80, 81, 90–91, 159; profanity, 6 ff., 189; Rabelaisianism, 6, 9, 10, 19, 58, 311, 329; voice, 6, 11, 12, 23, 46; lecturer, 7, 9, 10, 59, 114, 220; disasters in personal life, 14 ff., 21, 28, 352; businessman, 14, 24, 59; publisher, 15, 59; round-the-world tour, 15; "Mark Twain's Pageant," Oxford University, 16; "Belle of New York," 17; death, 21–22; reading habits, 35; reader of poetry, 46; printing office, 49, 59, 70, 71, 74, 78, 159; "Governor of the Third House," Nevada, 89; "Washoe Giant," 104; "Professor of Moral Culture and Dogmatic Humanities," 114
——, the writer: association with Negroes, 4, 13, 28–30, 42, 59, 60, 149, 281, 299, 320; "Wild Humorist of the Pacific Slope," 8, 112; evidences of artistic qualities, 9, 18, 23, 26, 29, 34–39, 41, 42, 46–49, 51, 58, 74, 85, 89, 96, 114, 118, 122, 128, 136, 139, 141, 146–47, 151, 154, 155, 175, 190, 197, 232, 245–47, 251, 262, 264, 265, 272, 274, 310, 316, 322, 323, 331, 332, 335, 336, 338, 341, 344–46, 349, 361, 362, 366; burlesque, 14, 56, 72, 75, 79, 80, 83, 84, 88, 91, 92, 95, 96, 104, 113, 122, 131, 132, 134, 136, 139, 145, 151, 173–74, 199, 346, 312, 313, 316, 331; rage and impatience, 18, 60, 63, 68, 82, 95, 97, 98, 188, 189, 191, 192, 196–97, 222, 230, 239, 283, 306, 323, 324, 331, 348, 371, 372, 375; sensitivity, 18, 19, 20, 42, 52, 56, 58, 59, 77, 80, 128, 187, 197, 323, 330, 341, 371; conflicts and contradictions, 20, 33, 40, 41, 54 ff., 64, 76, 118, 139, 154–55, 172, 175, 176, 180, 181, 186, 305–

306, 309–10, 316, 318, 331; pessimism, 25, 61 ff., 172, 179, 182 ff., 200, 218, 297, 301, 310, 313, 326, 348, 373–75; artistic defects, 26, 28, 29, 40, 42, 49, 50, 54, 56, 81, 96, 110, 117, 174, 176, 188, 190, 192, 197, 237, 308, 309, 326 ff., 331, 361, 362, 375; satire, 27, 40, 50, 56, 57, 71 ff., 75, 79, 81, 83 ff., 93, 94, 98, 100 ff., 109, 110, 124, 127, 131, 135, 139, 140, 144, 154, 159–60, 164, 167, 172, 290–95, 298, 300 ff., 312, 331, 338 ff., 344, 350, 371; Presbyterianism, 28, 55, 70, 105 ff.; pre-occupation with death, 32, 62, 123, 127, 194–96 198, 259–60, 296, 301, 347, 363, 370–71; frustration, 33, 118, 139, 372–73; determinism, 34, 48, 51, 56, 62–64, 109, 117, 134, 155, 182 ff., 222, 305, 307 ff., 313, 315, 317 ff., 331, 346, 347, 357; literary devices, 35–37, 49, 56–57, 83, 86, 88, 94 ff., 110, 113, 121, 124, 125, 128, 132, 135, 138, 139, 143, 167, 174, 175, 208, 215, 218, 230, 231, 263, 274, 281, 298, 316, 322, 334, 344, 346, 360 ff., 369 ff.; diminution and magnification, 48, 208, 209, 215, 216, 273, 356 ff.; Western sketches, 72, 121, 124, 137, 155, 167, 169, 173, 175, 209, 255, 274, 280, 356, 368; conscience, 76, 107, 115, 135, 174, 186, 223–24, 226, 313, 324, 325, 337, 343, 346 ff., 352, 359; "Josh," 78; "Mark Twain" pseudonym, 83; belief in press as re-forming agency, 85, 89 ff., 98–99, 133; irony, 52, 88, 93, 96 ff., 168, 169, 177, 223, 256, 300, 315, 323, 324, 358; romanticism, 55, 56, 59, 64, 100, 164, 205 ff., 275–77, 324, 338, 347; reformer, 56, 57, 70, 80 ff., 108 ff., 127, 128, 138, 151 ff., 161 ff., 167–69, 177 ff., 192, 238, 248; Calvinism, 57, 63, 69, 70, 106, 224, 320, 332; humanitarianism, 57, 163, 166, 170 ff., 180, 181, 197, 310; moralism, 57, 58, 63, 64, 71, 95, 105 ff., 131, 132, 134, 139, 140, 156, 159 ff., 186, 192, 196, 203, 224, 227, 248, 261, 265, 305 ff., 328 ff., 357, 358; sympathy, 60, 63, 330, 355, 356; pity, 63, 68, 98, 191, 192, 196–97, 324, 332; patheticism, 64, 197 ff., 324, 364–65, 372; twofold aspect of life, 64, 227 ff., 234, 236, 262, 263, 326, 327, 329, 332, 336, 349, 369, 370; "Moral Phenome-non," 104, 112; realism, 108, 109, 116, 149, 164, 246, 276, 338; "Moral-ist of the Main," 112; figures of speech, 128, 130, 152, 194, 241, 252 ff.; wit, 137–38; methods of characterization, 141 ff., 147, 148, 150, 154 ff., 244, 246, 247, 271, 338, 339, 342; escapism, 207, 213, 217 ff., 235, 265, 296, 360, 370, 372; see also Mark Twain. Attitudes and opinions and Mark Twain. Literary treatment

——. Attitudes towards and opinions on: governmental assemblies, 6, 59, 71, 82, 89, 90, 112, 292, 294; God, 14, 15, 21, 44, 50, 51, 60, 61, 63, 76, 107, 134, 176, 198, 256–57, 306–309, 320, 347, 353, 354, 359, 361, 364, 374; women, 17, 31, 32, 151; aesthetic considerations, 23, 41, 47, 81, 110, 113, 118, 139, 147, 154, 155, 170 ff., 187, 189, 203, 204, 219, 240, 242, 246, 254, 265, 310, 374; religion (his own un-orthodoxy), 33, 70, 75, 105, 299; worthlessness of mankind, 34, 60,

61, 63, 72, 77, 93, 94, 111, 116, 118, 123, 138, 144, 175, 177 ff., 182 ff.,
190, 191, 196, 200, 208, 210 ff., 222, 225, 273-74, 276, 283, 294, 304 ff.,
310, 313, 321, 325, 330, 331, 345, 348, 356, 358, 360, 361, 368, 373,
374; art, 43, 169-72, 177, 204; slavery, 49, 52, 53, 77, 103; Chinese,
83, 84, 91, 97 ff., 374; politics, 86, 87, 94, 114, 146, 150, 292-93, 295,
303, 306; police, 91, 94, 96, 97; Sunday school, 97, 193, 278, 300,
301, 336; oppressed races, 99, 179, 180; spiritualism, 106, 108, 127,
368; common people, 115, 152, 156, 163, 170 ff., 242, 287, 316, 348,
372-73; Satan, 179, 320, 329, 330, 353-59, 361, 364, 374; dignity of
mankind, 236, 237, 263, 349, 350, 351, 375-76; institutions, 339, 340,
347, 358-59; *see also* Mark Twain, the man

———. Literary treatment of: village, 29, 53, 59, 287-90, 301 ff., 319, 330,
348, 352, 358; sex, 30-32, 58, 162 ff., 173, 175, 177, 178, 321, 328,
329; war, 47, 75-77, 79, 256-57, 358, 359; Negroes, 49, 275, 279, 299,
318 ff., 338, 342; malign Nature, 62, 63, 107, 187, 196, 198, 200, 362;
religion, 72, 106-107, 169, 223, 233, 236, 299; dialect, 73, 79, 299,
300, 341; government, 73, 79, 101, 130, 293; good and evil, 107, 156,
218, 227, 236, 327, 330, 336, 360, 373; Sunday school tales, 111, 134,
334, 340; beauty, 156, 161, 170, 173, 187, 206 ff., 228, 230, 235, 237,
260, 263, 265, 355, 356, 358, 380; ugliness, 156, 185, 201 ff., 230, 235,
237, 260, 265, 360; *see also* Mark Twain, the writer

———. Works:
"About Barbers," 125
"About Play Acting," 113, 370-71
"Account of the Extraordinary Meteoric Shower, An," 108, 122, 129
Adventures of Huckleberry Finn, The, 39, 46, 52, 57, 82, 99, 150,
    228, 277, 279, 302, 310, 316, 322, 330, 336-47, 349, 350, 353, 361,
    369, 370, 371, 374
Adventures of Thomas Jefferson Snodgrass, The, 73, 75, 120, 122,
    141, 159
Adventures of Tom Sawyer, The, 72, 105, 231, 299 ff., 310, 332-36,
    339, 340, 342, 349, 359 n., 371
American Claimant, The, 303 304, 366&n., 315-17
"Aurelia's Unfortunate Young Man," 122
Autobiography, 31, 51, 57, 58, 69, 70, 89, 253, 269, 279-83, 295, 298,
    365, 366 n.
"Blabb, W. Epaminondas Adrastus," 70-71, 82, 141
"Blabbing Government Secrets," 70-71
"Black Hole of San Francisco, The," 97
"Bluejay Yarn," 146, 149-50, 246, 247
"Biographical Sketch of George Washington, A," 111, 126
"Boy's Manuscript," 333

Burlesque Biography, 121
"Californian's Tale, The," 145, 324, 370
"Cannibalism in the Cars," 123
"Canvasser's Tale,The," 135
"Captain Ed Montgomery," 150–51, 153, 155
Captain Stormfield's Visit to Heaven, 243, 368, 369–70, 372, 374
"Case of George Fisher, The," 101
"Celebrated Jumping Frog of Calaveras County, The," 12, 112, 130, 146, 147–48, 152, 153, 154, 155
Chinese Letters, 99
Christian Science, 250
"Christmas Fireside . . . by Grandfather Twain, The," 111
Colonel Sellers (play), 298
"Concerning Notaries," 88
"Concerning the Answer to That Conundrum," 120
"Concerning the Jews," 306, 329
Connecticut Yankee at King Arthur's Court, A, 27, 46, 303, 305, 311–16, 340, 350, 353
"Couple of Sad Experiences, A," 88, 95
Curious Republic of Gondour, The, 88, 95, 114n.
"Daniel in the Lion's Den—and Out Again All Right," 109–10, 130, 142
"Dandy Frightening the Squatter, The," 83, 141, 155
"Death Disk, The," 370
"Defence of General Funston, A," 323
"Disgraceful Persecution of a Boy, The," 97–98
Double-Barrelled Detective Story, A, 46
"Dutch Nick Massacre": *see* "Empire City Massacre"
"Earthquake Almanac, An," 100, 131
"Early Rising as Regards Excursions to the Cliff House," 123–24
"Empire City Massacre," 85, 278
"Evidence in the Case of Smith *vs.* Jones, The," 93, 116, 143, 356
"Fables for Good Old Boys and Girls," 121 ,130
"Facts Concerning the Recent Resignation, The," 101
"Facts in the Case of the Great Beef Contract, The," 73, 101, 122, 130
"Fenimore Cooper's Literary Offenses," 250
"Fitz Smythe's Horse," 150
"Five Boons of Life, The," 370
Following the Equator, 62, 69, 138, 177–78, 180, 185–87, 195–96, 199, 217–18, 221–22, 226–27, 232–37, 240–42, 247, 248, 252, 254–55, 260, 262–65, 354, 367
"Fourth of July Oration," 78

Gilded Age, The, 82, 112, 274, 287–301, 316, 333, 359n., 366

"Goldsmith's Friend Abroad Again": *see Chinese Letters*

"Gospel": *see What Is Man?*

"Grandfather's Old Ram," 35, 117, 146, 271

"Great Dark, The," 216, 352, 362, 363, 364, 365, 372, 374

"Great Prize Fight, The," 86–87, 100, 101, 122–23

"Great Revolution in Pitcairn, The," 315

"Greeting from the Nineteenth to the Twentieth Century, A," 179

"How I Edited an Agricultural Paper," 122

"How They Take It," 97

"How to Cure a Cold," 88

"How to Make History Dates Stick": 126–27

"How to Tell a Story," 148–49

"Hunting of the Cow, The," 283

"Important Correspondence Concerning the Occupancy of Grace Cathedral," 105

"Indignity Put Upon the Remains of George Holland, The," 92

"Ingomar Over the Mountains," 133

Innocents Abroad, The, 7, 9, 42, 45, 53, 109, 125, 164, 167–69, 171 ff., 175–77, 184, 190–95, 198–99, 201 ff., 211–15, 219, 224–25, 230, 231, 237, 239, 245, 251, 257–60, 261, 269, 271

"Interior Notes," 110

"Invalid's Story, The," 123

Is Shakespeare Dead? 329

Joan of Arc, 324, 340, 347–49, 359n.

"Johnny Skae's Item," 131–32, 135

"Journalism in Tennessee," 92

"Judge's Spirited Woman, The," 101, 151–52

"Kearney Street Ghost Story, A," 127

"Late Benjamin Franklin, The," 102

Lectures on the Sandwich Islands, 7, 220

Letter to Annie Taylor, 72, 73

Letters from the Earth, 368

Letters from the Sandwich Islands, 160–64, 180, 182, 187–88, 194, 207–11, 216, 219, 223–24, 227–29, 232–34, 237, 238, 242, 243, 251, 274, 360

Letters of Quintus Curtius Snodgrass, 75, 322–23

"Lick House Ball, The," 84, 290

Life on the Mississippi, 44, 58, 72, 83n., 93, 100, 269, 275–79, 282, 300, 344

"Lionizing Murders," 102

"London *Times* of 1904, The," 370

"Magnanimous Incident Literature," 134
Man That Corrupted Hadleyburg, The, 82, 287, 308, 309, 316, 328, 331, 340
Mark Twain in Eruption, 34, 35, 68, 91, 113, 269, 283
Mark Twain's Travels with Mr. Brown, 164–67, 182–83, 188–98, 201, 209 ff., 229, 238–39, 243–45, 253, 352, 353
"Map of Paris," 68
"Moral Statistician," 110
"My Bloody Massacre," 86, 95, 100, 127
"My Late Senatorial Secretaryship," 132–33
"My Platonic Sweetheart," 366–67
Mysterious Stranger, The, 28, 95, 216, 273, 329, 330, 348&n., 352–62, 368, 372 ff.
"Mysterious Visit, A," 101–102
"New Crime, A—Legislation Needed," 102
"Nicodemus Dodge," 246–47, 251
Notebook (Mark Twain's), 107, 160, 162, 163, 176, 210, 311–13, 353 ff., 362–66
"Office Bore, The," 151
"Old Times on the Mississippi," 275
"Notable Conundrum, A," 120
"Not a Suicide," 97
"Old Webster-Unabridged," 145–46
"On Murders," 87, 88
"Our Assistant's Column," 71
"Our Fellow Savages of the Sandwich Islands" (lecture), 10
"Pageant of Progress, A," 179
"Petrified Man, The," 131
"Playing Courier," 124–25
Prince and the Pauper, The, 37, 309–12, 317, 337
"Private History of a Campaign That Failed, The," 76–77
"Professor Personal Pronoun," 78
Pudd'nhead Wilson, 31, 39, 82, 299, 303–304, 317–22, 336, 340, 359n.
Pudd'nhead Wilson's maxims, 61, 121, 137–38, 197, 233 ff., 250, 305
"Recent Carnival of Crime in Connecticut, The," 107, 135
"Reflections on the Sabbath," 107
"Review of *The Crown Diamonds*," 133
Roughing It, 35, 49, 92, 100, 102, 116, 122, 143, 243, 250, 269–75, 279, 282, 295
"Sergeant Fathom" (Isaiah Sellers burlesque), 75, 142
"1601: A Fireside Conversation," 58, 311
Sketches New and Old, 86, 97, 111

"Slave-Girl Market Report, A," 175
"Some Rambling Notes of an Idle Excursion," 184, 243, 250
"Still Further Concerning That Conundrum," 120
"Stolen White Elephant, The," 331
"Stories of Good Little Boys and Girls," 111
"Story of the Bad Little Boy, The," 111, 134
"Story of the Good Little Boy, The," 111, 133–34
"Taming the Bicycle," 124
"Those Blasted Children," 83, 84, 110, 122, 153
"Those Extraordinary Twins," 303, 317
"3,000 Years Among the Microbes," 354, 367, 368
"To Miss Katie in H–l," 70
Tom Sawyer Abroad, 362, 372
Tom Sawyer, Detective, 359n., 369
"Tone-Imparting Committee, The," 102
Tramp Abroad, A, 19, 42, 43, 177, 195, 198, 199, 204, 215–16, 220–21, 225, 226, 231–32, 239, 240, 246–47, 251–53, 255, 262, 353
"True Story, A," 49, 300
"Turning Point of My Life, The," 38, 49
"Unbiased Criticism, An," 94, 145
"Uncle Lige," 132
"Undertaker's Chat, The," 123
"War Prayer, A," 256–57
Washoe Giant, The, 96
"Washoe, Information Wanted," 108, 121, 126
"What Have the Police Been Doing?" 96
What Is Man?, 28, 56, 63, 182, 184, 305, 307, 331, 350, 361, 364
"What Paul Bourget Thinks of Us," 39
"Wild Man Interviewed, The," 132
Twichell, Joseph: 8, 9, 12, 19, 20, 42, 47, 60, 128, 172, 221, 275, 306, 307, 311, 315, 323, 329

United States: 25, 47, 59, 80, 84, 162, 172, 179, 283, 294, 295, 304, 350

Van Doren, Carl: 103, 136, 279, 287, 332, 335
Victoria, princess of Hawaii: 161, 162, 182, 194
Virginia City (Nevada): 6, 50, 85, 107, 122, 129, 271, 293
Virginia City *Territorial Enterprise*: 6, 78, 80, 81–83 85, 87–90, 96
Voltaire, François Marie Arouet: 23, 62, 103

Wagenknecht, Edward: 24, 26, 35, 38n., 43n., 47n., 50, 57, 132n.;

quoted, 12, 20n., 23, 29, 33, 35, 37, 40, 54, 58, 59, 67, 155, 305, 311, 322, 324, 333

Wakeman, Captain Ned: 164, 243, 369

Walker, Franklin: 80, 87n., 100, 108n., 112, 128, 144n., 164n., 165

Wallace, Elizabeth: 7, 41

Ward, Artemus (Charles Farrar Browne): 74, 89, 120, 148, 153

Warner, Charles Dudley: 13, 290, 295ff., 306

Washington, George: 173, 323

Washington, D. C.: 17, 20, 101, 120, 290ff., 300

Washoe (Nevada): 81, 84, 86, 87, 103, 108, 126, 139, 155, 160, 209, 278, 280

Webb, Charles Henry: 99, 100, 112, 144, 154

West, the: 5-7, 9, 13, 26-27, 31, 49, 50, 52, 53, 55-57, 59, 67, 72, 77, 79, 80, 81-84, 89, 99, 100-103, 105, 107, 108, 112, 116, 122, 124, 127, 128, 130, 142, 144, 152, 159, 170, 245, 253, 269, 271, 273, 293, 360

Whitman, Walt: 152, 154, 172, 340

Wolfe, Jim: 246

Wordsworth, William: 190, 205

Wright, William: *see* Dan DeQuille